Hedge
FUNDS

FOR CANADIANS

W9-CQI-326

Hedge FUNDS

FOR CANADIANS

NEW INVESTMENT STRATEGIES FOR WINNING IN ANY MARKET

Second Edition

Peter Beck • Miklos Nagy

John Wiley & Sons Canada, Ltd.

Copyright © 2005 by Peter Beck and Miklos Nagy
All rights reserved. No part of this work covered by the copyright herein may be reproduced or used in any form or by any means—graphic, electronic or mechanical without the prior written permission of the publisher. Any request for photocopying, recording, taping or information storage and retrieval systems of any part of this book shall be directed in writing to The Canadian Copyright Licensing Agency (Access Copyright). For an Access Copyright license, visit www.accesscopyright.ca or call toll free 1-800-893-5777.

Care has been taken to trace ownership of copyright material contained in this book. The publisher will gladly receive any information that will enable them to rectify any reference or credit line in subsequent editions.

This publication contains opinions and ideas of the authors. They are not presented to provide a basis of action for any particular circumstances without consideration by a competent professional. The authors and publisher expressly disclaim any liability, loss, or risk, personal or otherwise, which is incurred as a consequence, direct or indirect, of the use or application of the contents of this book.

Library and Archives Canada Cataloguing in Publication Data

Beck, Peter, 1955-
    Hedge funds for Canadians : new investment strategies for winning in any market / Peter Beck, Miklos Nagy.—2nd ed.

Includes index.
ISBN-13 978-0-470-83636-9
ISBN-10 0-470-83636-9

    1. Hedge funds—Canada. I. Nagy, Miklos, 1959- II. Title.

HG5154.5.B42 2005   332.64'524   C2005-902302-3

Production Credits:
Cover and Interior text design: Interrobang Graphic Design Inc.
Printer: Printcrafters

John Wiley & Sons Canada Ltd
6045 Freemont Blvd.
Mississauga, Ontario
L5R 4J3

Printed in Canada

10 9 8 7 6 5 4 3 2 1

I want to dedicate this book to my sons: Philipp, Sebastian and Pierre.
Miklos

To my wife Sondra; for the smile that brings warmth to my heart.
Peter

Acknowledgements

The authors wish to thank Kit Hunt of SwiftTrade and Ferenc Schneman of Canadian Hedge Watch Inc. for their assistance. All errors are our own.

Contents

Preface

The traditional New Year's Eve dinner in Hungary is suckling pig with cabbage cooked in champagne and potatoes sautéed with onion. Because a whole piglet would not have fit into my father's oven (and we could have never consumed that much anyway), I decided to buy just a leg with the skin still on. After rubbing it generously with salt and spiking it with cloves of garlic, I roasted it slowly in the oven. Three hours and many bastings later, our "goodbye to 2004" dinner was ready; the golden-brown skin wrapped around the delicious and juicy dish, filling my father's place in Budapest with a wonderful aroma.

Having just celebrated his 95th birthday three days earlier did not prevent my father from enjoying the celebrations. It was past 10:30 p.m. by the time dinner was served and we welcomed midnight with glasses of champagne. Dad stayed up well past 2 a.m. watching my two young daughters dance and listening to my half-hearted efforts at explaining to them that not every night is New Year's Eve and yes, we do have to go to bed on other nights at the usual time.

By 4 a.m. everyone was sleeping, but regardless of how hard I tried I could not join my family in that exercise. So, I was sitting in the living room and looking ahead to see how the new year would shape up when suddenly I realized that in a few days I would have to hand in the changes to the second edition of *Hedge Funds for Canadians*. Call me crazy, but right now I am sitting in my hotel, typing these words into my notebook computer. The next few hours might be the only quiet time I will have on this vacation and this beats watching the early morning shows on one of the few channels the hotel has to offer.

More than two years have gone by since we wrote the first edition and a lot has changed. The book helped many individuals become more familiar with hedge funds and as a result it was a great success. That is why Wiley asked us to update the book and incorporate the changes that have taken place.

Looking at the overall landscape, we see staggering changes. At the writing of the first edition there may have been around 200 hedge funds in Canada, 50 of which we described in great detail in the book. Now we have over 350 funds available and the number is growing daily. Thus, in this edition, we are providing a detailed description of 100 of them.

Explaining an industry that's gaining more and more mainstream status on the Canadian financial landscape, let this book be the guide for all who want to find out about this sometimes mysterious financial instrument.
So let the fun begin. Start reading!

Peter Beck

Since the first edition of this book was published, people have been continually congratulating me on how successfully we described such a seemingly complicated investment as hedge funds. And in a relatively short period of two years, the industry has continued to grow both in the number of funds and in the total assets under management. This is despite numerous accusations and attacks by media and regulators globally and in Canada. Sadly, in most cases, these accusations and criticism have stemmed from ignorance of the structure of hedge funds, and an inability to grasp their characteristics. Having said that, the recent and still inconclusive probe to Portus Asset Management in Canada unfortunately did not help dispel criticism of this industry.

Despite the brisk growth, the number of books catering specifically to the Canadian hedge fund industry remains less than a handful. The goal of the second edition of *Hedge Funds for Canadians* is to update and expand on the original, and incorporate the many changes in the industry since 2003. And in order to stay current with the continued proliferation of funds available in Canada, we have expanded the number of featured funds from 50 to 100, giving detailed descriptions and statistical information as of December 31, 2004.

In writing the second edition, we also wish to shed some light on the hedge fund industry and remove some of the stigmas of secrecy and exoticness, bringing them more into the mainstream of investments. One of the problems has been media and regulators complaining that hedge funds can lose money rather spectacularly. In truth, that hedge funds lose money is actually a good sign. Why?

Suppose we lived in a world where funds did not lose big once in a while; this would mean that there would be three states in which hedge funds could exist: very successful, mediocre, and not losing very much. But this is impossible, as being very successful means making very high returns, which requires that we take on a higher amount of risk. And as we all know, with higher risk comes a higher probability of not just higher gains but also higher losses. Spectacular losses are a natural result of taking risks, as are spectacular gains. So if we eliminate the possibility of spectacular losses, we create an asset class that is merely mediocre—not very appealing!

So disregard much of the statistical mumbo-jumbo and "expert" advice, and use your head! Don't forget that increasing regulation will never result in the elimination of problems (it will only affect the frequency and magnitude of them) or improvement of products. Freedom (with as little intervention as possible) is, despite some shortcomings, our best hope. And this is not only true of hedge funds.

Happy hedgehogging!

Miklos Nagy

The History of Hedge Funds

ALFRED WINSLOW JONES

Unlike most investment strategies, which have evolved over many years and through many different theories and practices to their current forms, hedge funds can be traced to a single and truly remarkable individual. The son of an American father, Alfred Winslow Jones was born in Melbourne, Australia in 1901 and moved to the United States with his family at the age of four. As an adult, a long series of career changes and adventures led him to the ripe old age of 48, when he founded what is now recognized as the first hedge fund.

After graduating from Harvard in 1923, Jones traveled the world as a purser on a tramp steamer and in the early 1930s served as vice consul to the United States Embassy in Berlin while the rise of Hitler and Nazism was in full swing. During the Spanish Civil War, he reported on civilian relief for the Quakers; in 1941, he completed a doctorate in sociology at Columbia University. His thesis, "Life, Liberty and Property," became a standard sociology text of the time.

It was during the forties, however, that Jones developed the financial strategies that made him famous. He became an associate editor of *Fortune* magazine (as well as writing for *Time* and many other non-business periodicals), and it was while researching for an article entitled "Fashions in Forecasting" that Jones became well acquainted with many Wall Street analysts, technicians, and forecasters.

His research and conversations led him to formulate an entirely new kind of investment strategy. By the end of 1949, he had raised $100,000 (of which $40,000 was his own) and began a general investment partnership to test his theories. It was the beginning of a new and innovative industry, one that was to fundamentally

change the way investors thought about their business. But it was 17 years before it
was brought to light.

TRADITIONAL INVESTMENTS: THE PROBLEMS WITH "GOING LONG"

Jones realized that one of the fundamental problems with traditional investment
strategies was their vulnerability to the unpredictable declines of the stock market. Mutual funds, for instance, bought securities, held on to them until the price
of the securities went up, and then sold them for a profit. This is the "traditional"
model of investing, often referred to as a "buy and hold" strategy or "going long."
The flaw that Jones found in this was simple: *stock values simply don't always go up.*
When markets go down, stock prices go down, so funds that invest in stocks
go down as well. This means that investment funds, such as mutual funds, are
directly correlated to the directions of the markets.

The history of investment management in the United States dates back to
the beginning of the 19th century. It was founded on the three major principles
of fiduciary responsibility: acting solely in the best interests of the client; the
preservation of capital, where the primary goal was to make sure that the initial investment was secure, and *prudence*, which demanded that a fiduciary (money
manager) should gain a reasonable return *without speculation* (taking a risky gamble
on a stock). Upholding all three principles is extremely hard to do when markets
are declining, because the only way to make returns is to be a brilliant stock pick-
er—in other words, find the few securities that are gaining in a downward or
"bear" market. Speculation was severely frowned upon, as it was thought to be
against the moral responsibilities of money managers.

The mutual fund industry was actually the first notable departure from
these original tenets, in that mutual fund managers sought to *multiply* capital,
and not just *maintain* it. These new "performance-oriented" funds brought a
new and more aggressive approach to investing. Where investing had originally
been more of a side project for banks and insurance companies, mutual fund
managers did it *full-time*. And, more important, they were paid specifically for
managing money, and the more money they managed, the more they were paid.
Using full-blown marketing campaigns, they promoted themselves as money
makers, not capital *preservers*. The industry exploded, to say the least, and the
foundations of today's mutual fund industry were laid. Chapter 2 will go into
more detail on the history of mutual funds. For this chapter's purposes, however,
we just need to realize that *long only* (buy and hold), when used as a sole strategy,

will always be correlated to whether the markets are going up or down. Thus, investments such as mutual funds provide returns that are *relative* to the current market trend.

JONES'S SOLUTION

Jones saw two main objectives for his investments. First and foremost, he wanted to get rid of market correlation in order to reduce the risk of losing money in a down market. Second, he wanted to make profits (as is the goal of all investors) even in down markets. His solution was simple and brilliant.

By combining two separate techniques, *short selling* and *leverage*, and maintaining long positions as well, Jones was able to "hedge" his bets against market downturns, while still making profits from rising ones. In short, he could be profitable no matter what the markets were doing. How was this possible? To understand it, we need to start by defining the two techniques.

Short Selling

Short selling is the act of borrowing a stock and selling it in anticipation of being able to *repurchase* it at a lower price, at or before the time it must be returned to the lender. This may seem confusing at first, but the idea is fairly simple. A short analogy can help.

A high-tech video game player is the hottest new thing on the market. Everyone wants one. The player retails for $179, but because of the high demand (and because stores can't keep them in stock), people are prepared to pay ridiculous prices for them. Your brother, in fact, has just purchased one for a whopping $300. Being a little more market savvy than your brother, you analyze the situation and realize that this is a vastly overblown price. You are sure that as soon as the fad is over, prices will drop, because a newer, more advanced video game player will show up on the market and become the next hot item.

With this in mind, the short selling analogy goes like this:

1. You propose to borrow the video player from your brother, give it back in a month, and buy him a new game cartridge for it as payment. He agrees, and you take the player home.

2. The next day, you sell the player to a desperate buyer for $300, who figures it's a pretty good deal, since the few of them that are even on the market are now going for more than that. You put the money in your pocket.

   Over the next three weeks, your prediction comes true—in spades. A rival company produces a video player that vastly outperforms the existing one, and everyone is jumping in to buy the new players and trying desperately to sell the old ones.

3. Down at the local computer store, the old players are now on sale for $150, because there is no more demand for them. You pull out your $300, buy a player for $150 and a game cartridge for your brother for $25 (they're on sale now too!). You take the cartridge and the player back to your brother, thank him for the loan, and go home.

You've just made a net profit of $125, or $300 – ($150 + $25).

   Securities can be handled in the same way. A trader can borrow securities—there are many ways to do this—that he or she believes are overvalued (worth less than they are selling for) and then sell them in anticipation of the security losing value before the promised date of return. The profit is gained from repurchasing the security at the lower price. Figure 1.1 can help illustrate this. Assume that an investor sees a reason that shares in Company X will decline in value over a period of time. This could be due to any number of factors, depending on what Company X does and what the market conditions are.

   By using short selling, it is therefore possible to make money on losing shares, and in an overall declining market, this technique can be used to make profits (it must be noted here that predicting whether a share's price will go down is just as difficult as whether it will go up).

FIGURE 1.1

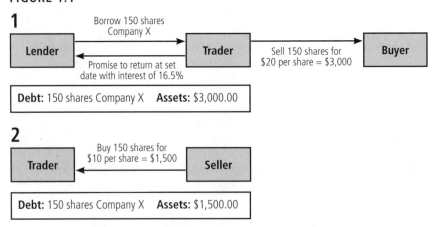

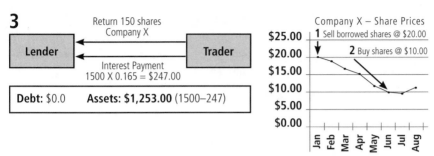

Leveraging

Leveraging is the act of borrowing money to amplify an investment's return. Again, analogies are useful:

Let's say you live next door to a prosperous strawberry farm. You find out that the farmer is willing to sell you strawberries for $1 per pint (lower than market price, because he doesn't have to do any shipping or marketing). You also find out that the small grocery store down the road is willing to buy strawberries for $1.50 a pint. This looks like an ideal way to make a profit. You can buy a pint of strawberries for $1 and sell it for 50% more—all that's involved is transportation! If you have $10 to spend, you can make $5 profit.

With this in mind, the leveraging analogy works like this:

1. You have $10. That's all there is in the bank. With $10, you are guaranteed a $5 profit, by buying $10 worth of strawberries and selling them for $15. You *borrow* $90 from your brother and promise to pay it back the next day and buy him an ice cream for his trouble (interest, in essence).

2. You take the $100 (your $10 and your brother's $90) and purchase 100 pints of strawberries from the farmer.

3. You sell the 100 pints to the grocery store for $150.

4. You return the $90 to your brother the next day, buy him a super double-dip jumbo ice cream cone for $2.75, and go home.

You have just made a net profit of $47.25, or $150 − ($90 + $2.75)—which is $42.25 more than you would have made using your own money.

Leveraging is a common instrument in investing. In essence, it amplifies the amount of return you receive. Using our Company X from the short selling description, we can represent this process in Figure 1.2.

It should be noted here, though, that leveraging is a dangerous business, as it also amplifies *losses* if you make a bad decision. For instance, if your 100 pints of strawberries turned out to be sour and the grocery store refused to buy them, you would not only lose your own $10, but would be in debt to the tune of $92.75, or the cost of the ice cream cone *plus* the borrowed $90.

FIGURE 1.2

Unleveraged

Assets: $10,000.00
Returns: $15,000.00
Profit: $ 5,000.00

Leveraged

Assets: $ 10,000.00
Debt: ($ 90,000.00)
Returns: $150,000.00
Profit: $ 50,000.00

Hedging

By having long investments on stocks he felt were undervalued (worth more than he paid for them), and short positions on stocks he felt were overvalued (worth less than he sold them for), Jones was able to balance his investments and make money in both advancing and declining markets.

We can demonstrate the way these techniques can combine to produce superior returns with a hypothetical example using events from recent history.

In Figure 1.3, a hedge fund manager in 1994 goes long on Microsoft stocks— that is, betting that they will increase in value. This position was taken based on a gamble that Microsoft was becoming the largest player in the computer market and would continue to grow—a pretty safe bet. At the same time, however, the manager goes "short"—betting the price will drop—in Novell Inc. This position was taken because Microsoft had just introduced Windows 95, which integrated a network application into its operating system. Novell sold the network application for its platform separately. Who would want to buy two separate pieces when you could get both in one package?

FIGURE 1.3

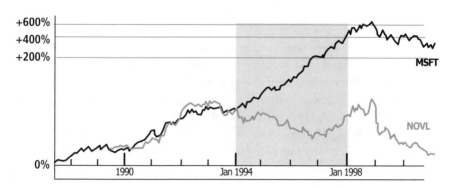

It turned out to be a good gamble. From January 1994 through January 1998, Microsoft stock increased its value by 600%, a tidy profit. During the same period, Novell stocks lost 70% of their value. Once again, the manager turns a hefty profit, having sold the shares previous to the decline.

This is a win-win scenario. The hedge fund strategy is actually twofold and is designed to not only make money in declining markets, but to minimize risk, so that losses on one side can be offset by gains on the other. Should Novell Inc. have gained rather than lost (by introducing a different popular software package, for instance), any subsequent return loss would have been more than adequately negated by gains on Microsoft—you would have bet on *both* sides of the table, so the only assets on one side you can "lose" are those that are not offset by assets "winning" on the *opposite* side.

To further understand Jones's system, we can use another example. Let's say you start out with $10,000 in capital. Using Jones's model, you would borrow money (leverage your position)—let's say you borrow $1,000, so you could buy $11,000 worth of shares. Then, you would *short* shares (borrow them hoping they decline in value) valued at $5,000. While the total amount you have invested is $16,000 (the $11,000 long and the $5,000 short positions), your *net market exposure* would only be $6,000 ($11,000 long minus $5,000 short). Jones would then say that your portfolio was 60% "net long," meaning that only 60% of your money is subject to decline in a downward market. His formula was as follows:

Market Exposure = (Long position – Short position) / Capital

This position is strengthened further by the fact that in an overall market decline, your short positions will *gain in value*, offsetting your losses on the *long side*.

Active Management

As we can see, the strategy requires a little more work than the traditional "buy and hold" model. It requires that the fund be *actively managed*, to take advantage of market swings and make sure that the investments are properly balanced.

So when the markets were down, Jones could shift a larger portion of his portfolio to the short side, and when they went up, he could shift back to the long side. And by applying leverage, he was able to greatly amplify his returns. Far from the traditional "buy and hold" strategy, Jones actively managed his capital, getting in and out of short and long positions to guard against swings in the market and make profits in every market climate. And amazing profits they were.

THE JONES THAT NOBODY KEEPS UP WITH

Jones operated in almost complete obscurity from 1949 until 1966, when an article in *Fortune* by Carol J. Loomis entitled "The Jones That Nobody Keeps Up With" profiled his partnership. The article detailed Jones's unique investment strategy and revealed that his fund had outperformed the best performing mutual fund by an impressive 44% and the best five-year mutual fund at the time by a staggering 85%, *net of all fees*.

In effect, the hedge concept puts Jones in a position to make money on both rising and falling stocks, and also partially shelters him if he misjudges the general trend of the market. He assumes that a prudent investor wants to protect part of his capital from such misjudgments. Most investors would build their defenses around cash reserve or bonds, but Jones protects himself by selling short.

To those investors who regard short selling with suspicion, Jones would simply say that he is using "speculative techniques for conservative ends." As illustration, he is given to contrasting his methods with those of an investor who has, say, $100,000 and elects to invest $80,000 of it in stocks and the rest in "safe" bonds. Jones would use the $100,000 to borrow perhaps another $50,000. . . . Of the $150,000 total, he might put $110,000 into stocks he likes and sell short $40,000 worth of stocks he thinks are overvalued. Thus he ends up with $40,000 of his long position hedged—i.e., offset by a short position—and the remaining $70,000 fully exposed. . . . His problem, therefore, is to buy stocks that will rise more than the general market, and sell stocks short that will rise less than the average (or will actually fall). If he succeeds in this effort, his rewards are multiplied because he's employing, not just a portion of his capital, but 150 percent of it. The main advantage of the hedge concept, then, is that the investor's short position enables him to operate on the long side with maximum aggressiveness. (Loomis, *Fortune*, April 1966)

Incentive Fees

The *Fortune* article attracted much attention from investors and managers alike. Investors, because of the remarkable returns, and managers, because of another unique twist in Jones's approach. As managing partner in 1952 (after transforming the general partnership into a limited partnership), Jones had introduced an *incentive fee* of 20% of all profits from the fund. This was an extremely attractive package for other fund managers, who were more than happy to give up large salaries in favour of profit participation in the portfolios they managed, as it created an opportunity to earn 10 to 20 times as much compensation (compared to long-only management) while managing smaller amounts of money.

Combined, these factors produced a minor explosion in the hedge fund industry, and from 1966 to 1968, nearly 140 new hedge funds were launched in the United States.

THE DOWN YEARS

Unfortunately, many of these new hedge fund managers weren't really "hedging" at all and didn't follow Jones's model for minimizing risk. For the most part, this was because of the stellar performance of the markets in the mid to late 1960s. As we have seen, when markets are up, hedge funds balance their returns by placing a larger portion of capital on the long side. Many of the equity markets rose by as much as 50% or more through 1967 and 1968. Under these conditions, the army of new and largely inexperienced hedge fund managers began realizing that shorting even a portion of their portfolios was becoming time consuming and costly. Most of them virtually stopped shorting at all and fell deeper into the more attractive (but inherently dangerous) strategy of high-leverage, long-only positions.

This was to be their downfall. Between the beginning of 1969 and the end of 1974, there were two very powerful downturns in the market. Most people are more familiar with the 1973–74 bear markets (remember the lineups at the gas stations?), but the previous market crash in 1969–70 was the most damaging to the new hedge fund industry. The savage conditions of 1973–74 finished off most of the already crippled hedge funds, and after the dust settled, only a scant 68 hedge funds were left, with assets under management by the largest 28 funds declining by more than 70%.

THE COMEBACK

The period between 1974 and 1986 was one in which only the shrewdest of managers survived, among them some of the biggest and most well known today: George Soros (who began his Quantum Fund in 1969), Michael Steinhardt (Steinhardt Partners in 1967), and, not surprisingly, Alfred Winslow Jones himself. Most importantly, this period saw the development of a new breed of hedge funds—funds that employed strategies and used tools unavailable to Jones and his disciples. Among the most successful, Julian Robertson (and his Tiger Fund Management, created in 1980) eventually became the poster child for the hedge fund revival in the late eighties and helped to establish a new and much larger milieu for the industry.

Tiger Fund Management applied the traditional "hedged equity" model to its $8 million in assets under management, and soon the financial world began to take notice, as Tiger posted a 24.3% gain in 1981, against a 5% drop by the Standard & Poor's 500 index—an average of the returns for the top 500 performing stocks. Over the next 18 years, Robertson averaged an annual return of 29%, better than anyone else at the time. With few hedge funds operating, he soon began piling up assets as more and more investors scrambled to get on board. This is when he was forced to diverge from the traditional "Jones" model. Why was this?

When picking stocks and working both the long and short sides of the market, it becomes very difficult to find enough strategies and ideas to handle large amounts of capital without disrupting the markets. This is because any large volume movements in a stock (caused by a large buy or sell order, for example) will most likely have an effect on its price and can alter the whole strategy of a fund. Imagine you hold stock in a company, and all of a sudden a hedge fund sells a million shares. What would you think? You'd assume that the manager knew something that you didn't, and you'd sell your shares before they started losing value—and so would everyone else. So when the Tiger Fund suddenly found itself with over $3 billion in assets, the hedged equity approach (Jones's model) became too cumbersome to manage, and Robertson turned to a style called "global macro" that he is well known for today (and indeed this is the style that both the media and the public have come to think of as "hedge funds" even though funds managed by this style represent less than 7% of the hedge fund industry—we'll discuss this later).

Global macro managers try to generate returns by recognizing differences between the price and the underlying value of stocks across a wide range of markets. Robertson's first "global macro play" was early in 1985, when he bet that the U.S. dollar would decline against the Swiss franc, deutsche mark, pound sterling, and yen. Spending $7 million on instruments known as "foreign currency call options," he managed to increase profits over a few months in excess of 200% of the capital risked. Investors began to sit up and take notice.

In 1986, *Institutional Investor* published an article that eerily paralleled Loomis's in *Fortune* from 20 years earlier. Appearing in the May issue of that year, "The Red Hot World of Julian Robertson" began another wave of interest from investors and managers alike. Bolstered by such swashbuckling hedge fund superstars as George Soros and his international bets (he made almost *$2 billion* betting that the English pound would fall), hedge funds were transformed from Jones's "speculative instruments for conservative purposes" to what the media touted as (and the public have come to know as) "freewheeling global playgrounds for the super rich." This and other controversial events of the nineties aided in creating a worldwide skepticism of hedge funds. This mistrust was further amplified in 1998 by the Long-Term Capital Management (LTCM) scandal, when a multi-billion-dollar bailout was organized by the U.S. Federal Reserve to avoid what the press was touting as a possible "global economic meltdown."

Literally hundreds of hedge funds with highly specialized strategies bearing no resemblance to Jones's original model have been created since 1980. The term "hedge fund" itself has been expanded to include any incentive-based investment vehicle employing non-traditional methods. Like ivy left unpruned, the industry, under the name "hedge fund," has grown and insinuated itself into virtually every part of the market. And it is the long periods of unchecked growth, the "gaps" between the media and the public's attention, that have allowed the industry to experiment with and exploit the many inefficiencies left open by more traditional investment vehicles.

THE MYTHS AND FACTS ABOUT LONG-TERM CAPITAL MANAGEMENT

One of the most infamous hedge fund stories is the relatively recent tale of LTCM. The Federal Reserve's organized multi-billion-dollar bailout (although no money came from them) in 1998 of this large global macro fund has given large financial institutions cause to rally behind renewed support of traditional investment vehicles and has caused investors to shy away from hedge funds and banks to become much more cautious in lending money to hedge funds. This is arguably a mistake.

Established in February 1994 and limited to investors who could afford a minimum of $10 million, LTCM generated billions of dollars in profits, logging astounding annual returns of nearly 30% in 1994 and more than 40% in 1995 and 1996. By the end of 1997, LTCM had nearly *tripled* its investors' money. Two of the firm's partners, Robert Merton and Myron Scholes, shared the Nobel Prize for economics in 1997 for their work on the pricing of options and other sophisticated financial instruments (which formed the basis of LTCM's investment strategies).

LTCM's strategy was a fairly traditional "Jones" style, aiming to make money no matter the direction of the markets, by buying assets that seemed cheaper than they should be and simultaneously short selling assets that seemed too expensive. Using complex computer models, LTCM believed it had a nearly foolproof strategy that found and then exploited temporary price "distortions" between the price of U.S., Japanese, and European bonds whose relative price had reflected a historical pattern of consistency ("undervalued" and "overvalued" securities). The theory was that over time, the value of these bonds would tend to become identical (the spread between the bonds would return to its historical level). While the two values remained "distorted," however, a profit could be realized by capturing the difference. We'll explain in more detail how this works in Chapter 4.

The plan worked spectacularly well, until the Asian economic crisis hit and the Russian government defaulted on its domestic debt in August and September 1998. Suddenly, there was a worldwide flight to safety (where investors quickly try to safeguard their capital by investing in "safer" vehicles), and historical patterns were completely abandoned as panicked investors sold Japanese and European bonds to buy U.S. bonds (traditionally a "safer" investment). The temporary distortions between the bonds, instead of narrowing as in the past, actually ballooned. Rather than making a profit on a narrowing gap, LTCM incurred huge losses on both sides of its bets.

THE MAIN PROBLEM: LEVERAGING

Not only did LTCM bet the wrong way on both sides of their hedge, but because the difference in the price between the bonds they were trading was minute, they had also leveraged themselves heavily (to amplify returns) and had borrowed that money from the largest banks and brokerage houses in the world. This endangered a world banking system that was already shaky from the huge losses in Russia and Asia. The fund had less than $2.5 billion in capital, which it used as collateral to purchase as much as $125 billion in securities. Using these securities as collateral, the firm was able to engage in complex financial transactions that affected as much as *$1.25 trillion* in securities worldwide. Because of the hedged positions, many of these transactions offset one another (Jones's "market exposure"), so LTCM's collapse would not have resulted in total losses anywhere near this size. However, the U.S. federal government was worried that if the fund were forced to "unwind" all its positions (sell off assets) over a very short time period, the entire global financial system might have been in trouble—you will remember our discussions about how difficult it is to move large blocks of shares without disrupting the markets—which is why, in September 1998, the president of the Federal Reserve Bank of New York called a meeting of the chief executives of some of the world's biggest commercial and investment banks. Using its position, the Fed successfully organized a massive private-sector rescue of LTCM by demanding that most of the banks contribute $300 million each to a $3.5-billion rescue fund.

A RARE CASE

Hedge funds, contrary to popular belief, do not speculate wildly, but rather see themselves as "arbitrageurs," meaning that they look for assets with prices they believe are temporarily higher or lower than their fundamental value. By taking one side of a trade that everyone else doesn't want, speculators improve *liquidity*, or the *amount* of stocks and bonds that are traded regularly. This keeps the markets "moving." In truth, the LTCM failure is an isolated and rare case. Regardless, the carefree late nineties' bull-market boom of hedge funds quickly changed to concern and pessimism as people started wrongly blaming hedge funds for the economic turmoil that, in fact, brought them down as well. The relative secrecy of hedge funds' operations, the charismatic and entrepreneurial nature of their managers, and the speculations concerning their involvement in manipulating markets worldwide, combined with a scant few examples of funds borrowing (leveraging) heavily to amplify their bets to create an overall skepticism that seriously tarnished hedge funds' reputation.

The combination of a low-risk strategy with enormous leverage is indeed rare, and other market-neutral funds earned an average of 14% returns over the five years leading up to 1998, compared with the incredible 40% per year for LTCM during the same period. This alone indicates that LTCM was a unique case.

It is also important to note that leveraging heavily is not only limited to so-called alternative investments. Many large banks regularly leverage their trading arms by as much as 20 to 1, and on a much larger scale. Some reports say that where LTCM had an exposure of $80 billion in the U.S. Treasuries, the banks had

$3 trillion tied up in similar bets. This was the reason that the banks felt they had to rescue LTCM. Had the fund been allowed to collapse, and all of its positions been liquidated, it would have drastically and negatively affected the banks' similar bets.

In truth, almost a third of all hedge funds don't borrow at all, and more than half borrow no more than the amount investors put into them. The rest rarely leverage more than 10 to 1, and only on certain positions.

HEDGE FUND GROWTH IN THE WORLD TODAY

Globally, hedge funds grew to almost 8,000 in 2004 from 4,000 in 2000 and about 500 in 1990. Assets under management in the industry similarly increased to over US$1 trillion in 2004 from about US$500 billion in 2000 and US$50 billion in 1990. To what factors do we owe this staggering growth? Tables 1.1 and 1.2 can give us an idea. As you can see, hedge funds managed to outperform the major indices regardless of the market condition over the periods shown.

TABLE 1.1: HISTORICAL HEDGE FUND PERFORMANCE VERSUS GLOBAL EQUITY AND FIXED INCOME INDICES, JANUARY 1998 TO DECEMBER 2004

	Annual ROR	Standard Dev.	Sharpe 4%
VAN Global Hedge Fund Index	15.96%	8.80%	1.36
MSCI World Index (C$)	8.08%	14.07%	0.29
S&P 500 TRI (C$)	11.87%	13.64%	0.58
Morningstar Average Equity Mutual Fund	10.04%	15.90%	0.38
Lehman Brothers Aggregate Bond Index	8.11%	5.42%	0.76

TABLE 1.2: PERFORMANCE AT THE HEIGHT OF THE BULL MARKET, JANUARY 1995 TO MARCH 2000

	VAN Global Hedge Fund Index	MSCI World Index
Annualized Return	20.21%	19.86%
Annualized Standard Deviation	8.51%	13.34%
Sharpe Ratio (4%)	1.90	1.19

TABLE 1.3: PERFORMANCE IN ONE OF THE MOST DIFFICULT PERIODS, APRIL 2000 TO DECEMBER 2004

	VAN Global Hedge Fund Index	MSCI World Index
Annualized Return	6.47%	-6.14%
Annualized Standard Deviation	5.97%	13.87%
Sharpe Ratio (4%)	0.41	-0.73

HEDGE FUNDS IN CANADA TODAY

The public perception of hedge funds in Canada as the new millennium began was dismal. In the events of the past few years leading up to today, however, we can see the rebirth of interest in hedge funds. Between 1995 (when there were fewer than 15 funds in Canada) and 2000, the hedge fund industry grew slightly in this country, but in the second half of 2000, it began a boom that continues today. At the end of 2004 there were about 200 active hedge funds in Canada (the total number is about 350, but many are duplicates or different classes of the same funds), and every indication is that this number is much lower than it will be 5 or 10 years from now. There has been consistent growth in the industry since 2000, with around 4 to 10 new hedge funds being launched each month. It seems obvious that the heavy losses suffered by investors in traditional long-only mutual funds and other vehicles during the bear market of 2000 to 2003 have created an increasing interest in alternatives. Although equity markets rebounded in 2003 and 2004, their performance was really not strong enough to suggest we will see anything like the numbers they were posting between 1982 and 2000. But even if equity markets deliver returns similar to those of the past, the risk associated with equity investing can make investors nervous, having lived through the recent dismal times.

The hedge fund market in Canada is still relatively small (although rapidly growing), representing only about 3% of mutual fund investments. The size of the hedge fund industry at the retail level is around $16 billion, versus $500 billion invested in mutual funds. On top of that there is about $10 billion invested in hedge funds by institutions. By contrast, the United States boasts around 5,000 hedge funds, accounting for about 7.5% of mutual fund assets. Even U.K. and Netherlands investors have around 3.5% of their capital in hedge funds.

The Canadian hedge fund market clearly has some more growing to do. The following chapters lead you through a more in-depth look at the current state of the investment industry in Canada, describe the various styles of hedge funds today, and talk about how investors should apply hedge funds to their existing portfolios. This information is essential to the prudent investor's goal of finding vehicles to continue portfolio growth through the volatile times of today and the future.

The Difference Between Hedge Funds and Mutual Funds

A SHORT HISTORY OF MUTUAL FUNDS

Mutual funds have been on the financial landscape for longer than most investors realize. The industry is usually traced back to Great Britain, where the Foreign and Colonial Government Trust, formed in London in 1868, is widely considered to be the first example of a "mutual-fund style" investment. Some would argue, however, that this kind of investing had been introduced almost a century prior to this in Holland, when a Dutch merchant named Adriaan van Ketwich invited investors to form an investment trust under the name of Eendragt Maakt Magt (loosely translated to mean "Unity Creates Strength") in 1774. The purpose of the trust was to let small investors diversify without a large investment. This diversification, or risk spreading, came from foreign bond investments in countries such as Austria, Denmark, Spain, Sweden, and Russia, as well as some European-owned plantations in Central and South America. With an initial capitalization of 1 million guilders (around US$500,000 today), the fund invested in 10 different groups of bonds and diversified its assets across these groups. The fund promised a 4% per year dividend, which was slightly *below* the average interest rate on the bonds in its portfolio. What this meant was that as long as the bonds did not default, investment income would be more than the promised dividend payments—creating a surplus. The interesting twist was a form of lottery embedded in the process to attract investors. The difference between the promised 4% return and the actual interest rate of the bonds was placed in a cash reserve. This reserve was then used to "retire" a specified number of fund shares each year at 10% more than their face value. The dividends for the retiring shares would then be split between neighbouring shares; when share number 67 was retired, for example, its 4% dividend would be split between shares numbered 66 and 68, which would then earn 6% (obviously, by today's standards, this was a highly suspect practice).

Other investment vehicles followed Eendragt Maakt Magt, with similar success and equally interesting names such as Voordeelig en Voorsigtig (Profitable and Prudent) in 1776, and a second by van Ketwich himself called Concordia Res Parvae Crescunt (Small Matters Grow by Consent) in 1779. The success of these ventures was, it is assumed, based on modest capital gains and not on creative nomenclature.

The Foreign and Colonial Government Trust in England some 90 years later had a similar mandate. It promised the "investor of modest means the same advantages as the large capitalist . . . by spreading the investment over a number of different stocks." Like its Dutch counterpart, it offered diversification, one of the few ways to minimize risk in a long-only investment (losing smaller amounts by spreading out the capital among a variety of vehicles). Most of the early British investment companies (including the early Dutch investment trusts) and their American counterparts resembled today's "closed-end" funds and sold a *fixed number of shares* (raising a certain amount of money to invest), with the price of those shares being determined by supply and demand (as a source for this section, see Investment Company Institute [ICI], *Mutual Funds Fact Book*, 1997).

The first "modern" mutual fund is widely considered to be the Massachusetts Investors Trust, which was introduced in Boston in March 1924 with a modest portfolio of 45 stocks and $50,000 in assets. It was the first so-called "open-end" mutual fund and introduced a concept that revolutionized the fund industry: a continuous offering of new shares, thus continuously raising money to invest. These shares were redeemable at any time, based on the current value of the fund's assets (the fund is still in existence today, and information about it can be found on the Internet at www.mfs.com).

The growth of the early mutual fund industry was hampered by the 1929 stock market crash and the Great Depression. With long-only portfolios, even the sharpest investors couldn't beat the staggering losses during this period. The result was that mutual funds began gaining popularity only in the forties and fifties, when the markets started to boom. In 1940 there were fewer than 80 funds in the United States, with total assets of $500 million. Twenty years later, there were 160 funds and $17 billion in assets. The industry truly exploded when huge amounts of money began flowing into mutual fund coffers in the mid-1980s, and by the end of 1999 more than 8,000 mutual funds were managing close to $7 trillion in assets.

The first mutual fund in Canada, the Canadian Investment Fund, was founded in 1932. Mutual fund growth in this country mirrored U.S. trends over the 50 years following this, but the actual explosion in the Canadian mutual fund industry happened slightly later, in the 1990s, with assets increasing from $25 billion in December 1990 to $500 billion by January 2005. Today, approximately 4,200 investment funds are available in Canada, offered by a variety of fund and insurance companies. Interestingly, the Canadian government's Department of Finance Web site (www.fin.gc.ca/fin-eng.html) states that there are approximately 50 million unit holder accounts in Canada. Since there are only around 30 million people living in this country and some of them are too young to even say "mutual fund" (never mind hold units in one), it is obvious that most investors have units in multiple funds. This is a good demonstration of the huge popularity of these investment vehicles in Canada today.

What has happened recently? What caused the serious declines in value leading up to 2002? Why have mutual funds not been able to gain back their former glory?. There are two main reasons: one, mutual funds, because of their long-only positions, are correlated to the markets (and thus provide returns that are relative to them), and two, the rules they must abide by *prohibit them from doing anything else*.

RULES FOR MUTUAL FUNDS

The United States *Investment Company Act of 1940* regulates the "dos and donts" of mutual funds. The Canadian counterpart to this is the *National Instrument 81-102*, which regulates the funds under the Department of Finance's definition:

Mutual Fund
A company that uses its capital to invest in other companies. Its capital is a pool of funds gathered from a number of investors and placed in securities selected to meet specific criteria and goals. Mutual fund companies fall under the jurisdiction of the provincial securities commissions.

Two fundamental guiding principles govern the investment techniques of mutual funds: *safety* and *liquidity*. Safety refers to the fact that fund managers are not allowed to invest in instruments that have very high risk, and liquidity means that they must invest in instruments that are easily sellable (so they can provide cash in case the investor redeems his or her shares). Both these tenets are a result of the fiduciary responsibility, preservation of capital, and prudence principles (discussed in the previous chapter) put in place to protect the investor from the risks of speculation and to satisfy government regulators who are concerned with the integrity and stability of the markets.

Let's look more closely at these two principles.

Liquidity

Liquidity is essentially a measurement of how easy it is to liquidate (convert to cash or equivalent) an investment. We can use a fairly common example to demonstrate the inherent risks in illiquid (not easily convertible into cash or equivalent) investments:

Jim, a young professional, inherited $250,000 from a distant aunt who died in Germany. He paid off some bills, bought some clothes, and took an extravagant European vacation, so by the time all was said and done he had about $200,000 left. He decided to invest his newly found wealth.

It was the spring of 2000, and Jim believed the stock market was showing signs of serious decline, so he figured that real estate would be a more solid investment (even though he also believed that some of the fibre optic companies looked like they might get better in the next few months). He purchased a small condominium downtown and rented it out to a couple who were more than happy to sign a two-year lease. After paying expenses, Jim was making a 5% return on his investment and betting that the condo would appreciate 6 to 7% every year until he sold it.

As fate had it, though, Jim met Cathy shortly after his transactions. It was love at first sight. Three weeks later he proposed to her, and in the summer of 2000 they were married. Two months after the wedding they were house hunting, as Cathy was pregnant and they could not imagine raising a child in Jim's small midtown condo (which they were living in at the time). Jim put both condos on the market—the one they were living in, and the one he had purchased for invest-ment purposes. By selling both of them, he figured they would have a large enough down payment for a nice house in a good neighbourhood. In a short six days, he had an offer for the unit they were living in, for *more* money than it was listed for. Jim was happy to sign. However, the other condo was a different story. There were many interested parties, but once potential buyers found out that there was a lease on the condo for another year and a half, they shied away. They wanted to move in, not sit on the property for investment purposes.

Three months later the unit still had not sold, and Jim had reduced its price to well below what he paid for it. In the meantime, the deal on their other condo had closed, and Jim and Cathy had to move into a rental, since they didn't have enough money for the down payment in the area where they wanted to purchase.

Time was *definitely* not on their side. Finally, at the end of January 2001, they received an offer for the rental unit. Once the deal was done, and commissions and legal fees were paid, Jim calculated that he had lost $37,000 on the deal. Though in the end Jim and Cathy managed to get enough money together for the down payment on their dream house, it was an agonizing experience living in limbo for months on end.

Jim's alternative, as he saw it, would have been to invest in a number of fibre optic stocks. Not only would he have made money during the summer of 2000 (due to the boom in technology stocks), he would have had no problem getting back into cash, or liquidating the shares—a call to his broker would have done it, and a small commission (small compared to what real estate agents get) would have been all it cost.

Stocks, for the most part, are very liquid instruments. Buyers and sellers can always be found on the major stock exchanges, so it is relatively easy to get a match for your needs (as long as your block of shares isn't too big!). This is why mutual funds are obliged to invest in instruments that are highly liquid—if you have to get your money back, they can just sell some of their holdings quickly and redeem your units.

Safety

The safety of an investment is the second major consideration. In the previous chapter we described what short selling is. Short selling involves borrowing a stock and selling it in anticipation of being able to repurchase it at a lower price, at or before the time it must be returned to the lender. But what happens if the price starts going up after you have made the commitment and borrowed it? By definition, you lose money. If you buy a stock, the most you can lose is the price you paid for it (i.e., the stock's value cannot go below zero), but on the short side the losses can be unlimited, since (theoretically) prices can continue to rise indefinitely. There is no limit to how much money you can lose. This is where safety comes in. The rules of mutual funds prohibit investing in a short position, thereby protecting the unit holders from the theoretically unlimited losses.

A number of other prohibitions exist, such as strict guidelines on the percentage of the fund's holdings that can be in one stock (or type of stock) and the percentage of stocks of a particular company a fund can hold. Both these rules are in place to minimize potential losses to the fund by forcing it to diversify its holdings and spread out risk. Mutual funds can therefore *hold only a diversified long portfolio*. These regulations serve as safeguards to protect the public's interest, but as we will see, they can become a hindrance under certain circumstances.

RELATIVE PERFORMANCE AND WHY MUTUAL FUNDS ARE MEASURED BY IT

Mutual fund performance is generally correlated to market performance, due to the buy and hold (long) strategy. Therefore, mutual funds are measured in light of that performance. This measurement is obtained by comparing their performance to the overall performance of various averages and indices, or amalgamations of top-performing securities ("blue chip" stocks) in the market.

In North America, there are four major stock markets: the New York Stock Exchange (NYSE), the American Stock Exchange (AMEX), the National Association of Securities Dealers Automated Quotient (NASDAQ), and the Toronto Stock Exchange (TSX). All these exchanges have an index that is one way or another tied to the performance of the stocks listed on the exchange.

The NYSE has the famous Dow Jones Industrial Average index, which reflects the price of 30 major stocks in important industry sectors, 28 of which are listed on the exchange itself and two of which, Intel and Microsoft, are actually NASDAQ stocks. The NASDAQ has the NASDAQ 100 index, which tracks the prices of its 100 top securities. The AMEX Composite Index is a similar index. In Canada, what was the TSE 300 Composite Index (or an average of the top 300 stocks on the old TSE) was recently converted to the S&P/TSX Composite Index, reducing the number of stocks averaged to 60 (this was largely because of the dot-com crash in 2001).

These indices, while useful for specific industries in specific places, are limited in scope when compared to the broader markets (since they measure only a few stocks). To measure the performance of broad markets, there are the so-called broad market indices. The most famous of these is the S&P 500. The Standard & Poor's corporation of Chicago publishes this index, which covers the 500 largest corporations in America, regardless of their home exchange. Because of the large number of stocks it covers, the S&P 500 is the most representative of the general markets of the United States, and as such, it serves as the "benchmark" for many mutual funds. This means that the performance of a fund is measured against the S&P 500 Index.

So, if in a given year a fund that uses the S&P 500 as its benchmark gains a 15% return while the index gains only 13%, we would say that the fund *outperformed the index* by 2 percentage points. In declining markets, if the index drops by 19% and the fund drops by only 14%, we would say that the fund *outperformed the index* by 5 percentage points.

This is what is called *relative* performance (relative to the index that is used as the benchmark for the fund). However, not all funds use the S&P 500 as their benchmark. Funds that invest in Canadian stocks, for instance, would use the S&P/TSX or the Toronto Stock Exchange's tracking index.

Why are mutual funds measured relative to the broad market indices? The practice is a combination of history and economic theory.

Modern Portfolio Theory

Mutual funds started to gain popularity in the 1950s when stock market performance was robust. After the Second World War, thousands of soldiers returned home to start families, enter the civilian workforce, and spend their money. The "baby boom" hit quickly, and the economy was fuelled by a need for everything from new and larger housing to new technologies.

This period also coincided with the evolution of new financial thinking in academia and the development in the 1950s of the modern portfolio theory by Harry Markowitz and William F. Sharpe, professors of economics at the University of Chicago. The theory was based on the observation that asset classes (securities in specific industries) all had different degrees and types of risk associated with them. Markowitz and Sharpe suggested that by analyzing these varying degrees and types of risk and quantifying them, one could put together a diversified portfolio that gave a return directly related to the amount of risk. This construction of the portfolio was done by carefully combining asset classes, so that they were not correlated to one another and they responded with different patterns to different market conditions. The relationship between the oil and gas industry and the oil and gas *service* industry would be correlated, for instance. When the oil industry is hurt because of a particular event, the service industry is hurt at the same time and to a greater or lesser degree (this also applies to a number of other industries, such as tourism and airlines). Thus, a portfolio containing stocks in both these classes would be more exposed to risk (of declining in value) in the event of a disaster in the industry.

Before this theory was put forward, investors had relied on one of two strategies in making stock choices: *technical analysis* or *fundamental analysis*. Technical analysts carefully examine historic market data, looking for patterns in the movements of particular stocks and investing in the hopes that the patterns will repeat themselves. Fundamental analysts analyze particular businesses and their prospects for growth based on factors within the industry, investing in companies they feel either are on the verge of growing faster than the economy or appear undervalued.

In the 1960s, researchers began to use computers for the first time to analyze historical data and pick apart the daily price movements of every stock listed since 1926. What they discovered changed investing yet again. They found, through their analysis, that stock prices, rather than having recurring patterns, were affected by *events*. Events are, by nature, random, so technical analysis—looking for repeating patterns—was worthless and even impossible. The researchers also concluded that the markets were highly efficient, meaning that any information affecting a stock's price (world events, accounting scandals, takeovers, etc.) was reflected almost immediately. This threw out fundamental analysis as well, for it was evident that investors were all using the same information from the same sources and would all arrive at the same conclusions.

The overall conclusion was that picking winning stocks was impossible, and investors should focus more on being in the right *asset class* (such as energy or high tech) and not just the right stock. The key was to formulate an asset allocation policy (based on risks and returns) and construct a portfolio based on the policy's objectives.

Asset allocation attempts to diversify holdings (the portfolio) so that no one industry downturn or collapse will hurt the portfolio too much. The idea is to find asset classes that are uncorrelated to one another. Almost all large institutions began using asset allocation as their main strategy, so much so that money managers in these institutions began specializing in particular asset classes and focusing their efforts in tightly defined styles.

All of this was combined with a raging bull market through the fifties and sixties, when companies in virtually every sector were booming. In this climate, the buy and hold strategy was extremely profitable, and mutual fund sales were driven by *performance*. Stock market analysts at the time were claiming that the general stock market gave higher returns over time than anything else, implying that investing and waiting would eventually pay off, and a couple of losing years were simply the price to be paid to achieve superior returns in the long run.

In this environment, the yardstick used by investors and advisers alike is the comparison of *relative* performance among available funds. To do this comparison, they adopted benchmarks such as the Dow Jones and the S&P 500.

HOW HEDGE FUNDS DIFFER FROM MUTUAL FUNDS

- *Hedge funds seek "absolute" returns.*
  Unlike mutual funds, hedge funds seek to benefit from both increasing and decreasing stock prices, while mutual funds make money only if the underlying investments they hold increase in value. Hedge funds have investments in long positions (investments that go up in value if the underlying asset goes up) and

short positions (investments that go up in value if the underlying asset goes down). By combining "longs" and "shorts" in a portfolio, hedge funds are able to reduce risk because in a falling market, short positions will offset or even reverse losses accumulated on long positions.

Hedge funds do not fully subscribe to the old idea that stocks are superior performers over the long term. Rather, they aim to reduce the risk usually associated with investing in stocks (whether they will gain or lose value depending on events). Because their structure has the potential of making money in any market condition, hedge funds seek to make positive returns every year rather than merely outperforming the market index. Hedge funds simply have more tools at hand to make money than mutual funds, and because of this, their goal is to achieve absolute (positive) returns, uncorrelated to the market.

- *Mutual funds are highly regulated.*

Mutual funds are restricted from using short selling and other hedging techniques. As we have seen, these rules were put in place many years ago to protect investors from the risks associated with what were deemed to be "speculative" investments. These regulations can, however, serve as a kind of straitjacket, making it more difficult to outperform the market and to protect the assets of the fund in sliding (downward) market conditions. Any kind of restriction means potentially less return. This is especially true in a falling market when, as more stocks lose ground, mutual fund portfolios are likely to decrease in value as well—how can you make money when your benchmark is negative? In this type of market only managers of superior insight can make money, and that has so far proved to be a very tall order.

- *Hedge funds are less regulated than mutual funds.*

Hedge funds are much less regulated than mutual funds. Less regulation means more options, which in turn leads to potentially better performance. Hedge funds also generally have higher-than-usual minimum investment thresholds. Because their investors are usually more knowledgeable about their investments, hedge funds are granted the option to pursue strategies and techniques not available to mutual fund managers.

This may not remain the case, however. As the manuscript for this book was being submitted, the Ontario Securities Commission announced that it had suspended the operations of Portus Alternative Asset Management Inc. for "questionable marketing practices." While there was no mention of specific violations, it is highly likely that should this kind of action continue, Canadian hedge funds will be more regulated in the future.

- *Remuneration of mutual fund managers is based on a percentage of the assets under their management (AUM).*

  Mutual fund managers are paid according to an annual management fee based on the value of assets under their management (AUM). The fee is usually 2 to 3% of AUM per year, and is *not dependent on the fund's performance.* This fee structure means that mutual fund managers are *not penalized for negative or poorer-than-average performance.* While logic might dictate that poor performance would slow the growth of a mutual fund's AUM (by failing to attract new investors), this fee structure provides little or no incentive for managers to perform, but rather encourages them to stick to their benchmarks and be "middle of the road."

- *Hedge fund managers typically receive a performance-related fee.*

  From Chapter 1, you will remember that hedge fund managers receive an incentive fee on top of the annual management fees (which are similar to mutual funds' management fees). This is because hedge fund management is more demanding and requires greater knowledge, skill, and talent. And it is because of this differing fee structure that hedge funds are able to attract the best talent in the market. Hedge fund managers also most often have a significant amount of their personal wealth invested in the funds they manage.

  This "incentive" or "performance fee" is usually 20% of the fund's performance in a calendar year. Simply put, posting a high positive return is financially much more rewarding for a hedge fund manager than for a mutual fund manager. The following example (Table 2.1) shows the effect of the incentive fee:

TABLE 2.1

	Hedge Fund A	Mutual Fund B
Size (start of year)	$150 Million	$150 Million
Management Fee	2.0%	2.5%
Performance	20%	10%
Performance Fee	20%	N/A
TOTAL FEES	$9.0 Million	$3.75 Million

The performance fee model of remuneration used by hedge funds transfers the pain of incurring a loss to the manager by depriving him or her of potential compensation (which is in many cases equal to or greater than the management fee).

- *Mutual funds cannot effectively protect portfolios in declining markets other than by going into cash.*

  In a falling market the value of mutual funds will probably decline since most of the stock in their portfolios will parallel the general market direction (that is, a relative return). Even if a mutual fund manager anticipates further drops in the market, regulations restrict mutual fund investments to long positions only (which will reflect the market trend). The only safe bet in this situation would be to liquidate losing investments into real money, or cash. Managers rarely take the action of going to cash, however, for three reasons:

1. Each mutual fund has a mandate to be in a specific sector of the market, or *asset class*. It is not the job of a mutual fund manager to deviate from this mandate by moving into cash, as each manager's asset class is often an integral part of an overall diversified portfolio. Thus the mandate to stay in their asset class is far more important than the safety of the investor's capital within that class.

2. Mutual funds are rated by their relative performance, therefore a negative performance by itself is not considered detrimental, as long as losses are comparable to other funds and their benchmarks.

3. The broad market increases about 60 to 70% of the time (increases rather than declines), and a cash position has only a 30 to 40% chance of outperforming funds relative to this. If a manager is wrong, and underperforms compared to other fund managers, the penalties of possible job loss and/or a reduction of assets under management outweigh any prospective gain.

- *Hedge funds use various "hedging" strategies to make money on the downside.*
  Because of their regulations and aims, hedge funds actively use techniques that have the potential to realize increased value in a falling market. By combining long and short positions in a portfolio, most hedge funds reduce their dependence on market direction in order to perform. It should be noted, however, that some funds that are termed hedge funds do not actually "hedge" against risk. For example, a global macro fund (see hedge fund strategies in Chapter 4) may speculate on changes in economic policies that have an impact on interest rates, while using high levels of leverage.

  Returns for these funds can be impressive, but so can their losses. In reality, they account for less than 5% of all hedge funds.

- *Performance of mutual funds depends on the direction of the equity markets.*
  As noted earlier, mutual funds will likely perform positively only if their benchmark market does the same. This is because they are limited to long positions and their investment levels are usually close to 100%.

Many hedge fund strategies do not depend on market direction. Accordingly, they have a very low correlation to traditional equity markets as well as to each other.

Because hedge funds may hold long and short positions at any point in time and because their relative share (compared to each other) can also be frequently changed, hedge funds are much less reliant on market direction than mutual funds. Due to this ability, hedge funds depend much more on the stock-picking abilities of their managers than on positive performance, a benchmark, or the market.

- **The mutual fund industry is homogeneous.**
  There is a high correlation among mutual funds, so diversification among equity mutual funds will only slightly change the overall risk of the portfolio. Because of their more limited choices, and because most of them are 90 to 95% invested in widely diversified, long-only positions in their respective markets, similar mutual funds exhibit very similar performance results. They are therefore *homogeneous*. As a result, diversification in similar types of mutual funds adds little to a portfolio's risk reduction. The problem is that many Canadians seek to diversify by spreading investments over several mutual funds, yet because of their homogeneity, most mutual funds are invested in the same companies. It is an "apples to apples" comparison and simply does not result in an effectively diversified portfolio.

- **The hedge fund industry is heterogeneous.**
  There is a low correlation among hedge funds, so diversification among hedge funds results in substantial reduction of risk. They are therefore *heterogeneous*.
  Hedge funds are a very diverse group of investment vehicles. Even similar types of hedge funds exhibit widely different results with regard to both risk and performance. As a result, hedge funds have low correlation with each other and to mutual funds. This is because

  1. Hedge funds have significantly more choices in products and strategies than mutual funds.

  2. Hedge funds are allowed to have a more focused portfolio because, unlike mutual funds, they are not restricted by a limit of 10% exposure to any one financial investment vehicle.

Because of their heterogeneity, hedge funds can provide excellent diversification benefits when investing in different hedge funds (or in a "fund of funds" hedge fund—see Chapter 4) within an individual portfolio.

We have seen that mutual funds, by their nature and history, are highly regulated instruments. The industry is founded on a buy and hold strategy, which correlates performance directly to the increases and declines of the broad markets. With trillions of dollars under management, mutual fund companies basically use themselves as benchmarks for returns, a policy that has created a culture that can see a loss as positive, as long as that loss is relatively less than the markets or that of other mutual funds.

Conversely, hedge funds are largely uncorrelated to the markets and are free to employ strategies and techniques for investment unavailable to mutual funds. This allows hedge funds to actively seek positive, absolute returns every year, by remaining uncorrelated to both the broad markets and other hedge funds.

Hedge Funds	Mutual Funds
Private investment vehicles	Regulated investment vehicles
Limited use of leverage	Use of leverage not permitted
Manager may short sell	Prohibited from short sell
Restricted from advertising	May freely advertise and promote
Manager is compensated on performance	Manager paid a salary and bonus
Manager invests own capital in the fund	Manager does not invest own capital in fund
Liquidity varies from daily to yearly	Daily liquidity and redemption
Offered by offering memorandum	Offered by prospectus
Flexibility in investment strategies	Relatively flexible
Seek to make positive returns (absolute returns)	Seek to outperform known market benchmark

With the uncertainty of today's markets, being able to manipulate investments to decrease risk and take advantage of any opportunity for positive returns is paramount. In Canada today, there is an obvious and growing need for these kinds of alternatives.

Why Canadians
Need Hedge Funds

MUTUAL FUND PERFORMANCE

In the first two years of the new century, the performance of mutual funds was disappointing, to say the least, with return levels of the average equity mutual fund in Canada declining to 4.1% in 2001 from 11% in 2000. Statistics for 2002 are even worse, with the average Canadian equity fund losing a painful 12%. This alone has made many Canadian investors not only concerned but inclined to actively seek at least stable, and at best profitable, investments. As a case in point, almost $6 billion was taken out of mutual funds in Canada from June 2002 to January 2003. The reason for this was that the overall market declined during the same period. As discussed in the previous chapters, mutual funds provide relative performance, and thus their volatility is parallel to the performance of the general markets. When the markets are down, mutual funds are down, too.

Table 3.1 shows the performance of the S&P 500 Index (generally representing U.S. stock markets), the S&P/TSX Composite Index (Canadian equity markets), and the Canadian and U.S. bond indices.

TABLE 3.1

	2000	2001	2002	2003	2004
S&P 500 TRI in US$	-9.10%	-11.90%	-21.10%	28.70%	10.90%
S&P/TSX Composite Index TRI	6.18%	-13.94%	-13.97%	25.26%	13.66%
U.S. 90-Day T-Bills Bonds	5.76%	3.56%	1.61%	1.03%	1.30%
Scotia McLeod Univers Bond	10.24%	8.08%	8.73%	6.70%	7.08%

All returns are calculated on index values converted into C$ unless otherwise indicated.

We can see from this information that in order for the relative performance-oriented mutual funds to get back to the stellar numbers of the nineties, there must be a bull market that matches the general market numbers of the same time frame. History shows us that there is simply no way to predict these swings or how long a particular trend will last.

THE ROLLER COASTER EFFECT

The outstanding performance of the markets for the last years of the 20th century was the result of a booming technology sector. Prices skyrocketed daily as both institutional and private investors bought up stocks at a feverish pace. The NASDAQ, where most tech stocks trade, ballooned well into the 5,000s (5,132, in fact, was the all-time high during trading on March 10, 2000. At market close on that day the NASDAQ stood at 5,048).

What happened to all that stock after the collapse in 2000? As the NASDAQ plunged more than 2,000 points over a four-week period through late March and April, why did people hold on to their investments? The answer is _hope_. Investors hold on to their overpriced stocks, hoping desperately that the prices will climb again and they can get out without huge losses. Look at Figure 3.1 and imagine that you invested in Nortel in October 1999. On the first of that month, you would have purchased the stock at US$28.38 (adjusted price). This was $20.62 or almost _four times_ as much as it was at the same time in 1998. Still, everyone was saying that it would continue to climb, with no end in sight.

FIGURE 3.1: THE NORTEL ROLLER COASTER

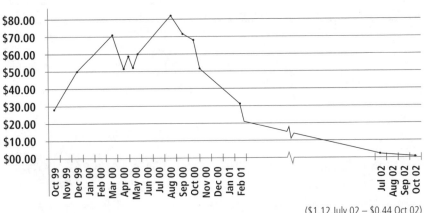

($1.12 July 02 – $0.44 Oct 02)

Sure enough, by the end of December 1999, your shares have grown to an astounding $50.35, a 56% return in only *three months*. Eureka! You've hit the jackpot. You're telling everyone about your incredible market skills, liquidating other investments to put more money into Nortel, and urging all your friends and family to buy it as well and enjoy the ride with you.

Three months later, the stock is at an incredible $70.42, almost a *110% return in six months*. You're planning early retirement as you sit and scan the Saturday morning business section. Like a gambler on a lucky streak, you just "let it ride."

But wait. The stock drops radically for a few weeks, and it stands at $51.10 on April 17. What's happening? Not to worry; it will come back. Sure enough, it's back to $58.23 on May 1. Whew. But then it tanks again to $51.60 the next week. Should you sell? No. No one else is selling. They must know something. Your hunch is correct; it's back to $59.88 on May 30. Not only that, it shoots up over the next three months to $82.51! The train is on the tracks again, and you're sitting on a stock that is worth almost *three times more* than you paid for it. Now it's not just early retirement, but you're eyeing the aging Buick in your garage and thinking about a BMW, or maybe *two*.

September comes with a bit of a jolt, though. The stock goes down to $72.47 on the fourth. No problem; you've seen this before. Heck, it went all the way down to $51 and change back in April. By October 16, it has dropped to $68.11. Still nothing to worry about; it's been worse. No problem.

The next week, however, it plunges over $25 to $42.44. Should you wait it out? Yes. It can come back from that, can't it? Only a year ago, it was worth a mere $28.38. This is a glitch.

The next three months are nail-biters. The stock goes up a little one week, only to lose again the next, on a small but steady decline. Nervous, but still confident in an upswing, you wait it out until the first part of February, when it suddenly dives $5 in a week and stands at $30.50. Now you're *really* scared. You bought the stock for $28.38, so you're dangerously close to being right back where you were. So much for the BMW, you think. There's still a spread worth keeping though, and the stock hasn't been *really* volatile. A few bucks here and there; you can afford to wait until it's a little closer to your original purchase price.

Too late! The next week the stock nosedives to $20. Now you're in a *losing* position. How can this have happened? What were you thinking? One thing is for sure, though; you're not going to sell it and lose money. No sir. Not until you're *sure* it won't come back.

The rest, as they say, is history. A long and steady decline in Nortel's stock price brought it to an unbelievable low of $0.44 on October 10, 2002. After being up almost 300%, your stock is now worth a mere 1/30th of its original purchase price. In hindsight, of course, you should have sold. The culprit here was a combination of hope and greed. Once a winning investment becomes a losing one, it is incredibly hard to sell. Most people will simply stand sadly by and watch the ship sink.

So when does it end? It doesn't. When markets do finally begin coming back up, it creates the same momentum. People think, "Aha! The stock is coming back, and I can buy it really cheap right now!" and on the other side, investors who've been burned by the stock's collapse are looking to "dump it" and recoup their losses. This creates selling pressure, and once again, the buying frenzy will over-inflate the stock's value, and the subsequent selling will eventually begin to drive the market down, and so on, and so on.

This roller coaster effect is expected to be the trend of the first part of this decade, and with these kinds of market conditions, it will be almost impossible for mutual funds to provide a consistent positive return. So the average investor, without spending considerable time on research and trading, will have an extremely difficult time making a reasonable return on his or her investments.

What can be done to protect investments from this roller coaster ride? Again, the answer is simple: invest in instruments that are *not correlated to market performance*. These are often referred to as *alternative investments*.

ALTERNATIVE INVESTMENT VEHICLES

Broadly defined, an alternative investment strategy is anything outside the traditional investments of stocks, bonds, and cash equivalents. Th s means it is defined by the fact that it is not correlated with the stock and bond markets. The simplest of these vehicles is leaving your money in a bank account or GIC. You receive an *absolute return* (the amount of interest guaranteed by the institution you entrust your money to) and the security that comes with it. At the writing of this book, however, a 12-month GIC will provide you with only a 1.6% interest income. This is hardly a handsome return and, in many cases, won't even keep up with the rate of inflation. Some other vehicles offer better returns, but come with added risk and many complications.

Real Estate

Since the writing of the first edition of this book, we have seen an unbelievable appreciation of real estate prices in Canada. The 2001, the average house price was $171,910. This increased to $226,400 by 2004 and is expected to reach $236,588 by the end of 2005 (from www.canoe.ca). Considering that the inflation rate in the same time frame hovered around 2 to 3%, these are excellent returns. And the picture gets even brighter if you look at certain high-demand neighbour-hoods in places like Toronto and Vancouver. So should we sell everything we own, sink it into real estate, and wait to get rich? Don't bank on it.

While tight rental markets in major cities across this country created inflated rental rates in the eighties and nineties, the declining interest rates of the early 21st century made mortgage payments more affordable. Under these circum-stances, it became much cheaper to own than to rent an apartment or house, bringing individuals and families to the market that otherwise would never have thought of buying. Increased demand pushed prices up, and declining interest rates fuelled the buying spirit. The result of this cocktail is an almost bubble-like housing market, with grossly inflated valuations.

So hold on to that old Spiderman #2 comic book—don't auction it on eBay for cash to buy property just yet! At the writing of this second edition, we are al-ready seeing the market slow down, and with increasing interest rates looming on the horizon, the whole trend is bound to reverse itself.

We are not saying that you should forget real estate altogether. The industry's low correlation and typically modest returns can provide a valuable cushion when markets are down. Some advisers recommend allocating up to 10% of a portfolio in real estate. In most cases, it can serve as a potential hedge against inflation and deflation due to the relative predictability of long-term returns.

Much like the stock market, it is the intelligent and informed selection of real estate ventures that offers the greatest possibility for positive returns. Recognizing an undervalued piece of property can be highly profitable, if you're willing to wait. However, if you guess wrong, it can be disastrous. Industry closures, water con-tamination, highway construction—property can depreciate in many ways, most of them unpredictable. Some real estate ventures are private sales, that is, individuals buying and selling properties. People who prefer to leave the property picking to more informed professionals can turn to real estate investment trusts, or REITs. These are a form of income trusts, another alternative investment vehicle.

Income Trusts

A uniquely Canadian animal, income trusts have been rapidly growing in popular-ity over the past few years. In fact, they hold more than $100 billion of Canadians' money at the writing of this book (2005), more than four times the amount they held in 2000.

Income trusts have been growing in popularity because for many Canadians they are a lower-risk alternative to stocks, and they offer a significantly better return than bonds, with returns averaging anywhere from 8 to 14%. With the presently volatile and unpredictable markets, this has meant a boom for this relatively small class of investments—there are almost 200 income trusts in Canada in 2005, with more being created every month. Although income trusts have generally operated in the energy and real estate sectors, the offerings have expanded to include everything from cold storage facilities to pizza parlours.

But while income trusts are a good investment option to help diversify a portfolio, keep in mind that they are not all created equal: income trusts are vehicles best created by businesses that don't need a lot of capital, since they pay out most of their profits to investors.

One of the most popular types of income trusts is the real estate investment trust (REIT). A REIT is a security that uses investor capital to purchase or manage real estate, either by buying properties or securing mortgages. REITs operate just like stocks and are traded on major exchanges. They work by selling units to investors, who then receive regular and stable cash returns from the company's real estate holdings.

Some of the advantages of REITs include affordability and liquidity. Instead of putting down a large sum of money to purchase property, an investor can buy units of a REIT and convert them to cash whenever necessary. In this sense, REITs resemble "closed end" (having a fixed investment amount) mutual funds. REITs also offer a tax shelter, since they are taxed less heavily than interest income. Since the property holdings in a REIT are typically spread out in a number of areas, they are more diverse and therefore less risky than sinking all of your money into one property. They also offer the bonus of being professionally managed, so you don't have to stay awake at night wondering when the best time is to sell. No matter how good the manager is at picking properties, though, the volatility of the real estate market makes any large investment in REITs a risky one.

Gold and Precious Metals

The allure of gold has, for as long as recorded history, been a representation of wealth at every level. As an investment, however, the numbers don't shine. The volatility of this once-stable investment has been an insane roller coaster over the last 20-odd years, with prices reaching staggering numbers in the early eighties (US$850 on January 21, 1980), and tanking to new lows in 1982 and 1985 (as low as US$296 by late June 1982). A volatile up-and-down history led to the four years from 1998 to 2001 when it couldn't even manage to break through the "floor" US$300 barrier. It was only in 2002 that it managed to do this.

Traditionally, gold has been seen as a safe investment—a hedge against market swings. When stocks and currencies start to slide, investors will get out and purchase gold as a "stable" commodity to sit on until the markets come back. The problem is that people still think that gold has some kind of direct relationship to *money*. It doesn't. True, the history of this unique metal is practically defined by its use as an exchangeable currency, but in fact, it has had no global connection to the value of currency since 1973, when the world's currencies were "floated"—that is, countries no longer valued their money by some set amount of actual, physical gold bullion (or promissory notes) hidden in a vault somewhere.

There are two primary sources of gold supply—mining and central bank vaults. Should the supply of gold through mining not be sufficient for demand, the difference may be provided by the central banks, partially through sales and leasing in order to keep the price stable. It is estimated that in 2003, about 32,000 tons of gold are still being held by central banks worldwide, despite the selling of significant portions of gold reserves by major banks in the 1990s.

The average price of gold in 1975 was US$161.02 per ounce (See Figure 3.2). At the time of this book's writing, gold was trading at US$426.00 per ounce. This is less than a 165% gain in 30 years and again, with inflation, you have actually realized a small *loss*, hardly a good investment.

FIGURE 3.2: GOLD PRICES, 1975–2005 (AVERAGE)

Having said that, gold has been shining lately, and its price has been going up steadily over the past four years. This is largely attributable to the U.S. government policy of increasing their debt. The significant drop in the U.S. dollar value over the past year, as well as anticipation of more of the same in the future, has seen many governments and their citizens holding onto and even increasing their gold holdings (at the expense of the U.S. dollar). With the re-election of the Bush administration, we can expect prices to rise even further as these forces remain in play.

Other precious metals have had similar problems. Platinum and silver have mirrored the up and down swings of gold over the past few decades. Platinum reached a whopping US$659 in 1987, and silver topped US$11.25 in the same year. At the time of this book's publishing, their prices are US$867 and US$6.77, respectively.

Given the international situation and continuing U.S. government policy, investment in precious metals (either in bullion or mining stocks) may be warranted for diversification purposes. However, due to their past volatile behaviour and associated riskiness, no more than 10% of investments in a portfolio should be here (and we would recommend around 5%).

Fine Art

Another alternative investment strategy is investing in art. Collecting can be a highly enjoyable form of investment, but it comes with many potential pitfalls, not least of which is getting too attached to your investments and not wanting to sell them.

The main problems with investing in art come with the highly unpredictable whims of what society will see as *precious*. Vincent Van Gogh sold only *one painting* in his entire career. Rooting around in garage sales looking for the next Andy Warhol or Pablo Picasso can be fun, but it is hardly a secure form of investing.

Art prices also have demonstrated a historic correlation to stock prices—as commodities, their price fluctuates with the amount of available disposable income.

LIQUIDITY

The main problem with many of these alternative vehicles is lack of liquidity. Liquidity is the ability of an investor to get out of—or liquidate—a given investment, and turn it back into cash. This is one of the most important features an investment should have, as even the most long-term plans can be derailed by any number of circumstances requiring actual money.

Any immediate need for cash will require that you sell an investment. The amount of time and effort you have to put into that exercise represents the level of liquidity for that investment. As an example, stocks, bonds, and gold are extremely liquid. One phone call can immediately convert these vehicles to cash. Using the Internet, it's even simpler—you have the money, literally, in minutes.

Real estate is more complicated. Agents, advertising, open houses, market offers, lawyers, and all the details can take time, but the effort involved is never a guarantee of a sale. Even if you accept an offer, it takes an additional 30 to 60 days for the official close. Real estate is not a liquid investment by any means. You will remember the predicament Jim found himself in from the last chapter, when circumstances meant he needed to sell his property immediately.

THE IMPORTANCE OF CONSISTENT RETURNS

Every investor wants a consistent, reliable (and hopefully positive) return. Table 3.2 shows the returns of two funds for 12 months. For simplicity's sake, monthly numbers are not compounded, but totalled. Fund A returned 18% for the year, 2% more than Fund B. Is Fund A a better investment? It's a matter of how you handle risk and the stress that comes from seeing your investments losing money.

TABLE 3.2

	Jan	Feb	Mar	Apr	May	Jun	Jul	Aug	Sep	Oct	Nov	Dec	Total
Fund A	+5%	-7%	+4%	+8%	-7%	-1%	+11%	+2%	+1%	-5%	+9%	-2%	**+18%**
Fund B	+1%	+1%	+2%	+2%	+1%	+1%	+2%	+1%	+1%	+2%	+1%	+1%	**+16%**

Imagine you've invested in Fund A at the beginning of January and have just checked Saturday's paper at the end of February. Your total investment is down 2%, and suddenly you're asking questions, wondering if you should get out now, and frustrated because your broker doesn't work on the weekends. By the time you see the March numbers, you've had an entire month of uncertainty. April makes you feel better, but you do it all over again in May. This is *not* worry-free investing.

Now imagine that you've invested in Fund B. It only returned 16%, but did you ever question your judgment? The returns are consistent and reliable. To most people, the slight drop in potential profit is more than acceptable when it comes to your health and emotional state.

With the roller coaster effect predicted to continue for the next three to five years, investors are seeking a vehicle that will provide protection from volatility and still achieve better returns than GICs. Enter the hedge fund.

HEDGE FUND PERFORMANCE

As we understand from the previous chapter, hedge funds can utilize techniques such as short selling and leverage—techniques not available to mutual fund managers—to continue to achieve positive returns in a declining market. Table 3.3 shows the 16 negative quarters starting from 1990 leading up to the last quarter of 2004.

The S&P 500 Index declined cumulatively 69.4%. During the same negative quarters, the average U.S. equity mutual fund declined 70.80%, while the average U.S. hedge fund had a cumulative negative return of only 8.80%. Furthermore, during this negative and highly volatile time, hedge funds had a much more consistent return rate—smoothing out the roller coaster.

TABLE 3.3

	S&P 500	VAN U.S. Hedge Fund Index	Morningstar Average Equity Mutual Fund
1Q90	-3.00%	2.20%	-2.80%
3Q90	-13.70%	-3.70%	-15.40%
2Q91	-0.20%	2.30%	-0.90%
1Q92	-2.50%	5.00%	-0.70%
1Q94	-3.80%	-0.80%	-3.20%
4Q94	-0.02%	-1.20%	-2.60%
3Q98	-9.90%	-6.10%	-15.00%
3Q99	-6.20%	2.10%	-3.20%
2Q00	-2.70%	0.30%	-3.60%
3Q00	-1.00%	3.00%	0.60%
4Q00	-7.80%	-2.40%	-7.80%
1Q01	-11.90%	-1.10%	-12.60%
3Q01	-14.70%	-3.80%	-17.20%
2Q02	-13.40%	-1.40%	-10.70%
3Q03	-17.3%	-3.60%	-16.70%
1Q03	-3.20%	-0.70%	-3.70%
TOTAL	**-69.40%**	**-8.80%**	**-70.80%**

HEDGE FUNDS AND CONSISTENT RETURNS

Performance in the long run (during both bear and bull markets) shows the overall strength of hedge funds. Table 3.4 shows a 17-year history ending in 2004. Far from simply providing positive returns on a consistent, annual basis, hedge funds also, again, "smooth out the ride." The average global hedge fund (measured by Van Global Hedge Fund Index) provided a 15.96% compounded return, as compared to the 10.04% of the average equity mutual fund (measured by Morningstar Equity Mutual Fund Index). At the same time, the S&P 500 Index returned 12.40% and the U.S. bond market managed 8.11%, while the MSCI World gained just 6.61%.

Figure 3.3 and Table 3.4 clearly show that hedge funds not only provide superior returns but give a much smoother ride. Even in the worst years, they still remained positive. Mutual funds, on the other hand, were negative 5 out of 17 years.

FIGURE 3.3: VAN GLOBAL HEDGE FUND INDEX VERSUS MORNINGSTAR EQUITY MUTUAL FUND, ANNUAL RETURNS, 1988–2004

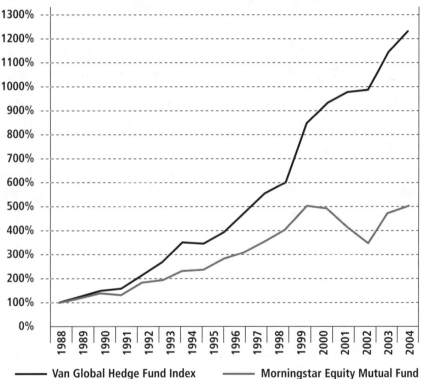

TABLE 3.4

	1988	1989	1990	1991	1992	1993	1994	1995	1996
Van Global Hedge Fund Index	25.9%	25.3%	6.4%	32.0%	18.2%	30.0%	1.2%	18.8%	19.0%
MSCI World Equity	23.3%	16.7%	-18.7%	16.0%	-7.1%	20.4%	3.4%	18.7%	11.8%
S&P 500	16.6%	31.7%	-3.1%	30.5%	7.6%	10.1%	1.3%	37.6%	23.0%
Morningstar Average Equity Mutual Fund	14.9%	25.5%	-7.1%	31.9%	6.4%	19.3%	-2.3%	24.5%	14.7%
Lehman Brothers Aggregate Bond Index	7.9%	14.5%	10.3%	14.6%	7.4%	9.8%	-2.9%	18.5%	3.6%

	1997	1998	1999	2000	2001	2002	2003	2004	Compounded Annual Return
Van Global Hedge Fund Index	15.8%	6.3%	40.3%	8.4%	6.3%	0.1%	18.6%	7.7%	**15.96%**
MSCI World Equity	14.1%	22.8%	23.6%	-14.0%	-17.8%	-21.1%	30.8%	12.8%	**6.61%**
S&P 500	33.4%	28.6%	21.0%	-9.1%	-11.9%	-22.1%	28.7%	10.9%	**12.40%**
Morningstar Average Equity Mutual Fund	15.7%	10.7%	28.4%	-5.1%	-12.6%	-20.3%	32.7%	12.7%	**10.04%**
Lehman Brothers Aggregate Bond Index	9.7%	8.7%	-0.8%	11.6%	8.4%	10.3%	4.1%	4.3%	**8.11%**

HEDGE FUND LIQUIDITY

Currently, some funds require a lock-up period of one year or more, meaning redemptions will not be honoured for that time period. However, more and more startup funds in Canada allow investors to make quarterly, monthly, or, more commonly, weekly withdrawals. Some even provide for daily redemptions, allowing almost complete liquidity.

As the industry grows and more products are offered on the market, there will be choices between many different funds with alternative redemption rules. An investor can pick a fund that best suits his or her needs, parcelling out a portfolio that balances superior returns and shorter lock-up periods. The key is flexibility.

THE FUTURE OF HEDGE FUNDS IN CANADA

Like any investment vehicle, some hedge funds may invest in esoteric areas of the market or use strategies that are difficult to understand, but the majority will utilize securities that are familiar to the average investor and strategies that are relatively easy to understand. Chapter 4 discusses hedge fund styles in detail.

It is not surprising that since the end of the bull market in 2000, there has been an exponential rise in interest in hedge funds in Canada. At the beginning of 2000, there were approximately 20 hedge funds in the country, managing around $1.5 billion; by December 2004 there were about 350 funds with a combined asset value of around $16 billion (at the retail level). This huge growth is not likely to slow down.

Fuelling this growth is a change in regulations in the Canadian securities markets combined with more innovative financial instruments. In 2000, investment in a hedge fund required a minimum of $25,000 to $150,000 (depending on province of residence). In the last couple of years, however, the most popular hedge funds, called Guaranteed Investment Notes (GIN), enabled smaller investors to take part. Normally GINs allocate a substantial portion of their principal to bonds, which provide a guaranteed return at maturity (usually between 7 and 10 years). While they generally come with higher fees and less liquidity, they are usually available at a $5,000 minimum regardless of the class of investor. In addition, recent changes in some provinces allow investors to contribute as little as $5,000 to hedge funds provided they simply sign a "Risk Acknowledgement Form."

As investment in hedge funds becomes easier and as more and more investors realize that hedge funds (on average) are not only safer investments than mutual funds (in that they attempt to provide absolute returns as well as smooth out the roller coaster effect), there will be an even larger influx of cash into these vehicles. In turn, this will encourage the industry to come up with an even larger variety of funds, providing a large number of choices currently only available in mutual funds.

Trouble on the Horizon? The Portus Alternative Asset Management Case

On February 13, 2005, the Ontario Securities Commission ordered Portus Alternative Asset Management Inc. to cease trading. This was done as a result of some practices being deemed "questionable" by the OSC. With more than $700 million in assets under management, Portus was one of the largest and fastest-growing hedge funds in Canada until the order was put in place.

The fund company is accused of diverting almost $90 million to commissions, referral fees, and other related expenses, representing more than 12% of the fund's total value. Many authorities believe that this is entirely too much for investors to be able to receive any returns, saying that it would take a 15% return annually just to cover these costs. The case is still being investigated, with the temporary cessation of trading extended to May 17th, 2005.

Depending on the outcome of the case, this could mean increased regulations for hedge funds in Canada, which could in turn be a problem for the justification of lower minimum investments, among other things. It remains to be seen.

CHAPTER FOUR

Hedge Fund Styles

Looking back, we can see that since the days of Mr. Jones, the hedge fund industry has gone through considerable changes. Jones's first fund (his "long/short equity" style) held both long and short positions to make profits by taking advantage of increasing and decreasing markets. Since that time, however, managers have had to become more innovative and have developed different styles and methods to manage the money that is entrusted to them.

While there are several different classification systems for hedge funds, we will be looking at the system developed by Morgan Stanley Capital International (MSCI). The following table lists the five major MSCI hedge fund classifications, as well as the corresponding sub-strategies under each category.

Do not worry if some of the terminology is foreign—we will be explaining each style in detail in this chapter.

TABLE 4.1: MAJOR TYPES OF HEDGE FUNDS

MSCI Classification	Definition	Sub-strategies
Directional Trading	Based on speculation of market direction in multiple asset classes	Discretionary trading
		Systematic Trading
	Both model-based systems and subjective judgement are used to make trading decisions	Tactical Allocation

continued

MSCI Classification	Definition	Sub-strategies
Relative Value	Focus on spread relationship between pricing components of financial assets Market risk is kept to a minimum Many managers use leverage to enhance returns	Arbitrage Convertible Arbitrage Merger Arbitrage Statistical Arbitrage
Security Selection	Combine long and short positions, primarily in equities, in order to exploit under- or over-valued securities Market exposure can vary substantially	Long Bias Short Bias Variable Bias No Bias
Specialist Credit	Based on lending to credit sensitive issuers Funds in this style conduct a high level of due diligence in order to identify relatively inexpensive securities	Distressed Securities Long–Short Credit Private Placements
Multi-process Group	Combine different hedge fund strategies	Event Driven

DIRECTIONAL TRADING

Directional trading managers speculate on the direction that a variety of instruments in both the cash and futures markets, including currencies, commodities, equities, and bonds, will take. It should be noted that managers using directional trading strategies are quite far removed from the original hedging concept pioneered by Alfred Winslow Jones. Instead of hedging risk, directional trading managers will make large bets on the direction a particular market will follow. This strategy often makes use of large amounts of leverage in order to generate the greatest possible return.

Because the typical investment horizon can vary considerably in this strategy, managers using this approach will quickly change their strategy to adapt to changing market conditions. Managers rely upon one of two different methods: a model-based approach, or a more subjective method where trading decisions are made using discretionary judgment.

Directional trading includes three separate methods:

• discretionary trading
• systematic trading
• tactical allocation

Discretionary Trading

Most funds in the discretionary style are based on the assumption that fashions change—what is hot this year may not be in great demand 12 months from now. How does this principle apply to the stock market? It is based on movements of shares in similar industries. The New York Stock Exchange has approximately 2,100 listed companies. These companies represent different industries, such as oil and gas or financial services. These are called sectors (you may have heard people refer to the "financial services sector" or "oil and gas sector"). To make classification more precise, each sector has sub-sectors. The financial services sector, for instance, has the following sub-sectors:

• banking
• trust savings and loan companies
• investment companies and funds
• insurance companies
• finance and leasing
• investment houses
• credit unions

Traditionally, share prices of companies in the same sub-sector tend to move together. For example, if there is a regulatory change that affects insurance companies positively, chances are that all insurance company stocks will rise. Managers of discretionary funds take advantages of such changes. They find the sectors or sub-sectors that are hot and invest in them. As soon as the wave of fashion changes, they move on by liquidating their positions in the declining sector and going into the next "hot" one.

In 1999, for instance, Internet stocks were hot. Prices were not only going up, they were catapulted to levels that reason could no longer justify. Then, in April 2000, the dot-coms came hurtling down. But in the summer of 2000, the fibre optic companies were still flying high. A successful manager of a discretionary fund would have been invested in Internet stocks in 1999 (and making triple-digit returns). At the first sign of trouble, however, the manager would have moved the fund's investments over to the fibre optic sector until the end of the 2000, when *that* sector started to decline.

Sound easy? It's not. There are two fundamental difficulties in applying this strategy. First, you need to be able to anticipate what is going to be hot. For most of us, by the time we read about a hot sector in the papers, it is too late, and most of the potential profit has already been pulled out. A manager has to be able to anticipate the next hot sector, and put the fund's money on the line before everybody else does. If the guess is right, then the rewards are great, but if you're wrong (the sector is going no-where or even worse, going down), the potential losses are great as well.

Second, you need to know when to get out. This can be even more difficult than guessing hot sectors. Again, by the time the public reads about problems in the papers, it is too late—you have to anticipate it. Returning to our Internet stocks example, in March 1999 the Internet stocks were making higher highs every day. However, the best managers were already selling. Based on their research, they knew the end was in sight. But think of the temptation. "Why should I sell? Prices just keep going up. I should stay in for a few more days. It may not collapse for a month and in that case I'll kick myself for selling too soon." But think this way and the unavoidable eventually happens, and most of the gains on the positions evaporate, or worse, the positions turn into losses.

The secrets of success in discretionary trading are to *sell too soon* rather than too late, and to have the skills to anticipate the next "fashion" sector.

A high degree of portfolio turnover is therefore often characteristic of discretionary trading. Although discretionary traders do not generally hedge their positions, they do take a disciplined approach to risk management. We will discuss various risk management tools later in this book.

Systematic Trading

Since computers were invented, the temptation to harness their data-crunching capabilities has been hard to resist. Can computers find some kind of order in the chaos of stock price movements? Systems traders think so. In the early days of computers, major investment firms and banks were the only ones who could afford to buy the equipment and hire the talent needed to conduct research in this field. Today, however, for a few hundred dollars anyone can buy a powerful computer that packs the equivalent processing power of machines that as recently as 10 years ago would have cost a few million dollars to acquire.

The Internet has made it possible to have access to real-time stock market data at relatively reasonable prices, and a number of Web sites deliver complex tools to analyze the data streams. Using the computer to find certain patterns in the price movements of stocks, futures, options, or bonds that can be exploited by the manager of the fund is only the beginning of systematic trading, though. Most managers use much more sophisticated systems than the ones you can find on the Internet. They hire roomfuls of mathematicians, statisticians, and computer scientists to develop their own algorithms.

There are a number of pitfalls in this strategy, however. There is no good evidence to prove that markets move in any kind of pattern whatsoever; rather, they are event driven. A computer could not predict the events of September 11, 2001, for instance (or, for that matter, any unpredictable event that affects the stock market). In a case where a systematic trading fund is making profits on their investments by using patterns in an industry that is affected by a sudden event, the results can be catastrophic.

As a side note, the investment process used by commodity trading advisers (CTAs) is generally included under systematic trading as well. A CTA manages separate commodity trading accounts for individuals. He or she will often make a large bet on the direction of a commodity, such as oil, or the near-term direction of a financial instrument, such as stock index futures. These positions are often highly leveraged, with the CTA only depositing 20% of his or her market exposure on a futures contract. For instance, suppose a CTA deposits $20 million (20% of his or her position) for a commodity trade. He or she will then leverage this position up to $100 million.

Tactical Allocation

In the tactical allocation method, a hedge fund manager allocates capital across a wide array of both markets and strategies. The largest funds in the hedge fund universe (that is, the global macro funds) will sometimes use tactical allocation, because increased asset size (the amount of money being managed) often makes it necessary to move that capital to areas of perceived opportunity. As a result, managers using this process tend to seek opportunities with the greatest liquidity.

Managers using the tactical allocation method often take a top-down, "thematic" investment approach, shifting capital among various processes to take advantage of perceived investment opportunities wherever they occur.

RELATIVE VALUE

Relative value strategies focus on the difference between the prices of financial assets or commodities, with the emphasis on managing risk. Because in most cases the investment opportunities related to this strategy are low risk, many managers will engage in leverage as a means of increasing their returns.

In a lot of cases, managers using a relative value strategy employ statistical and mathematical techniques to identify and hedge an opportunity. The use of these techniques is particularly useful in situations where hedging activity requires frequent trading.

The following processes are sub-strategies of relative value:

• arbitrage
• convertible arbitrage
• merger arbitrage
• statistical arbitrage

Arbitrage

What is arbitrage? According to Investorwords.com, an online financial dictionary, arbitrage is defined as "attempting to profit by exploiting price differences of identical or similar financial instruments, on different markets or in different forms." Why is this so tempting? Because theoretically, you can make money without any risk.

A hedge fund is making use of arbitrage strategy if each position in the portfolio tries to capitalize upon a feature of an asset (or combination of assets) that is mispriced, according to its theoretical fair value. In this style, all pricing factors, other than the identified element, are fully hedged or managed, first within the position and then within the total portfolio.

One of the classic variants of an arbitrage strategy involves the use of inter-listed stocks (stocks that trade on two or more markets). A manager can take advantage of any pricing discrepancy by taking a long position in the stock on one market and a short position in another market. In this way, the position is completely hedged, since the manager holds equal weights of the stock on both the long and short side. He or she makes a profit if the stock is priced differently on the two exchanges and/or the currency exchange is favourable. An example can help to illustrate this technique:

A hedge fund manager decides to use an arbitrage strategy using Ridgeway Developments Inc., which trades simultaneously on the NYSE and TSX (See Table 4.2). In the U.S., Ridgeway trades in U.S. dollars; in Canada, it trades in Canadian dollars. If the manager knows the exchange rate at any given point in time, he or she can determine if there is any price difference between the two quotes.

TABLE 4.2: MARKET PRICE OF RIDGEWAY SHARES

NYSE	$4.75 US
TSX	$6.17 Cdn
Exchange rate	$1 US = $1.3297 Cdn

Our manager decides to buy 10,000 shares of Ridgeway on the TSX, and at the same time sell 10,000 shares on the NYSE. By engaging in this arbitrage strategy, he has earned a profit of $1,460.75 on the two transactions. Table 4.3 below gives an illustration of his results.

TABLE 4.3: RESULTS OF RIDGEWAY ARBITRAGE STRATEGY

Buy 10,000 shares Ridgeway TSX	$61,700.00 Cdn
Sell 10,000 shares Ridgeway NYSE	$47,500.00 US
Value of shares adjusted for exchange rate	$63,160.75 Cdn
Profit	**$1,460.75 Cdn**

The greatest danger for arbitrageurs is *other* arbitrageurs. The more people trying to perform the same arbitrage, the less likely it is that opportunities will happen. If they do happen, they will last for only a very short time before someone else grabs them. Once an opportunity is exploited, it becomes obsolete. The method in the above example is practised by so many individuals and institutions that it is now very hard to make any reasonable profit at it.

The most frequently traded vehicles in this style include convertibles, equities, and fixed income. In many cases, the spread between instruments is quite narrow and the returns are small. Leverage will often be used to increase the size of the returns, particularly when the downside risk is relatively low. Since hedge funds using an arbitrage strategy rely upon the ability to borrow, it is very important for these funds to have access to substantial lines of credit.

Convertible Arbitrage

In order to understand the convertible arbitrage, or convergence arbitrage, strategy, we have to define a number of financial terms:

Bond (not James): By definition, a bond is a debt instrument issued for a period of more than one year, for the purpose of raising capital by borrowing. The federal government, provinces, cities, corporations, and many other types of institutions sell bonds. A bond, then, is generally a promise to repay the principal along with interest on a specified date (at maturity).

Corporate Bond: A corporate bond is any bond issued by a corporation (as opposed to a government).

Convertible Bond: This is a corporate bond that can be exchanged, at the option of the holder, for a specific number of shares of the company's stock on a certain date. This date is often referred to as the exercise date.

So why do corporations issue bonds? The answer is relatively simple: they need money to grow business.

Corporations can raise money in two fundamentally different ways: they can *sell equity* or *borrow money*. Selling equity is issuing stocks. The money received through selling these stocks becomes the company's and does not have to be paid back. The drawback is that a certain percentage of the company is given away in the process (stockholders "own a piece" of the company). By borrowing (through issuing bonds), the corporation does not give up any equity but must instead pay back the borrowed money with interest.

Market conditions will dictate which method companies will choose. When the stock markets are high, for instance, selling equity may seem the better alternative—the share prices are up. When interest rates are very low, however, issuing bonds would be a more economic alternative—the company pays less interest on borrowed money.

Why would a company issue convertible bonds? In order to attract more investors by sweetening the deal a little. Since there are a number of companies issuing bonds all the time, and they compete for the investors' money, a bond may be more attractive if investors can potentially participate in the appreciation of the underlying stock price.

A hedge fund manager can capitalize on the above situation when he or she believes that the current price of the convertible bond reflects a lower level of stock volatility than what is actually the case for the underlying stock over a certain time frame. In other words, the manager expects the convertible bond to have more value than its current market price indicates.

Convertible or convergence arbitrage is one of the more popular forms of arbitrage. Hedge funds using this style will take long positions in convertible bonds and short sell the underlying stock. By establishing a short position in the underlying stock, the hedge fund manager creates positive cash flow. The net effect of the hedge is a lower overall cost for the convertible bonds.

In the case of the convertible bonds, the manager establishes an explicit hedge to deal with credit risk. As an alternative to explicitly hedging the risk associated with the convertible bonds, the manager will invest in a well-diversified portfolio of convertible bonds, or find convertibles with high hedge ratios that trade well above their value as a straight bond. As a result, they have minimal credit spread risk.

Compared to straight investments in bonds, convertible arbitrage strategies have produced significantly greater returns with only slightly higher volatility.

Unfortunately, convertible arbitrage does have a serious limitation—a lack of product. The convertible bond market is a relatively small universe, with too many hedge fund managers trying to invest in the same instruments. In the same way that the profits from relative value arbitrage decline as more and more managers try to exploit existing opportunities, the margins from convertible arbitrage shrink from too much competition.

Example of a Convertible Arbitrage Hedge

As we mentioned, in order to attract investors, a company may decide to issue bonds with a feature to convert the bonds to a specific number of shares on a certain date. With that in mind, consider the following scenario:

Neptune Resources is a junior mining company that trades on the TSX. Currently, the stock is trading at $2.60 per share. The company wants to raise $9,000,000 in capital and decides to issue convertible bonds to finance its expansion plans. The bonds are issued at par, carrying a coupon of 7% and a term of 15 years.

Samantha is optimistic about Neptune's prospects, but doesn't want to purchase the stock now. Instead, she decides to purchase $10,000 worth of the bond. If the bond were held to maturity, she would receive total interest payments of $10,500 (7% X $10,000 X 15 years).

Alternatively, she could exchange the $10,000 bond for Neptune's common stock during set times over the 15-year period, at $5 per share. Suppose that five years later, the stock price increases to $9.00 per share. Samantha could then convert her bond and receive 2,000 shares ($10,000 ÷ $5 per share). She would then sell the stock on the market and receive $18,000 ($9.00 X 2,000 shares), making a profit of $8,000 ($18,000 − $10,000). Over the five-year period, Samantha would also receive $3,500 in interest income (7% X $10,000 X 5 years).

The nice thing about this situation is that even if the share price *falls* instead of rising over the 15 years, Samantha would still receive interest payments and the full amount of the bond's principal at maturity.

Hedge funds can take advantage of this situation. Once issued, convertible bonds trade on the market in the same way as regular bonds. The price of bonds depends upon a number of considerations, including the level of interest rates, the maturity date of the bonds, the price of the underlying stock, and the growth of the company's earnings.

A hedge fund manager wants to acquire convertible bonds that are priced in such a way that, by buying the bond, he or she is able to acquire the company stock at a discount from its current market value. The manager takes a long position in the convertible bond, based upon the assumption that it will rise in price because the stock is undervalued. The stock is then sold short because the manager is betting that the majority of investors will convert the bonds (which represent a potential profit) to stock. When this happens, it depresses the value of the stock.

The best environment for this particular strategy is a combination of a rising bond market and a falling stock market. The hedge fund manager can benefit from the increase in bond prices and the fall in stock prices. As well, the manager will generate interest income from the bonds. Going back to Samantha, then, we can see how her situation plays out with a hedge fund manager engaged in convertible arbitrage:

Interest rates fall and Samantha's $10,000 bond is now worth $11,200, and the company's stock is trading at $7 per share. In the meantime, Samantha has decided to purchase a house and wants to use the bond to finance the down payment.

If Samantha converts her bond to stock, she would make a profit of $4,000 (($7 X 2,000 shares) – $10,000). Unfortunately for her, however, the conversion date for the bond is six months away, and the house she wants is available right now.

Karim, a hedge fund manager, offers to buy the bond from Samantha so that she can make her house purchase. He then pays Samantha $11,200 for the bond (what it will be worth in six months—hooray for Samantha). He then *borrows* 2,000 shares of Neptune Resources and sells them short on the market. You can see that effectively, Karim has generated a profit of $2,800 (($7 x 2,000 shares) – $11,200). He has locked in a profit because six months from now, he will return the shares he borrowed when he converts the bond to the underlying stock. And again, in the interim, he also receives interest payments on the convertible bond.

So to sum up, a manager using convertible arbitrage is making a profit by utilizing the price differences of similar financial instruments in different forms. These types of strategies have produced significantly higher returns, with only marginally higher volatility, than investing solely in bonds. Because of the popularity of this strategy, a number of hedge fund managers have migrated to it. The major downside, though, is the lack of products. Only a limited number of convertible bonds are available, and too many managers are chasing after the same deals. As you saw earlier, the number one enemy of arbitrageurs is other arbitrageurs. Thus, the margins are getting thinner and thinner, and it is getting harder and harder to make a profit.

Merger Arbitrage

A merger is simply the combination of two or more companies through a purchase. In a basic merger, there are two companies—the company making the acquisition and the company being acquired. The pursuit of greater growth is the primary reason one company would want to acquire another. By combining their activities, the new, larger entity can eliminate duplicate expenses and achieve greater profitability.

In most instances, the acquiring company is willing to pay a premium over the target company's stock price. This is because the merger will generally create additional long-term growth, and because after the merger is announced the stock of the target company usually rises, moving closer to the acquisition (takeover) price. However—and this is where the hedge fund comes in—the share price of the target company will likely not reach the acquisition price, because there is some risk that the merger will not be completed.

In the majority of cases, the key determinant of success in merger arbitrage is the successful completion of the transaction. A hedge fund manager using merger arbitrage tries to capture the price spread between the current price of a security and its value upon the successful completion of a takeover, merger, or restructuring. The manager studies these risks, looking at all the possible reasons that the merger could fail. If the merger is a cash transaction, the manager simply buys the shares in the company being sold, and then surrenders those shares to the acquiring company at the higher price.

In the majority of cases, companies do not acquire other companies for cash; instead, the owners of the target company receive stock in the company making the acquisition. In this case, the spread reflects the difference between the *current* value (i.e., before the merger or acquisition) of the target company's stock and that of the acquiring company's stock. In order to capture the difference between these two values, the hedge fund manager usually purchases the stock of the target company and *sells short* an appropriate amount of the acquiring company's stock.

Because of the uncertainties surrounding these deals, merger arbitrage managers usually wait for the announcement of a merger before taking a position. They generally do not speculate upon stocks that are expected to become takeover candidates, or trade in instruments that are mispriced relative to other securities. A simple example can help illustrate this style:

Clear Mountain Resorts owns and operates several ski resorts in Quebec. It wants to expand into Ontario and decides to acquire another ski operator, Blue Sky Ski Resorts, on a share-for-share basis. Presently, Clear Mountain's stock is trading at $30 per share, while Blue Sky's stock sits at $19 per share.

Clear Mountain issues a press release stating that it is offering one share of its stock for each share of Blue Sky. Hiroshi, a merger arbitrageur, sees an opportunity: he purchases Blue Sky stock at a price of $22 (its price immediately after the merger announcement—remember, target company stock usually goes up after an announcement). He then sells short the same amount of Clear Mountain's stock, which is now at $28 because of short selling pressure from other fund managers trying to do the same thing as Hiroshi.

As the deadline for the merger approaches, the $6 spread between the prices of Clear Mountain and Blue Sky narrows, as the stock price of the two companies converge. These price movements reflect the reduced risk that the merger will not be completed. If the deal closes and Blue Sky stock is converted to Clear Mountain stock, Hiroshi locks in the gain of $6, regardless of Clear Mountain's current price!

Key Problems for Merger Arbitrageurs

For this strategy to be a success, Hiroshi must deal with three fundamental problems.

1. The risk that the merger will not happen.

   If the merger does not go through, the target company's stock will fall back to its starting level, most likely creating a loss for the arbitrageur. Simultaneously, the price of the acquiring company's stock will rise, as all other arbitrageurs cancel their short positions by buying the stock. This upward drive in price creates a potential loss for the fund on the short side as well.

2. Insufficient opportunities available for merger arbitrage.

   With the onset of the bear market in early 2000, there has been a marked decline in merger activity. Eventually, however, market conditions will improve and should produce renewed merger activity.

3. Increased competition from other arbitrageurs.

   As more participants enter the market, they reduce the profit potential for merger arbitrage activity. With more competition, managers are forced to look at other opportunities, where there is greater risk that the merger will not be completed. This can obviously be dangerous!

Statistical Arbitrage

Statistical arbitrage uses various models, and focuses on constructing long and short positions where the relative value is currently different from its quantitative or theoretically determined value. This may sound complex, but it is relatively simple in practice. Basically, statistical arbitrage assumes that the mispricing of securities is not based on any economic fundamentals, and that the price of the security can be measured against an abstract, model-driven benchmark.

The models used in statistical arbitrage play a central role and serve two purposes:

- the identification of securities (either individual or groups) that are mispriced relative to an internal benchmark
- the construction of a market-neutral portfolio

All of the models used in statistical arbitrage strategies assume that the particular set of data (a stock's price or fundamental data, for example) contains information relevant to the future price performance of that security. The assumption is that this information has not yet been accounted for in the stock's current price (i.e., the price is either too high or too low, and the market hasn't figured it out yet).

In statistical arbitrage, the methods used to identify this information are quantitative in nature and generally automated (computerized). Portfolio performance depends upon the future price of securities moving toward the equilibrium price defined by the model.

SECURITY SELECTION

Much like Mr. Jones's original concept, hedge fund managers using a security selection style combine both long and short positions, relying on their ability to select investments while offsetting systematic market risk at the same time. In this particular strategy, there can be substantial differences in the level of market exposure, producing a wide array of risk and return profiles. Security selection funds are primarily equity-based, but can include other asset classes.

We've seen this before; managers using the security selection style focus their attention on investments that appear over- or undervalued, and buy or sell these positions before the market reacts to the (perceived) mispricing. In general, and again just like Mr. Jones, the idea is to try to generate positive returns in any market environment through hedging (balancing long and short positions to remain market-neutral). At least, this is the idea—some managers can have substantial market exposure if they are betting on the market's anticipated direction.

Security selection sub-strategies include:

• long bias
• short bias
• variable bias
• no bias

Long Bias

Basically what you see is what you get here. In a long-bias portfolio, the long side of the portfolio has greater representation in the fund than the short side. But wait a minute; doesn't this go against the whole market-neutral philosophy? Yes, it does. So why would a manager want to do this? Let's use a simple example to explain.

It is easy to understand that during a bull market, a long-bias portfolio will do very well because the general market increases in value. But how about during a bear market? How can a hedge fund manager make money when the majority of the capital is invested on the long side, and most of the stocks are trending down? The key word in the above sentence is "most."

Regardless of how strong the market decline is, there are *always* stocks that defy the trend—there are always companies that flourish in declining markets. These are generally companies whose stock price is contrary to general market trends. In 2002, a year of severe market decline, gold stocks did very well. "Gold stocks" does not refer to the precious metal itself, but rather companies involved in the mining and refining of gold bullion. This impressive performance was because of an increase in the price of gold (which traditionally represents a "flight to safety" during a bear market and subsequently sees gains in overall market declines). As gold prices go up, these companies can and will make more money, so it is logical that their share price should rise. A good hedge fund manager of a long-bias portfolio has to find the sectors that buck the trend during declining markets and invest the long side of the portfolio in companies in those sectors. On the short side of the portfolio, the manager will place stocks that trend along with the market (i.e., that are going down in value), thus making money on both sides.

Short Bias

As you might expect, the short-bias strategy is the exact opposite of the long-bias strategy. Short-bias portfolios maintain a significant net short market exposure. In a bear market, the hedge fund manager goes with the flow (shorting the stocks that follow the downward trend of the markets), making money on overvalued securities and picking stocks on the long side that buck the trend, as in the long-bias strategy, to earn profits on both sides. The art of running a short-bias fund comes to the fore during a bull market, when the manager has to find companies on the short side that will decline even though the general market trend is going up (i.e., bucking the trend in the opposite direction). Interestingly, the gold sector did this in the latter stages of the 2002 bear market.

Managers with a short bias do not borrow to invest, and most have large cash positions from their short selling activities. The short-bias category can also include "short only" funds which, obviously, hold only short positions in their portfolios.

Variable Bias

If you thought that variable bias was a combination of the short- and long-bias strategies, you were right again. In this case, the manager goes with the flow, regardless of direction, and manages the fund in the traditional Jones style. When the market is going up, the manager will have a long-bias portfolio; the stronger the bull market, the larger the percentage of the fund's investments that will be on the long side. When the market turns down and the bear roars onto Wall Street, the manager will switch to a short bias. Sounds simple, doesn't it?

The challenge lies in *knowing when the market will turn*. Predicting or recognizing this change is much more difficult than it sounds. A bear market can have a temporary "pull-back" when prices inexplicably go up for a while (you may have heard of these moves as "hiccups").

A perfect example of this occurred in October and November of 2001. Figure 4.1 shows how the Dow Jones Industrial Average and the S&P 500 behaved during that time. As we can see, there was a general downward trend in the market that started back in June 2001 and really dived after September 11. But, by the end of September 2001, the markets started going up. And they continued that upward trend until March 2002, when the markets turned again and the downward movement resumed. What would our variable manager do at the beginning of October 2001? The fund holds a *short-bias portfolio* (because of market trends), and now the market is going *against it*.

FIGURE 4.1

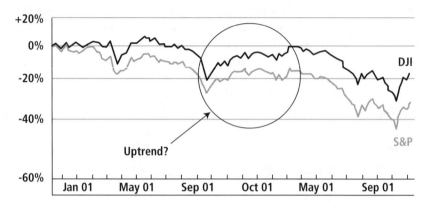

The questions that have to be asked are the following: Are we in an up trend now? If this is a pull-back, how long will it last? Even if the manager realizes that this is a pull-back that could last for weeks or even months, the rebalancing of the portfolio could be prohibitively expensive. We must not forget that hedge fund managers pay commissions to their brokers just like any other investor. In fact, they pay more in commissions than most investors who have discount brokerage accounts. Since funds need to sell large blocks of shares when they try to get in and out of positions (to make the switch to a long or short bias), just dumping them into the market can seriously affect the price of their stocks (and thus the profit of the fund). So it is very important that the broker the fund utilizes "works" the order (to buy or sell the large amount of shares) and *slowly* trades into the market or finds another institution to buy the large block of shares. This requires considerably more work than just executing a discount brokerage order for 500 shares, and it's why the cost of realigning a portfolio for a relatively short pull-back can be prohibitive.

The manager has to be certain that the market direction has changed before he or she attempts to realign. In our example in Figure 4.1, imagine what the manager would have thought on October 5 (or on November 5, for that matter). For over six weeks, the market was trending *against* the fund. Should the manager change?

If, in this case, the manager had made the move to realign, he or she would have regretted it, unless the execution cost was low enough to warrant a short switch. With today's technology, many of the managers in this category are switching over to *direct-access execution brokers*, a system in which they can perform their own executions at a fraction of the cost of the traditional brokerage houses. This practice has helped this strategy flourish by lowering costs and increasing the speed with which funds can realign their portfolios.

No Bias

The no-bias, market-neutral category is a very interesting one and, again, raises a lot of questions. A hedge fund is following a no-bias approach when the average net exposure for the portfolio does not exceed either 20% short or 20% long over any 90-day period. In addition, a no-bias portfolio will never intentionally have a net long or short position of more than 50% at the end of any trading day. It is essentially split evenly 50–50. Theoretically, such a portfolio is not affected by market movements. If markets go up, the portfolio will lose on the short positions and gain on the long ones, and if markets go down the exact opposite will happen. So how can the manager make money at it? The answer comes down, once again, to excellent stock-picking skills. As explained earlier, the market has different sectors, such as the gold sector. This sector includes companies that explore for, mine for, or refine gold. When gold prices go up, all the companies in the gold sector tend to move up. Some of them, however, move up at a faster pace than others. They simply gain more than their peers. These are called the strong companies of the sector. Each sector also has weak companies, which tend to go down more than their peers when the sector trends down.

A good no-bias manager will go long on stocks that are strong in a particular sector and short on the ones that are weak. The logic is that when the market goes up, the portfolio will lose less money on the short side than it will gain on the long side. The opposite is true for a bear market, making more money on the short side than is lost on the long side. The greatest challenge for the manager is to know *when to rebalance*. A stock that was weak in a sector can become strong overnight in response to news of better-than-expected earnings, for example, or in the case of the gold sector, a large strike in mining exploration. Most of the time, however, the sign of a stock changing characteristics is much more subtle, and the manager has to realize this very quickly. No-bias, market-neutral is probably the most conservative of the hedge fund strategies, and as such, it generally offers a relatively low return.

SPECIALIST CREDIT

This strategy is based on lending to credit-sensitive issuers. Funds using this style conduct extensive research in order to identify relatively inexpensive securities that may be inexpensive for a number of reasons, including regulatory anomalies or other constraints on traditional lenders (for example, speed of decision making or disclosure rules).

Hedge funds following this particular approach are extending credit in some form to a company. As a result, it is sometimes difficult to distinguish this process from private equity investors or other non-hedge fund providers of credit.

The following processes fall under specialist credit:

- distressed securities
- long/short credit
- private placements

Distressed Securities

To begin with, we should define what "distressed" securities are. Essentially, they are securities (stocks), bonds, and any bank loans or "trade claims" (claims held by suppliers owed for goods or services) outstanding from a company that is about to be subject to bankruptcy or financial distress. Distressed-securities fund managers attempt to capitalize on this situation. They are essentially the scavengers of the investment world. Sounds risky, doesn't it? In many cases it is, but there are exceptions.

So where is the "hedge"? Distressed securities are hedged investments because their returns have little or no correlation to stock market returns.

When news of a company's financial trouble starts surfacing, investors will often react emotionally and start dumping the securities of the organization (the many cases of accounting scandals in 2002 demonstrate this well). The question is, are the investors all just focusing on the bad news and selling instinctively, or is there a real problem? Maybe they are haunted by the memory of a similar situation when they had huge losses. Or maybe they just believe they can put their money somewhere else and generate much better returns. Regardless, they sell and sell and sell. During this process, it is conceivable (and quite often true) that the price of that security will fall to below its true value. This is when hedge fund managers who specialize in this type of trading and understand the true risk of the situation start buying and potentially realizing value from the rubble.

An opportunity typically arises when a company, unable to meet all its debts, files for bankruptcy protection or liquidation. *Liquidation* involves shutting a company's doors and dividing its assets among its creditors. *Bankruptcy protection* gives the company court protection to continue operating while working out a repayment plan, known as a *plan for reorganization*, with a committee of its major creditors. These creditors can be banks that have made loans, utilities and other vendors owed for their goods and services, and investors who own bonds. Stockholders are compensated only with what is left over, and when it comes to dividing up the assets of the company, they are generally paid very little, if anything (in a bankruptcy, if a company does not have sufficient assets to repay all claims, the stockholders will get wiped out as they are last in line to receive any of the proceeds from the liquidation or reorganization). So, when looking for bargain-priced securities, a distressed-securities investor focuses mostly on the bank debt, the trade claims, and the bonds (which can vary in their place on the bankruptcy-claim totem pole, with senior bonds paid ahead of junior, for example).

The approach is essentially to be patient and to use strategies and instruments that are either unavailable to or not used by the creditors. Most institutional investors, for instance (such as pension funds), are banned from buying or holding below-investment-grade securities (often called "junked" securities) even if the company is a potentially profitable one. Because of this constraint, they may sell these newly junked bonds at bargain basement prices, which has the net effect of lowering prices even further. Banks usually prefer to sell their bad loans (ones no longer paying interest) in order to remove them from their books. As well, a bank is not in the business of trying to figure out how a reorganization process (which can last several years) will work and if there is any potential profit in waiting it out. Holders of trade claims are in the business of producing goods or providing services and have no interest in speculating on the outcome of the reorganization process. Creditors generally don't have the knowledge, interest, ability, or time to make decisions like this (such as how to keep the company alive) and will usually sell their claims at much lower prices than they would ultimately be worth, in which case the investor who buys the claims or securities can realize a profit—if all goes well.

Sorting out the value of all these different claims is the specialty of the distressed-securities fund manager. Managers ask themselves how much a claim might be worth if the company's assets were divided among the creditors. As always, an example can help here:

Ethan, a hedge fund manager, specializes in distressed securities. He is interested in a company called Alliance Energy Inc., which has recently filed for bankruptcy protection. The company has $91 million of assets and $140 million of debt. On average, the company's creditors would receive $0.65 on the dollar for each dollar of debt (excluding related expenses).

The Ontario Teachers' Pension Plan (OTPP) holds $30 million worth of Alliance bonds. Since their mandate does not allow the pension fund to hold below-investment-grade securities, the pension managers must now somehow dispose of their Alliance shares.

Ethan, our manager, makes a deal with the OTPP fund managers to buy the $30 million debt for $0.40 on the dollar. Hence, he pays $12,000,000 ($30,000,000 X $0.40) for the bonds. Ethan believes that if the company can restructure, it will be profitable again. If the restructuring fails, Ethan believes that he can receive $0.65 on the dollar (what the creditors will be paid), or a total of $19,500,000 ($30,000,000 X $0.65).

In addition to owning a company's debt, the hedge fund manager may also own "orphan" equity. Orphan equity is new stock issued by newly reorganized companies emerging from bankruptcy. However, the manager can also take a short position in the company's stock, should he or she feel that the company's prospects could deteriorate further over the short term.

To be successful, the hedge fund manager must undertake intensive research. Analyzing the different kinds of claims involved in reorganization or bankruptcy is a difficult job, as not all of them are paid back evenly and at the same time. Managers look at the debt structures to figure out where the priorities are. A mortgage backed by the collateral of a company's property, for instance, would be higher on the priority list than an uncollateralized loan or trade claim, which, in turn, would take priority over publicly held bonds and shares.

The reason distressed-securities investing is considered a hedge is that it has little or no correlation to the overall performance of the stock market and bases its success on the manager's research and analysis of the variables and debt structures of a distressed company. It is, again, a daunting task, requiring in-depth knowledge of not only the distressed company itself, but all the involved creditor companies as well (the complexity of the claims, the creditor companies' regulations and patience, how long the reorganization will last, how the assets will be distributed, and much more). Some managers will go as far as buying up enough of the distressed company's debt to get a seat on the creditor committee and aid in making decisions on distribution of assets (now *there's* a good premise for a Wall Street movie).

Long/Short Credit

Long/short credit funds invest in credit-sensitive securities, taking either a long or a short position. Trading activity in these instruments is based upon credit analysis of the issuer and the particular security. It may incorporate credit market reviews, and may be dependent upon either anticipated price movements of the security or "positive carry." Positive carry involves the exploitation of investment opportunities where the cost of borrowed funds is below the return earned from an investment.

In long/short credit funds, the manager assumes credit risk as a core part of his or her investment strategy. However, interest rate risk is not a significant factor since it is either explicitly hedged, or is irrelevant relative to credit risk.

Private Placements

Private placement is the sale of securities directly to institutional investors, such as banks, mutual funds, insurance companies, pension funds, and hedge funds, and does not require regulatory registration (provided the securities are bought for investment purposes only, rather than for resale). This means that the issuing company *does not have to go through the prospectus offering*. Offering a prospectus is a time-consuming and expensive—and legally required—process that a company has to go through if it wants to issue an IPO (initial public offering, or the first time a company sells shares publicly) or even a secondary offering of public shares. The cost of a prospectus offering can easily be in the millions of dollars, while a private placement offering can be done for a few thousand.

When companies try to raise money through share offerings (selling equity), cost can be a major issue, especially if they do not need large sums of money. To raise $6 to $7 million, and then spend over a million on items such as a prospectus, is just not efficient. So, if a corporation whose shares are publicly traded needs to raise, say, $7 million, the most efficient way to do it is through a private placement. The company will find an institution (in this case, a hedge fund) that is willing to buy the shares. The company draws up the private placement document (at a cost of a few thousand dollars in legal fees) and closes the deal.

Obviously, the question remains: how can the hedge fund make money on this transaction? After all, it could have simply bought the shares on the open market. The key is that because there is no prospectus issued, regulators put restrictions on what can be done with any shares acquired in this manner. Most often, there is a period during which the shares cannot be sold. This is why the definition states that they are for *investment purposes only*. In Ontario, for example, that period is currently four months—for four months, the hedge fund cannot sell those shares. After the four-month period, however, the shares become tradable. The trick is that to compensate the fund for that risk (which could be a serious drop in the liquidity of the investment), the issuing company will give a discount to the investor on the current market price. Depending on the price of the security, this discount can be up to 25% for TSX-traded stocks.

The job of the hedge fund manager is to find companies whose shares are *stable enough to last four months without a major fall*. If the share price is the same four months after the purchase, the manager will be able to realize a profit, depending on the discount he or she received from the issuing entity. In the case of a 25% discount, a share would have to lose more than a quarter of its underlying value in only four months for the manager to realize a loss.

There is another trick to this. If the hedge fund manager buys the shares at a discount by organizing a private placement, he or she can then borrow shares and short-sell them. This, as in the convertible bond strategy, locks in the profit for the manager, who will simply pocket the money from the sale of the borrowed shares, collect interest for four months, and then give the restricted shares back to the lender at the end of the four-month period. This guarantees the profit. However, most companies will put a clause in any private placement agreement to restrict this practice—for obvious reasons; short-selling a company's stock tends to drive the price down.

MULTI-PROCESS GROUP

This style is, again, pretty much what it sounds like. Managers using a multi-process method use two or more styles simultaneously, with no one style accounting for more than 80% of the fund's capital. As an example, a fund in this style might have 50% of its capital involved in systematic trading, and the other 50% in statistical arbitrage.

The only sub-strategy under multi-process group is event driven.

Event Driven

The event driven approach is a multi-process strategy that focuses upon the selection of securities that will experience a change in valuation because of corporate events (and we have seen an awful lot of them recently!). Announcements of new corporate events are the triggers for activity by hedge fund managers using this approach. These events cover a wide spectrum and include filing for bankruptcy protection, proxy battles, the outcome of litigation, and leveraged buyouts. In many cases, the hedge fund manager must weigh the expected return from an investment against the probability that a particular event will occur. For instance, a manager might target companies involved in acquisition and bankruptcy activity, and combine elements of both merger arbitrage and distressed securities to attempt to profit from a given situation.

Managers using event driven strategies may also take positions of a more directional nature, and these positions may not be directly hedged.

COMPARING THE VARIOUS HEDGE FUND CATEGORIES

Table 4.4 below illustrates the risk and return characteristics for each of the Morgan Stanley process groups or strategies. In each case, the constituent hedge funds in each index are equally weighted, rather than weighted by asset size. The performance of these various strategies is compared against the performance of the MSCI World Equity and Sovereign Debt Indices.

TABLE 4.4

Process group/ strategy index	Year to Date Performance	Year ended 31/07/04	Annualized Return 4 Years ended 31/05/04	3-Year Standard Deviation	3-Year Sharpe Ratio
Directional Trading	-3.40%	1.05%	7.55%	7.90%	0.76
Relative Value	1.34%	4.04%	5.30%	1.35%	2.75
Security Selection	0.99%	10.09%	6.18%	5.58%	0.82
Specialist Credit	6.08%	15.34%	13.26%	4.05%	2.88
Multi-process	3.19%	12.17%	8.50%	4.42%	1.56
MSCI Equity and Fixed Income Indices					
World Equity Index	0.14%	17.58%	0.21%	16.08%	N/A
World Sovereign Debt Index	-2.10%	8.22%	10.83%	7.93%	N/A

Note: All performance figures are for the period ended July 31, 2004.

HEDGE FUND CLASSIFICATIONS

Besides MSCI, other organizations, such as Van Hedge Fund Advisors International and Credit Suisse First Boston (CSFB)/Tremont, have also developed classification systems for the hedge fund industry. While many systems use some of the same categories to describe hedge funds (for example, merger arbitrage and statistical arbitrage), others use groupings that differ from those used by MSCI.

The table below shows the categories used by Van Hedge Fund Advisors International and CSFB/Tremont.

TABLE 4.5: ALTERNATIVE HEDGE FUND CLASSIFICATIONS

Van Hedge Fund Advisors International	CSFB/Tremont
• marke-neutral group	• convertible arbitrage
• long/short equity group	• dedicated short bias
• directional trading group	• emerging markets
• specialty strategies group	• equity market-neutral
• fund of funds	• event-driven
	• fixed income arbitrage
	• global macro
	• long/short equity
	• managed futures
	• multi-strategy

Fund of Hedge Funds

A fund of hedge funds is, put simply, a hedge fund that invests in other hedge funds. At this point, you, the reader, know more about hedge funds than 90% of the population. So when you ask, "Why would anyone invest in something like that?" you are asking a very logical question. So let's look at it again. A fund of hedge funds collects investment capital from its customers and then puts the money into a number of different hedge funds. The investor receives a return that is the average return of the different hedge funds invested in, minus the management and performance fees charged by the fund of funds.

The question you likely have is this: why would I do that, when I could just as well invest in one or more funds and not pay a second layer of management and performance fees? Again, you are 100% correct to ask this. However, many very successful hedge funds have a *minimum investment* requirement that can be in the hundreds of thousands of dollars. If you have that kind of money to invest in a fund and you can do it a few times over, you can actually create your own fund of hedge funds. Most of us, however, cannot invest such large sums into one place, and that is where a fund of funds fills a void—by consolidating investments from a number of individuals. This consolidation allows these individuals to easily invest in any of the successful funds that have huge minimum investment requirements, investments that would be otherwise out of the question.

The second reason you might want to invest in a fund of hedge funds is *diversification*. Different funds of hedge funds create different types of diversification options. As you saw in earlier chapters, hedge funds are not relative to market performance. And you have seen above that there are many different hedge fund styles that for all intents and purposes are completely unrelated to each other, with no correlation of their performances whatsoever. By investing in a number of different, unrelated hedge funds, you can achieve true diversification. In understanding the strategies described above, it is easy to see that there is a normally low correlation among, for example, a long/short, a fixed income arbitrage, and a distressed securities fund. Rather than investing all your money into only one of them, spreading it across all three will minimize risk and potentially provide a better return.

The third reason you might want to invest in a fund of hedge funds is the *due diligence* the manager will have to apply. A prudent fund-of-funds manager will not just put his or her clients' money blindly into any hedge fund. Rather, he or she will go through a due diligence process, examining each of the potential funds in great detail, interviewing the managers, and making sure that these investments are the right ones for the clients. Not only will the manager do this at the beginning, he or she will maintain the process during the entire existence of the fund. Being close to the individual managers of these funds, the fund-of-funds manager can notice a potential "red flag" much sooner than the general public and take the necessary steps to minimize exposure. As a result, the manager might reduce investment in the troubled fund in question or just eliminate it completely from the portfolio. Undertaking this due diligence is extremely difficult for the average investor. Most of us have all kinds of other obligations in any given day that do not leave enough time to do serious research into investment vehicles. Doing that research is why a fund-of-funds manager can justify the second layer of fees.

TABLE 4.6

	Fund 1	Fund 2	Fund 3	Fund 4	Fund of Funds
2000	35%	22%	7%	(8%)	14%
2001	27%	(2%)	29%	19%	18%
2002	(10%)	39%	35%	45%	27%
2003	19%	25%	35%	35%	28%
2004	36%	20%	(1%)	16%	18%
5-year Compounded Return	20%	20%	20%	20%	**21%**

As you can see in Table 4.6, it is possible for a fund of hedge funds to provide the same return as single-strategy hedge funds while protecting investors better against large losses.

Advantages of a Fund-of-Funds Strategy

A fund-of-funds approach can be a very effective investment strategy. A fund of funds

- uses a variety of strategies that have little or no correlation with each other
- can provide better returns than single-strategy funds, with lower overall risk
- cushions investors from the poor performance of an underperforming fund
- can provide returns that are largely uncorrelated to the stock market
- eliminates the need for time-consuming due diligence by the investor
- permits easier administration of widely diversified investments across a large number of hedge funds
- allows access to a wider spectrum of leading hedge funds not available to the general public due to their high minimum requirements and/or domicile

While it is evident that a fund of funds is an attractive investment, there are, of course, some disadvantages. The second level of management and performance fees associated with a fund of funds creates a significant increase in costs.

HEDGE FUND INFORMATION ON THE WORLD WIDE WEB

While the amount of information provided by the hedge fund industry is still small relative to that provided to mutual fund investors, recent signs suggest that this is changing. In the U.S., Barron's (www.barrons.com) regularly publishes in-depth interviews with hedge fund managers. As well, *The Financial Times* offers real-time information on the performances and risk profiles of hedge funds through a new Web-based service known as PlusFunds (www.plusfunds.com).

In Canada, hedge funds are gaining greater visibility through the efforts of organizations such as the Alternative Investment Management Association (AIMA) Canada (www.aima-canada.org) and Canadian Hedge Watch (www.canadianhedgewatch.com). Canadian Hedge Watch, along with The Canadian Institute of Financial Planners (CIFP), sponsors an annual hedge fund forum called the World Hedge Funds Summit (www.worldhedgefundssummit.com). In addition, Canadian Hedge Watch provides a regular flow of information about new and existing hedge funds.

The maturation of the hedge fund industry has led to other developments, including the establishment of hedge fund indices. In 1999, Tremont Advisors, in conjunction with Credit Suisse First Boston, created the CSFB/Tremont Hedge Fund Index (www.hedgeindex.com). In early 2000, Hedge Fund Research launched another index with Zurich Capital Markets (www.zcmgroup.com).

Morgan Stanley Capital International (www.msci.com) established its hedge fund indices in July 2002. The MSCI Hedge Fund Indices consist of over 190 indices based on the MSCI Hedge Fund Classification Standard. The MSCI hedge fund database currently contains more than 1,700 hedge funds representing more than US$230 billion in assets.

Historically, the hedge fund industry operated without the usual professional trappings of associations, conventions, or newsletters. This is also beginning to change. AIMA, established in 1990, provides a forum where members can disseminate accurate information about their industry.

Advisers and their clients will discover that there is no single depository for hedge fund information. Consequently, a number of organizations have emerged to make it easier for investors to access information. The three largest suppliers of data include Hedge Fund Research (www.hedgefundresearch.com) in Chicago, Managed Account Reports (www.marhedge.com) in New York City, and TASS International Research in London (www.tassresearch.com). In addition, several other groups collect their own statistics, including the Hennessee Group (www.hennesseegroup.com) in New York and Van Hedge Advisors International (www.vanhedge.com) in Nashville, Tennessee.

Prospective investors need to be aware of one essential caveat: the quality of hedge fund data is open to question. Its value depends upon the willingness of hedge funds to provide both accurate and timely information. Another consideration is whether the collectors of hedge fund data verify the information received. In some cases, the reluctance of hedge funds to supply data reflects inertia; in other cases, funds do not supply fund details because of poor investment performance.

THE CURRENT HEDGE FUND INDUSTRY

Compared to the huge asset base of traditional asset classes, hedge funds still occupy only a small segment of the investment universe. Presently, there are more than 8,000 hedge funds in the world. Assets of U.S. hedge funds total between $400 and $500 billion, with fewer than 5% of funds having holdings of more than $500 million under management.

Although still quite small, the hedge fund industry has experienced rapid growth over the last few years, with the increasing number of funds reflecting developments on both the supply and demand sides. Particularly in the U.S., the technology boom of the late 1990s greatly increased the ranks of high-net-worth individuals. In addition, many institutional investors have turned their attention to alternative investments in search of a greater variety of investment opportunities.

On the supply side of the equation, there has been no shortage of investment managers joining the hedge fund business. Given the greater flexibility offered by hedge funds, it is easy to see why hedge funds attract the best and brightest of the investment business. By investing through hedge funds, they can both invest in their own way and receive considerable compensation for their success.

The growth of hedge funds has also been aided by the increased expertise of major brokerage firms. This increased expertise has allowed hedge funds to more easily process their trades. A number of these major firms have provided assistance to the hedge fund industry by helping hedge fund managers to set up their operations.

Picking a Hedge Fund That's Right for You

So you want to buy a hedge fund. What should you look for? The Canadian hedge fund industry is still relatively small, but there are almost 350 funds to choose from nonetheless—where to begin?

First of all, we should review a couple of main points. If you think investing in hedge funds will be anything like investing in mutual funds, think again. You will remember from Chapter 2 that mutual funds are correlated to the broad markets and are homogeneous, meaning that they all have relatively similar performances and risk characteristics. This is because the mutual fund industry is based on a long-only strategy that prohibits them from holding short positions and restricts them to allocating no more than 10% of their assets to any one financial instrument.

These restrictions result in mutual funds delivering returns that are relative to the broad markets (when the markets go down, for the most part so do mutual funds). As well, mutual funds measure their returns relative to a benchmark, such as the S&P 500. The mutual fund culture is to outperform the benchmark. So if the benchmark loses 15% and the mutual fund loses only 10%, the fund managers rejoice. "We've outperformed the benchmark by 5 percentage points!" they cry. Wait a minute. Your fund still *lost* 10%. What are you smiling about?

The other pitfall in mutual fund investing is the difficulty of assembling a diversified portfolio based solely on mutual funds. Because they are, by design, all widely diversified, long-only portfolios, they all move similarly to the markets and as a result end up being very similar to each other.

Because of the severely declining markets in 2001 and 2002, and because mutual funds move with the markets, over $6 billion was taken out of mutual funds in Canada between June 6, 2002 and January 3, 2003 (as we saw at the beginning of Chapter 3). While the major North American markets produced relatively good numbers for 2003 and 2004 (thanks to the November–December rally) performance remains "shaky" at best.

So forget about looking at the S&P or other benchmarks. Stop watching the TSX wobbling unsteadily up and down. Grab a pencil, put on your slippers, and have a look at hedge funds.

HEDGE FUNDS AND MARKET CORRELATION

You will remember from Chapter 2 that hedge funds are heterogeneous, meaning that they all have widely different performances and risk characteristics. So when a number of them are put together in a portfolio, they are good material for diversification. This is highly desirable, as it lowers the risk of being exposed to a particular market decline.

You also learned that hedge funds have a low correlation to the broad markets, because they are not restricted to long-only positions and are not subject to an asset allocation straitjacket. Again, this is a great advantage, as it protects the investor from overall declines in the market. This lack of correlation to the markets (and to each other) means that hedge funds can look for positive, absolute returns every year and can be highly diversified in a properly created portfolio.

So how do you choose a hedge fund? There are a number of important steps, beginning with a little research.

DUE DILIGENCE

First and foremost, due diligence must be exercised. This fancy term has a simple definition. Due diligence is simply gaining a solid understanding of risk in an investment through research. Due to hedge funds' diversity, proper due diligence for these funds is more complicated than for mutual funds. As well, mutual funds are relatively transparent—strategies, risk factors, and histories are easily obtained. Most information can be obtained merely by looking at the financial pages of the Saturday paper or by visiting Web sites such as www. globefund.com or www.fundlibrary.com. By contrast, hedge fund managers are a fairly secretive bunch and are not required to post their performances or strategies publicly.

Fund managers often defend this lack of transparency among hedge funds as one of their greatest advantages. The argument is that if they had to openly report current portfolio holdings, other funds could see the opportunity and jump in, destroying the delicate balance of a strategy. Regardless, obtaining information on hedge funds can be a difficult but not impossible task.

By now we hope we've convinced you that investing in hedge funds will provide you with superior returns and less risk. But we are also telling you that there is a considerable amount of research and work involved in investing wisely. You will need to find out the answers to some very detailed questions regarding the funds, their managers, their returns, and their risks. Maybe you are the type of person who likes to do a lot of research. Some people enjoy looking at every possibility, lining up candidates, searching every nook and cranny, reading through every related document, and coming up with informed decisions. In this case, looking for a hedge fund will be one of your greatest and most enjoyable challenges.

What if you're not like that? What if you don't know where to start?

Finding detailed information about anything is hard, so get someone else to do it for you. A financial adviser or broker is a good place to start. Since these professionals earn money on your hedge fund investment, you can get them to do the digging to answer your questions. It's their job! Again, the Canadian hedge fund market is still relatively small, so it may be difficult to find an adviser with experience in this market. But don't let this be an excuse! An adviser or broker's duty is to become educated on your behalf. If your adviser or broker isn't doing what you ask or producing the results you want, simply tell him or her that there are plenty of other people out there who will! Remember that these people have a *client*-based business, and someone who has recently entered the field may want to work harder to get your business than someone who already has an established clientele.

You should come up with a list of questions to get your adviser to answer. Some of the information you will need is listed below. And remember: if the fund seems reluctant to answer your questions, you should ask yourself why!

THE MANAGER

By far the most important consideration in assessing any fund is the quality and reliability of its manager. As you have seen, hedge funds rely much more heavily on the talent of their managers than mutual funds do. They have a wide range of strategies and tools available to them, but they also need to be much more innovative, market savvy, and ahead of the game as they use these strategies and tools. Actively managing money in a hedge fund is a difficult and complicated task, so make sure you get the best. If you had a rare disease and needed a good medical specialist, wouldn't you research very carefully and ask a lot of questions? Wouldn't you want the best in the field? If you're not comfortable with a fund manager's background and experience, don't go any further.

Background

The background profile of the manager can tell you a lot about his or her style and help in assessing the potential risks of the fund. What is the manager's family situation? Single, married, 11 kids—it may seem funny, but a manager's family and lifestyle can have a large effect on his or her ability to actively manage a hedge fund. What is the manager's past credit history? This can certainly be an indicator of reliability and credibility.

Getting this information—even admitting you want these details—may seem a little "cloak-and-dagger" at first, but you *are* trusting the manager with *your* money, after all. And because of the lack of regulations in the hedge fund industry, managers tend to be more flamboyant (and talented), traits that can create risks. Many superstars (not only the ones in sports and pop music) have lost their edge because of personal or emotional problems!

Licensing

Intelligence, creativity, and wily money-management skills can come from a number of places. Some managers study widely, some gain experience through examining other managers, and some just have an inherent knack for the job. Regardless of where you think this kind of talent comes from, you at least need to find out if the manager is properly licensed. You may run across some funds that are private and that have found ways to get around the licensing rules. Be *very* careful here.

Since many provinces have different laws, it is important to make sure that the manager is licensed under the appropriate security legislation for the province it is operating in. Your adviser or broker can find this information for you, or you can contact your provincial securities commission to see which licences apply in your province.

Experience

Knowing about the manager's experience is very important information, and besides the obvious (you want someone with a good track record), it uncovers a number of concerns.

Did the manager ever manage more traditional investments (mutual funds or a similar investment)? This can tell you a lot about the potential risks. If a manager worked for a large mutual fund company for, say, 10 years, it is extremely important that you look carefully at the reasons he or she is now managing a hedge fund. The temptation to run a hedge fund because of the potential performance fees is a big one, and many mutual fund managers have left their salaried jobs in favour of making big bucks on profit sharing.

The question to ask is "How can a manager who has only held a long portfolio and never shorted stocks be an effective hedge fund manager?" The long-side (markets going up) mindset can be a very hard habit to kick, and in our opinion the relatively poor performance of some Canadian hedge funds can be traced to former mutual fund managers simply taking long positions and leveraging themselves to the neck. All those disciples of Alfred Winslow Jones in the late sixties and early seventies found out the hard way that no matter what the market climate, a short portfolio is *always* necessary. This is not to say that every mutual fund manager would make a bad hedge fund manager, but if *you* thought the only way to make money in the markets was to go long and wait it out, how would you handle the short side?

Good hedge fund managers will have experience in managing prior hedge funds, in trading, or in managing discretionary accounts (building and managing an investment portfolio for individual investors).

THE FUND

Information on the fund itself (for the most part, anyway) should be a little easier to obtain, because funds are required by law to publish certain details in the offering memorandum for the fund. This is the creation document for the fund—its "bible"—and is invaluable to the investor.

The Offering Memorandum

The offering memorandum (OM) is designed to explain the details of the fund's structure. And be warned; it's *not* light reading. Rather, it is a very detailed, lengthy, "lawyerspeak" document that must be read *thoroughly*, as it is the investor's primary source of information. Understanding the OM completely will give you ammunition if the fund strays from its path, as it will also point out the potential risks of the investment and the legal rights of investors to sue the fund if the OM contains misrepresentations.

The OM is a confidential document that will often have its own identification number attached to it, so the fund can keep track of how many they have given out. It will include pricing, investment minimums, and legal and financial information on all parties involved. The Web sites of some funds may have the OM in a file you can download. Otherwise, call the fund and they will send you one.

An investor can usually get a good idea of the fund's general risks and returns by looking through the summary at the beginning—a lot of time and effort can be saved if you can just look at it quickly and say, "Nope." Therefore, it's a good idea to start with the summary, and if you find a section that is not clear or one that interests you, go to the relevant section of the OM to get information. If you don't get the information there, start asking questions!

You will also find the dealer compensation amounts in the OM. Read them so you don't feel so badly about making your broker or adviser work hard to get you the information you want.

And on the whole, the larger the document and the more fine print there is, the more likely the fund is to be above board. So if the offering memorandum is written in crayon on a napkin, run!

Strategy of the Fund

In the previous chapter, you read about a number of different strategies and styles in the hedge fund world. It is very important to have a basic understanding of the kind of strategy a hedge fund has. Under what conditions will the fund likely make money? More importantly, under what conditions will it likely *lose* money? What is the fund's risk control mechanism? Not knowing this information is inviting disaster.

Much like choosing a mutual fund, picking a hedge fund means considering your own risk tolerance—what are you willing to bet? If someone asked you to give them a quarter and said they would bet you a dollar that the quarter would come up heads five times in a row, would you take the bet? Most people would; the odds are pretty good that the quarter will turn up tails at least *once*.

But what if the bet was $100? Or $1,000? Would you still be as confident? Assessing your risk tolerance is a very important step in choosing a style that's right for you. As we mentioned in the previous chapter, only someone with a large amount of disposable income would think about investing in a global macro fund, for instance.

So have a look at the different strategies and ask yourself how much risk you are willing to take for a certain return. This should give you a good idea of the kinds of styles that are right for you.

A Few Words About "Style Drift"

"Style drift" is a much-discussed topic in the funds-management world, and there are a variety of opinions about it. Style drift describes the situation when a fund manager moves away or drifts from a specific style that is described in the OM. For example, a hedge fund manager might drift from a merger arbitrage style to a long/short equity style. Why would this happen? There can be any number of reasons. Maybe the manager realized that only a few mergers were available, and many other funds were competing for them, so it would be very hard to make any money. Then again, maybe the manager simply saw a great opportunity in the market and flipped the portfolio over to take advantage of it.

The question remains: is it a good or a bad thing? Should a manager be forced to remain in his or her OM-mandated style? Most experts would reply with a resounding "Yes!" This is because for mutual fund investment, style drift is *absolutely* unacceptable. Money managers in mutual funds are hired to handle capital in a particular asset class, with a particular style. The whole industry is founded on the diversification of capital over a wide range of asset classes, so if a single manager drifts from his or her style, it places that diversity in jeopardy by throwing everything off balance. For example, if a mutual fund manager is maintaining a growth fund and suddenly sells 40% of the fund's stocks and puts the capital into cash and bonds, the growth fund is changed to a balanced fund, and the risks, returns, and liquidity of the investment are changed, too. Once again, the long-only, diversified portfolio mindset, based in prudent, fiduciary responsibility, comes into play.

But we must ask a few questions here. From an investor's perspective, if your fund manager saw that the current style he or she was in was going to result in losses, what would you like that manager to do? Would you prefer that he or she simply watch the losses accumulate and do nothing? Or maybe change style without telling you? Or would you rather that the manager inform you of his or her concerns regarding the possible change (in a monthly newsletter, for instance) and give you the choice of staying in or getting out?

And one more important question: is standing by, watching money go down the drain when one knows that there are alternatives, *really* a good example of fiduciary responsibility?

Having said that, you have to make sure whatever "new" investment the manager makes it is still covered by the documentation in the OM and the OM is ammended accordingly.

Size of the Fund (Asset Ceiling)

Once you have identified the strategy of the fund, it is also vital that you find out what limits it puts on the amount of assets under management (AUM), or its *asset ceiling*. This limit is generally put in place to allow flexibility for the manager's strategy. As you learned in Chapter 3, hedge funds, because of their unique strategies, have varying amounts of AUM they can manage at any one time, depending on a number of constraints. If a fund invests in a narrow market niche, it can be very hard to put loads of money into a tight space without affecting the markets. Smaller funds are able to make large returns mainly because it is easier to trade in and out of 5,000 shares than 500,000. Remember our discussion about variable-bias funds in Chapter 4? We explained that to sell large blocks of shares when a fund is trying to get in and out of positions, just dumping them into the market can seriously affect the price of the security (and thus the profit of the fund). So it is very important that the broker the fund utilizes "works" the order (to buy or sell the large amount of shares) and *slowly* trades it into the market. These larger orders make the fund much more cumbersome and less able to capitalize on profits.

Then there is the simple problem of market liquidity, or how much product is out there. Let's assume that there is about $500 million worth of mergers available in a given year. This means that an M/A (merger arbitrage) fund cannot, by definition, have a cumulative value of over $500 million. And there is certainly more than just one M/A fund out there competing for that money. So if in this situation an M/A fund has assets of $250 million, simple math tells you that the chances of that fund finding enough opportunities to supply that demand are slim to none!

So you need to look at the potential amount of product and ask a few questions. How much liquidity (product) is there to support the strategy?

You will also want to ask how far the fund is from its asset ceiling. If you think that the fund's ceiling is too high, getting in just as it starts to become too big to manoeuvre can be a mistake. A fund that works well at $10 million may not be effective at $100 million.

Past Performance

This is where the fun really starts—examining the actual numbers (when you get to start thinking about how much money you might make!). What returns did the fund produce, and what were the risks involved? First of all, you need a basic understanding of how to read some of the numbers you'll be looking at. We can all relate to a "15% return," but how do you measure something like risk? How does a fund manage that risk?

A large dose of caution should be used when analyzing hedge fund returns: data is usually limited to only a couple of years of monthly returns, under a limited set of conditions within that time period. How a hedge fund might perform under different market conditions that it may not have yet experienced is a question that is very difficult to answer with any precision, so treat any analysis of hedge fund performance with a large grain of salt!

MEASURING RISK

There are a number of ways to assess the potential risks in a hedge fund, and an outline of return and risks is almost always found in the OM. Managers are generally required to publicize their "numbers" in statistics such as the famous *Sharpe ratio* (see below). It is necessary to understand this calculation, as it is a very useful tool in assessing "risk-adjusted performance," or the ratio of the *amount of excess return (over and above the risk-free rate of return) to the amount of risk involved in achieving it.*

Let's look at an example of how the Sharpe ratio can be useful for you. If Hedge Fund A returned 25%, and Hedge Fund B returned 15%, you would think that Hedge Fund A was a better choice. But if you were to examine the amount of *risk* that Hedge Fund A took, it might be much more extreme than B's. Therefore, Hedge Fund A stands a better chance of losing money than B and will be a much more volatile investment.

The Sharpe ratio is a way of putting these two funds on a level playing field. The calculation of the ratio is complicated and really not necessary to spell out in great detail (unless you have an affection for complex calculations). Your adviser can tell you what the Sharpe ratio is—even if you don't figure it out yourself, it is worthwhile knowing what it is and what it means. One main component of the ratio is important to understand, however, as it is used to measure the volatility of a fund's returns. This measure is called *standard deviation.*

Standard deviation is a way to assess data, showing potential volatility. This calculation is achieved by measuring how far a fund's returns strayed from the average or "mean." For example, for the numbers 1, 2, and 3, the "mean" is 2. Let's look at another example. Hedge Fund A has an annual return of 12%. This means that on average, it returned 1% per month (12 months X 1% each month = 12%). In a perfect world, the fund actually did this; that is, returned 1% *consistently* every month. In this case, the fund would have no *standard deviation from the mean.* It returned 1% every month 100% of the time. Figure 5.1 illustrates this.

FIGURE 5.1: HEDGE FUND A—MONTHLY RETURNS

Jan	Feb	Mar	Apr	May	Jun	Jul	Aug	Sep	Oct	Nov	Dec
1%	1%	1%	1%	1%	1%	1%	1%	1%	1%	1%	1%

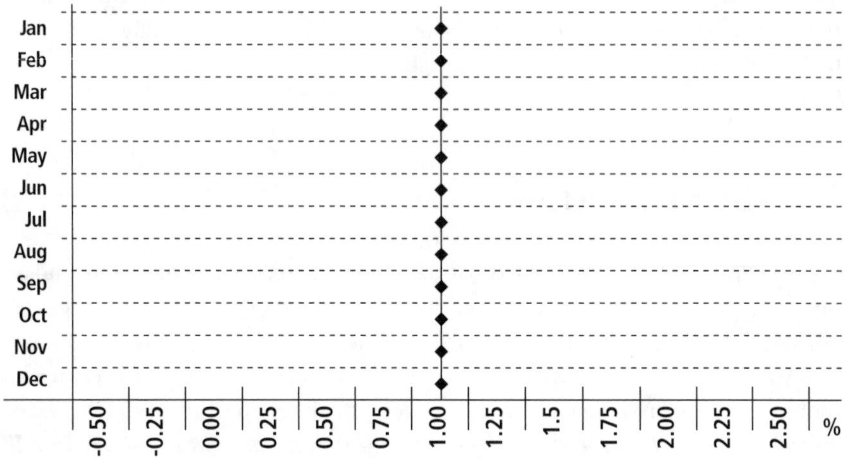

This, of course, is almost impossible in investment vehicles, but your savings account would look like this graph (although with a lot lower monthly returns), as the bank guarantees you a steady, monthly interest rate (though unfortunately nothing *like* 12%).

Now let's look at Hedge Fund B. It returned 12% as well over the same year, but had a number of months in which it deviated from the mean of 1%. Figure 5.2 illustrates this.

FIGURE 5.2: HEDGE FUND B—MONTHLY RETURNS

Jan	Feb	Mar	Apr	May	Jun	Jul	Aug	Sep	Oct	Nov	Dec
1%	1.1%	0.9%	1%	1.3%	1%	0.6%	1%	1.2%	0.8%	1%	1.1%

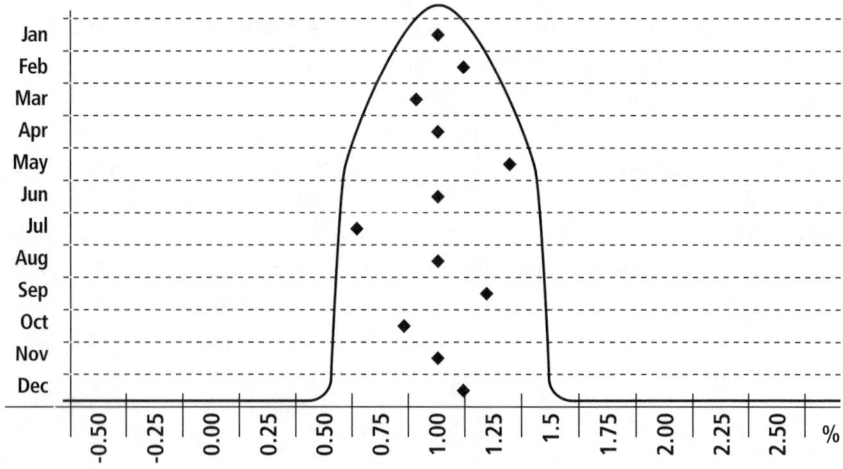

If you look at the numbers, this fund had a great success rate in returning the mean of 1%. As to the rest of the returns, they fell within either .6% on the low side or 1.3% on the high side. This is a more-than-acceptable deviation in most cases. If you are an investor in this fund, you can feel fairly confident in the manager's ability to provide consistent, reliable returns within the target range.

But now let's have a look at Hedge Fund C. This fund, while also returning 12% over the year, swung crazily back and forth, with returns as high as 2.5% and as low as -.5%.

FIGURE 5.3: HEDGE FUND C—MONTHLY RETURNS

Jan	Feb	Mar	Apr	May	Jun	Jul	Aug	Sep	Oct	Nov	Dec
-0.5%	1.8%	0.8%	2.0%	2.5%	-0.25%	1.7%	1.4%	-0.5%	2.1%	0%	0.95%

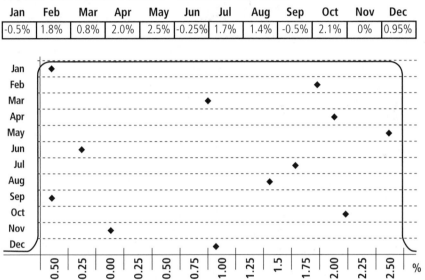

What a ride *this* fund was on (compared to the previous ones)! One month you have great returns, the next you lose

These are illustrations of the volatility of fund performance, and it is from these data that we calculate the standard deviation of a fund's returns. We won't bore you with the actual calculations—they're easy enough to find if you want to look for them. The bottom line is that standard deviation is the *average distance of the values from the mean.*

So, the lower the standard deviation, the less volatile a fund's returns will be.

FIGURE 5.4: HEDGE FUND B—STANDARD DEVIATION

Jan	Feb	Mar	Apr	May	Jun	Jul	Aug	Sep	Oct	Nov	Dec
1%	1.1%	0.9%	1%	1.3%	1%	0.6%	1%	1.2%	0.8%	1%	1.1%

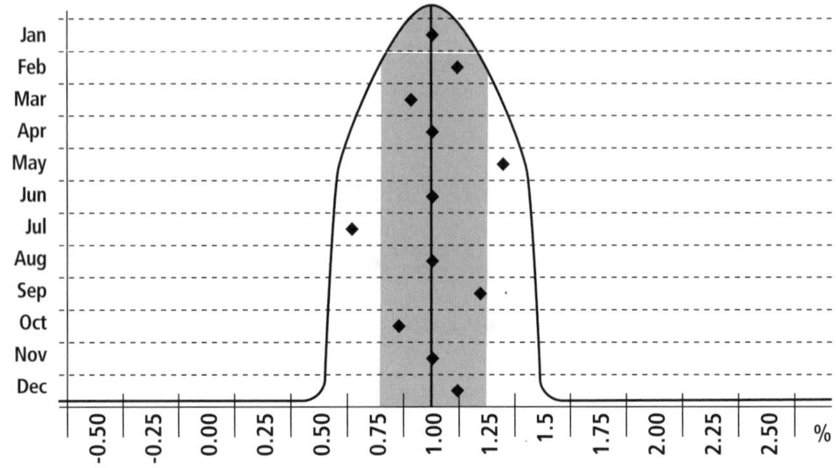

The shaded area in Figure 5.4 represents returns where most of the monthly returns were falling, meaning within 1 standard deviation "distance" from the mean.

Table 5.1 illustrates how standard deviation can show the volatility of a particular fund. Five managers are represented, and their returns shown over a five-year period. The compounded return of each fund over these five years is the same—20%. But look at the standard deviations. Manager 5 has a considerably lower standard deviation than the others. Why is this? The answer lies in the consistency of his or her returns. Look at Manager 5's returns: they varied between 14% and 27%. Manager 1, on the other hand, may have also returned 20%, but look at the huge swings between returns over the five-year period—from -10% all the way to 36%. So we can see that a higher standard deviation number indicates a higher volatility (or risk).

TABLE 5.1

	Manager 1	Manager 2	Manager 3	Manager 4	Manager 5
2000	35%	22%	7%	(8%)	14%
2001	27%	(2%)	29%	19%	17%
2002	(10%)	39%	35%	45%	25%
2003	19%	25%	35%	35%	27%
2004	36%	20%	(1%)	16%	18%
5-year Compounded Return	20%	20%	20%	20%	20%
Standard Deviation	16.86	13.20	15.07	18.12	5.51

THE SHARPE RATIO

As we have said, the Sharpe ratio is a measure of the risk-adjusted return of an investment, essentially allowing a calculation based not only on annualized (average) returns, but on the potential risk involved as well. The major advantage of using the Sharpe ratio over other models is that the Sharpe ratio takes into consideration not only the fund's return but it's return in relation to it's risk.

The ratio was derived by Professor William Sharpe (one of three economists who received the Nobel Prize for economics in 1990 for their contributions to what is now called modern portfolio theory—see Chapter 2). The ratio takes the excess return (over and above the risk-free rate of return) and divides it by something called the *annualized standard deviation of returns*. Don't panic; it's fairly simple.

The excess return is a measure of how much more return your investment provided than that of the risk-free return did. A risk-free return rate is usually the return of a very stable investment, such as Canadian treasury bills. It basically tells you how much better your investment performed relative to something that is a "safe bet."

The annualized standard deviation of returns is exactly what it says it is: the average amount of deviation of the returns of the fund in question relative to its mean return. This represents the risk, because if a fund's standard deviation is high, we know that its returns swing wildly above and below the mean.

Again, a lot of the calculations are mind-boggling, but when the dust clears, the Sharpe ratio provides us with a scale of sorts, where the lower the number, the less return you receive for the same unit of risk, and the higher the number, the *more* return you receive for the same unit of risk. So the higher the number, the better!

The only real drawback to using Sharpe ratios to assess a single investment's risk-adjusted return rate is that it is expressed as just a number, meaning that it is very hard for an investor to evaluate the Sharpe ratio of an individual fund without seeing the ratios of other funds in the same category. A Sharpe ratio of 1.5 is usually considered good (even great), but what if all the other funds in that category had ratios above 2.0?

So it is very important to compare Sharpe ratios among funds in the same category. This will give you a good understanding of how the funds are performing relative to each other.

BETA

You will come across a number of different ways in which people attempt to analyze risk in the hedge fund world. Because hedge funds are relatively uncorrelated to the markets, you would think that there would be no way (or reason) to measure their performance relative to the markets—it would be like comparing apples to oranges.

However, if you think of hedge funds as oranges and market indices, such as the S&P 500, as apples, there is actually a lot of value in measuring how much less or more certain apples are like—or *not* like—oranges. This may seem confusing, but it makes sense. Using these statistics, a hedge fund can show how uncorrelated it actually is to the markets and their benchmarks. This is the role of *beta*.

Beta is the risk of an investment (in our case, a hedge fund) relative to that of the S&P 500 (or other index). A stock with a beta of 1 is considered as volatile as the market. Less than 1 means it is less volatile, and more than 1 means it is more. So obviously you're looking for funds with betas of less than 1. (If you're looking for less risky funds.)

JENSEN'S ALPHA

Jensen's alpha, named for its creator, Michael Jensen, an influential Harvard Business School professor, is another complicated calculation to assess risk-adjusted performance. Alpha is basically a representation of a fund manager's ability to achieve a return that is above what would be expected, given the risk the fund takes; that is, much better the manager is doing than the numbers say he or she should. In this sense, it is similar to the Sharpe ratio in measuring performance.

By providing a basis of comparison for portfolios that have different risk exposures, this measurement is used to identify the part of the performance that can be attributed to the manager and not to blind luck. Calculated over a relatively extended period of time (most suggest no less than three years), positive alphas generally mean the fund manager is performing well, and negative ones mean he or she is not.

For example, if two hedge funds both have a 12% return, it stands to reason that an investor would want to buy the one with less risk. By analyzing the alpha, you can determine if a fund is earning the proper return for its level of risk. If the alpha is positive, then the portfolio is earning excess returns, or returns above and beyond what are expected. So a positive value for alpha means a fund manager has superior performance due to his or her strategy and experience.

CORRELATION TO A BENCHMARK

Correlating to a benchmark may seem like a strange concept. With all our talk of how hedge funds are uncorrelated to the markets and don't use benchmarks to measure their performance, why are we all of a sudden talking about correlation to a benchmark?

Essentially, it is because if you can see just *how* uncorrelated a hedge fund is to the markets, you can get a good idea of how to place it in your portfolio. In a diversified portfolio, you want each investment to be as uncorrelated to the others as possible. By using the correlation to benchmark calculation, you can place hedge funds into the portfolio to give maximum diversity.

Using the S&P 500 as the benchmark, we can demonstrate how this information is useful. Correlation is measured between -1 and +1, where -1 means that a fund will be completely negatively correlated to the benchmark (when the S&P 500 goes down, the hedge fund will go up in an exact mirror reflection), and where +1 means that the fund is perfectly positively correlated to the benchmark (when the S&P 500 goes down, the fund will go down exactly parallel to it). A correlation of 0 means that there is absolutely no correlation between the hedge fund and its benchmark.

If we look at the correlation of a certain hedge fund to the S&P 500 in a declining market, we want to see numbers below 0, meaning that the hedge fund is going up as the market is going down.

RISK CONTROL MECHANISMS

Think of risk control mechanisms as being like the floodgates on a hydroelectric dam. When everything is running smoothly, water runs through the dam and power is generated. But when too much water is running through and the area below the dam is starting to flood, the engineers close the floodgates until the area dries up again. The floodgates help to minimize the risk of flooding.

With hedge funds, there can be any number of potential risks, and the manager has to put in place "floodgates" to help keep those risks to a minimum. These control mechanisms can include the following:

When to Cut Losses?

We all know the downfall of most gamblers. "Letting it ride" usually ends in disaster—anyone can tell you that there is no such thing as a lucky streak. With investing, the trick is to know when to get out of a bad situation. You will remember our discussions from Chapter 3 about the crash of tech stocks in 2002. Investors saw huge gains over a relatively short period of time and became greedy. When the stocks started falling, the investors held on, thinking that the downward movement would turn around. It never did, and in some cases investors lost literally everything.

A good hedge fund manager will know when to say "when" and will try to anticipate declines and get out before they happen. And when an unexpected decline does happen, they will know to sell even at a loss, to avoid further losses. It is important to ask questions about the fund's history and expectations of its risk control. What is the likely maximum drawdown (losses) a fund will endure before action?

Types of Investments Allowed

This is a simple question. Does the fund invest in any high-risk instruments? If so, what are the risks, and how much of the assets are dedicated to them? The more assets that are allocated to a high-risk venture, the greater the potential for loss. This information will be in the offering memorandum for the fund.

Net Market Exposure

You will remember Mr. Jones's formula from the first chapter. In a long/short equity hedge fund, he measured risk by calculating the amount of short positions versus long positions.

Net Market Exposure = (Long position – Short position) / Capital

This gave him a way to measure the minimum and maximum levels of market exposure, or how much of the assets were "exposed" to potential market fluctuations. By looking at how the assets are spread between long and short positions, you can get a good idea of what the potential risks are. By and large, the further the Net Market Exposure is from 0%, the more risk the hedge fund has. Good long/short managers will usually report the current percentages of asset allocation, as they are constantly juggling positions to get the most out of the current market conditions.

There are other risk-assessing methods as well. In the hedge fund world, risks, as with many other aspects, are dependent on the manager, the correlation of strategy, style, and asset ceiling. Again, it is important to match up your risk tolerance with the volatility level of a given fund's strategy and their methods of controlling that volatility, or risk.

Leverage—How Much?

You will recall from Chapter 1 that the collapse of Long-Term Capital Management in 1998 was due, for the most part, to extensive leveraging. Besides being wrong on both sides of its arbitrage strategy, it had borrowed huge amounts of money to amplify its returns. And as we saw, the company suffered extensive losses instead and had to be bailed out by the banks.

When leverage becomes high, we can see the potential risks expressed in raw numbers. This is rooted in the fact that losses tend to hurt more than gains help. If your investment loses, say, 10% in one month, it will take an 11% positive return the next month to get even again.

This is simple math. If you have $100 and lose 10% of that, you're left with $90. The question is, what percentage gain do you have to make to get back to having $100? The answer is a simple formula: $(100/90) - 1 = 11.1\%$. So you need an 11.1% gain to top up to your original $100.

Knowing this, we can see that with a leverage of 2 to 1, this investment would lose 20% in that same month. This requires a 25% gain to get back to where you started. And with a leverage of 5 to 1, you lose 50%, and you would need a 100% gain to get even. And of course, with a 10 to 1 leverage, this investment would lose 100% in that month, and you're broke!

You can assess the potential risk associated with investing in the hedge fund given the leverage range. Once again, the offering memorandum will have this information in it. You may want to ask questions about any reasons for increasing or decreasing leverage, however.

Return and Risk Characteristics

While past performance does not tell you the whole story, the past risk characteristics of a fund can tell you much more about its risk. The longer the past history (the longer the fund has been in existence), the better "feel" investors can get when analyzing the fund's risks. It is important to pay special attention to any losing months the fund may have had in periods of market upheaval (especially on the downside!).

How well did the manager preserve the fund's assets in a down market? Also, it is a good idea to compare the fund's risk objectives to its risk record. If they are wildly different, you have more serious questions to ask before going any further.

Auditors

It is important to find out who the auditors of the fund are. Auditors add an extra layer of comfort for an investor. Obviously, a well-respected auditing firm lends credibility to the fund's offering. This information should be in the fund's OM.

Location of the Fund and Its Management

Many hedge funds operate offshore. This tactic is mostly undertaken for tax purposes and to add tools and strategies to the fund's arsenal by getting around onshore regulations. It is important to be extremely cautious with these operations. From where exactly is the fund operating? How accessible is information on the fund and its principals? It is much easier to conduct potentially fraudulent activities from outside the territory of regulatory watchdogs, so be careful!

Some people also have a moral dilemma in investing with firms who don't pay the same taxes as they do. We'll leave this decision up to you.

Management and Performance Fees

Remember, there are accepted standards in hedge fund fees, so if the fund's fees look a little wonky, make sure you find out why. The fee structure will be part of the offering (found in the OM), so it's important to see if the fees correlate with the standards and are relative to the other factors in the fund. Management fees are usually between 2 and 3% of your investment per year, and performance fees are generally around 20% of the fund's positive calendar year return.

Hurdle Rate

Most hedge funds will charge performance fees only on positive (anything over 0%) calendar-year performance. This means that unless the fund is net positive, you won't have to pay any performance fees. This feature is one of the best of hedge funds, as, unlike mutual fund managers who make their money regardless of performance, hedge fund managers get paid a performance fee only if the fund is positive. This incentive makes for good performance.

However, some hedge funds will charge a fee only when a certain performance level has been reached. This is called the *hurdle* rate. What this means is that the fund puts a *minimum* on calendar-year performance, say, 10%. It is only on returns *above* this hurdle rate in these funds that investors must pay a performance fee (as opposed to anything above 0%). Thus, the higher the hurdle rate, the better the fund is for the investor.

You may see hedge funds that use market indices, such as the S&P 500, as their hurdle rate. While this may seem a little odd, as we have been spending so much time talking about the lack of correlation between hedge funds and market indices, it actually makes sense when you realize that it is another way to see how the fund is performing relative to the markets.

Again, any hurdle rate will be outlined in the fund's OM. Be sure to ascertain if it seems reasonable by looking at historic returns for the fund.

High-Water Mark

The "high-water mark" is another unique twist in hedge fund investing. Simply put, the high-water mark is the number that represents the highest net asset value (adjusted to dividends and net investments) the fund has attained in its history. Most hedge funds put this measure in place to ensure that investors don't have to pay performance fees more than once on the same return. This is how it works:

Let's say John bought 150 units of Hedge Fund A, at $1,000 per unit, in 1999. He has not added any units or redeemed any to date.

In Figure 5.5, scenario one shows Hedge Fund A with a performance fee in place of 20%. In 2001, the fund made a return of 20%, meaning that John's units were worth $1,200 each—a $200 profit. But in 2002 it was negative 10%, decreasing the unit value to $1,080. It then made a return of plus 11% in 2003, bringing the unit price back up to its previous high of $1,200. Remember: performance fees apply only if the fund makes a profit. So John would have paid a performance fee in 2001 of 20% of his $200 gain. But in 2002 the fund was negative, so John didn't have to pay any performance fees at all.

The insurance provided by the high-water mark is that John didn't have to pay any performance fees in 2003 either. This is because he had only regained his losses from 2002, and the fund had *not exceeded its high-water mark*. The fund would consider $1,200 per unit as the high-water mark, or the highest level of net asset value the fund attained. You can do the math: if John lost 10% in 2002 and gained 11% in 2003, he's only back where he started in 2002, with units that were worth $1,200 (you will remember that in order to regain a 10% loss, you need an 11.111% gain). So the high-water mark is the level the fund must attain in order for performance fees to kick in. If the fund had made a 15% return in 2003, as in scenario two, the fund would have exceeded its previous high-water mark and established a new one. John would have therefore paid a 20% fee on the amount over and above the previous high-water mark, or 20% of his $42 per unit gain.

The high-water mark, and the stipulations surrounding it in a particular fund, are required to be in the OM.

FIGURE 5.5

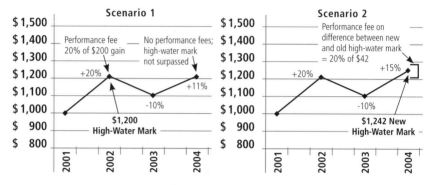

Liquidity

We have discussed liquidity thus far in great detail, with good reason. The liquidity of a hedge fund is a measure of how much notice the investor must give to the hedge fund manager before he or she can sell (redeem) units in the fund. Obviously, the longer this period is, the more careful you must be.

Most hedge funds in Canada are redeemable on a weekly basis, but it is best to make sure. And make sure you find out if the fund has a "lock-up" period. Some hedge funds will put in place a date, upon investment, before which you cannot redeem your units (even for a fee). This lock-up period can vary widely, and you need to examine the time frame to see if it seems too long.

As well, pay close attention to any "early redemption charge." Many hedge funds charge a 5% fee if redemption occurs within six months after the purchase of the fund. Again, this information will be in the OM.

PASSING THE DUE DILIGENCE BUCK: FUND OF FUNDS HEDGE FUNDS

There are some real advantages to fund of funds hedge funds, as they can take a lot of work out of the investor's hands.

As we saw in the last chapter, fund of funds managers, by definition, must perform on-going due diligence of hedge funds in their portfolio. This undertaking provides real benefits to the individual investor by conducting the due diligence on the investor's behalf. As well, these managers can diversify across a larger number of hedge funds than the average investor. And because of the high minimum investment levels in some high-performance funds, fund of funds managers can pool resources from a number of smaller investors to take advantage of better opportunities.

Using the same table as in our discussion about standard deviation, we can see the fictitious results of five years of performance with four single-strategy hedge funds and a fund of funds (Table 5.2). The fund of funds had the same rate of return but achieved this with a lot lower volatility or risk because of its unique ability to exploit a number of hedge fund styles to widely diversify its portfolio.

TABLE 5.2

	Fund 1	Fund 2	Fund 3	Fund 4	Fund 5
2000	35%	22%	7%	(8%)	14%
2001	27%	(2%)	29%	19%	18%
2002	(10%)	39%	35%	45%	27%
2003	19%	25%	35%	35%	28%
2004	36%	20%	(1%)	16%	18%
5-year Compunded Return	20%	20%	20%	20%	**20%**

Investors in a fund of funds are advised, however, to still perform the due diligence process outlined in this chapter so far, although not on the underlying hedge funds, but on the fund of hedge funds instead. In addition to these guidelines, though, the following points need to be considered in the case of a fund of funds investment.

How Many Hedge Funds Are in the Portfolio?

A number of research papers on hedge funds show that the optimal number of hedge funds for diversification is somewhere between 10 and 14. Fund of funds hedge funds having fewer funds in their portfolio than this are not true "fund of funds" hedge funds and therefore can be much more volatile because of their inability to effectively diversify.

Hands Off or On Approach?

Are the funds included in the fund of funds constant (or can they be changed only in remotely possible cases)? Does the fund swing within a wide basket of hedge funds? It is wise to seek a fund of funds with constant on-going management and that conducts its due diligence process on an ongoing basis. This means that the manager is constantly monitoring the performances of all the hedge funds in the portfolio and is quick to sense trouble, knowing when to get out or to cut losses in a particular fund.

Diversification Across Hedge Fund Styles

One of the biggest benefits of investing in a fund of funds hedge fund is the ease of diversification among other hedge funds. As stated earlier, hedge fund strategies allow for much wider and uncorrelated performances, so pay close attention to proper diversification. Funds included in the fund of funds must be as diverse as possible in order to achieve significant risk reduction in the fund of funds portfolio.

The OM will include a list of all funds (or at least name their styles) in the fund of funds portfolio and will usually tell you the percentage of assets that are allocated to each one.

What Are the Total Fees?

The ease of diversification, the risk reduction it creates, and entrusting a specialist to conduct a due diligence process all come with a price tag. Funds of funds charge performance fees (usually 10%) and management fees (usually 1.5 to 2.5%) on top of the individual hedge funds' performance and management fees. It is important to evaluate the combined management and performance fees charged by the individual and fund of funds managers. Ask your adviser to give you a detailed calculation of the combined management and performance fees.

So in evaluating a fund of funds, you have to factor in the amount of fees with the return rates, and ask yourself just what you are willing to pay for it. How much more are the returns for the fund of funds than that for a single hedge fund, and even more importantly with how much less risk? Once again, knowing your own risk tolerances is key to making these decisions.

OTHER RESOURCES

Don't be dismayed. What we've outlined may seem like a lot of work, but most of it is a combination of a little understanding and common sense. There is a surprising amount of information available, if you just start looking around. The Internet is invaluable, and a number of sites are dedicated to hedge fund education and analysis. While most information you will come across will be for hedge fund investors in the United States, there are a few good Canadian sites to surf through. We have included a list of resources at the back of this book and urge you to do a little digging of your own.

Remember, this should be fun! You are embarking on a financial journey that has potentially great rewards, so think of it as an adventure. With proper due diligence, you won't be disappointed!

CHAPTER SIX

Buying, Managing, and Selling Your Hedge Fund

Even after your short list has been completed and you are comfortable with the hedge funds you have selected, you may still run into a few obstacles. Maybe one hedge fund manager didn't return your calls, for instance, and you found yourself feeling uncomfortable, so you dropped that fund from the list, as one of the criteria for your "perfect" fund is decent customer service. Another fund turned out to have hit its asset ceiling while you were researching, so you had to shelve that one, too. Finally, though, you have come to an informed, confident decision.

Once you have picked the fund (or funds) you want to invest in, there are still a few more important things to look at and consider. Owning a hedge fund is not like owning a piece of art; rather, it is an on-going process. This chapter will give you some tools for understanding this process by guiding you through the buying, managing, and selling of your hedge fund.

BUYING A HEDGE FUND

Due diligence complete, fund (or funds) chosen, and chequebook in hand, it's time to take the plunge. What's next? There are still a few aspects to consider.

How Is the Fund Priced?

It is important to know how the fund is priced, as it gives you a good idea of the relative value of the fund's units and some insight into performance. Unit pricing in hedge funds is based on *net asset value* or NAV. If you have already invested in mutual funds, you are probably familiar with this term.

Net asset value is pretty much exactly what it says it is: *the total value of the fund.* This number is calculated by adding up all the fund's assets, then subtracting all liabilities, such as any leverage the fund utilizes, and subtracting accrued expenses.

Based on what you already know about hedge funds, you won't be surprised to learn that it can be a difficult job to arrive at this final figure. Assets in hedge funds can vary from ones with a solid, identifiable value (such as cash) to ones that have value in theory only (like shares in a private company, for instance). So how do funds establish a value for their assets? Funds that trade highly liquid instruments (stock, futures, bonds) will simply use the closing price for the day as the basis to calculate the total assets. However, with less liquid instruments, such as thinly traded stocks or shares in private companies, the situation is much trickier. The manager will have to use *estimates* based on realistic criteria.

It is good to know at this point whether the fund is *internally* or *externally* priced, that is, is the NAV calculated by an outside source or does the fund handle it? An investor might be concerned about the potential for fraud in an *internally* priced fund, particularly a fund that deals in highly illiquid assets (ones with *theoretical* value), because the NAV requires *estimation* on the part of the manager In this case, *external* pricing is much more credible because the pricing will be done by an outside, unbiased agency. You will most likely find this information in the OM.

Once the total value of the fund's assets are calculated, liabilities, such as leverage, loans, etc., are deducted. The next step is to deduct all accrued expenses, such as management fees, performance fees, audit fees, etc. What is left is the *net asset value*. This number is then *divided by the number of units the fund has outstanding* (the number that have been sold to date). The resulting number is the *NAV per unit*, which translates into the price you are being quoted for purchasing units.

So, when you're investing in a fund, the fund will give you the price for a unit, based on the calculation described above. If you decide to invest $10,000 and the unit price is $11.56, you will receive 865.052 units ($10,000 / $11.56). Why is this important to know?

Most (but not all) funds start selling their units at $10, $100, or $1,000 per unit. As the fund makes or loses money, the unit price goes up or down. This means you can see some hard evidence of performance. If, for instance, you are quoted the price of a fund's units at $11.56, you can be fairly sure that the units started out priced at $10, and that the fund has therefore made $1.56 profit for each unit since its inception. This, of course, is dependent on the history of the fund—if the fund in question started out 40 years ago at $1, then the returns are *much* better!

How Much Should You Invest?

How much you should invest really depends on the individual, but there are some good rules of thumb to consider. Let's say you have $1,000 to invest. If you find a hedge fund you like, there is really no good reason not to invest the whole $1,000. Why? Because you can't realistically diversify as little as $1,000. This relatively small amount of money will not perform well at all if it is spread out over 10 funds in $100 lots. However, if you have $5 million, you would most certainly be a fool to put the whole thing into a single fund, no matter how confident you were. Five million dollars is a lot of money to risk in one place even for extremely wealthy people, so you should seek to diversify that capital and spread out the risk of losing it.

Be sure to consider the amount of money you have to invest in hedge funds, and think carefully about how much risk you are willing to undertake. You should probably have a good idea of your goals by now, but you may want to have a quick self-examination! Most experts agree that hedge fund allocation should be at least 10% to a maximum of 35% in an overall portfolio.

Where Are You in Life?

This isn't a personal question! It's a way of assessing (again—we can't stress this enough) your risk level and what you have in mind for the future. What are your long- and short-term goals? Are you looking to strike it rich quick? Or are you hoping for long-term, better-than-a-bank-account performance that you can count on and still preserve your capital?

Once again, this is determined solely by the individual. If you are 25 years old, for instance, and have been working at a high-paying job, you have probably accumulated a reasonable amount of money. If you're not married and are healthy, you will more than likely have a fairly high risk tolerance. At only 25, there are many money-making years ahead, and you can afford to take a loss or two, betting on a big gain somewhere.

If, on the other hand, you are 75 and living on a fixed income, preserving that nest egg will probably be your main goal. In this case a guaranteed return will be what you are looking for. As you can imagine, though, there are virtually endless variations to the situations people find themselves in, and only you can assess your own.

If you are not sure about how to assess your situation, financial planners can be a great help. Their job is to look at such things as past investment history, your lifestyle, and your comfort level to give you a good basis from which to consider the appropriate strategies.

If you already have a number of investments, you may want to ask how much of your assets you should allocate to hedge funds in conjunction with other vehicles. The fact is, most decisions in hedge fund investment rely heavily on simple common sense and knowing your tolerances. The size of your portfolio, your income level, and the types of investments and assets contained in your portfolio besides hedge funds should, along with your adviser or broker, help you to make an informed decision.

Most experts agree that hedge fund allocation should be at least 10% to a maximum of 35% in an overall portfolio.

The Purchasing Process

The first part of the purchasing task is simple. Call the fund (or your adviser or broker) and ask for a copy of the *subscription agreement (unless the hedge fund is offered as a guaranteed note or principal-protected note)*. Most funds will include a subscription agreement with the OM in their promotional package, but if not, you will require one.

The Subscription Agreement

With the exception of those structured as guaranteed or principal-protected notes, investors in hedge funds must fill out a subscription agreement.

The subscription agreement is your application to be allowed to buy units in your chosen fund. It will require that you supply basic personal information. Some funds will require that you sign a certificate stating that you qualify as a "sophisticated investor." Or if you wish to invest much less than the usual provincial "non-accredited investor minimum" you may, in certain provinces, be required to sign a "risk acknowledgement form." These rules have been put into place to protect people from investing in instruments that are deemed too risky for their financial means (a kind of fiduciary responsibility).

All Canadian provinces have different sophisticated investor rules, which are managed by their respective securities commissions. Your adviser or broker will be able to tell you what the rules are where you live, or you can check with your home province's Securities Commission.

Once you have filled out the subscription agreement and been accepted, all that's left is to pay your money. You are now the proud owner of a well-researched, properly placed high-performance investment!

MANAGING YOUR HEDGE FUND

So now you own units in a hedge fund. What next? As we have said, due diligence and purchasing are far from the only things to consider in hedge fund investment, as investing in these funds is a *process*, requiring on-going management and analysis. How does this work? To start with, you need to monitor the fund's performance.

Hedge funds calculate their net asset value either daily, weekly, or monthly, depending on the fund, its manager, and its strategy. Some hedge funds print returns in the business section of the newspaper, but not all do.

You, as an investor, should receive at least a quarterly or semi-annually statement of the value of your "piece of the pie." This information should also be available to you on demand, either by calling the fund or accessing the fund's Web site, if it has one, via a password. Some funds even post daily returns on their Web sites. Tracking the fund in this way can be fun for investors, as they can watch the progress of the fund on a daily basis!

Better managers will issue monthly or quarterly newsletters that explain their on-going strategy and views on the economy and the markets. Your job as an investor is to decide whether you agree and assess why. Just because you disagree with the manager doesn't mean that he or she is wrong. After all, he or she has much more experience than you do—that's why you invested with that fund in the first place!

Think of yourself as a voting member on the fund's board of directors —if the manager believes that buggy whips are poised to be the next hot thing, what kind of questions are you going to ask and how are you going to vote if he or she decides to put all the fund's assets into Acme Buggy Whips Inc.? You can "vote" against this move by pulling out of this hedge fund.

Remember, you need to be comfortable with your investment. It's your money, and regardless of how smart or experienced you believe the manager to be, do not, under any circumstances, let yourself be convinced of a strategy or idea that you are not comfortable with.

And also remember, all of this on-going management is not to monitor the fund's success (although that can be a source of great enjoyment if it is doing well), but to safeguard you against possible losses. Selling a hedge fund, like stepping away from a perceived "winning streak," can be a very difficult thing to do. So if a manager starts losing after four years of consistent profits, you need to have in place your own criteria for getting out.

SELLING YOUR HEDGE FUND

As stated above, selling a hedge fund can be a big decision and needs to be a quick, decisive, and well-thought-out move. We hinted above at the potential for losses, but there may be other reasons for selling.

Need Some Money Immediately?

One of the bonuses of owning investments is the flexibility it potentially gives you in case you need immediate cash. Reasons for needing cash vary widely, from buying a home, starting a business, attending to a family emergency, or even to whimsical purchases such as engagement rings, cars, and much-needed vacations (you will recall our numerous discussions throughout the book about liquidity). If you are likely to need cash for any of these reasons, you will have factored this expectation in to the liquidity of your hedge fund units and purchased a fund that has no "lock-up" period and little or no penalty or time restrictions on redemption of units. Selling these funds is a relatively simple transaction. Call the fund (or your adviser or broker) and declare that you wish to sell all or a certain number of your units, depending on the amount of cash you require. Remember, you are not required to tell anyone why you are selling, so don't let them make you feel guilty!

Found a Better Investment Vehicle?

Perhaps you have been smart and have continued to look around for investments that are even better than the ones you currently own. Then again, maybe your lifestyle or financial situation has changed, and with it, your risk tolerances and long-term goals. Either way, these can be compelling reasons to sell your units in a hedge fund.

But beware: hedge fund units are not something you can just convert into a different investment without potential tax liabilities from your profits. It is a very good idea to not only perform due diligence on the new investment, but to factor in the value of that investment against potential gains in the existing fund and potential tax liabilities.

Is the Fund Performing Badly?

Here is where the hard decisions come in, and they need to be assessed very carefully, as they go right to the heart of some of your fundamental beliefs and behaviours that may or may not need some modifications.

If a fund is not living up to your expectations, what mechanisms should you have in place to handle the situation? How stringently should you abide by your expectations, no matter what your gut feeling is? A number of issues can come into play here, and they need to be addressed.

Greed

We have spoken extensively about greed. In Chapter 3, we talked about the reasons that so many people lost huge amounts of money during the crash of tech stocks through 2000. We have also talked about the need for prudent hedge fund managers to be proactive in getting out while the "getting's good" and cutting losses when necessary. Selling your hedge fund because it is performing badly is a very similar situation, but the responsibility for the decision whether to sell lies solely on your shoulders.

Staying in too long and losing is almost human nature, and it takes almost a Herculean effort to resist the temptation to hang on, yet resisting it is the key to prudent investment and financial success.

Don't let us make you think that greed is necessarily bad, as it is greed that has made you decide to invest so you can improve your material and social well-being. Rather, greed has the *ability* to take over and cloud your judgment.

Hope

Another uniquely human trait, hope, can be as disastrous as greed, and they often go hand in hand. When things go wrong, the tendency is to hope they will get better. While this is a nice sentiment, hoping will do nothing to change the situation either way. It takes courage and discipline to jump from a sinking ship early, but it's something that every investor must learn to do.

Setting Your Own Risk Control

It is vital, in your on-going diligence, that you create and strictly adhere to rules about the level of loss below which you will not hold on to your units. This is your own version of a risk-control mechanism. Let's illustrate with Figure 6.1, showing performances of a hedge fund over a period of time.

FIGURE 6.1

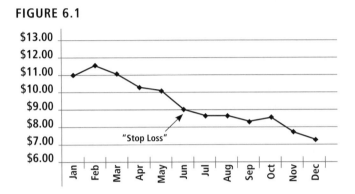

The figure assumes you bought units in this fund on January 1 with a net asset value of $11. Obviously this was not a wise choice, as the fund went up by 50 cents and then started a solid downward slide.

What should your risk-control mechanism be here? You should put in place loss restrictions and abide by them no matter what.

Stop Loss

What you should have done was to have a *stop loss* in place. A stop loss is just what it sounds like: when to *stop* your *losses*. In this case, you bought in at $11. Let's say you decide, based on your risk tolerance, that the most you can afford to lose on this investment is $2 per unit. This means that when the price hits $9, you *sell no matter what*. This is where the discipline comes in—selling at a loss is one of the hardest things to do in life. As we can see in the above example, however, if you sold at $9, you would have avoided much more *extensive* losses.

The Rolling Stop

Look at Figure 6.2 below, and think about why you invested in the first place: to make money and improve your financial stability, right? So when you look at your investment three months after you bought it, it has gained $3. Excellent!

FIGURE 6.2

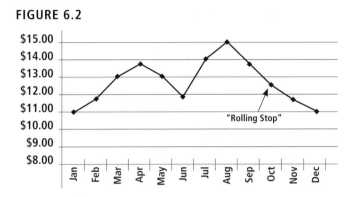

In May, however, it comes down to $13. Still $2 more than you paid for it. But the next month, it's down to just below $12. Should you sell? You have lost another $1 in a month, but you're still up $1. Thankfully, while you are contemplating this, it goes back up to $14. Relax.

Suddenly the unit value jumps to over $14, and you're "on a roll" again (we're sure you can see where this is going by now). By August, your $11 investment is now worth $15, and life is grand.

Over the next few months, sadly, the price begins to drop steadily. When do you sell? Probably, you would sell when the price hits $11 (you wouldn't have sold it at $12, because the last time it was there it went right back up); you'd end up actually *losing* money because you were hoping it would eventually come back.

Sometimes a fund will go up and down in small fits and starts, like the one depicted in Figure 6.2. This can be a hair-raising ride (and hopefully the fund you have chosen moves more evenly than this!), but you can smooth it out by putting in place a *rolling stop*. This is a mechanism stating that there is a certain amount *below the most recent high* at which point you will sell. It is vital that your adviser or broker know where your "rolling stop" is.

In the above case, let's say you set a rolling stop at $2.50 (rolling stop levels are usually higher than stop losses, because at that point you are still in a *winning* situation). This means that at any point if the fund is $2.50 below its most recent high, you will sell your units—again, *no matter what*. So here, you would have sold it in October, when it dipped to $12.50 from its previous August high of $15.00, eight months into the investment. You would have made a little money and could sit back and begin looking for a new venture.

Discipline, Discipline, Discipline

We've given you an example where your rolling stop was absolutely the right decision: you sold while you still had a profit and before you started losing. The thing
to remember is that *no matter what*, you must stick to your rules. Even if the above
fund had continued to rise through the *roof* after your rolling stop happened and
you sold, you made the best decision and lived to invest another day.

And believe us, this will happen. You will set your risk management, stick
rigidly to it, and get out when your own rules tell you to, only to sadly watch the
fund start to gain, and gain, and gain. These are the stories you hear about—*not*
the ones where it continued to lose. The "one that got away" is a major fear of
investors. How many times have you heard someone whining about how they
could have bought Microsoft in 1985 or IBM in 1960?

But know this: if you choose to ignore your risk control, over the long run,
you will lose. If, however, you stick to your guns, the payoff will be great.

Hedge Funds in Canada Today

INTRODUCTION TO THE SELECTION AND RATING OF 100 CANADIAN HEDGE FUNDS

As of the end of 2004, there are about 350 hedge funds available in Canada. Many of these funds are "duplicates," though. In most cases, the reason for this is that the fund company offers investors a U.S.-dollar-based version, different series dependent on the sales charge option, or a 100% RSP-eligible version of the same hedge fund. New funds are also created simply to offer the same fund with a different fee structure. One of the oldest hedge funds in Canada, the BPI Global Opportunities (its name has been recently changed to CI Global Opportunities) offered by CI Mutual Funds, actually operates under six slightly different names. Since all of these "twins" (and there are many of them) are essentially the same, we will feature only one of them in our list—usually the one with the longest track record.

We do not show all the funds available in Canada; rather, our selection process was designed to give investors a good cross-section of what is available, based on the size of the fund, its length of operation, and return and risk records. In our information pages we deliberately omitted the minimum-investment information, as it became very complicated depending on the fund's structure and/or place of residence requirements and/or income/net worth thresholds.

THE NAGY–BECK HEDGEHOG
RATING SYSTEM (NBHRS)

In the interest of simplifying the following 100 hedge fund analyses, we have devised our own rating system, called the "Nagy–Beck Hedgehog Rating System." And in the interest of keeping the whole exercise lighthearted, we've decided that one hedgehog will represent our worst rating, and five hedgehogs will be the best (we're financial analysts, not movie critics).

Our rating system starts with an evaluation of each fund based on the following criteria:

Risk	between 0 and 1.5
Return	between 0 and 1.5
Efficiency	between 0 and 1.5
Correlation	between 0 and 1.5

We have rated funds based on three years of statistics for each fund (funds that have not been around that long are not rated). The reason for this is twofold: not many hedge funds have longer than a three-year history and older historical data will, in our opinion, worsen rather than improve the accuracy of the rating.

Risk was measured with annualized standard deviation and largest drawdown; return with annualized return; efficiency with the Sharpe ratio; and correlation with the correlation coefficient to the S&P 500/TSX. The reason for this last measure is simple; the majority of Canadian investments are highly correlated to the TSX, because it is the largest national stock exchange. Our rating is purely quantitative and takes no qualitative properties into consideration.

The end result of the above exercise is a number between 0 and 6. The ratings are given according to the following formula:

0–1.49	1 hedgehog	
1.5–2.49	2 hedgehogs	
2.5–3.49	3 hedgehogs	
3.5–4.49	4 hedgehogs	
4.5 - 6	5 hedgehogs	

So there you have it. Hopefully we have given you a good insight into the rapidly growing world of hedge funds in Canada, and have demonstrated the value of including them in your portfolio. Hedge funds are not the playground of the super rich any more, and with their continued growth, we can only hope that these nimble, absolute-return-oriented investments will become more and more available to all investors so that everyone can benefit from these unique, fascinating, and potentially profitable vehicles.

Happy Hedgehogging!

@RGENTUM CANADIAN L/S EQUITY PORTFOLIO

FUND SPONSOR COMPANY

@rgentum Management & Research Corp.
Tel: 416-640-0282   Toll-Free: 800-465-1812
Fax: 416-351-8225   Web site: www.rgentum.com

PORTFOLIO MANAGER(S)

@rgentum Management & Research Corporation, a wholly owned subsidiary of Merchant Capital Securities Corporation (MCSC), employs time-proven techniques of fundamental money management and supplements them with the most advanced technological and quantitative resources available. To achieve superior investment performance, a portfolio must contain characteristics that better the overall market.
Management Team — ChabotPage Investment Counsel

FUND DESCRIPTION

Seeks to provide consistent long-term growth through capital appreciation while maintaining minimal portfolio exposure to general equity market risk by holding securities in both long and short position.

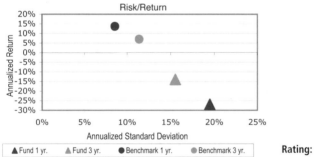

Rating:

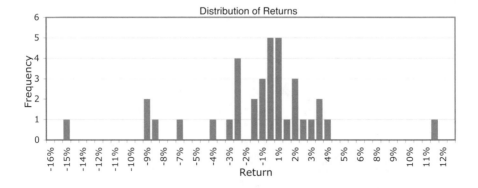

	1 yr.	3 yr.
Annualized rate of return	-26.95%	-13.97%
Annualized standard deviation	19.48%	15.55%
Percentage of negative months	66.67%	58.33%
Largest monthly drop	-14.95%	-14.95%
Maximum drawdown	-31.87%	-44.39%
Sharpe ratio	-1.59	-1.16
Semideviation	17.28%	14.16%
Sortino ratio	-1.79	-1.27
Jensen's alpha	-36.00%	-17.81%
Beta	0.52	-0.05
Up capture ratio	-77.98%	-42.72%
Down capture ratio	138.92%	12.25%
Omega -0%	24%	44%
Appraisal ratio	-1.07	-1.20
Average α over benchmark	-3.53%	-1.76%
Tracking error	5.55%	5.67%
Information ratio	-63.62%	-31.09%
Sterling ratio	-0.97	-0.40
Treynor measure	-0.59	3.28
M^2 – Modigliani measure	-23.30%	-16.17%
Burke ratio	-1.56	-0.75
Skewness	-120.67%	-60.67%
Kurtosis	84%	298%
Correlation to S&P/TSX	0.251	-0.041
R squared	0.063	0.002
Benchmark: S&P/TSX		

TERMS AND CONDITIONS

Inception:	March 1, 2000
Style:	Security Selection
Sub-style:	Variable Bias
Valuation:	Daily
RRSP:	Yes
Management fee:	2.00%
Performance fee:	20.00%
High-water mark:	Yes
Hurdle rate:	0.00%
NAV:	$3.42
Asset Size (million):	$0.05
Maximum leverage:	100%
Early red'n period:	2 mo.
Early red'n fee:	N/A

PERFORMANCE (as of December 31, 2004)

	1 mo.	3 mo.	6 mo.
Funds	-14.95%	-21.88%	-23.56%
S&P/TSX	2.40%	6.67%	8.41%
Van Global HF Index	1.50%	4.87%	5.48%

	1 yr.	2 yr.	3 yr.
Funds	-26.95%	-19.11%	-13.97%
S&P/TSX	13.66%	19.32%	6.99%
Van Global HF Index	7.79%	13.04%	8.40%

Year	Jan	Feb	Mar	Apr	May	Jun	Jul	Aug	Sep	Oct	Nov	Dec	Total
2004	3.22%	3.88%	-0.49%	-8.93%	-1.23%	-0.44%	-2.73%	1.20%	-0.59%	0.77%	-8.86%	-14.95%	-26.95%
2003	0.02%	1.24%	-1.02%	-2.51%	-3.32%	-0.94%	-0.28%	-2.43%	0.51%	2.69%	-0.45%	-4.25%	-10.41%
2002	0.09%	0.41%	1.95%	0.30%	11.40%	-1.21%	-2.88%	1.35%	-0.71%	-6.58%	-8.93%	3.46%	-2.71%

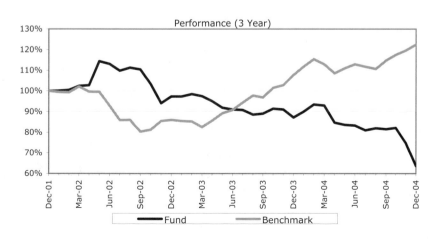
Performance (3 Year)

@RGENTUM POOLED MARKET NEUTRAL PORTFOLIO C$

FUND SPONSOR COMPANY

@rgentum Management & Research Corp.

Tel: 416-640-0282   Toll-Free: 800-465-1812

Fax: 416-351-8225   Web site: www.rgentum.com

PORTFOLIO MANAGER(S)

@rgentum Management & Research Corporation, a wholly owned subsidiary of Merchant Capital Securities Corporation (MCSC), employs time-proven techniques of fundamental money management and supplements them with the most advanced technological and quantitative resources available. To achieve superior investment performance, a portfolio must contain characteristics that better the overall market.

Management Team — ChabotPage Investment Counsel

FUND DESCRIPTION

The investment objective of the fund is to provide consistent and above-average long-term growth regardless of the general direction of the stock market by taking both long positions (anticipating an increase in the price of the stock) and short positions (anticipating a decrease in the price of the stock) in selected large and medium capitalization stocks.

Rating: 🦔🦔

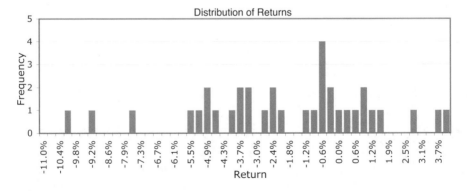

	1 yr.	3 yr.
Annualized rate of return	-20.61%	-21.28%
Annualized standard deviation	10.84%	11.86%
Percentage of negative months	75.00%	72.22%
Largest monthly drop	-5.61%	-10.35%
Maximum drawdown	-23.21%	-52.36%
Sharpe ratio	-2.27	-2.13
Semideviation	4.14%	8.12%
Sortino ratio	-5.95	-3.11
Jensen's alpha	-27.14%	-25.22%
Beta	0.89	0.01
Up capture ratio	21.49%	-28.64%
Down capture ratio	246.17%	81.57%
Omega -0%	25%	22%
Appraisal ratio	-0.93	-2.09
Average α over benchmark	-2.45%	-1.81%
Tracking error	1.68%	5.28%
Information ratio	-145.52%	-34.30%
Sterling ratio	-1.06	-0.48
Treynor measure	-0.28	-27.40
M^2 – Modigliani measure	-24.32%	-23.83%
Burke ratio	-2.19	-1.15
Skewness	64.35%	-45.32%
Kurtosis	-63%	18%
Correlation to S&P/TSX	-0.022	-0.173
R squared	0.712	0.000
Benchmark: MSCI World C$		

TERMS AND CONDITIONS

Inception:	April 15, 1998
Style:	Security Selection
Sub-style:	No Bias
Valuation:	Daily
RRSP:	Yes
Management fee:	2.50%
Performance fee:	20.00%
High-water mark:	Yes
Hurdle rate:	2.00%
NAV:	$3.99
Asset Size (million):	$0.16
Maximum leverage:	100%
Early red'n period:	2 mo.
Early red'n fee:	N/A

PERFORMANCE (as of December 31, 2004)

	1 mo.	3 mo.	6 mo.
Funds	0.86%	-4.86%	-17.82%
S&P/TSX	5.25%	6.76%	0.07%
Van Global HF Index	1.50%	4.87%	5.48%

	1 yr.	2 yr.	3 yr.
Funds	-20.61%	-24.17%	-21.28%
S&P/TSX	6.85%	8.58%	-2.18%
Van Global HF Index	7.79%	13.04%	8.40%

Year	Jan	Feb	Mar	Apr	May	Jun	Jul	Aug	Sep	Oct	Nov	Dec	Total
2004	2.50%	-0.39%	-5.14%	4.05%	-0.78%	-3.38%	-4.98%	-3.70%	-5.61%	-3.48%	-2.27%	0.86%	-20.61%
2003	-7.79%	-0.90%	-3.67%	-5.29%	-10.35%	-0.61%	3.81%	0.25%	-4.70%	0.85%	-0.09%	-2.44%	-27.58%
2002	1.54%	-2.69%	-0.48%	0.45%	-4.02%	-1.43%	1.01%	-0.68%	3.64%	-9.32%	-2.94%	-0.78%	-15.15%

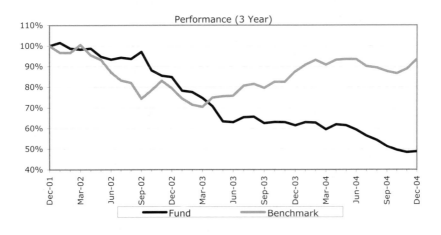

Performance (3 Year)

@RGENTUM U.S. MARKET NEUTRAL PORTFOLIO C$

FUND SPONSOR COMPANY

@rgentum Management & Research Corp.

Tel: 416-640-0282   Toll-Free: 800-465-1812
Fax: 416-351-8225   Web site: www.rgentum.com

PORTFOLIO MANAGER(S)

@rgentum Management & Research Corporation, a wholly owned subsidiary of Merchant Capital Securities
Corporation (MCSC), employs time-proven techniques of fundamental money management and supplements them
with the most advanced technological and quantitative resources available. To achieve superior investment
performance, a portfolio must contain characteristics that better the overall market.
Management Team — ChabotPage Investment Counsel

FUND DESCRIPTION

Seeks to provide consistent long-term growth through capital appreciation while maintaining minimal portfolio exposure
to general equity market risk by holding securities in both long and short position.

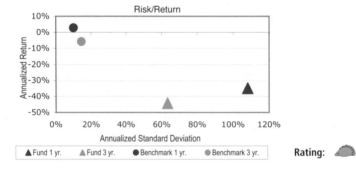

Rating: 🦔

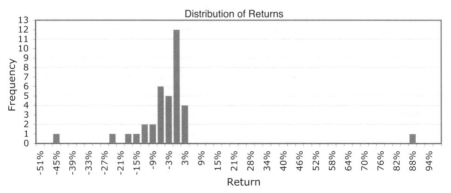

	1 yr.	3 yr.
Annualized rate of return	-34.96%	-44.19%
Annualized standard deviation	108.09%	63.32%
Percentage of negative months	83.33%	77.78%
Largest monthly drop	-46.72%	-46.72%
Maximum drawdown	-65.24%	-90.73%
Sharpe ratio	-0.36	-0.76
Semideviation	52.81%	36.82%
Sortino ratio	-0.74	-1.31
Jensen's alpha	-40.54%	-54.74%
Beta	-1.34	-0.67
Up capture ratio	-309.58%	-114.59%
Down capture ratio	-313.14%	32.92%
Omega -0%	103%	44%
Appraisal ratio	-0.66	-1.62
Average α over benchmark	-0.03%	-2.97%
Tracking error	31.72%	19.38%
Information ratio	-0.10%	-15.30%
Sterling ratio	-0.60	-0.53
Treynor measure	0.29	0.72
M² – Modigliani measure	-2.42%	-1.24%
Burke ratio	-0.71	-0.73
Skewness	197.79%	327.21%
Kurtosis	668%	1901%
Correlation to S&P/TSX	-0.264	-0.234
R squared	0.018	0.025
Benchmark: S&P 500		

TERMS AND CONDITIONS

Inception:	March 1, 2000
Style:	Security Selection
Sub-style:	No Bias
Valuation:	Daily
RRSP:	No
Management fee:	2.00%
Performance fee:	20.00%
High-water mark:	Yes
Hurdle rate:	2.00%
NAV:	$1.03
Asset Size (million):	$0.00
Maximum leverage:	100%
Early red'n period:	2 mo.
Early red'n fee:	—

PERFORMANCE (as of December 31, 2004)

	1 mo.	3 mo.	6 mo.
Funds	0.05%	-0.22%	86.99%
S&P/TSX	4.80%	4.07%	-3.39%
Van Global HF Index	1.50%	4.87%	5.48%

	1 yr.	2 yr.	3 yr.
Funds	-34.96%	-51.98%	-44.19%
S&P/TSX	2.81%	4.32%	-5.78%
Van Global HF Index	7.79%	13.04%	8.40%

Year	Jan	Feb	Mar	Apr	May	Jun	Jul	Aug	Sep	Oct	Nov	Dec	Total
2004	-11.02%	-46.72%	-26.03%	-0.63%	-0.04%	-0.15%	-0.07%	87.91%	-0.19%	-0.17%	-0.11%	0.05%	-34.96%
2003	-6.05%	-3.27%	-2.51%	-4.49%	-7.37%	-5.45%	-2.87%	-6.01%	-12.43%	-13.24%	-14.86%	-18.98%	-64.54%
2002	0.20%	-7.22%	-4.06%	0.28%	-5.93%	3.02%	2.11%	-0.76%	2.09%	-10.70%	-6.60%	0.75%	-24.65%

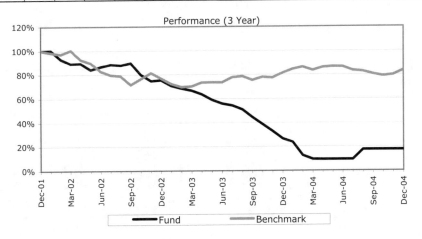

Performance (3 Year)

Fund — Benchmark

ABRIA DIVERSIFIED ARBITRAGE TRUST CLASS C

FUND SPONSOR COMPANY

Abria Financial Group

Tel: 416-367-4777   Toll-Free: 877-902-2742

Fax: 416-367-4555   Web site: www.abriafunds.com

PORTFOLIO MANAGER(S)

Mr. Henry Kneis, the Chief Executive Officer of Abria, has over 15 years of securities industry experience, specializing in equity derivative and proprietary arbitrage trading. He was the CEO of a Canadian investment dealer that was a member firm of the Toronto Stock Exchange and the Investment Dealers Association of Canada, capitalized at $100 million. He managed a proprietary trading portfolio for the firm and its affiliates, with aggregate balance sheet assets of $3 billion.

FUND DESCRIPTION

The Trust has the following objectives: to achieve capital appreciation at the U.S. treasury bill rate plus 5% to 7% (net of fees and expenses); to generate these returns at volatility levels similar to mid-term bond indices; to minimize the frequency and extent of losses under hostile market conditions; and to have a low correlation with the major equity and fixed income markets.

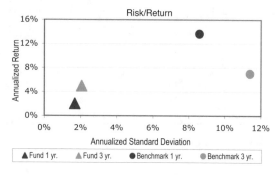

Rating:

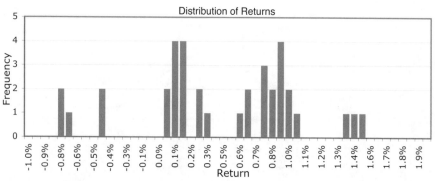

	1 yr.	3 yr.
Annualized rate of return	2.03%	4.98%
Annualized standard deviation	1.69%	2.06%
Percentage of negative months	16.67%	13.89%
Largest monthly drop	-0.74%	-0.79%
Maximum drawdown	-1.20%	-1.57%
Sharpe ratio	-1.17	0.47
Semideviation	1.13%	1.30%
Sortino ratio	-1.74	0.75
Jensen's alpha	-2.72%	0.98%
Beta	0.08	0.00
Up capture ratio	9.87%	11.02%
Down capture ratio	3.36%	-20.30%
Omega -0%	268%	554%
Appraisal ratio	-1.77	0.48
Average α over benchmark	-0.93%	-0.21%
Tracking error	2.31%	3.35%
Information ratio	-40.30%	-6.30%
Sterling ratio	-1.65	0.62
Treynor measure	-0.26	-4.81
M^2 – Modigliani measure	-19.70%	2.41%
Burke ratio	-2.27	0.66
Skewness	-9.36%	-33.74%
Kurtosis	12%	-36%
Correlation to S&P/TSX	0.426	-0.012
R squared	0.182	0.000
Benchmark: S&P/TSX		

TERMS AND CONDITIONS

Inception:	March 1, 2000
Style:	Fund of Hedge Funds
Sub-style:	N/A
Valuation:	Daily
RRSP:	Yes
Management fee:	1.95%
Performance fee:	10.00%
High-water mark:	Yes
Hurdle rate:	0.00%
NAV:	$111.27
Asset Size (million):	$162.00
Maximum leverage:	N/A
Early red'n period:	N/A
Early red'n fee:	N/A

PERFORMANCE (as of December 31, 2004)

	1 mo.	3 mo.	6 mo.
Funds	0.60%	1.89%	2.06%
S&P/TSX	2.40%	6.67%	8.41%
Van Global HF Index	1.50%	4.87%	5.48%

	1 yr.	2 yr.	3 yr.
Funds	2.03%	4.06%	4.98%
S&P/TSX	13.66%	19.32%	6.99%
Van Global HF Index	7.79%	13.04%	8.40%

Year	Jan	Feb	Mar	Apr	May	Jun	Jul	Aug	Sep	Oct	Nov	Dec	Total
2004	0.87%	0.23%	0.05%	-0.46%	-0.74%	0.02%	0.09%	0.06%	0.02%	0.33%	0.95%	0.60%	2.03%
2003	1.44%	0.74%	-0.45%	0.98%	0.89%	0.11%	-0.79%	-0.79%	1.35%	0.87%	0.94%	0.72%	6.14%
2002	0.86%	0.16%	0.72%	0.62%	0.24%	0.16%	0.56%	0.83%	0.83%	0.13%	0.07%	1.45%	6.83%

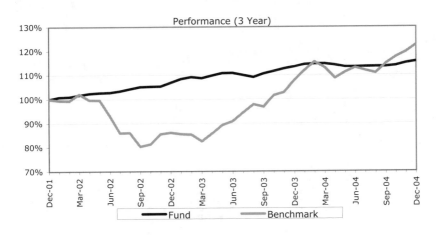

Performance (3 Year)

— Fund   — Benchmark

ACCUMULUS TALISMAN FUND

FUND SPONSOR COMPANY
Strategic Analysis Corporation
Tel: 416-594-3100   Toll-Free: 866-278-8696
Fax: 416-594-3101   Web site: www.accumulus.ca

PORTFOLIO MANAGER(S)

Mr. C. Ross Healy is the co-founder of one of Canada's leading money managers and was Director of Investment Research of the Canadian arm of a large, U.S.-based brokerage and investment firm. He is past president of the Toronto Society of Financial Analysts and served on the board of the Financial Analysts Federation (now the CFA Institute).

FUND DESCRIPTION

The objective of this Fund is to generate income and capital appreciation by investing primarily in North American securities believed to be undervalued due to prevailing conditions or specific company or sector circumstances. It will invest primarily in equity instruments, including common and preferred shares, equity derivatives, and fixed-income securities that have equity-like characteristics. This Fund may also engage in limited short selling.

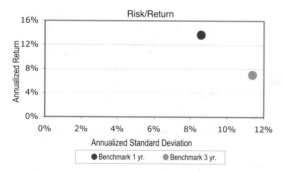

Rating: Not Rated

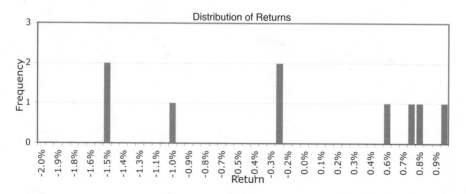

	1 yr.	3 yr.
Annualized rate of return		
Annualized standard deviation		
Percentage of negative months		
Largest monthly drop		
Maximum drawdown		
Sharpe ratio		
Semideviation		
Sortino ratio		
Jensen's alpha		
Beta		
Up capture ratio		
Down capture ratio		
Omega -0%		
Appraisal ratio		
Average α over benchmark		
Tracking error		
Information ratio		
Sterling ratio		
Treynor measure		
M^2 – Modigliani measure		
Burke ratio		
Skewness		
Kurtosis		
Correlation to S&P/TSX		
R squared		
Benchmark: S&P/TSX		

TERMS AND CONDITIONS

Inception:	February 19, 2004
Style:	N/A
Sub-style:	N/A
Valuation:	Daily
RRSP:	Yes
Management fee:	1.95%
Performance fee:	N/A
High-water mark:	N/A
Hurdle rate:	N/A
NAV:	$9.60
Asset Size (million):	$21.37
Maximum leverage:	N/A
Early red'n period:	N/A
Early red'n fee:	N/A

PERFORMANCE (as of December 31, 2004)

	1 mo.	3 mo.	6 mo.
Funds	0.74%	0.46%	0.41%
S&P/TSX	2.40%	6.67%	8.41%
Van Global HF Index	1.50%	4.87%	5.48%

	1 yr.	2 yr.	3 yr.
Funds			
S&P/TSX	13.66%	19.32%	6.99%
Van Global HF Index	7.79%	13.04%	8.40%

Year	Jan	Feb	Mar	Apr	May	Jun	Jul	Aug	Sep	Oct	Nov	Dec	Total
2004				-1.55%	-0.24%	-0.25%	0.55%	-1.56%	0.97%	-1.07%	0.80%	0.74%	-1.63%
2003													
2002													

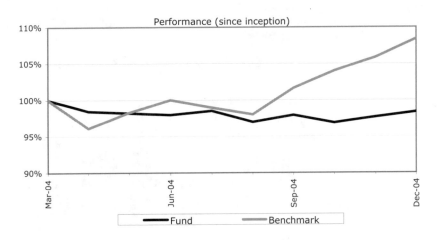

Performance (since inception)

ADALY OPPORTUNITY FUND CLASS A

FUND SPONSOR COMPANY
Strategic Advisors Corporation
Tel: 416-861-0774   Toll-Free: 866-557-0774
Fax: 416-867-9771   Web site: www.strategic-ac.com

PORTFOLIO MANAGER(S)

Martin Braun is the President of Strategic Advisors Corp., which he founded in April 1998. Prior to SAC, Martin was a partner and portfolio manager at Gluskin Sheff + Associates, a Toronto-based investment counselling firm. During his 10 years there, he was responsible for the analysis and management of Canadian and U.S. equity portfolios. Prior thereto, Martin was a Vice President of Research with Richardson Greenshields, where he was responsible for the banking and real estate sectors.

FUND DESCRIPTION

The Advisor's objective is to first protect, and then grow the Partnership's capital through the construction of a diversified portfolio of publicly traded securities that exhibit low correlation to general market direction.

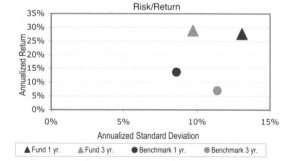

Rating:

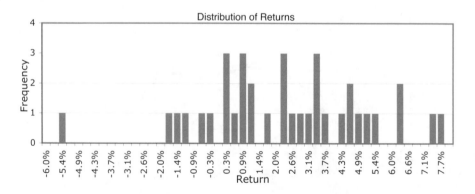

	1 yr.	3 yr.
Annualized rate of return	27.68%	28.91%
Annualized standard deviation	13.07%	9.71%
Percentage of negative months	25.00%	16.67%
Largest monthly drop	-5.66%	-5.66%
Maximum drawdown	-7.06%	-7.06%
Sharpe ratio	1.81	2.57
Semideviation	9.26%	6.11%
Sortino ratio	2.56	4.07
Jensen's alpha	12.17%	23.25%
Beta	1.19	0.55
Up capture ratio	162.52%	131.25%
Down capture ratio	94.14%	-16.19%
Omega -0%	431%	784%
Appraisal ratio	-0.61	-3.71
Average α over benchmark	1.02%	1.56%
Tracking error	2.10%	2.52%
Information ratio	48.63%	61.72%
Sterling ratio	3.35	3.53
Treynor measure	0.20	0.45
M^2 – Modigliani measure	5.90%	26.25%
Burke ratio	4.03	3.95
Skewness	-43.39%	-26.23%
Kurtosis	30%	50%
Correlation to S&P/TSX	0.854	0.667
R squared	0.729	0.445
Benchmark: S&P/TSX		

TERMS AND CONDITIONS

Inception:	December 31, 1999
Style:	Security Selection
Sub-style:	N/A
Valuation:	Quarterly
RRSP:	No
Management fee:	1.50%
Performance fee:	20.00%
High-water mark:	Yes
Hurdle rate:	4.00%
NAV:	$3,884
Asset Size (million):	N/A
Maximum leverage:	N/A
Early red'n period:	N/A
Early red'n fee:	N/A

PERFORMANCE (as of December 31, 2004)

	1 mo.	3 mo.	6 mo.
Funds	4.52%	14.76%	22.75%
S&P/TSX	2.40%	6.67%	8.41%
Van Global HF Index	1.50%	4.87%	5.48%

	1 yr.	2 yr.	3 yr.
Funds	27.68%	35.59%	28.91%
S&P/TSX	13.66%	19.32%	6.99%
Van Global HF Index	7.79%	13.04%	8.40%

Year	Jan	Feb	Mar	Apr	May	Jun	Jul	Aug	Sep	Oct	Nov	Dec	Total
2004	4.78%	3.17%	-1.49%	-5.66%	0.72%	2.80%	0.29%	-0.55%	7.25%	2.05%	7.59%	4.52%	27.68%
2003	2.99%	1.12%	0.45%	3.54%	6.23%	0.05%	4.33%	6.25%	0.65%	5.02%	3.25%	3.39%	43.98%
2002	2.20%	5.20%	0.22%	1.10%	1.48%	0.61%	-1.20%	2.30%	-1.77%	4.01%	2.25%	-0.79%	16.51%

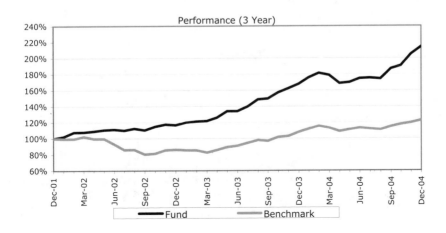

Performance (3 Year)

— Fund — Benchmark

AGF MANAGED FUTURES FUND

FUND SPONSOR COMPANY
AGF Funds Inc.
Tel: 416-367-1900   Toll-Free: 800-268-8583
Fax: 416-865-4321   Web site: www.agf.com

PORTFOLIO MANAGER(S)

AGF began managing mutual funds including the first U.S. mutual fund available to Canadian investors in 1957. AGF is an independent, Canadian-owned company, publicly traded on the Toronto Stock Exchange. As at November 2004, AGF had over $31.4 billion in assets under management. AGF is registered in Ontario as a mutual fund dealer, and as an investment counsel and portfolio manager.

FUND DESCRIPTION

To provide superior investment returns through investment in a diversified portfolio of commodity contracts, while reducing the risk of loss of capital through the implementation of prudent risk controls.

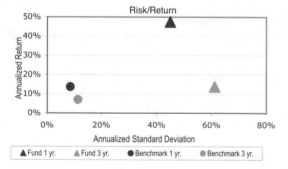

Rating:

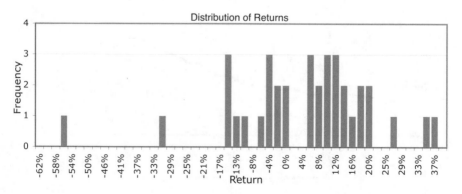

	1 yr.	3 yr.
Annualized rate of return	47.47%	13.82%
Annualized standard deviation	44.95%	61.13%
Percentage of negative months	33.33%	41.67%
Largest monthly drop	-15.82%	-56.39%
Maximum drawdown	-19.62%	-64.39%
Sharpe ratio	0.97	0.16
Semideviation	17.13%	50.31%
Sortino ratio	2.54	0.20
Jensen's alpha	24.44%	9.87%
Beta	1.97	-0.02
Up capture ratio	251.44%	65.51%
Down capture ratio	88.90%	9.02%
Omega -0%	200%	154%
Appraisal ratio	-0.50	0.16
Average α over benchmark	2.97%	2.26%
Tracking error	12.17%	17.96%
Information ratio	24.39%	12.61%
Sterling ratio	2.22	0.15
Treynor measure	0.22	-6.51
M² – Modigliani measure	-1.35%	-1.16%
Burke ratio	1.67	0.13
Skewness	-58.34%	-101.60%
Kurtosis	-118%	264%
Correlation to S&P/TSX	0.411	-0.003
R squared	0.169	0.000
Benchmark: S&P/TSX		

TERMS AND CONDITIONS

Inception:	March 28, 1995
Style:	Directional Trading
Sub-style:	N/A
Valuation:	Daily
RRSP:	Yes
Management fee:	3.00%
Performance fee:	18.00%
High-water mark:	Yes
Hurdle rate:	N/A
NAV:	$1.51
Asset Size (million):	$30.14
Maximum leverage:	N/A
Early red'n period:	3 mo.
Early red'n fee:	N/A

PERFORMANCE (as of December 31, 2004)

	1 mo.	3 mo.	6 mo.
Funds	-15.61%	-0.68%	0.69%
S&P/TSX	2.40%	6.67%	8.41%
Van Global HF Index	1.50%	4.87%	5.48%

	1 yr.	2 yr.	3 yr.
Funds	47.47%	-7.33%	13.82%
S&P/TSX	13.66%	19.32%	6.99%
Van Global HF Index	7.79%	13.04%	8.40%

Year	Jan	Feb	Mar	Apr	May	Jun	Jul	Aug	Sep	Oct	Nov	Dec	Total
2004	20.20%	12.61%	17.91%	-15.82%	15.04%	-5.23%	-12.41%	7.09%	8.09%	9.52%	7.45%	-15.61%	47.47%
2003	35.29%	-13.48%	-3.52%	16.67%	4.02%	-7.30%	10.19%	12.19%	4.12%	-32.01%	20.11%	-56.39%	-41.76%
2002	-16.16%	-4.82%	25.32%	-3.03%	8.33%	-4.81%	13.13%	5.36%	-1.70%	33.62%	10.97%	-1.16%	71.72%

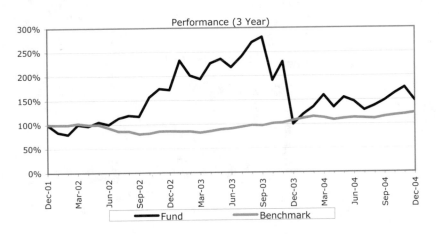

Performance (3 Year)

AIC AMERICAN FOCUSED PLUS FUND

FUND SPONSOR COMPANY
AIC Limited
Tel: 905-331-4242   Toll-Free: 800-263-2144
Fax: 905-331-7160   Web site: www.aic.com

PORTFOLIO MANAGER(S)

James Cole joined AIC in February 2000 as senior Vice President and Portfolio Manager, bringing almost 20 years of investment experience to AIC, including eight years as a portfolio manager for Canadian equity portfolios. James has been lead portfolio manager of AIC Canadian Focused Fund since its inception and was appointed as lead manager of AIC Canadian Balanced Fund in September 2002.

FUND DESCRIPTION

The investment objective of the Fund is to obtain capital preservation and appreciation by investing directly in a select number of U.S. equities, and through the use of derivatives, leverage, and short selling.

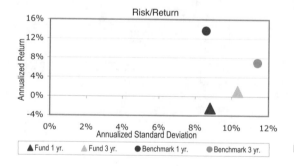

Rating: 🦔🦔

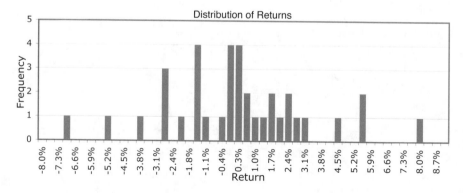

	1 yr.	3 yr.
Annualized rate of return	-2.42%	1.06%
Annualized standard deviation	8.82%	10.32%
Percentage of negative months	33.33%	47.22%
Largest monthly drop	-7.26%	-7.26%
Maximum drawdown	-8.59%	-20.30%
Sharpe ratio	-0.73	-0.28
Semideviation	10.91%	6.82%
Sortino ratio	-0.59	-0.43
Jensen's alpha	-6.41%	-0.68%
Beta	0.01	0.23
Up capture ratio	-14.71%	20.10%
Down capture ratio	-0.79%	18.52%
Omega -0%	80%	113%
Appraisal ratio	-0.72	-0.07
Average α over benchmark	-0.44%	0.54%
Tracking error	3.82%	4.25%
Information ratio	-11.59%	12.72%
Sterling ratio	-0.75	-0.14
Treynor measure	-6.15	-0.13
M² – Modigliani measure	-6.10%	5.66%
Burke ratio	-0.86	-0.25
Skewness	-211.45%	14.68%
Kurtosis	581%	103%
Correlation to S&P/TSX	0.549	0.482
R squared	0.000	0.110
Benchmark: S&P 500		

TERMS AND CONDITIONS

Inception:	September 24, 2001
Style:	Security Selection
Sub-style:	No bias
Valuation:	Daily
RRSP:	No
Management fee:	2.00%
Performance fee:	N/A
High-water mark:	N/A
Hurdle rate:	N/A
NAV:	$10.76
Asset Size (million):	$32.49
Maximum leverage:	N/A
Early red'n period:	N/A
Early red'n fee:	N/A

PERFORMANCE (as of December 31, 2004)

	1 mo.	3 mo.	6 mo.
Funds	1.97%	4.72%	4.22%
S&P/TSX	4.80%	4.07%	-3.39%
Van Global HF Index	1.50%	4.87%	5.48%

	1 yr.	2 yr.	3 yr.
Funds	-2.42%	9.10%	1.06%
S&P/TSX	2.81%	4.32%	-5.78%
Van Global HF Index	7.79%	13.04%	8.40%

Year	Jan	Feb	Mar	Apr	May	Jun	Jul	Aug	Sep	Oct	Nov	Dec	Total
2004	1.17%	0.09%	0.00%	-7.26%	-0.48%	0.19%	-1.15%	2.13%	-1.42%	0.39%	2.30%	1.97%	-2.42%
2003	-2.95%	-2.37%	-3.00%	4.29%	5.37%	7.91%	5.22%	2.77%	-1.58%	0.94%	2.52%	1.64%	21.99%
2002	-2.85%	-4.00%	-1.42%	-5.26%	-1.53%	-0.33%	-0.22%	0.22%	-0.33%	-0.11%	0.33%	1.56%	-13.28%

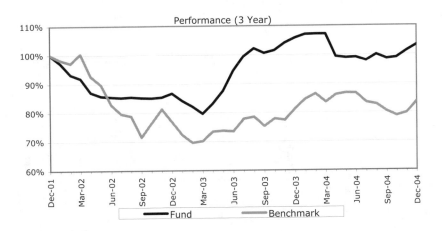

Performance (3 Year)

ARROW CLOCKTOWER GLOBAL FUND

FUND SPONSOR COMPANY
Arrow Hedge Partners Inc.
Tel: 416-323-0477   Toll-Free: 877-327-6048
Fax: 416-323-3199   Web site: www.arrowhedge.com

PORTFOLIO MANAGER(S)

David M. Benwell — Clocktower Capital, Managing Director

FUND DESCRIPTION

Platinum Asset Mgmt. applies its unique stock selection methodology to the objective of achieving above-average returns for its clients. The emphasis of the organization is on managing clients' money rather than gathering funds under management. The approach is to identify overlooked or out-of-favour situations in which there is a significant difference between inherent business value and current market price and there is a catalyst that will close the gap.

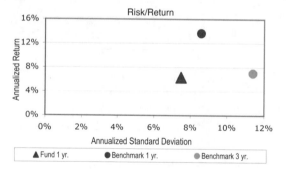

Rating: Not Rated

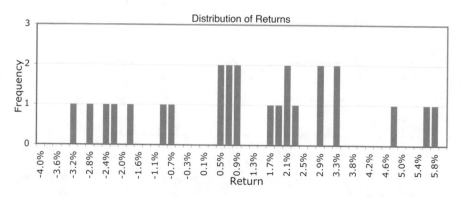

	1 yr.	3 yr.
Annualized rate of return	6.32%	
Annualized standard deviation	7.49%	
Percentage of negative months	25.00%	
Largest monthly drop	-3.20%	
Maximum drawdown	-5.94%	
Sharpe ratio	0.31	
Semideviation	5.93%	
Sortino ratio	0.39	
Jensen's alpha	2.19%	
Beta	0.05	
Up capture ratio	4.15%	
Down capture ratio	-57.61%	
Omega -0%	181%	
Appraisal ratio	0.30	
Average α over benchmark	-0.05%	
Tracking error	3.37%	
Information ratio	-1.60%	
Sterling ratio	0.39	
Treynor measure	0.50	
M² – Modigliani measure	0.08%	
Burke ratio	0.50	
Skewness	-54.72%	
Kurtosis	-70%	
Correlation to S&P/TSX	0.373	
R squared	0.004	
Benchmark: MSCI World C$		

TERMS AND CONDITIONS

Inception:	December 31, 2002
Style:	Security Selection
Sub-style:	N/A
Valuation:	Weekly on Friday
RRSP:	No
Management fee:	2.25%
Performance fee:	20.00%
High-water mark:	N/A
Hurdle rate:	N/A
NAV:	$12.05
Asset Size (million):	$15.96
Maximum leverage:	N/A
Early red'n period:	N/A
Early red'n fee:	N/A

PERFORMANCE (as of December 31, 2004)

	1 mo.	3 mo.	6 mo.
Funds	1.70%	5.58%	5.32%
S&P/TSX	5.25%	6.76%	0.07%
Van Global HF Index	1.50%	4.87%	5.48%

	1 yr.	2 yr.	3 yr.
Funds	6.32%	14.13%	
S&P/TSX	6.85%	8.58%	-2.18%
Van Global HF Index	7.79%	13.04%	8.40%

Year	Jan	Feb	Mar	Apr	May	Jun	Jul	Aug	Sep	Oct	Nov	Dec	Total
2004	0.50%	0.80%	3.30%	-3.20%	-2.20%	1.90%	-2.50%	0.30%	2.00%	0.50%	3.30%	1.70%	6.32%
2003	-1.90%	-2.80%	-1.10%	5.40%	5.60%	0.80%	2.80%	2.90%	2.30%	2.00%	0.30%	4.60%	22.52%
2002												-0.80%	-0.80%

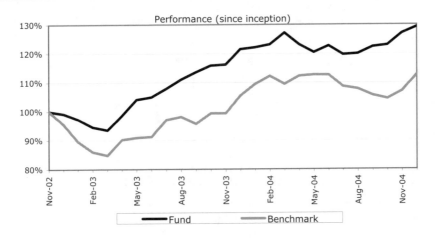

Performance (since inception)

ARROW ELKHORN U.S. LONG/SHORT FUND

FUND SPONSOR COMPANY

Arrow Hedge Partners Inc.
Tel: 416-323-0477   Toll-Free: 877-327-6048
Fax: 416-323-3199   Web site: www.arrowhedge.com

PORTFOLIO MANAGER(S)

Eric Kilcollin is a co-founder of Sanborn Kilcollin Partners and is responsible for the business and operational aspects of Sanborn. Mr. Kilcollin has extensive business management experience as well as expertise in business development, investment management operations, and the evaluation and management of financial risk. He was President and CEO of the Chicago Mercantile Exchange. Mr. Kilcollin also served as CEO of The Investments Group.

FUND DESCRIPTION

The objective of the Fund is to achieve superior capital appreciation with volatility below that of the S&P 500.

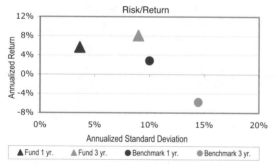

Rating: 🦔🦔🦔

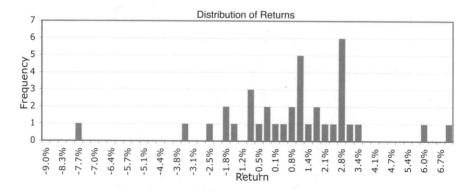

	1 yr.	3 yr.
Annualized rate of return	5.68%	8.09%
Annualized standard deviation	3.65%	8.99%
Percentage of negative months	33.33%	36.11%
Largest monthly drop	-1.00%	-7.90%
Maximum drawdown	-1.10%	-9.69%
Sharpe ratio	0.46	0.46
Semideviation	2.00%	7.18%
Sortino ratio	0.84	0.57
Jensen's alpha	1.68%	6.69%
Beta	0.00	0.27
Up capture ratio	12.12%	28.25%
Down capture ratio	-28.99%	-11.21%
Omega -0%	300%	202%
Appraisal ratio	0.46	0.98
Average α over benchmark	0.20%	1.09%
Tracking error	3.08%	3.83%
Information ratio	6.40%	28.55%
Sterling ratio	1.53	0.42
Treynor measure	-7.18	0.15
M^2 – Modigliani measure	5.80%	16.37%
Burke ratio	1.06	0.42
Skewness	20.24%	-68.70%
Kurtosis	-16%	280%
Correlation to S&P/TSX	0.032	0.463
R squared	0.000	0.194
Benchmark: S&P 500		

TERMS AND CONDITIONS

Inception:	April 17, 2003
Style:	Security Selection
Sub-style:	N/A
Valuation:	Weekly on Friday
RRSP:	No
Management fee:	2.50%
Performance fee:	20.00%
High-water mark:	N/A
Hurdle rate:	N/A
NAV:	$10.48
Asset Size (million):	$14.00
Maximum leverage:	N/A
Early red'n period:	N/A
Early red'n fee:	N/A

PERFORMANCE (as of December 31, 2004)

	1 mo.	3 mo.	6 mo.
Funds	0.90%	3.73%	4.66%
S&P/TSX	4.80%	4.07%	-3.39%
Van Global HF Index	1.50%	4.87%	5.48%

	1 yr.	2 yr.	3 yr.
Funds	5.68%	4.85%	8.09%
S&P/TSX	2.81%	4.32%	-5.78%
Van Global HF Index	7.79%	13.04%	8.40%

Year	Jan	Feb	Mar	Apr	May	Jun	Jul	Aug	Sep	Oct	Nov	Dec	Total
2004	-1.00%	0.80%	0.70%	-0.10%	-1.00%	1.60%	-0.70%	1.10%	0.50%	0.30%	2.50%	0.90%	5.68%
2003	-3.50%	-1.00%	-1.90%	2.60%	2.10%	1.10%	-0.20%	-0.50%	-1.70%	2.20%	2.50%	2.50%	4.03%
2002	2.80%	6.70%	2.60%	2.50%	1.60%	1.20%	-2.70%	3.30%	-7.90%	1.00%	5.70%	-2.00%	14.87%

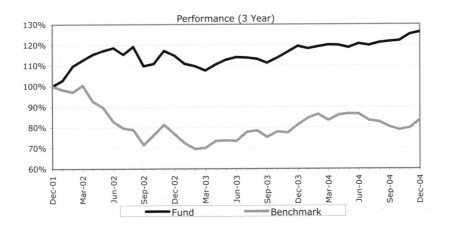

ARROW ENSO GLOBAL FUND

FUND SPONSOR COMPANY
Arrow Hedge Partners Inc.
Tel: 416-323-0477   Toll-Free: 877-327-6048
Fax: 416-323-3199   Web site: www.arrowhedge.com

PORTFOLIO MANAGER(S)

Paul Durose was most recently a Senior Research Analyst at Triton Partners. Previously, Mr. Durose helped manage the top-performing High Yield Fund and a Worldwide High Income Fund at Morgan Stanley Asset Management.
Joshua Fink was most recently a Managing Director at Argonaut Capital Management.

FUND DESCRIPTION

The Fund's investment objective is to attain superior after-tax returns with volatility less than that of the S&P 500 Index. The Fund will seek to achieve its investment objective primarily by investing both long and short in a diversified portfolio of global equity securities. The Fund's portfolio will be broadly diversified with respect to both industry and geography, and will consist entirely of securities of public companies.

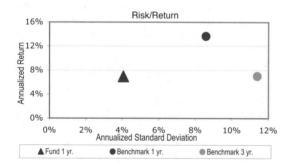

Rating: Not Rated

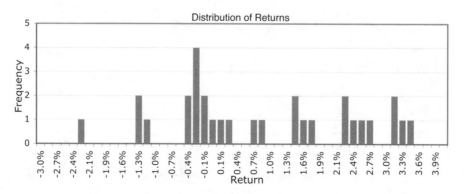

	1 yr.	3 yr.
Annualized rate of return	6.94%	
Annualized standard deviation	4.06%	
Percentage of negative months	50.00%	
Largest monthly drop	-0.50%	
Maximum drawdown	-2.08%	
Sharpe ratio	0.72	
Semideviation	0.84%	
Sortino ratio	3.49	
Jensen's alpha	2.47%	
Beta	0.16	
Up capture ratio	26.69%	
Down capture ratio	-20.76%	
Omega -0%	424%	
Appraisal ratio	0.84	
Average α over benchmark	-0.02%	
Tracking error	2.49%	
Information ratio	-0.83%	
Sterling ratio	1.41	
Treynor measure	0.18	
M² – Modigliani measure	3.99%	
Burke ratio	3.22	
Skewness	100.05%	
Kurtosis	-7%	
Correlation to S&P/TSX	0.516	
R squared	0.170	
Benchmark: MSCI World C$		

TERMS AND CONDITIONS

Inception:	July 12, 2002
Style:	Security Selection
Sub-style:	N/A
Valuation:	Monthly
RRSP:	No
Management fee:	2.25%
Performance fee:	20.00%
High-water mark:	Yes
Hurdle rate:	N/A
NAV:	$11.82
Asset Size (million):	$21.39
Maximum leverage:	N/A
Early red'n period:	N/A
Early red'n fee:	N/A

PERFORMANCE (as of December 31, 2004)

	1 mo.	3 mo.	6 mo.
Funds	1.40%	4.98%	5.50%
S&P/TSX	5.25%	6.76%	0.07%
Van Global HF Index	1.50%	4.87%	5.48%

	1 yr.	2 yr.	3 yr.
Funds	6.94%	10.48%	
S&P/TSX	6.85%	8.58%	-2.18%
Van Global HF Index	7.79%	13.04%	8.40%

Year	Jan	Feb	Mar	Apr	May	Jun	Jul	Aug	Sep	Oct	Nov	Dec	Total
2004	3.00%	-0.50%	-0.30%	-0.20%	-0.20%	-0.40%	-0.50%	0.20%	0.80%	2.20%	1.30%	1.40%	6.94%
2003	-0.30%	-0.30%	-2.40%	0.10%	2.50%	1.50%	3.20%	3.30%	-1.20%	2.60%	2.30%	2.20%	14.15%
2002							-0.10%	-1.40%	3.00%	-1.40%	1.60%	0.70%	2.35%

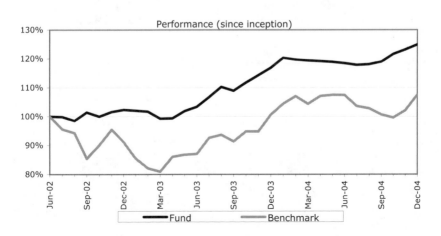

Performance (since inception)

Fund — Benchmark

ARROW GLOBAL LONG/SHORT FUND

FUND SPONSOR COMPANY
Arrow Hedge Partners Inc.
Tel: 416-323-0477   Toll-Free: 877-327-6048
Fax: 416-323-3199   Web site: www.arrowhedge.com

PORTFOLIO MANAGER(S)

Arrow Hedge Partners Inc. was founded in December 1999. The company is headquartered in Toronto, Canada with representative offices in Montreal, Calgary, Vancouver, Geneva, and Barbados. Arrow Hedge currently manages in excess of CDN$125 million in hedge funds. Arrow Hedge Partners is an investment counsel, portfolio manager and a limited market dealer.

FUND DESCRIPTION

The Arrow Global Long/Short Fund is an investment fund of funds offered only to sophisticated investors, and managed by Arrow Hedge Partners Inc. The Arrow Global Long/Short Fund is currently allocated to a number of underlying funds. The Fund's objective is to outperform the MSCI World Index over a market cycle with a correlation of less than 0.50 and half the index volatility.

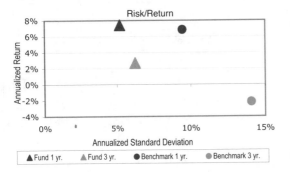

Rating: 🦔🦔

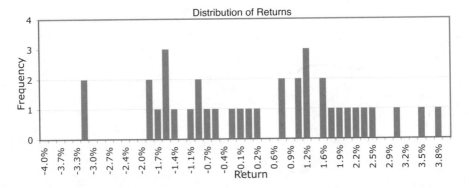

	1 yr.	3 yr.
Annualized rate of return	7.42%	2.68%
Annualized standard deviation	5.20%	6.23%
Percentage of negative months	25.00%	44.44%
Largest monthly drop	-1.80%	-3.30%
Maximum drawdown	-3.47%	-15.90%
Sharpe ratio	0.66	-0.21
Semideviation	3.15%	3.40%
Sortino ratio	1.09	-0.39
Jensen's alpha	3.23%	0.17%
Beta	0.07	0.24
Up capture ratio	17.26%	32.47%
Down capture ratio	-43.29%	27.79%
Omega -0%	274%	136%
Appraisal ratio	0.69	0.03
Average α over benchmark	0.02%	0.34%
Tracking error	2.94%	3.40%
Information ratio	0.72%	9.98%
Sterling ratio	0.98	-0.08
Treynor measure	0.51	-0.05
M^2 – Modigliani measure	3.37%	3.20%
Burke ratio	1.35	-0.20
Skewness	12.61%	-4.99%
Kurtosis	78%	-75%
Correlation to S&P/TSX	0.505	0.720
R squared	0.018	0.314
Benchmark: MSCI World C$		

TERMS AND CONDITIONS

Inception:	April 30, 2004
Style:	Multi Manager
Sub-style:	Security Selection
Valuation:	Weekly on Friday
RRSP:	No
Management fee:	2.50%
Performance fee:	20.00%
High-water mark:	Yes
Hurdle rate:	N/A
NAV:	$10.32
Asset Size (million):	$22.00
Maximum leverage:	N/A
Early red'n period:	N/A
Early red'n fee:	N/A

PERFORMANCE (as of December 31, 2004)

	1 mo.	3 mo.	6 mo.
Funds	0.70%	5.99%	7.04%
S&P/TSX	5.25%	6.76%	0.07%
Van Global HF Index	1.50%	4.87%	5.48%

	1 yr.	2 yr.	3 yr.
Funds	7.42%	10.74%	2.68%
S&P/TSX	6.85%	8.58%	-2.18%
Van Global HF Index	7.79%	13.04%	8.40%

Year	Jan	Feb	Mar	Apr	May	Jun	Jul	Aug	Sep	Oct	Nov	Dec	Total
2004	1.10%	1.10%	0.90%	-1.80%	-1.60%	0.70%	-0.80%	0.20%	1.60%	1.50%	3.70%	0.70%	7.42%
2003	-1.20%	-1.60%	-2.00%	2.10%	2.30%	2.40%	2.90%	1.80%	0.00%	2.00%	1.40%	3.40%	14.16%
2002	-0.10%	-1.00%	0.90%	-0.30%	-1.60%	-1.90%	-3.30%	-3.20%	-0.90%	-1.40%	1.10%	-0.60%	-11.72%

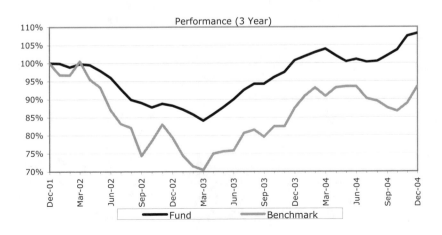

Performance (3 Year)

— Fund   — Benchmark

ARROW HIGH YIELD FUND

FUND SPONSOR COMPANY
Arrow Hedge Partners Inc.
Tel: 416-323-0477   Toll-Free: 877-327-6048
Fax: 416-323-3199   Web site: www.arrowhedge.com

PORTFOLIO MANAGER(S)

Barry Allan is the founding partner of Marret Asset Management Inc., a Canadian company incorporated in November 2000. Barry has 24 years of investment experience and has successfully operated in virtually all areas of the fixed income arena.

Greg Foss has 10 years of investment experience. Greg started his career in finance as an analyst with Royal Bank, spent seven years at TD Securities and 3 years with Midland Walwyn and prior to that 3 years consulting on credit risk.

FUND DESCRIPTION

The objective of the Fund is to achieve a high level of income and potential capital gains with an attractive risk return profile and moderate volatility.

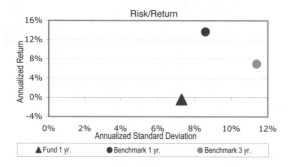

Rating: Not Rated

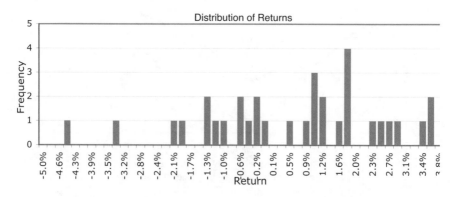

	1 yr.	3 yr.
Annualized rate of return	-0.42%	
Annualized standard deviation	7.29%	
Percentage of negative months	50.00%	
Largest monthly drop	-4.45%	
Maximum drawdown	-8.46%	
Sharpe ratio	-0.61	
Semideviation	6.44%	
Sortino ratio	-0.69	
Jensen's alpha	-4.76%	
Beta	0.04	
Up capture ratio	-1.53%	
Down capture ratio	0.86%	
Omega -0%	98%	
Appraisal ratio	-0.65	
Average α over benchmark	-1.12%	
Tracking error	3.18%	
Information ratio	-35.08%	
Sterling ratio	-0.52	
Treynor measure	-1.26	
M² – Modigliani measure	-14.86%	
Burke ratio	-0.77	
Skewness	-117.93%	
Kurtosis	70%	
Correlation to S&P/TSX	0.045	
R squared	0.002	
Benchmark: S&P/TSX		

TERMS AND CONDITIONS

Inception:	January 1, 2002
Style:	Directional
Sub-style:	N/A
Valuation:	Weekly on Friday
RRSP:	No
Management fee:	2.25%
Performance fee:	20.00%
High-water mark:	Yes
Hurdle rate:	0.00%
NAV:	$8.91
Asset Size (million):	$61.86
Maximum leverage:	300%
Early red'n period:	6 mo.
Early red'n fee:	N/A

PERFORMANCE (as of December 31, 2004)

	1 mo.	3 mo.	6 mo.
Funds	-0.60%	2.13%	4.61%
S&P/TSX	2.40%	6.67%	8.41%
Van Global HF Index	1.50%	4.87%	5.48%

	1 yr.	2 yr.	3 yr.
Funds	-0.42%	7.10%	
S&P/TSX	13.66%	19.32%	6.99%
Van Global HF Index	7.79%	13.04%	8.40%

Year	Jan	Feb	Mar	Apr	May	Jun	Jul	Aug	Sep	Oct	Nov	Dec	Total
2004	2.29%	-3.50%	-0.32%	-0.41%	-4.45%	1.66%	-0.38%	1.05%	1.75%	1.49%	1.24%	-0.60%	-0.42%
2003	2.88%	2.37%	-2.06%	1.10%	-1.30%	1.63%	0.42%	-0.05%	3.47%	3.51%	1.68%	0.76%	15.20%
2002				3.28%	-0.66%	-1.14%	-2.23%	1.01%	-1.39%	-1.42%	1.04%	2.71%	1.04%

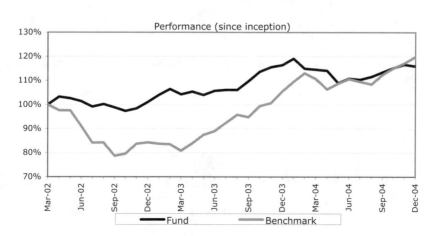

Performance (since inception)

Fund — Benchmark

ARROW MULTI-STRATEGY FUND

FUND SPONSOR COMPANY
Arrow Hedge Partners Inc.
Tel: 416-323-0477   Toll-Free: 877-327-6048
Fax: 416-323-3199   Web site: www.arrowhedge.com

PORTFOLIO MANAGER(S)

Arrow Hedge Partners is an investment counsel, portfolio manager and a limited market dealer.
The Fund invests in 11 hedge fund styles and 25 hedge fund managers.

FUND DESCRIPTION

The Fund's investment objective is to generate an absolute return of 300 to 500 basis points over LIBOR. The Fund attempts to deliver bond like volatility (5%–7% annual standard deviation) and very low correlation to major stock and bond market indices.

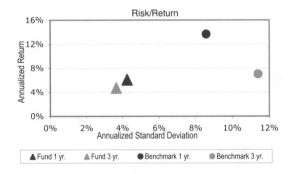

Risk/Return

Rating:

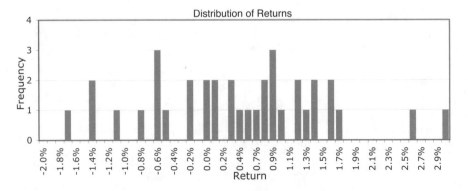

Distribution of Returns

	1 yr.	3 yr.
Annualized rate of return	6.08%	4.70%
Annualized standard deviation	4.25%	3.65%
Percentage of negative months	25.00%	30.56%
Largest monthly drop	-1.40%	-1.70%
Maximum drawdown	-2.78%	-4.14%
Sharpe ratio	0.49	0.19
Semideviation	2.72%	2.16%
Sortino ratio	0.76	0.32
Jensen's alpha	1.91%	1.32%
Beta	0.06	0.10
Up capture ratio	13.51%	19.83%
Down capture ratio	-36.91%	0.12%
Omega -0%	300%	254%
Appraisal ratio	0.49	0.42
Average α over benchmark	-0.09%	0.49%
Tracking error	2.83%	3.77%
Information ratio	-3.09%	13.05%
Sterling ratio	0.75	0.17
Treynor measure	0.35	0.07
M^2 – Modigliani measure	1.78%	8.89%
Burke ratio	1.05	0.22
Skewness	18.64%	13.41%
Kurtosis	63%	14%
Correlation to S&P/TSX	0.547	0.641
R squared	0.021	0.158
Benchmark: MSCI World C$		

TERMS AND CONDITIONS

Inception:	January 1, 2002
Style:	Fund of Hedge Funds
Sub-style:	N/A
Valuation:	Weekly on Friday
RRSP:	No
Management fee:	2.50%
Performance fee:	20.00%
High-water mark:	Yes
Hurdle rate:	0.00%
NAV:	$11.38
Asset Size (million):	$67.14
Maximum leverage:	N/A
Early red'n period:	6 mo.
Early red'n fee:	N/A

PERFORMANCE (as of December 31, 2004)

	1 mo.	3 mo.	6 mo.
Funds	0.80%	5.17%	6.54%
S&P/TSX	5.25%	6.76%	0.07%
Van Global HF Index	1.50%	4.87%	5.48%

	1 yr.	2 yr.	3 yr.
Funds	6.08%	8.61%	4.70%
S&P/TSX	6.85%	8.58%	-2.18%
Van Global HF Index	7.79%	13.04%	8.40%

Year	Jan	Feb	Mar	Apr	May	Jun	Jul	Aug	Sep	Oct	Nov	Dec	Total
2004	1.10%	0.40%	0.10%	-1.40%	-1.40%	0.80%	-0.20%	0.00%	1.50%	1.30%	3.00%	0.80%	6.08%
2003	0.00%	0.70%	-0.60%	0.80%	1.20%	1.50%	1.10%	0.70%	0.30%	2.50%	0.90%	1.60%	11.20%
2002	0.10%	-0.80%	1.30%	0.60%	-0.50%	-1.10%	-1.70%	-0.60%	-0.20%	0.50%	-0.60%	0.30%	-2.70%

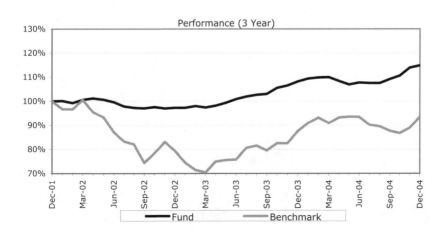

Performance (3 Year)

Fund — Benchmark

ARROW EPIC NORTH AMERICAN DIVERSIFIED FUND

FUND SPONSOR COMPANY

Arrow Hedge Partners Inc.

Tel: 416-323-0477   Toll-Free: 877-327-6048
Fax: 416-323-3199   Web site: www.arrowhedge.com

PORTFOLIO MANAGER(S)

The Fund is advised by **David Fawcett** and **Tom Schenkel** of Epic Capital, which is an asset management company based in Toronto, Canada.

FUND DESCRIPTION

The Fund's investment objective is to maximize capital appreciation and income through the purchase and short sale of Canadian or U.S. listed or over the counter quoted securities.

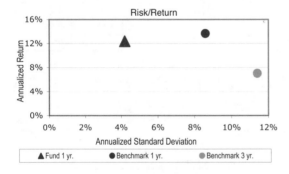

Rating: Not Rated

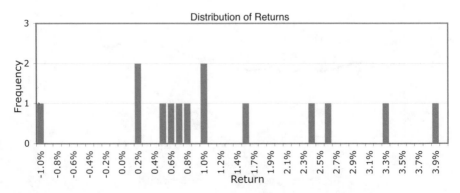

	1 yr.	3 yr.
Annualized rate of return	12.37%	
Annualized standard deviation	4.20%	
Percentage of negative months	8.33%	
Largest monthly drop	-1.00%	
Maximum drawdown	-1.00%	
Sharpe ratio	1.99	
Semideviation	2.12%	
Sortino ratio	3.95	
Jensen's alpha	8.59%	
Beta	0.19	
Up capture ratio	58.16%	
Down capture ratio	-18.09%	
Omega -0%	1280%	
Appraisal ratio	4.51	
Average α over benchmark	0.71%	
Tracking error	2.53%	
Information ratio	28.16%	
Sterling ratio	8.37	
Treynor measure	0.45	
M² – Modigliani measure	21.12%	
Burke ratio	8.37	
Skewness	104.26%	
Kurtosis	215%	
Correlation to S&P/TSX	0.562	
R squared	0.232	
Benchmark: S&P 500		

TERMS AND CONDITIONS

Inception:	December 31, 2000
Style:	N/A
Sub-style:	N/A
Valuation:	Weekly on Friday
RRSP:	No
Management fee:	2.50%
Performance fee:	20.00%
High-water mark:	Yes
Hurdle rate:	N/A
NAV:	$11.35
Asset Size (million):	$21.42
Maximum leverage:	N/A
Early red'n period:	N/A
Early red'n fee:	N/A

PERFORMANCE (as of December 31, 2004)

	1 mo.	3 mo.	6 mo.
Funds	2.50%	4.25%	4.45%
S&P/TSX	4.80%	4.07%	-3.39%
Van Global HF Index	1.50%	4.87%	5.48%

	1 yr.	2 yr.	3 yr.
Funds	12.37%		
S&P/TSX	2.81%	4.32%	-5.78%
Van Global HF Index	7.79%	13.04%	8.40%

Year	Jan	Feb	Mar	Apr	May	Jun	Jul	Aug	Sep	Oct	Nov	Dec	Total
2004	1.50%	3.80%	0.80%	0.20%	0.60%	0.50%	0.20%	-1.00%	1.00%	0.70%	1.00%	2.50%	12.37%
2003											3.20%	2.30%	5.57%
2002													

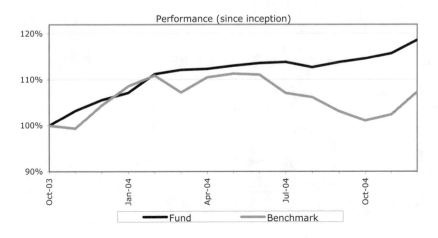

Performance (since inception)

ARROW NORTH AMERICAN MULTIMANAGER FUND

FUND SPONSOR COMPANY
Arrow Hedge Partners Inc.
Tel: 416-323-0477   Toll-Free: 877-327-6048
Fax: 416-323-3199   Web site: www.arrowhedge.com

PORTFOLIO MANAGER(S)

Arrow Hedge Partners Inc. was founded in December 1999. The company is headquartered in Toronto, Canada with representative offices in Montreal, Calgary, Vancouver, Geneva and Barbados. Arrow Hedge currently manages in excess of CDN$125 million in hedge funds. Arrow Hedge Partners is an investment counsel, portfolio manager and a limited market dealer.

FUND DESCRIPTION

The Fund is an investment fund offered only to sophisticated investors, and managed by Arrow Hedge Partners Inc. The fund allocates to three separate Arrow single manager funds to create a North American fund with regional specialists. The funds are committed to providing our clients with access to broadly diversified equity hedge or long/short portfolios that are diversified by manager, investment style, and regional focus.

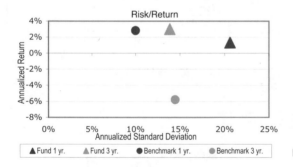

Rating:

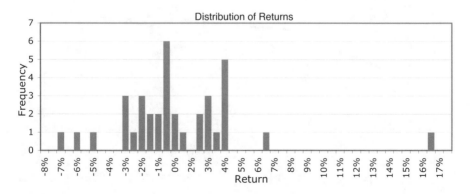

	1 yr.	3 yr.
Annualized rate of return	1.33%	3.01%
Annualized standard deviation	20.59%	13.87%
Percentage of negative months	58.33%	55.56%
Largest monthly drop	-7.27%	-7.27%
Maximum drawdown	-9.77%	-17.74%
Sharpe ratio	-0.13	-0.07
Semideviation	9.84%	7.10%
Sortino ratio	-0.27	-0.14
Jensen's alpha	-2.46%	2.40%
Beta	0.17	0.35
Up capture ratio	55.19%	51.73%
Down capture ratio	60.70%	38.56%
Omega -0%	116%	127%
Appraisal ratio	-0.12	0.19
Average α over benchmark	-0.01%	0.73%
Tracking error	6.36%	4.58%
Information ratio	-0.10%	15.95%
Sterling ratio	-0.27	-0.06
Treynor measure	-0.15	-0.03
M² – Modigliani measure	-0.11%	8.74%
Burke ratio	-0.26	-0.08
Skewness	185.59%	166.97%
Kurtosis	538%	684%
Correlation to S&P/TSX	-0.012	0.438
R squared	0.009	0.139
Benchmark: S&P 500		

TERMS AND CONDITIONS

Inception:	June 29, 2001
Style:	Multi Manager
Sub-style:	N/A
Valuation:	Weekly on Friday
RRSP:	No
Management fee:	2.50%
Performance fee:	20.00%
High-water mark:	Yes
Hurdle rate:	N/A
NAV:	$10.89
Asset Size (million):	$0.33
Maximum leverage:	N/A
Early red'n period:	N/A
Early red'n fee:	N/A

PERFORMANCE (as of December 31, 2004)

	1 mo.	3 mo.	6 mo.
Funds	-7.27%	1.51%	-2.04%
S&P/TSX	4.80%	4.07%	-3.39%
Van Global HF Index	1.50%	4.87%	5.48%

	1 yr.	2 yr.	3 yr.
Funds	1.33%	12.98%	3.01%
S&P/TSX	2.81%	4.32%	-5.78%
Van Global HF Index	7.79%	13.04%	8.40%

Year	Jan	Feb	Mar	Apr	May	Jun	Jul	Aug	Sep	Oct	Nov	Dec	Total
2004	1.67%	2.26%	-0.13%	-0.41%	-2.16%	2.24%	-0.56%	0.15%	-3.10%	-6.03%	16.50%	-7.27%	1.33%
2003	-0.25%	-1.39%	-2.35%	3.20%	1.87%	3.14%	3.26%	3.23%	-0.17%	5.83%	3.63%	3.63%	25.96%
2002	-0.60%	-1.51%	0.71%	-2.02%	-1.86%	-3.05%	-5.32%	-0.92%	-2.89%	0.36%	2.26%	-0.35%	-14.37%

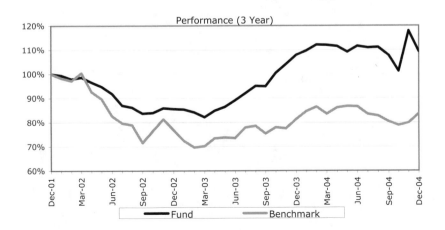

Performance (3 Year)

ARROW WF ASIA FUND

FUND SPONSOR COMPANY
Arrow Hedge Partners Inc.
Tel: 416-323-0477   Toll-Free: 877-327-6048
Fax: 416-323-3199   Web site: www.arrowhedge.com

PORTFOLIO MANAGER(S)

Peter Ferry was Fixed Income Investment Specialist & Chief Marketing Officer at Lloyd George Management. Mr. Ferry has over 22 years of investment banking experience in equity research, sales and trading.
Scobie Ward was Chief Investment Officer of Lloyd George Management.

FUND DESCRIPTION

The objective of this Fund is to achieve capital appreciation through investment primarily in the securities of companies that are listed, quoted, or traded on stock exchanges and the over-the-counter markets in Asia, and through investment in American Depository Receipts and/or Global Depository Receipts representing securities companies in Asia.

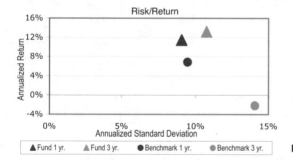

Rating:

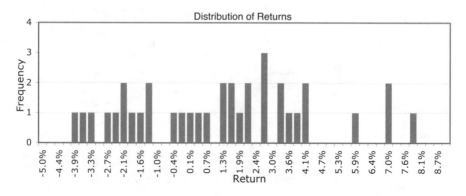

	1 yr.	3 yr.
Annualized rate of return	11.49%	13.22%
Annualized standard deviation	9.05%	10.76%
Percentage of negative months	33.33%	38.89%
Largest monthly drop	-4.10%	-4.10%
Maximum drawdown	-6.21%	-17.88%
Sharpe ratio	0.83	0.86
Semideviation	6.33%	4.92%
Sortino ratio	1.18	1.87
Jensen's alpha	7.85%	11.10%
Beta	-0.13	0.30
Up capture ratio	3.40%	58.01%
Down capture ratio	-112.72%	-2.57%
Omega -0%	257%	237%
Appraisal ratio	0.75	1.65
Average α over benchmark	0.35%	1.19%
Tracking error	4.04%	3.98%
Information ratio	8.76%	29.92%
Sterling ratio	1.21	0.52
Treynor measure	-0.59	0.30
M^2 – Modigliani measure	4.98%	18.24%
Burke ratio	1.59	1.05
Skewness	-15.37%	30.12%
Kurtosis	52%	-49%
Correlation to S&P/TSX	0.106	0.452
R squared	0.021	0.168
Benchmark: MSCI World C$		

TERMS AND CONDITIONS

Inception:	July 27, 2001
Style:	Security Selection
Sub-style:	Long Bias
Valuation:	Weekly on Friday
RRSP:	No
Management fee:	2.25%
Performance fee:	20.00%
High-water mark:	Yes
Hurdle rate:	0.00%
NAV:	$14.31
Asset Size (million):	$19.47
Maximum leverage:	200%
Early red'n period:	6 mo.
Early red'n fee:	N/A

PERFORMANCE (as of December 31, 2004)

	1 mo.	3 mo.	6 mo.
Funds	0.50%	8.99%	12.06%
S&P/TSX	5.25%	6.76%	0.07%
Van Global HF Index	1.50%	4.87%	5.48%

	1 yr.	2 yr.	3 yr.
Funds	11.49%	22.40%	13.22%
S&P/TSX	6.85%	8.58%	-2.18%
Van Global HF Index	7.79%	13.04%	8.40%

Year	Jan	Feb	Mar	Apr	May	Jun	Jul	Aug	Sep	Oct	Nov	Dec	Total
2004	-0.60%	1.60%	3.90%	-2.20%	-4.10%	1.10%	-0.30%	1.10%	2.00%	2.60%	5.70%	0.50%	11.49%
2003	-2.50%	-3.30%	-2.40%	3.80%	4.00%	7.00%	7.80%	3.30%	3.00%	2.70%	0.40%	6.90%	34.38%
2002	3.00%	1.30%	1.40%	2.60%	-1.70%	-2.10%	-0.10%	-3.70%	-1.30%	-2.80%	2.00%	-1.50%	-3.13%

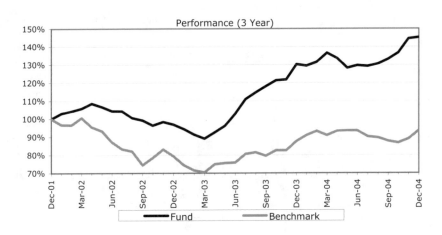

Performance (3 Year)

— Fund   — Benchmark

ASSET LOGICS INDEX TRACTION FUND

FUND SPONSOR COMPANY

Asset Logics Capital Management
Tel: 604-801-5577   Toll-Free: N/A
Fax: 604-801-5580   Web site: www.assetlogics.com

PORTFOLIO MANAGER(S)

Douglas W. Sereda co-founded Matisse Investment Management Ltd. in 1997. He has 20 years of experience in the derivatives industry and has worked closely with StrategicNova to build a pre-eminent managed futures product for Canadian investors.

FUND DESCRIPTION

The investment objective of the Fund is to maximize the absolute return for investors by achieving high capital appreciation over a medium-term horizon for investors who are willing to accept the risks inherent in investing in futures, forwards, currencies, and other derivatives.

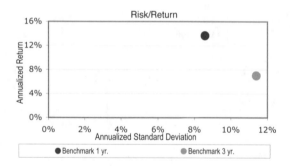

Rating: Not Rated

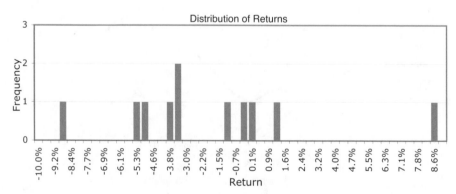

	1 yr.	3 yr.
Annualized rate of return		
Annualized standard deviation		
Percentage of negative months		
Largest monthly drop		
Maximum drawdown		
Sharpe ratio		
Semideviation		
Sortino ratio		
Jensen's alpha		
Beta		
Up capture ratio		
Down capture ratio		
Omega -0%		
Appraisal ratio		
Average α over benchmark		
Tracking error		
Information ratio		
Sterling ratio		
Treynor measure		
M^2 – Modigliani measure		
Burke ratio		
Skewness		
Kurtosis		
Correlation to S&P/TSX		
R squared		
Benchmark: S&P/TSX		

TERMS AND CONDITIONS

Inception:	January 1, 2004
Style:	Directional Trading
Sub-style:	N/A
Valuation:	Monthly
RRSP:	Yes
Management fee:	2.50%
Performance fee:	20.00%
High-water mark:	N/A
Hurdle rate:	N/A
NAV:	$7.78
Asset Size (million):	$1.30
Maximum leverage:	N/A
Early red'n period:	N/A
Early red'n fee:	N/A

PERFORMANCE (as of December 31, 2004)

	1 mo.	3 mo.	6 mo.
Funds	8.29%	3.88%	-7.48%
S&P/TSX	2.40%	6.67%	8.41%
Van Global HF Index	1.50%	4.87%	5.48%

	1 yr.	2 yr.	3 yr.
Funds			
S&P/TSX	13.66%	19.32%	6.99%
Van Global HF Index	7.79%	13.04%	8.40%

Year	Jan	Feb	Mar	Apr	May	Jun	Jul	Aug	Sep	Oct	Nov	Dec	Total
2004		0.00%	-0.51%	-8.87%	-1.19%	-5.73%	-3.73%	-3.55%	-4.08%	-5.14%	1.12%	8.29%	-21.86%
2003													
2002													

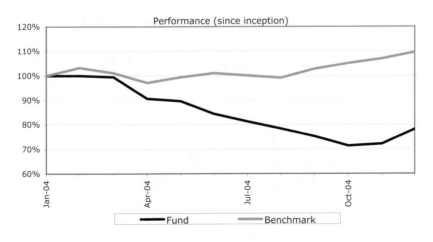

Performance (since inception)

ASSET LOGICS MANAGED FUTURES FUND

FUND SPONSOR COMPANY

Matisse Investment Management Ltd.

Tel: 604-801-5577   Toll-Free: N/A

Fax: 604-801-5580   Web site: www.assetlogics.com

PORTFOLIO MANAGER(S)

Douglas W. Sereda co-founded Matisse Investment Management Ltd. in 1997. He has 20 years of experience in the derivatives industry and has worked closely with StrategicNova to build a pre-eminent managed futures product for Canadian investors.

FUND DESCRIPTION

The investment objective is to provide value-added capital appreciation through speculation in derivatives across a broad spectrum of global markets.

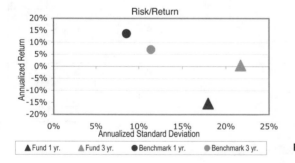

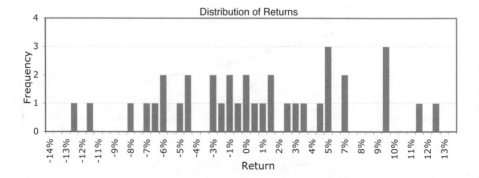

	1 yr.	3 yr.
Annualized rate of return	-15.43%	0.45%
Annualized standard deviation	17.96%	21.70%
Percentage of negative months	58.33%	50.00%
Largest monthly drop	-11.16%	-12.59%
Maximum drawdown	-26.99%	-32.08%
Sharpe ratio	-1.08	-0.16
Semideviation	11.36%	12.56%
Sortino ratio	-1.71	-0.28
Jensen's alpha	-32.47%	-2.94%
Beta	1.35	-0.20
Up capture ratio	24.59%	13.46%
Down capture ratio	257.40%	26.57%
Omega -0%	51%	109%
Appraisal ratio	-0.84	-0.13
Average α over benchmark	-2.36%	-0.39%
Tracking error	3.86%	7.39%
Information ratio	-61.20%	-5.28%
Sterling ratio	-0.72	-0.11
Treynor measure	-0.14	0.17
M^2 – Modigliani measure	-18.95%	-4.86%
Burke ratio	-1.35	-0.14
Skewness	16.84%	1.98%
Kurtosis	99%	-58%
Correlation to S&P/TSX	0.704	-0.110
R squared	0.496	0.012
Benchmark: S&P/TSX		

TERMS AND CONDITIONS

Inception:	June 8, 1999
Style:	Directional Trading
Sub-style:	N/A
Valuation:	Daily
RRSP:	Yes
Management fee:	1.50%
Performance fee:	25.00%
High-water mark:	Yes
Hurdle rate:	0.00%
NAV:	$9.09
Asset Size (million):	$10.90
Maximum leverage:	N/A
Early red'n period:	3 mo.
Early red'n fee:	N/A

PERFORMANCE (as of December 31, 2004)

	1 mo.	3 mo.	6 mo.
Funds	-0.49%	4.42%	-2.50%
S&P/TSX	2.40%	6.67%	8.41%
Van Global HF Index	1.50%	4.87%	5.48%

	1 yr.	2 yr.	3 yr.
Funds	-15.43%	-10.47%	0.45%
S&P/TSX	13.66%	19.32%	6.99%
Van Global HF Index	7.79%	13.04%	8.40%

Year	Jan	Feb	Mar	Apr	May	Jun	Jul	Aug	Sep	Oct	Nov	Dec	Total
2004	0.62%	9.05%	-2.50%	-11.16%	-2.88%	-6.03%	-4.79%	-3.00%	1.10%	0.09%	4.85%	-0.49%	-15.43%
2003	6.33%	5.12%	-12.59%	-0.60%	6.30%	-7.55%	-0.97%	5.41%	-6.81%	2.89%	-1.84%	1.07%	-5.23%
2002	-1.48%	-4.44%	2.10%	-5.16%	3.24%	12.54%	11.21%	5.22%	9.02%	-8.58%	-6.16%	9.10%	26.46%

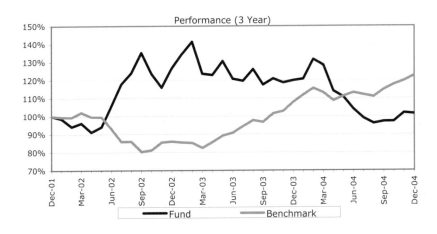

Performance (3 Year)

Fund   Benchmark

BLUMONT CANADIAN OPPORTUNITIES FUND

FUND SPONSOR COMPANY

BluMont Capital Inc.

Tel: 416-216-3566   Toll-Free: 866-473-7376
Fax: 416-216-3559   Web site: www.blumontcapital.com

PORTFOLIO MANAGER(S)

BluMont Capital Corporation
Hillsdale Investment Management Inc.
SciVest Capital Management Inc.

FUND DESCRIPTION

The Fund's objective is to achieve above-average, long-term capital growth by investing primarily in Canadian corporations with superior growth profiles while mitigating the overall market risk of the portfolio through various hedging strategies. The Fund's investment approach is designed to deliver consistent returns by combining three complementary strategies, managed 50% by BluMont Capital Corporation (Veronika Hirsch), 25% by Hillsdale Investment Management Inc., and 25% by SciVest Capital Management Inc.

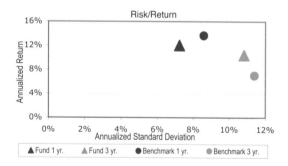

Rating: 🦔🦔🦔

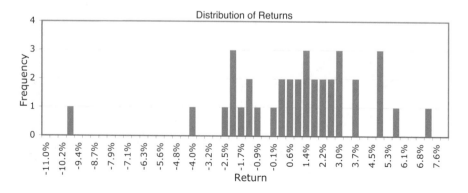

	1 yr.	3 yr.
Annualized rate of return	12.03%	10.42%
Annualized standard deviation	7.24%	10.82%
Percentage of negative months	33.33%	30.56%
Largest monthly drop	-2.53%	-9.86%
Maximum drawdown	-3.65%	-13.80%
Sharpe ratio	1.11	0.59
Semideviation	4.31%	8.94%
Sortino ratio	1.86	0.72
Jensen's alpha	2.43%	4.61%
Beta	0.58	0.60
Up capture ratio	75.63%	71.40%
Down capture ratio	60.61%	44.16%
Omega -0%	325%	208%
Appraisal ratio	9.20	1.02
Average α over benchmark	-0.13%	0.26%
Tracking error	1.66%	2.67%
Information ratio	-7.83%	9.71%
Sterling ratio	2.20	0.47
Treynor measure	0.14	0.11
M² – Modigliani measure	-0.13%	3.77%
Burke ratio	2.60	0.53
Skewness	6.34%	-99.71%
Kurtosis	-41%	282%
Correlation to S&P/TSX	0.750	0.655
R squared	0.563	0.429
Benchmark: S&P/TSX		

TERMS AND CONDITIONS

Inception:	January 1, 2001
Style:	Multi Manager
Sub-style:	Equity Long/Short
Valuation:	Weekly on Friday
RRSP:	Yes
Management fee:	2.50%
Performance fee:	20.00%
High-water mark:	Yes
Hurdle rate:	0.00%
NAV:	$161.03
Asset Size (million):	$60.85
Maximum leverage:	200%
Early red'n period:	N/A
Early red'n fee:	N/A

PERFORMANCE (as of December 31, 2004)

	1 mo.	3 mo.	6 mo.
Funds	2.14%	8.38%	9.38%
S&P/TSX	2.40%	6.67%	8.41%
Van Global HF Index	1.50%	4.87%	5.48%

	1 yr.	2 yr.	3 yr.
Funds	12.03%	14.45%	10.42%
S&P/TSX	13.66%	19.32%	6.99%
Van Global HF Index	7.79%	13.04%	8.40%

Year	Jan	Feb	Mar	Apr	May	Jun	Jul	Aug	Sep	Oct	Nov	Dec	Total
2004	0.96%	3.53%	-0.93%	-2.53%	-0.23%	1.71%	0.17%	-1.49%	2.28%	1.36%	4.68%	2.14%	12.03%
2003	0.67%	-1.75%	-2.10%	1.22%	1.90%	0.40%	2.73%	1.58%	0.17%	5.34%	2.90%	2.90%	16.91%
2002	1.17%	3.38%	4.67%	0.59%	4.85%	-4.28%	-9.86%	6.94%	-2.19%	-2.32%	-1.51%	2.54%	2.78%

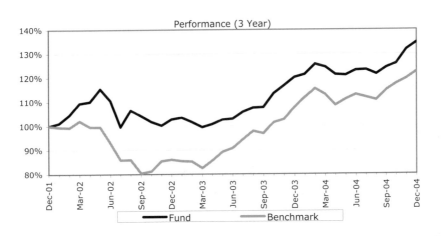

Performance (3 Year)

BLUMONT HIRSCH LONG/SHORT FUND

FUND SPONSOR COMPANY

BluMont Capital Inc.
Tel: 416-216-3566   Toll-Free: 866-473-7376
Fax: 416-216-3559   Web site: www.blumontcapital.com

PORTFOLIO MANAGER(S)

Veronika Hirsch is Chief Investment Officer of BluMont Capital Corporation and lead Portfolio Manager of the BluMont Canadian Opportunities Fund, the BluMont Hirsch Long/Short Fund, and the BluMont Hirsch Performance Fund. Ms. Hirsch, who has been in the investment management industry for 20 years, is recognized as one of Canada's premier equity investment managers.

FUND DESCRIPTION

The BluMont Hirsch Long/Short Fund's objective is to achieve above-average returns each year independent of the performance of the S&P/TSX Total Return Index by investing primarily in Canadian issuers and mitigating overall market risk of the portfolio through various hedging strategies.

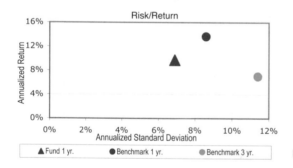

Rating: Not Rated

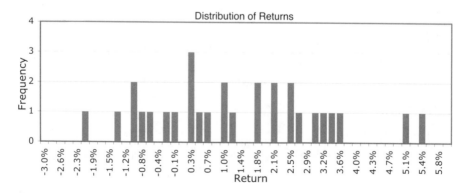

	1 yr.	3 yr.
Annualized rate of return	9.72%	
Annualized standard deviation	6.90%	
Percentage of negative months	33.33%	
Largest monthly drop	-2.17%	
Maximum drawdown	-4.38%	
Sharpe ratio	0.83	
Semideviation	3.31%	
Sortino ratio	1.73	
Jensen's alpha	0.02%	
Beta	0.59	
Up capture ratio	69.01%	
Down capture ratio	69.99%	
Omega -0%	272%	
Appraisal ratio	0.02	
Average α over benchmark	-0.31%	
Tracking error	1.48%	
Information ratio	-20.68%	
Sterling ratio	1.31	
Treynor measure	0.10	
M² – Modigliani measure	-2.53%	
Burke ratio	1.95	
Skewness	13.15%	
Kurtosis	-134%	
Correlation to S&P/TSX	0.802	
R squared	0.642	
Benchmark: S&P/TSX		

TERMS AND CONDITIONS

Inception:	August 2, 2002
Style:	Security Selection
Sub-style:	Equity Long/Short
Valuation:	Weekly
RRSP:	Yes
Management fee:	2.50% (Cl. F:1.50%)
Performance fee:	20.00%
High-water mark:	Yes
Hurdle rate:	0.00%
NAV:	$138.86
Asset Size (million):	$35.13
Maximum leverage:	200%
Early red'n period:	N/A
Early red'n fee:	N/A

PERFORMANCE (as of December 31, 2004)

	1 mo.	3 mo.	6 mo.
Funds	3.58%	7.21%	7.28%
S&P/TSX	2.40%	6.67%	8.41%
Van Global HF Index	1.50%	4.87%	5.48%

	1 yr.	2 yr.	3 yr.
Funds	9.72%	15.62%	
S&P/TSX	13.66%	19.32%	6.99%
Van Global HF Index	7.79%	13.04%	8.40%

Year	Jan	Feb	Mar	Apr	May	Jun	Jul	Aug	Sep	Oct	Nov	Dec	Total
2004	1.10%	3.42%	-1.12%	-2.17%	0.24%	0.87%	-1.38%	-0.88%	2.37%	0.28%	3.21%	3.58%	9.72%
2003	-0.72%	-0.21%	-1.00%	0.28%	1.66%	2.01%	2.43%	4.97%	0.33%	5.38%	2.03%	2.98%	21.84%
2002							2.63%	1.00%	-0.41%	0.53%	1.66%	5.50%

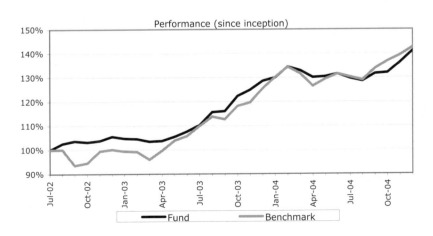

Performance (since inception)

BLUMONT HIRSCH PERFORMANCE FUND

FUND SPONSOR COMPANY

BluMont Capital Inc.
Tel: 416-216-3566   Toll-Free: 866-473-7376
Fax: 416-216-3559   Web site: www.blumontcapital.com

PORTFOLIO MANAGER(S)

Veronika Hirsch is Chief Investment Officer of BluMont Capital Corporation and lead Portfolio Manager of the BluMont Canadian Opportunities Fund, the BluMont Hirsch Long/Short Fund, and the BluMont Hirsch Performance Fund. Ms. Hirsch, who has been in the investment management industry for 20 years, is recognized as one of Canada's premier equity investment managers.

FUND DESCRIPTION

The objective of the Fund is to strive to deliver consistently positive returns by investing primarily in securities issued by Canadian corporations and mitigating the overall risk of the portfolio by varying market exposure and through the use of option strategies.

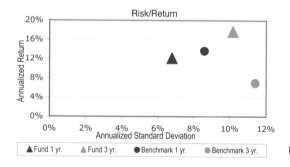

Rating:

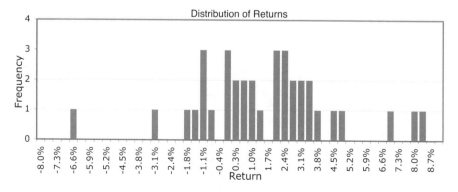

	1 yr.	3 yr.
Annualized rate of return	12.13%	17.71%
Annualized standard deviation	6.78%	10.17%
Percentage of negative months	41.67%	30.56%
Largest monthly drop	-1.73%	-6.88%
Maximum drawdown	-4.05%	-9.83%
Sharpe ratio	1.20	1.35
Semideviation	2.99%	6.52%
Sortino ratio	2.72	2.10
Jensen's alpha	2.29%	11.87%
Beta	0.60	0.61
Up capture ratio	75.57%	94.05%
Down capture ratio	59.40%	20.48%
Omega -0%	344%	378%
Appraisal ratio	-4.10	-17.86
Average α over benchmark	-0.12%	0.79%
Tracking error	1.37%	2.41%
Information ratio	-9.13%	32.79%
Sterling ratio	2.01	1.39
Treynor measure	0.13	0.22
M^2 – Modigliani measure	0.64%	12.37%
Burke ratio	3.31	1.66
Skewness	13.49%	0.03%
Kurtosis	-140%	144%
Correlation to S&P/TSX	0.836	0.705
R squared	0.699	0.497
Benchmark: S&P/TSX		

TERMS AND CONDITIONS

Inception:	September 1, 1997
Style:	Equity non-hedge
Sub-style:	Long Only
Valuation:	Weekly
RRSP:	Yes
Management fee:	0.00%
Performance fee:	20.00%
High-water mark:	Yes
Hurdle rate:	0.00%
NAV:	$20.18
Asset Size (million):	$53.34
Maximum leverage:	150%
Early red'n period:	N/A
Early red'n fee:	N/A

PERFORMANCE (as of December 31, 2004)

	1 mo.	3 mo.	6 mo.
Funds	2.67%	7.10%	7.56%
S&P/TSX	2.40%	6.67%	8.41%
Van Global HF Index	1.50%	4.87%	5.48%

	1 yr.	2 yr.	3 yr.
Funds	12.13%	20.93%	17.71%
S&P/TSX	13.66%	19.32%	6.99%
Van Global HF Index	7.79%	13.04%	8.40%

Year	Jan	Feb	Mar	Apr	May	Jun	Jul	Aug	Sep	Oct	Nov	Dec	Total
2004	2.41%	4.15%	-1.13%	-1.73%	-0.10%	0.70%	-1.12%	-0.72%	2.30%	1.04%	3.23%	2.67%	12.13%
2003	0.88%	0.12%	-1.80%	0.46%	2.80%	2.19%	2.93%	4.55%	1.77%	7.89%	1.96%	3.43%	30.43%
2002	0.62%	1.74%	8.11%	-0.04%	6.69%	-3.17%	-6.88%	3.55%	-1.31%	-0.23%	0.21%	2.56%	11.50%

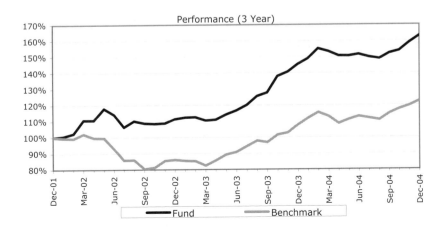

Performance (3 Year)

Fund — Benchmark

BLUMONT MAN-IP 220 SERIES 1 NOTES

FUND SPONSOR COMPANY
BluMont Capital Inc.
Tel: 416-216-3566   Toll-Free: 866-473-7376
Fax: 416-216-3559   Web site: www.blumontcapital.com

PORTFOLIO MANAGER(S)

MAN INVESTMENTS; Man, a division of Man Group plc, is a global leader in the fast-growing alternative investment industry. Established in 1987, Man has aspired to make alternative investments available to a wide range of institutional and private investors. Man strives to develop unique and innovative solutions that offer its clients the range of risk and reward outcomes they seek. Man has launched approximately 450 products worldwide. It manages approximately US$39.1 billion (as of September 30, 2004).

FUND DESCRIPTION

The Fund's objective is to achieve consistent medium-term growth. The IP 220 Fund targets double-digit annual returns while aiming to perform independently of, and with low correlation to, traditional stock and bond markets.

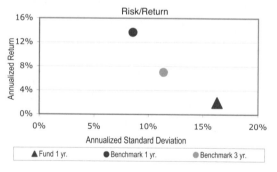

Rating: Not Rated

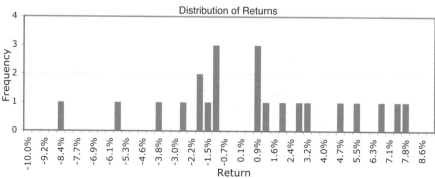

	1 yr.	3 yr.
Annualized rate of return	2.00%	
Annualized standard deviation	16.29%	
Percentage of negative months	41.67%	
Largest monthly drop	-8.70%	
Maximum drawdown	-19.23%	
Sharpe ratio	-0.12	
Semideviation	10.79%	
Sortino ratio	-0.19	
Jensen's alpha	-2.44%	
Beta	0.15	
Up capture ratio	14.07%	
Down capture ratio	5.77%	
Omega -0%	115%	
Appraisal ratio	-0.15	
Average α over benchmark	-0.32%	
Tracking error	5.21%	
Information ratio	-6.16%	
Sterling ratio	-0.10	
Treynor measure	-0.13	
M² – Modigliani measure	-4.01%	
Burke ratio	-0.18	
Skewness	-38.45%	
Kurtosis	-11%	
Correlation to S&P/TSX	0.580	
R squared	0.009	
Benchmark: MSCI World C$		

TERMS AND CONDITIONS

Inception:	March 1, 2003
Style:	Fund of Funds
Sub-style:	Structured Note Prod.
Valuation:	Monthly
RRSP:	Yes
Management fee:	N/A
Performance fee:	N/A
High-water mark:	N/A
Hurdle rate:	N/A
NAV:	$10.99
Asset Size (million):	$67.19
Maximum leverage:	N/A
Early red'n period:	N/A
Early red'n fee:	N/A

PERFORMANCE (as of December 31, 2004)

	1 mo.	3 mo.	6 mo.
Funds	0.80%	13.44%	17.30%
S&P/TSX	5.25%	6.76%	0.07%
Van Global HF Index	1.50%	4.87%	5.48%

	1 yr.	2 yr.	3 yr.
Funds	2.00%		
S&P/TSX	6.85%	8.58%	-2.18%
Van Global HF Index	7.79%	13.04%	8.40%

Year	Jan	Feb	Mar	Apr	May	Jun	Jul	Aug	Sep	Oct	Nov	Dec	Total
2004	1.20%	5.20%	-2.10%	-8.70%	-2.90%	-5.90%	-1.10%	1.90%	2.60%	4.40%	7.80%	0.80%	2.00%
2003			-1.20%	0.80%	7.40%	-3.80%	-2.10%	-1.30%	2.90%	0.60%	-1.80%	6.60%	7.80%
2002													

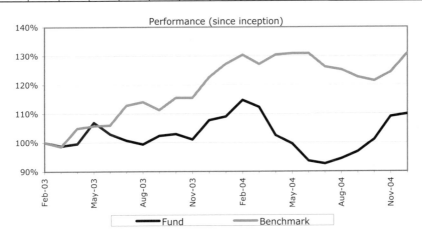

Performance (since inception)

Fund   Benchmark

BLUMONT MAN MULTI-STRATEGY SERIES 1 NOTES

FUND SPONSOR COMPANY

BluMont Capital Inc.

Tel: 416-216-3566   Toll-Free: 866-473-7376

Fax: 416-216-3559   Web site: www.blumontcapital.com

PORTFOLIO MANAGER(S)

MAN INVESTMENTS; Man, a division of Man Group plc, is a global leader in the fast-growing alternative investment industry. Established in 1987, Man has aspired to make alternative investments available to a wide range of institutional and private investors. Man strives to develop unique and innovative solutions that offer its clients the range of risk and reward outcomes they seek. Man has launched approximately 450 products worldwide. It manages approximately US$39.1 billion (as of September 30, 2004).

FUND DESCRIPTION

The investment objective of the Multi-Strategy Fund is to achieve double-digit annual returns with lower-than-equity-market volatility. The funds assets will be invested in a diversified and flexible portfolio of complementary investment strategies that generally have a low level of correlation to one another and that collectively have the potential to achieve positive returns on a consistent basis during both rising and falling market periods.

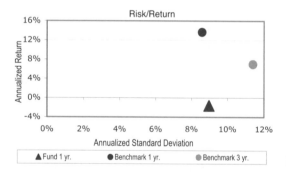

Rating: Not Rated

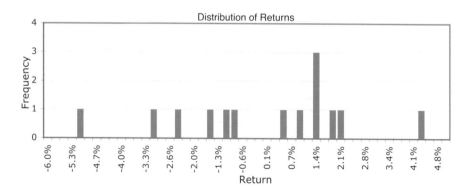

	1 yr.	3 yr.
Annualized rate of return	-1.60%	
Annualized standard deviation	8.97%	
Percentage of negative months	41.67%	
Largest monthly drop	-5.20%	
Maximum drawdown	-12.22%	
Sharpe ratio	-0.62	
Semideviation	6.04%	
Sortino ratio	-0.93	
Jensen's alpha	-5.95%	
Beta	0.12	
Up capture ratio	-1.55%	
Down capture ratio	11.31%	
Omega -0%	92%	
Appraisal ratio	-0.65	
Average α over benchmark	-0.67%	
Tracking error	3.49%	
Information ratio	-19.22%	
Sterling ratio	-0.46	
Treynor measure	-0.46	
M² – Modigliani measure	-8.75%	
Burke ratio	-0.84	
Skewness	-48.31%	
Kurtosis	9%	
Correlation to S&P/TSX	0.540	
R squared	0.020	
Benchmark: MSCI World C$		

TERMS AND CONDITIONS

Inception:	November 18, 2003
Style:	Fund of Funds
Sub-style:	Structured Note Prod.
Valuation:	Monthly
RRSP:	Yes
Management fee:	N/A
Performance fee:	N/A
High-water mark:	N/A
Hurdle rate:	N/A
NAV:	$9.80
Asset Size (million):	$34.54
Maximum leverage:	N/A
Early red'n period:	N/A
Early red'n fee:	N/A

PERFORMANCE (as of December 31, 2004)

	1 mo.	3 mo.	6 mo.
Funds	1.30%	7.60%	8.60%
S&P/TSX	5.25%	6.76%	0.07%
Van Global HF Index	1.50%	4.87%	5.48%

	1 yr.	2 yr.	3 yr.
Funds	-1.60%		
S&P/TSX	6.85%	8.58%	-2.18%
Van Global HF Index	7.79%	13.04%	8.40%

Year	Jan	Feb	Mar	Apr	May	Jun	Jul	Aug	Sep	Oct	Nov	Dec	Total
2004	0.40%	1.80%	-0.90%	-5.20%	-2.50%	-3.10%	-1.10%	1.20%	0.90%	2.00%	4.20%	1.30%	-1.60%
2003											-1.70%	1.20%	-0.50%
2002													

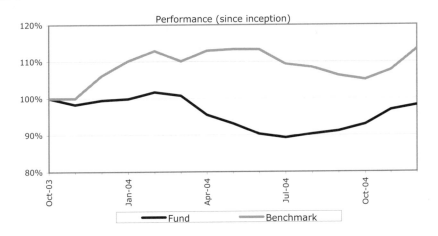

Performance (since inception)

Fund   Benchmark

BLUMONT STRATEGIC PARTNERS HEDGE FUND

FUND SPONSOR COMPANY
BluMont Capital Inc.
Tel: 416-216-3566   Toll-Free: 866-473-7376
Fax: 416-216-3559   Web site: www.blumontcapital.com

PORTFOLIO MANAGER(S)

Front Street Investment Management Inc., Hillsdale Investment Management Inc.,
BluMont Capital Corporation, Sprott Asset Management Inc., J.C. Clark Ltd.

FUND DESCRIPTION

The BluMont Strategic Partners Hedge Fund aims to achieve capital appreciation while managing risk through the use of a diversified hedged equity investment program. The Fund pursues this objective by allocating assets across a diversified portfolio, using distinct long/short equity hedge styles.

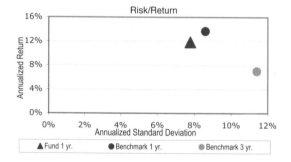

Rating: Not rated

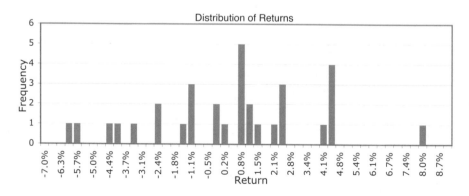

	1 yr.	3 yr.
Annualized rate of return	11.85%	
Annualized standard deviation	7.77%	
Percentage of negative months	33.33%	
Largest monthly drop	-2.67%	
Maximum drawdown	-3.04%	
Sharpe ratio	1.01	
Semideviation	4.32%	
Sortino ratio	1.81	
Jensen's alpha	2.97%	
Beta	0.50	
Up capture ratio	62.78%	
Down capture ratio	30.76%	
Omega -0%	334%	
Appraisal ratio	1.65	
Average α over benchmark	-0.14%	
Tracking error	2.10%	
Information ratio	-6.69%	
Sterling ratio	2.58	
Treynor measure	0.16	
M² – Modigliani measure	-0.99%	
Burke ratio	2.50	
Skewness	32.64%	
Kurtosis	-58%	
Correlation to S&P/TSX	0.608	
R squared	0.370	
Benchmark: S&P/TSX		

TERMS AND CONDITIONS

Inception:	May 16, 2002
Style:	Multi Manager
Sub-style:	Structured Note
Valuation:	Daily
RRSP:	Yes
Management fee:	N/A
Performance fee:	20.00%
High-water mark:	Yes
Hurdle rate:	0.00%
NAV:	$10.12
Asset Size (million):	$73.49
Maximum leverage:	200%
Early red'n period:	N/A
Early red'n fee:	N/A

PERFORMANCE (as of December 31, 2004)

	1 mo.	3 mo.	6 mo.
Funds	-0.30%	4.12%	8.04%
S&P/TSX	2.40%	6.67%	8.41%
Van Global HF Index	1.50%	4.87%	5.48%

	1 yr.	2 yr.	3 yr.
Funds	11.85%	9.03%	
S&P/TSX	13.66%	19.32%	6.99%
Van Global HF Index	7.79%	13.04%	8.40%

Year	Jan	Feb	Mar	Apr	May	Jun	Jul	Aug	Sep	Oct	Nov	Dec	Total
2004	1.17%	4.03%	0.82%	-2.67%	-0.38%	0.63%	1.06%	-1.56%	4.31%	0.16%	4.27%	-0.30%	11.85%
2003	0.63%	-1.13%	-2.64%	-3.59%	-1.40%	-1.31%	4.37%	0.68%	2.42%	4.20%	1.91%	2.33%	6.29%
2002					0.67%	-4.51%	-4.34%	2.46%	1.15%	-6.24%	-5.87%	7.75%	-9.38%

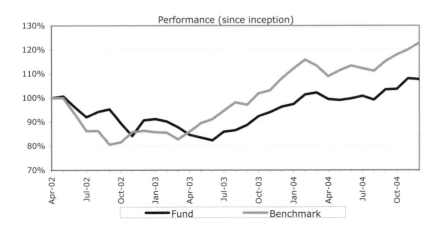

Performance (since inception)

CEO FUND

FUND SPONSOR COMPANY
Elysium Wealth Management Inc.
Tel: 204-989-6200   Toll-Free: N/A
Fax: 204-989-6209   Web site: www.ceofund.com

PORTFOLIO MANAGER(S)

Elysium Wealth Management Inc. (Elysium), formerly D.V. McQueen Ltd., has been providing portfolio management services to a select group of clients since 1986. It is known for its innovative approach and for providing personalized investment services. In addition to the management of individual segregated accounts, Elysium is also the manager of a unique and innovative mutual fund called the CEO Fund.

FUND DESCRIPTION

The investment objective of the Fund is to achieve long-term capital appreciation, with relatively low volatility, by buying and holding a portfolio of stocks of large capitalization U.S. companies, hedging the portfolio against major market risk, and buying and selling options on the individual stocks and/or market indices.

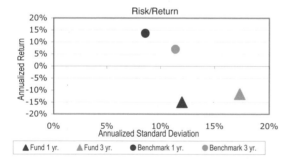

Rating:

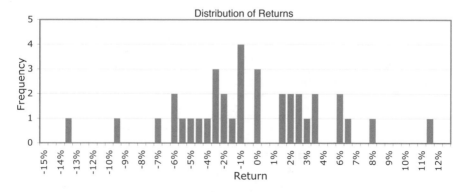

	1 yr.	3 yr.
Annualized rate of return	-15.03%	-11.53%
Annualized standard deviation	12.00%	17.30%
Percentage of negative months	66.67%	61.11%
Largest monthly drop	-6.12%	-13.57%
Maximum drawdown	-22.09%	-44.52%
Sharpe ratio	-1.59	-0.90
Semideviation	5.38%	10.90%
Sortino ratio	-3.54	-1.42
Jensen's alpha	-18.23%	-15.58%
Beta	-0.08	0.02
Up capture ratio	-35.32%	-13.21%
Down capture ratio	95.72%	71.73%
Omega -0%	42%	63%
Appraisal ratio	-1.69	-0.89
Average α over benchmark	-2.39%	-1.51%
Tracking error	4.39%	5.95%
Information ratio	-54.54%	-25.41%
Sterling ratio	-0.86	-0.35
Treynor measure	2.30	-8.60
M^2 – Modigliani measure	-23.28%	-13.22%
Burke ratio	-1.79	-0.65
Skewness	45.02%	-2.19%
Kurtosis	-80%	71%
Correlation to S&P/TSX	-0.065	0.012
R squared	0.004	0.000
Benchmark: S&P/TSX		

TERMS AND CONDITIONS

Inception:	July 1, 1998
Style:	Security Selection
Sub-style:	Index
Valuation:	Monthly
RRSP:	No
Management fee:	1.50%
Performance fee:	20.00%
High-water mark:	Yes
Hurdle rate:	10.00%
NAV:	$9.53
Asset Size (million):	$29.15
Maximum leverage:	100%
Early red'n period:	6 mo.
Early red'n fee:	5.00%

PERFORMANCE (as of December 31, 2004)

	1 mo.	3 mo.	6 mo.
Funds	5.12%	-0.95%	-15.40%
S&P/TSX	2.40%	6.67%	8.41%
Van Global HF Index	1.50%	4.87%	5.48%

	1 yr.	2 yr.	3 yr.
Funds	-15.03%	-23.01%	-11.53%
S&P/TSX	13.66%	19.32%	6.99%
Van Global HF Index	7.79%	13.04%	8.40%

Year	Jan	Feb	Mar	Apr	May	Jun	Jul	Aug	Sep	Oct	Nov	Dec	Total
2004	-1.75%	2.14%	-0.71%	2.47%	1.60%	-3.18%	-4.96%	-4.28%	-6.12%	-3.78%	-2.08%	5.12%	-15.03%
2003	1.62%	-3.06%	-5.87%	-0.54%	-5.80%	-2.98%	3.85%	-0.41%	1.54%	-7.15%	-1.81%	-13.57%	-30.25%
2002	2.73%	-2.83%	1.15%	-1.62%	-1.71%	-3.29%	-10.41%	11.54%	6.11%	3.45%	7.44%	5.01%	16.85%

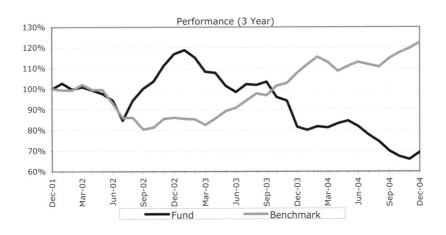

Performance (3 Year)

Fund ——— Benchmark ———

CI AMERICAN OPPORTUNITIES FUND

FUND SPONSOR COMPANY

CI Mutual Funds

Tel: 416-364-1145   Toll-Free: 800-268-9374
Fax: 416-364-6299   Web site: www.cifunds.com

PORTFOLIO MANAGER(S)

This Fund has recently changed its manager to **Nandu Narayanan**, founder and CIO of Trident Inv. Mgmt., LLC, who has 12 years of investment industry experience. Prior to founding Trident, he worked as an independent consultant on emerging markets to Credit Suisse Asset Management, as well as managing CI's Asian and emerging markets funds. He also worked as Chief Equity and Emerging Market Strategist at hedge fund manager Caxton Corporation, and as an investment analyst at Tiger Management, another hedge fund firm.

FUND DESCRIPTION

The objective of CI American Opportunities Fund is to achieve long-term capital appreciation by investing in a diversified portfolio consisting primarily of stocks, bonds, and other securities of U.S. issuers likely to benefit in the near term from structural change affecting specific companies and industries.

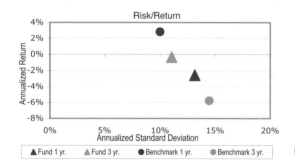

Rating: (2 hedgehogs)

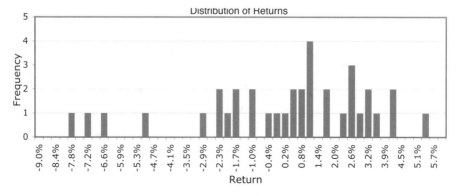

	1 yr.	3 yr.
Annualized rate of return	-2.59%	-0.32%
Annualized standard deviation	13.15%	11.06%
Percentage of negative months	33.33%	38.89%
Largest monthly drop	-7.95%	-7.95%
Maximum drawdown	-11.66%	-14.47%
Sharpe ratio	-0.50	-0.39
Semideviation	14.00%	9.09%
Sortino ratio	-0.47	-0.48
Jensen's alpha	-6.41%	-0.49%
Beta	0.16	0.39
Up capture ratio	10.82%	42.82%
Down capture ratio	35.77%	46.66%
Omega -0%	89%	102%
Appraisal ratio	-0.47	-0.04
Average α over benchmark	-0.42%	0.43%
Tracking error	4.46%	3.68%
Information ratio	-9.42%	11.74%
Sterling ratio	-0.57	-0.30
Treynor measure	-0.42	-0.11
M² – Modigliani measure	-3.82%	4.12%
Burke ratio	-0.61	-0.29
Skewness	-140.71%	-90.24%
Kurtosis	118%	58%
Correlation to S&P/TSX	0.751	0.634
R squared	0.017	0.279
Benchmark: S&P 500		

TERMS AND CONDITIONS

Inception:	October 29, 1999
Style:	Security Selection
Sub-style:	Long bias
Valuation:	Weekly on Friday
RRSP:	No
Management fee:	2.25%
Performance fee:	20.00%
High-water mark:	No
Hurdle rate:	No
NAV:	$118.49
Asset Size (million):	$54.60
Maximum leverage:	N/A
Early red'n period:	N/A
Early red'n fee:	N/A

PERFORMANCE (as of December 31, 2004)

	1 mo.	3 mo.	6 mo.
Funds	0.84%	5.48%	-1.89%
S&P/TSX	4.80%	4.07%	-3.39%
Van Global HF Index	1.50%	4.87%	5.48%

	1 yr.	2 yr.	3 yr.
Funds	-2.59%	6.44%	-0.32%
S&P/TSX	2.81%	4.32%	-5.78%
Van Global HF Index	7.79%	13.04%	8.40%

Year	Jan	Feb	Mar	Apr	May	Jun	Jul	Aug	Sep	Oct	Nov	Dec	Total
2004	0.02%	2.88%	-0.21%	-7.95%	2.54%	2.44%	-7.35%	-1.18%	1.59%	0.59%	3.99%	0.84%	-2.59%
2003	0.81%	0.71%	1.00%	4.13%	2.05%	1.67%	3.23%	3.29%	-2.53%	0.31%	-2.34%	3.12%	16.30%
2002	-1.25%	0.44%	-0.43%	1.06%	-2.89%	-2.08%	-1.69%	-1.80%	-6.65%	2.51%	5.31%	-5.32%	-12.58%

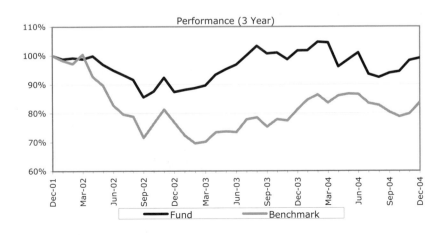

CI GLOBAL OPPORTUNITIES III FUND

FUND SPONSOR COMPANY
CI Mutual Funds
Tel: 416-364-1145   Toll-Free: 800-268-9374
Fax: 416-364-6299   Web site: www.cifunds.com

PORTFOLIO MANAGER(S)

This Fund has recently changed its manager to **Nandu Narayanan**, founder and CIO of Trident Inv. Mgmt., LLC, who has 12 years of investment industry experience. Prior to founding Trident, he worked as an independent consultant on emerging markets to Credit Suisse Asset Management, as well as managing CI's Asian and emerging markets funds. He also worked as Chief Equity and Emerging Market Strategist at hedge fund manager Caxton Corporation, and as an investment analyst at Tiger Management, another hedge fund firm.

FUND DESCRIPTION

The Fund's objective is to achieve long-term capital appreciation by investing in a globally diversified portfolio of stocks, bonds, and other securities that are likely to benefit in the near term from structural change affecting specific companies, industries, and national economies.

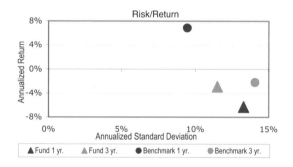

Rating: 🦔🦔

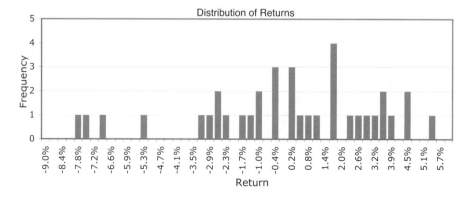

	1 yr.	3 yr.
Annualized rate of return	-6.31%	-2.92%
Annualized standard deviation	13.29%	11.51%
Percentage of negative months	50.00%	44.44%
Largest monthly drop	-7.96%	-7.96%
Maximum drawdown	-12.56%	-17.07%
Sharpe ratio	-0.78	-0.60
Semideviation	13.04%	8.86%
Sortino ratio	-0.79	-0.78
Jensen's alpha	-10.96%	-4.25%
Beta	0.23	0.43
Up capture ratio	-4.58%	31.00%
Down capture ratio	57.57%	55.38%
Omega -0%	70%	86%
Appraisal ratio	-0.74	-0.33
Average α over benchmark	-1.06%	-0.09%
Tracking error	4.30%	3.59%
Information ratio	-24.65%	-2.47%
Sterling ratio	-0.82	-0.41
Treynor measure	-0.45	-0.16
M² – Modigliani measure	-10.18%	-2.28%
Burke ratio	-0.92	-0.44
Skewness	-116.08%	-71.70%
Kurtosis	75%	20%
Correlation to S&P/TSX	0.700	0.608
R squared	0.032	0.294
Benchmark: MSCI World C$		

TERMS AND CONDITIONS

Inception:	October 29, 1999
Style:	Directional
Sub-style:	Long Bias
Valuation:	Weekly on Friday
RRSP:	30%
Management fee:	2.25%
Performance fee:	20.00%
High-water mark:	No
Hurdle rate:	No
NAV:	$87.51
Asset Size (million):	$76.30
Maximum leverage:	N/A
Early red'n period:	N/A
Early red'n fee:	N/A

PERFORMANCE (as of December 31, 2004)

	1 mo.	3 mo.	6 mo.
Funds	-0.43%	3.82%	-3.71%
S&P/TSX	5.25%	6.76%	0.07%
Van Global HF Index	1.50%	4.87%	5.48%

	1 yr.	2 yr.	3 yr.
Funds	-6.31%	3.90%	-2.92%
S&P/TSX	6.85%	8.58%	-2.18%
Van Global HF Index	7.79%	13.04%	8.40%

Year	Jan	Feb	Mar	Apr	May	Jun	Jul	Aug	Sep	Oct	Nov	Dec	Total
2004	-1.28%	2.99%	-0.55%	-7.96%	2.13%	2.38%	-7.67%	-1.05%	1.51%	0.06%	4.21%	-0.43%	-6.31%
2003	1.68%	0.47%	0.98%	4.22%	1.47%	1.44%	3.29%	3.64%	-3.33%	0.04%	-2.66%	3.31%	15.21%
2002	-2.86%	0.10%	-0.54%	0.69%	-2.90%	-2.38%	-1.56%	-1.83%	-7.03%	2.64%	5.34%	-5.47%	-15.24%

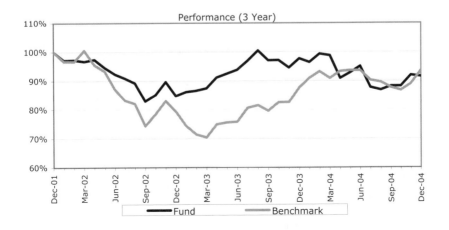

Performance (3 Year)

— Fund　　— Benchmark

CI ALTRINSIC OPPORTUNITIES FUND

FUND SPONSOR COMPANY

CI Mutual Funds

Tel: 416-364-1145   Toll-Free: 800-268-9374

Fax: 416-364-6299   Web site: www.cifunds.com

PORTFOLIO MANAGER(S)

John Hock has more than 12 years of investment experience focused on the analysis and selection of international securities. Previously, he was Senior Vice-President, Portfolio Manager and member of the Investment Strategy Committee at Hansberger Global Investors. He began his career at Merrill Lynch and then joined the firm's Global Securities Research and Economics Group, where he became Vice-President and Senior Analyst.

FUND DESCRIPTION

The investment objective of the Fund is to earn superior, absolute, risk-adjusted returns over the long term with a low correlation to, and lower volatility than, broad market indices such as the Morgan Stanley Capital International World Index (MSCI) and the Standard & Poor's 500 Total Return Index (S&P 500).

Rating: Not Rated

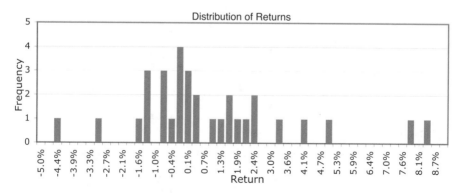

	1 yr.	3 yr.
Annualized rate of return	10.81%	
Annualized standard deviation	8.54%	
Percentage of negative months	50.00%	
Largest monthly drop	-1.74%	
Maximum drawdown	-3.03%	
Sharpe ratio	0.80	
Semideviation	2.21%	
Sortino ratio	3.08	
Jensen's alpha	5.35%	
Beta	0.51	
Up capture ratio	78.21%	
Down capture ratio	31.11%	
Omega -0%	431%	
Appraisal ratio	1.77	
Average α over benchmark	0.30%	
Tracking error	2.29%	
Information ratio	13.05%	
Sterling ratio	2.25	
Treynor measure	0.13	
M² – Modigliani measure	4.70%	
Burke ratio	3.43	
Skewness	222.68%	
Kurtosis	602%	
Correlation to S&P/TSX	-0.366	
R squared	0.380	
Benchmark: MSCI World C$		

TERMS AND CONDITIONS

Inception:	April 12, 2002
Style:	Security Selection
Sub-style:	Variable Bias
Valuation:	Weekly on Friday
RRSP:	30%
Management fee:	1.25%
Performance fee:	20.00%
High-water mark:	Yes
Hurdle rate:	0.00%
NAV:	$124.72
Asset Size (million):	N/A
Maximum leverage:	150%
Early red'n period:	2 mo.
Early red'n fee:	N/A

PERFORMANCE (as of December 31, 2004)

	1 mo.	3 mo.	6 mo.
Funds	2.05%	1.89%	-1.04%
S&P/TSX	5.25%	6.76%	0.07%
Van Global HF Index	1.50%	4.87%	5.48%

	1 yr.	2 yr.	3 yr.
Funds	10.81%	9.73%	
S&P/TSX	6.85%	8.58%	-2.18%
Van Global HF Index	7.79%	13.04%	8.40%

Year	Jan	Feb	Mar	Apr	May	Jun	Jul	Aug	Sep	Oct	Nov	Dec	Total
2004	2.16%	1.60%	-0.15%	7.80%	0.06%	0.17%	-1.74%	-0.27%	-0.88%	-0.12%	-0.03%	2.05%	10.81%
2003	-0.97%	-0.35%	0.27%	3.07%	1.50%	0.75%	3.94%	1.35%	-0.32%	-1.38%	-0.52%	1.13%	8.67%
2002					-0.79%	-1.48%	-1.44%	2.25%	-4.55%	8.33%	4.99%	-3.01%	3.71%

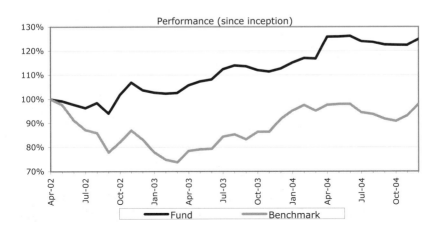
Performance (since inception)

CI LANDMARK GLOBAL OPPORTUNITIES FUND

FUND SPONSOR COMPANY
CI Mutual Funds
Tel: 416-364-1145   Toll-Free: 800-268-9374
Fax: 416-364-6299   Web site: www.cifunds.com

PORTFOLIO MANAGER(S)

John Hock has more than 12 years of investment experience focused on the analysis and selection of international securities. Previously, he was Senior Vice-President, Portfolio Manager and member of the Investment Strategy Committee at Hansberger Global Investors. He began his career at Merrill Lynch and then joined the firm's Global Securities Research and Economics Group, where he became Vice-President and Senior Analyst.

FUND DESCRIPTION

The Fund seeks to achieve absolute returns that have a low correlation with the broader indices while protecting clients at all times.

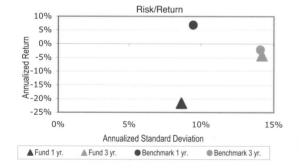

Rating: 🦅🦅

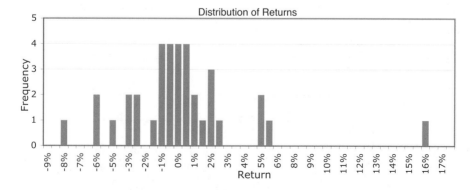

	1 yr.	3 yr.
Annualized rate of return	-21.57%	-4.24%
Annualized standard deviation	8.65%	14.18%
Percentage of negative months	75.00%	58.33%
Largest monthly drop	-6.19%	-8.33%
Maximum drawdown	-23.37%	-30.83%
Sharpe ratio	-2.96	-0.58
Semideviation	4.97%	7.58%
Sortino ratio	-5.14	-1.09
Jensen's alpha	-26.32%	-8.51%
Beta	0.26	-0.04
Up capture ratio	-51.37%	0.84%
Down capture ratio	140.71%	27.39%
Omega -0%	9%	81%
Appraisal ratio	-1.84	-0.61
Average α over benchmark	-2.56%	-0.18%
Tracking error	3.07%	5.89%
Information ratio	-83.55%	-3.03%
Sterling ratio	-1.09	-0.27
Treynor measure	-0.97	1.89
M^2 – Modigliani measure	-30.81%	-1.99%
Burke ratio	-2.43	-0.54
Skewness	-30.22%	171.07%
Kurtosis	-55%	675%
Correlation to S&P/TSX	0.582	0.170
R squared	0.099	0.002
Benchmark: MSCI World C$		

TERMS AND CONDITIONS

Inception:	August 3, 2001
Style:	Security Selection
Sub-style:	Long bias
Valuation:	Weekly on Friday
RRSP:	No
Management fee:	2.25%
Performance fee:	20.00%
High-water mark:	Yes
Hurdle rate:	0.00%
NAV:	$92.38
Asset Size (million):	$20.70
Maximum leverage:	150%
Early red'n period:	2 mo.
Early red'n fee:	N/A

PERFORMANCE (as of December 31, 2004)

	1 mo.	3 mo.	6 mo.
Funds	2.11%	2.07%	-2.03%
S&P/TSX	5.25%	6.76%	0.07%
Van Global HF Index	1.50%	4.87%	5.48%

	1 yr.	2 yr.	3 yr.
Funds	-21.57%	-5.78%	-4.24%
S&P/TSX	6.85%	8.58%	-2.18%
Van Global HF Index	7.79%	13.04%	8.40%

Year	Jan	Feb	Mar	Apr	May	Jun	Jul	Aug	Sep	Oct	Nov	Dec	Total
2004	-3.34%	-1.09%	-6.19%	-5.74%	-1.72%	-3.65%	-3.16%	0.09%	-0.98%	-0.27%	0.24%	2.11%	-21.57%
2003	-0.49%	-0.68%	-3.53%	0.74%	4.81%	0.14%	1.69%	5.77%	-0.43%	16.14%	-1.54%	-8.33%	13.19%
2002	1.32%	0.63%	-0.76%	5.24%	-1.21%	0.32%	-1.90%	-1.50%	1.59%	-1.52%	-4.74%	1.79%	-1.07%

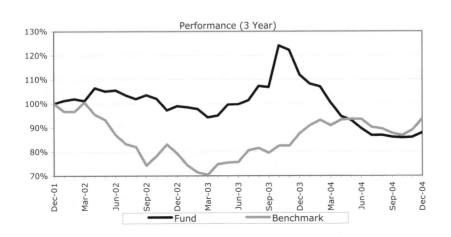

Performance (3 Year)

CI MULTI-MANAGER OPPORTUNITIES FUND

FUND SPONSOR COMPANY

CI Mutual Funds
Tel: 416-364-1145   Toll-Free: 800-268-9374
Fax: 416-364-6299   Web site: www.cifunds.com

PORTFOLIO MANAGER(S)

John Hock, Chief Investment Officer of Altrinsic Global Advisors, LLC
Nandu Narayanan, founder and Chief Investment Officer of Trident Investment Management, LLC

FUND DESCRIPTION

The fundamental investment objective of CI Multi-Manager Opportunities Fund is to achieve long-term capital appreciation.

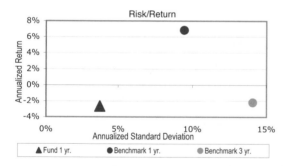

Rating: Not Rated

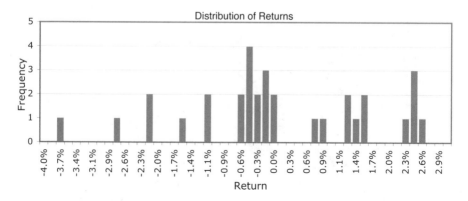

	1 yr.	3 yr.
Annualized rate of return	-2.64%	
Annualized standard deviation	3.71%	
Percentage of negative months	75.00%	
Largest monthly drop	-2.85%	
Maximum drawdown	-5.51%	
Sharpe ratio	-1.79	
Semideviation	3.17%	
Sortino ratio	-2.10	
Jensen's alpha	-7.34%	
Beta	0.24	
Up capture ratio	11.65%	
Down capture ratio	48.60%	
Omega -0%	55%	
Appraisal ratio	-1.68	
Average α over benchmark	-0.80%	
Tracking error	2.15%	
Information ratio	-37.41%	
Sterling ratio	-1.21	
Treynor measure	-0.27	
M² – Modigliani measure	-19.76%	
Burke ratio	-2.16	
Skewness	-94.55%	
Kurtosis	299%	
Correlation to S&P/TSX	0.462	
R squared	0.461	
Benchmark: MSCI World C$		

TERMS AND CONDITIONS

Inception:	April 12, 2002
Style:	Multi Manager
Sub-style:	Sec Sel'n, Long bias
Valuation:	Weekly on Friday
RRSP:	Yes
Management fee:	2.25%
Performance fee:	20.00%
High-water mark:	Yes
Hurdle rate:	0.00%
NAV:	$99.37
Asset Size (million):	$0.30
Maximum leverage:	N/A
Early red'n period:	2 mo.
Early red'n fee:	N/A

PERFORMANCE (as of December 31, 2004)

	1 mo.	3 mo.	6 mo.
Funds	0.61%	1.78%	-1.93%
S&P/TSX	5.25%	6.76%	0.07%
Van Global HF Index	1.50%	4.87%	5.48%

	1 yr.	2 yr.	3 yr.
Funds	-2.64%	3.73%	
S&P/TSX	6.85%	8.58%	-2.18%
Van Global HF Index	.79%	13.04%	8.40%

Year	Jan	Feb	Mar	Apr	May	Jun	Jul	Aug	Sep	Oct	Nov	Dec	Total
2004	-0.21%	1.36%	-0.57%	-0.38%	-0.51%	-0.40%	-2.85%	-0.61%	-0.22%	-0.08%	1.24%	0.61%	-2.64%
2003	-0.45%	-0.25%	-0.61%	2.33%	1.46%	0.85%	2.28%	2.57%	-0.54%	2.43%	-1.21%	1.27%	10.51%
2002					-1.16%	-2.20%	-1.59%	-0.11%	-3.80%	2.42%	1.46%	-2.19%	-7.08%

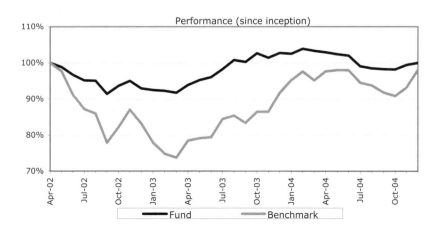

Performance (since inception)

Fund   Benchmark

CI TRIDENT GLOBAL OPPORTUNITIES FUND C$

FUND SPONSOR COMPANY

CI Mutual Funds

Tel: 416-364-1145   Toll-Free: 800-268-9374
Fax: 416-364-6299   Web site: www.cifunds.com

PORTFOLIO MANAGER(S)

Nandu Narayanan, founder and Chief Investment Officer of Trident Investment Management, LLC, has 12 years of investment industry experience. Prior to founding Trident, he worked as an independent consultant on emerging markets to Credit Suisse Asset Management, as well as managing CI's Asian and emerging markets funds. He also worked as Chief Equity and Emerging Market Strategist at hedge fund manager Caxton Corporation, and as an investment analyst at Tiger Management, another hedge fund firm.

FUND DESCRIPTION

The fundamental investment objective of the Fund is to generate superior, risk-adjusted, long-term rates of return through investments in global securities.

Rating:

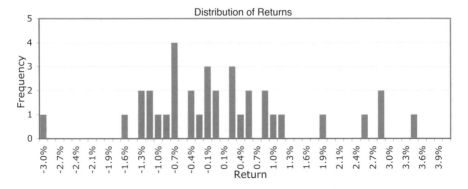

	1 yr.	3 yr.
Annualized rate of return	1.10%	1.62%
Annualized standard deviation	6.69%	5.26%
Percentage of negative months	66.67%	55.56%
Largest monthly drop	-3.15%	-3.15%
Maximum drawdown	-5.83%	-5.83%
Sharpe ratio	-0.43	-0.45
Semideviation	3.40%	2.47%
Sortino ratio	-0.85	-0.96
Jensen's alpha	-2.75%	-2.21%
Beta	-0.05	0.03
Up capture ratio	-3.19%	5.12%
Down capture ratio	-17.62%	-2.28%
Omega -0%	117%	130%
Appraisal ratio	-0.41	-0.42
Average α over benchmark	-0.48%	0.25%
Tracking error	3.47%	4.23%
Information ratio	-13.81%	5.87%
Sterling ratio	-0.50	-0.41
Treynor measure	0.55	-0.85
M² – Modigliani measure	-6.95%	-0.20%
Burke ratio	-0.78	-0.48
Skewness	67.97%	76.72%
Kurtosis	68%	75%
Correlation to S&P/TSX	-0.083	0.102
R squared	0.007	0.006
Benchmark: MSCI World C$		

TERMS AND CONDITIONS

Inception:	February 1, 2001
Style:	Security Selection
Sub-style:	Variable bias
Valuation:	Weekly on Friday
RRSP:	No
Management fee:	2.25%
Performance fee:	20.00%
High-water mark:	Yes
Hurdle rate:	0.00%
NAV:	$110.26
Asset Size (million):	$16.80
Maximum leverage:	150%
Early red'n period:	2 mo.
Early red'n fee:	N/A

PERFORMANCE (as of December 31, 2004)

	1 mo.	3 mo.	6 mo.
Funds	-1.12%	0.39%	-1.48%
S&P/TSX	5.25%	6.76%	0.07%
Van Global HF Index	1.50%	4.87%	5.48%

	1 yr.	2 yr.	3 yr.
Funds	1.10%	3.31%	1.62%
S&P/TSX	6.85%	8.58%	-2.18%
Van Global HF Index	7.79%	13.04%	8.40%

Year	Jan	Feb	Mar	Apr	May	Jun	Jul	Aug	Sep	Oct	Nov	Dec	Total
2004	-0.26%	2.84%	4.02%	-0.54%	-3.15%	-0.15%	-0.83%	-1.23%	0.18%	-0.24%	1.77%	-1.12%	1.10%
2003	-0.75%	-0.05%	-0.52%	-1.35%	0.86%	1.05%	-1.68%	3.35%	2.81%	0.20%	-0.90%	2.56%	5.57%
2002	-0.39%	0.72%	0.37%	0.47%	0.18%	-1.35%	0.48%	-0.14%	-0.74%	0.73%	-0.72%	-1.27%	-1.68%

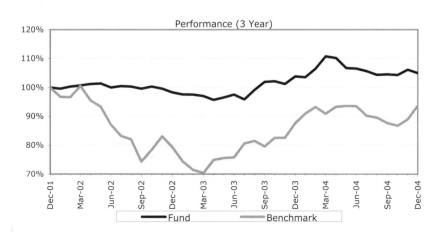

Performance (3 Year)

Fund   Benchmark

DELTAONE ENERGY FUND L.P.

FUND SPONSOR COMPANY
DeltaOne Capital Partners Corp.
Tel: 416-815-1692   Toll-Free: 866-227-2224
Fax: 416-365-3669   Web site: www.deltaonecapital.com

PORTFOLIO MANAGER(S)

DeltaOne Capital Partners

FUND DESCRIPTION

The investment objective of the Fund is to generate absolute returns through the purchase and sale of listed equitites and other securities related to the North American energy sector. The Fund also considers preservation of capital a key tenat in its investment philosophy. The Fund will seek a low correlation to the S&P/TSX Canadian Energy Index. The Fund will employ long and short strategies on the basis of intensive fundamental and quantitative research.

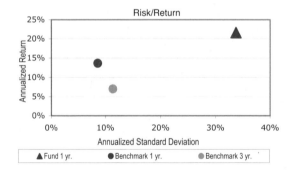

Rating: Not Rated

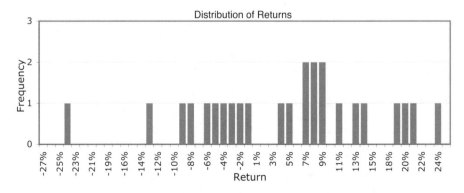

	1 yr.	3 yr.
Annualized rate of return	21.62%	
Annualized standard deviation	33.76%	
Percentage of negative months	41.67%	
Largest monthly drop	-13.32%	
Maximum drawdown	-26.36%	
Sharpe ratio	0.52	
Semideviation	14.21%	
Sortino ratio	1.24	
Jensen's alpha	7.55%	
Beta	1.04	
Up capture ratio	137.47%	
Down capture ratio	100.68%	
Omega -0%	164%	
Appraisal ratio	0.67	
Average α over benchmark	0.97%	
Tracking error	9.33%	
Information ratio	10.44%	
Sterling ratio	0.67	
Treynor measure	0.17	
M^2 – Modigliani measure	-5.18%	
Burke ratio	0.91	
Skewness	-8.23%	
Kurtosis	-90%	
Correlation to S&P/TSX	0.289	
R squared	0.084	
Benchmark: S&P/TSX		

TERMS AND CONDITIONS

Inception:	October 1, 2002
Style:	Security Selection
Sub-style:	L/S Equity
Valuation:	Monthly
RRSP:	No
Management fee:	2.00%
Performance fee:	20.00%
High-water mark:	Yes
Hurdle rate:	2%/Quarter
NAV:	$21.01
Asset Size (million):	$15.00
Maximum leverage:	N/A
Early red'n period:	N/A
Early red'n fee:	N/A

PERFORMANCE (as of December 31, 2004)

	1 mo.	3 mo.	6 mo.
Funds	6.20%	27.86%	29.33%
S&P/TSX	2.40%	6.67%	8.41%
Van Global HF Index	1.50%	4.87%	5.48%

	1 yr.	2 yr.	3 yr.
Funds	21.62%	36.61%	
S&P/TSX	13.66%	19.32%	6.99%
Van Global HF Index	7.79%	13.04%	8.40%

Year	Jan	Feb	Mar	Apr	May	Jun	Jul	Aug	Sep	Oct	Nov	Dec	Total
2004	18.81%	-8.30%	-4.15%	3.36%	-9.80%	-3.41%	7.34%	-13.32%	8.71%	10.81%	8.65%	6.20%	21.62%
2003	17.58%	23.11%	-5.52%	-24.35%	7.81%	20.06%	3.98%	-0.71%	13.46%	-6.65%	6.91%	-1.98%	53.45%
2002												12.60%	12.60%

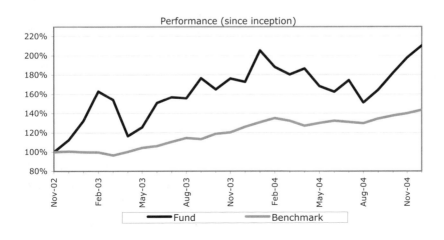

Performance (since inception)

Fund Benchmark

DELTAONE NORTHERN RIVERS FUND L.P.

FUND SPONSOR COMPANY

DeltaOne Capital Partners Corp.

Tel: 416-815-1692   Toll-Free: 866-227-2224

Fax: 416-365-3669   Web site: www.deltaonecapital.com

PORTFOLIO MANAGER(S)

DeltaOne Capital Partners

FUND DESCRIPTION

The Fund's objective is to maximize absolute returns on investments through securities selection and asset allocation, while using hedging activities and asset allocation in an attempt to manage market risk. The Fund will focus on achieving growth of capital through superior securities selection. The Fund will pursue a long-term investment program with the aim of generating capital gains.

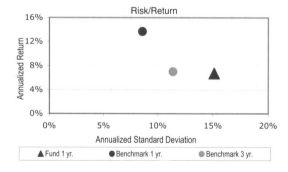

Rating: Not Rated

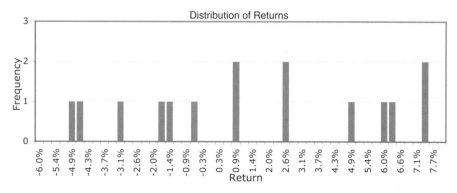

	1 yr.	3 yr.
Annualized rate of return	6.71%	
Annualized standard deviation	15.12%	
Percentage of negative months	50.00%	
Largest monthly drop	-5.09%	
Maximum drawdown	-13.34%	
Sharpe ratio	0.18	
Semideviation	6.17%	
Sortino ratio	0.44	
Jensen's alpha	-6.05%	
Beta	0.91	
Up capture ratio	87.57%	
Down capture ratio	145.86%	
Omega -0%	144%	
Appraisal ratio	-0.67	
Average α over benchmark	-0.47%	
Tracking error	3.61%	
Information ratio	-13.08%	
Sterling ratio	0.20	
Treynor measure	0.03	
M² – Modigliani measure	-8.12%	
Burke ratio	0.34	
Skewness	43.12%	
Kurtosis	-103%	
Correlation to S&P/TSX	0.562	
R squared	0.316	
Benchmark: S&P/TSX		

TERMS AND CONDITIONS

Inception:	September 1, 2003
Style:	Enhanced Equity
Sub-style:	N/A
Valuation:	Monthly
RRSP:	No
Management fee:	2.00%
Performance fee:	20.00%
High-water mark:	Yes
Hurdle rate:	2.00%/Quarter
NAV:	$12.74
Asset Size (million):	N/A
Maximum leverage:	N/A
Early red'n period:	N/A
Early red'n fee:	N/A

PERFORMANCE (as of December 31, 2004)

	1 mo.	3 mo.	6 mo.
Funds	0.82%	7.50%	-0.49%
S&P/TSX	2.40%	6.67%	8.41%
Van Global HF Index	1.50%	4.87%	5.48%

	1 yr.	2 yr.	3 yr.
Funds	6.71%		
S&P/TSX	13.66%	19.32%	6.99%
Van Global HF Index	7.79%	13.04%	8.40%

Year	Jan	Feb	Mar	Apr	May	Jun	Jul	Aug	Sep	Oct	Nov	Dec	Total
2004	5.98%	7.29%	-1.61%	-1.93%	-4.69%	2.54%	-3.18%	-5.09%	0.74%	-0.62%	7.29%	0.82%	6.71%
2003										4.81%	2.35%	6.17%	13.89%
2002													

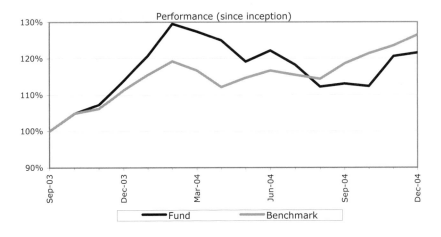

Performance (since inception)

Fund ■ Benchmark

DYNAMIC ALPHA PERFORMANCE FUND

FUND SPONSOR COMPANY

Dynamic Mutual Funds Ltd.

Tel: 416-365-5100   Toll-Free: 866-977-0477

Fax: 416-363-5850   Web site: www.dynamic.ca

PORTFOLIO MANAGER(S)

After joining Dynamic in 1997, **Noah Blackstein** became a founding member of the Dynamic Power Growth team. Prior to joining Dynamic, Noah was an Associate Portfolio Manager at BPI Mutual Funds. Noah has been featured in many well known publications, including the *National Post* and *The Wall Street Journal* and has also been a featured guest on CNBC and other respected financial news programs.

FUND DESCRIPTION

The investment objective of the Fund is to protect capital during a wide range of economic and market environments while earning superior equity or equity-related returns that are not correlated to major stock market indices. The objective is to reduce risk and invest in a diversified portfolio.

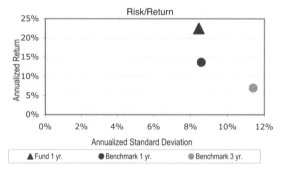

Rating: Not Rated

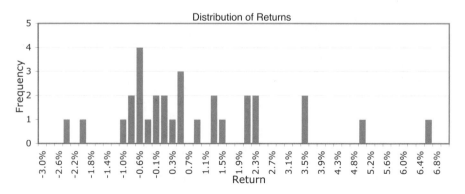

	1 yr.	3 yr.
Annualized rate of return	22.50%	
Annualized standard deviation	8.45%	
Percentage of negative months	25.00%	
Largest monthly drop	-2.01%	
Maximum drawdown	-2.01%	
Sharpe ratio	2.19	
Semideviation	2.99%	
Sortino ratio	6.19	
Jensen's alpha	12.96%	
Beta	0.57	
Up capture ratio	110.69%	
Down capture ratio	32.93%	
Omega -0%	829%	
Appraisal ratio	-2.91	
Average α over benchmark	0.63%	
Tracking error	2.10%	
Information ratio	30.10%	
Sterling ratio	9.22	
Treynor measure	0.32	
M² – Modigliani measure	9.15%	
Burke ratio	8.73	
Skewness	46.87%	
Kurtosis	-10%	
Correlation to S&P/TSX	0.636	
R squared	0.405	
Benchmark: S&P/TSX		

TERMS AND CONDITIONS

Inception:	June 7, 2002
Style:	Security Selection
Sub-style:	Long Bias
Valuation:	Weekly on Friday
RRSP:	No
Management fee:	2.25%
Performance fee:	20.00%
High-water mark:	Yes
Hurdle rate:	No
NAV:	$5.69
Asset Size (million):	$1.13
Maximum leverage:	N/A
Early red'n period:	N/A
Early red'n fee:	N/A

PERFORMANCE (as of December 31, 2004)

	1 mo.	3 mo.	6 mo.
Funds	2.27%	11.22%	11.32%
S&P/TSX	2.40%	6.67%	8.41%
Van Global HF Index	1.50%	4.87%	5.48%

	1 yr.	2 yr.	3 yr.
Funds	22.50%	12.74%	
S&P/TSX	13.66%	19.32%	6.99%
Van Global HF Index	7.79%	13.04%	8.40%

Year	Jan	Feb	Mar	Apr	May	Jun	Jul	Aug	Sep	Oct	Nov	Dec	Total
2004	4.82%	2.30%	0.00%	-0.66%	-0.19%	3.49%	-2.01%	0.09%	2.05%	2.10%	6.52%	2.27%	22.50%
2003	1.15%	-0.82%	0.00%	0.83%	-1.13%	-0.63%	-0.42%	3.37%	1.12%	-0.20%	-0.81%	1.32%	3.75%
2002							0.41%	-0.71%	-0.61%	0.31%	0.31%	-2.54%	-2.83%

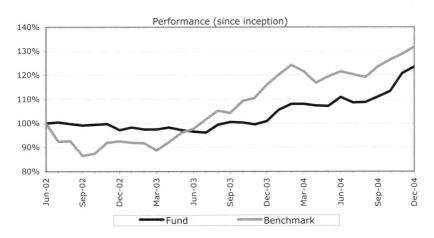

Performance (since inception)

DYNAMIC EQUITY HEDGE FUND

FUND SPONSOR COMPANY
Dynamic Mutual Funds Ltd.
Tel: 416-365-5100   Toll-Free: 866-977-0477
Fax: 416-363-5850   Web site: www.dynamic.ca

PORTFOLIO MANAGER(S)

Orbital Management Team: Brian Chait, B.Compt, CA, RFA; Morton Cohen, MBA, CFA

FUND DESCRIPTION

The investment objective of the Fund is to protect capital during a wide range of economic and market environments while earning superior equity or equity-related returns that are not correlated to major stock market indices. The objective is to reduce risk and invest in a diversified portfolio.

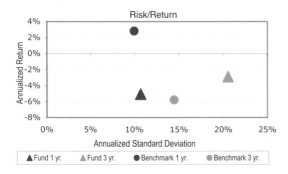

Rating:

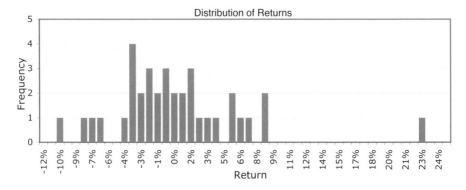

	1 yr.	3 yr.
Annualized rate of return	-5.07%	-2.88%
Annualized standard deviation	10.72%	20.55%
Percentage of negative months	58.33%	58.33%
Largest monthly drop	-4.37%	-10.94%
Maximum drawdown	-14.08%	-27.96%
Sharpe ratio	-0.85	-0.33
Semideviation	5.30%	9.81%
Sortino ratio	-1.71	-0.70
Jensen's alpha	-8.27%	1.11%
Beta	0.67	0.82
Up capture ratio	53.57%	91.61%
Down capture ratio	106.86%	86.88%
Omega -0%	73%	96%
Appraisal ratio	-0.59	0.05
Average α over benchmark	-0.66%	0.33%
Tracking error	2.39%	4.83%
Information ratio	-27.54%	6.82%
Sterling ratio	-0.64	-0.25
Treynor measure	-0.14	-0.08
M² – Modigliani measure	-7.27%	4.93%
Burke ratio	-1.21	-0.33
Skewness	65.09%	151.60%
Kurtosis	11%	510%
Correlation to S&P/TSX	0.315	0.676
R squared	0.466	0.350
Benchmark: S&P 500		

TERMS AND CONDITIONS

Inception:	August 3, 2001
Style:	Security Selection
Sub-style:	Long Bias
Valuation:	Weekly on Friday
RRSP:	No
Management fee:	2.25%
Performance fee:	20.00%
High-water mark:	Yes
Hurdle rate:	0.00%
NAV:	$10.11
Asset Size (million):	$10.10
Maximum leverage:	N/A
Early red'n period:	N/A
Early red'n fee:	N/A

PERFORMANCE (as of December 31, 2004)

	1 mo.	3 mo.	6 mo.
Funds	3.15%	-0.38%	-5.83%
S&P 500	4.80%	4.07%	-3.39%
Van Global HF Index	1.50%	4.87%	5.48%

	1 yr.	2 yr.	3 yr.
Funds	-5.07%	2.11%	-2.88%
S&P 500	2.81%	4.32%	-5.78%
Van Global HF Index	7.79%	13.04%	8.40%

Year	Jan	Feb	Mar	Apr	May	Jun	Jul	Aug	Sep	Oct	Nov	Dec	Total
2004	6.06%	-0.43%	-0.77%	0.95%	-1.71%	-3.05%	-3.95%	-2.99%	1.45%	-4.37%	0.99%	3.15%	-5.07%
2003	-8.85%	-2.62%	-7.62%	2.55%	7.92%	0.33%	8.19%	5.25%	-1.63%	6.14%	-0.55%	2.03%	9.84%
2002	-2.64%	-3.93%	0.64%	-4.61%	-1.42%	-6.83%	-10.94%	5.10%	-2.65%	-3.85%	22.62%	-0.84%	-12.15%

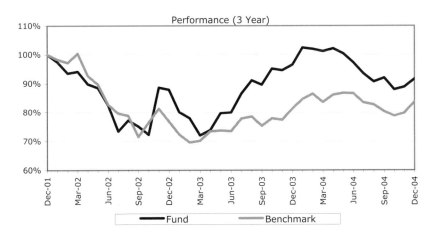

Performance (3 Year)

Fund   Benchmark

DYNAMIC POWER HEDGE FUND

FUND SPONSOR COMPANY
Dynamic Mutual Funds Ltd.
Tel: 416-365-5100   Toll-Free: 866-977-0477
Fax: 416-363-5850   Web site: www.dynamic.ca

PORTFOLIO MANAGER(S)

Veteran manager **Rohit Sehgal** heads up the Power team. Rohit's outstanding track record has been built over numerous markets cycles throughout his three decades in the investment business. As Chief Investment Strategist, he follows world economic and market developments closely, bringing exceptional global expertise to all of his portfolios.

FUND DESCRIPTION

The investment objective of the Fund is to protect capital during a wide range of economic and market environments while earning superior equity or equity-related returns that are not correlated to major stock market indices. The objective is to reduce risk and invest in a diversified portfolio. The Fund will be managed in a flexible manner and will use investment strategies and instruments beyond the reach of a typical mutual fund.

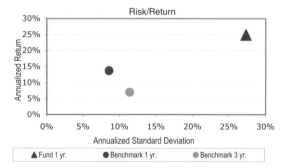

Rating: Not Rated

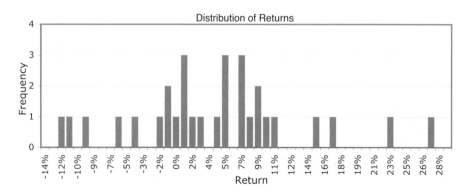

	1 yr.	3 yr.
Annualized rate of return	24.91%	
Annualized standard deviation	27.33%	
Percentage of negative months	33.33%	
Largest monthly drop	-9.93%	
Maximum drawdown	-17.98%	
Sharpe ratio	0.77	
Semideviation	13.94%	
Sortino ratio	1.50	
Jensen's alpha	3.15%	
Beta	1.84	
Up capture ratio	211.07%	
Down capture ratio	208.38%	
Omega -0%	209%	
Appraisal ratio	-0.17	
Average α over benchmark	1.05%	
Tracking error	6.61%	
Information ratio	15.81%	
Sterling ratio	1.16	
Treynor measure	0.11	
M² – Modigliani measure	-3.09%	
Burke ratio	1.59	
Skewness	41.83%	
Kurtosis	-27%	
Correlation to S&P/TSX	0.631	
R squared	0.398	
Benchmark: S&P/TSX		

TERMS AND CONDITIONS

Inception:	June 7, 2002
Style:	Security Selection
Sub-style:	Long Bias
Valuation:	Daily
RRSP:	No
Management fee:	1.25%
Performance fee:	20.00%
High-water mark:	Yes
Hurdle rate:	6.00%
NAV:	$24.54
Asset Size (million):	N/A
Maximum leverage:	N/A
Early red'n period:	N/A
Early red'n fee:	N/A

PERFORMANCE (as of December 31, 2004)

	1 mo.	3 mo.	6 mo.
Funds	0.15%	23.69%	34.79%
S&P/TSX	2.40%	6.67%	8.41%
Van Global HF Index	1.50%	4.87%	5.48%

	1 yr.	2 yr.	3 yr.
Funds	24.91%	58.66%	
S&P/TSX	13.66%	19.32%	6.99%
Van Global HF Index	7.79%	13.04%	8.40%

Year	Jan	Feb	Mar	Apr	May	Jun	Jul	Aug	Sep	Oct	Nov	Dec	Total
2004	2.16%	4.88%	-1.93%	-9.93%	-6.55%	4.78%	-5.17%	0.05%	14.86%	6.56%	15.90%	0.15%	24.91%
2003	6.57%	-1.13%	-12.30%	1.10%	10.51%	3.86%	-0.43%	22.38%	5.10%	26.50%	7.36%	8.08%	101.54%
2002							-11.51%	9.32%	0.32%	-1.47%	8.09%	6.76%	10.35%

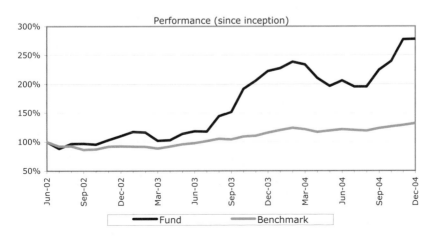

Performance (since inception)

Fund   Benchmark

EPIC LIMITED PARTNERSHIP

FUND SPONSOR COMPANY

Epic Capital Management Inc.

Tel: 416-703-3768   Toll-Free: N/A

Fax: 416-598-0118   Web site: www.epiccapital.ca

PORTFOLIO MANAGER(S)

David Fawcett has over seven years' experience analyzing equity investments. Recently David was an institutionally ranked Research Analyst at Deutsche Bank Securities in the context of a global research team.

Tom Schenkel has over seven years of equity analysis experience with the top-ranked Nesbitt Burns Research Dept. Prior to Epic, Tom was a top-ranked Consumer Products Analyst at BMO Nesbitt Burns.

FUND DESCRIPTION

The Epic Capital Fund is a Canadian long/short hedge fund. The investment objective of the Fund is to generate absolute returns through the purchase and short sale of primarily Canadian listed securities.

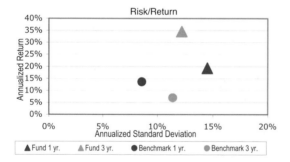

Rating:

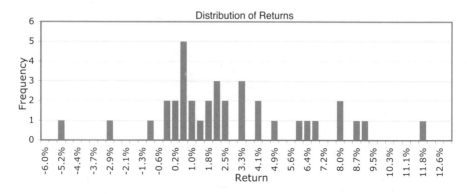

	1 yr.	3 yr.
Annualized rate of return	19.28%	34.53%
Annualized standard deviation	14.50%	12.19%
Percentage of negative months	41.67%	16.67%
Largest monthly drop	-5.26%	-5.26%
Maximum drawdown	-9.90%	-9.90%
Sharpe ratio	1.05	2.50
Semideviation	7.36%	6.18%
Sortino ratio	2.08	4.94
Jensen's alpha	3.78%	28.83%
Beta	1.19	0.57
Up capture ratio	138.34%	167.30%
Down capture ratio	125.24%	-15.24%
Omega -0%	278%	968%
Appraisal ratio	-0.45	-3.88
Average α over benchmark	0.46%	1.94%
Tracking error	2.77%	3.25%
Information ratio	16.51%	59.78%
Sterling ratio	1.54	3.08
Treynor measure	0.13	0.54
M^2 – Modigliani measure	-0.61%	25.54%
Burke ratio	2.42	4.83
Skewness	29.94%	50.59%
Kurtosis	-33%	40%
Correlation to S&P/TSX	0.770	0.546
R squared	0.592	0.298
Benchmark: S&P/TSX		

TERMS AND CONDITIONS

Inception:	November 30, 2001
Style:	Security Selection
Sub-style:	Variable Bias
Valuation:	Monthly
RRSP:	No
Management fee:	2.00%
Performance fee:	20.00%
High-water mark:	Yes
Hurdle rate:	0.00%
NAV:	$3,252
Asset Size (million):	$55.15
Maximum leverage:	N/A
Early red'n period:	24 mo.
Early red'n fee:	N/A

PERFORMANCE (as of December 31, 2004)

	1 mo.	3 mo.	6 mo.
Funds	1.76%	13.18%	12.35%
S&P/TSX	2.40%	6.67%	8.41%
Van Global HF Index	1.50%	4.87%	5.48%

	1 yr.	2 yr.	3 yr.
Funds	19.28%	40.86%	34.53%
S&P/TSX	13.66%	19.32%	6.99%
Van Global HF Index	7.79%	13.04%	8.40%

Year	Jan	Feb	Mar	Apr	May	Jun	Jul	Aug	Sep	Oct	Nov	Dec	Total
2004	7.75%	4.64%	-0.43%	-5.26%	0.29%	-0.47%	-1.09%	-3.26%	3.74%	2.17%	8.87%	1.76%	19.28%
2003	1.95%	0.97%	0.19%	2.05%	0.32%	3.93%	8.42%	6.69%	3.07%	11.49%	7.70%	5.88%	66.34%
2002	3.28%	1.17%	0.78%	1.65%	2.32%	0.22%	-0.13%	0.34%	0.42%	3.06%	1.42%	6.28%	22.70%

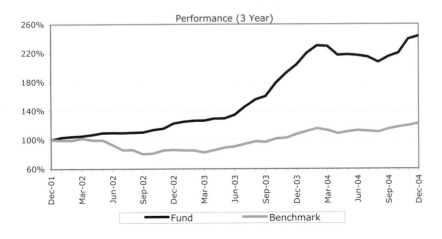

Performance (3 Year)

FULL CYCLE ENERGY LIMITED PARTNERSHIP I

FUND SPONSOR COMPANY

Full Cycle Energy Investment Mgmt. Ltd.

Tel: 416-850-0193   Toll-Free: N/A

Fax: 416-850-0374   Web site: www.fcenergy.com

PORTFOLIO MANAGER(S)

Henry Cohen has been an energy analyst for close to 25 years, and has also worked in Investment Banking, Portfolio Management, Research Management and Retail brokerage. He has been ranked in the top decile by various independent surveys for much of his career. Henry's specialty lies in: 1) energy business cycles; 2) corporate strategies and 3) valuation. Henry is a graduate of McGill University and holds the Chartered Financial Analyst (CFA) and the Derivative Market Specialist (DMS) designations.

FUND DESCRIPTION

The Fund's investment objective will be to generate above average long-term capital appreciation in energy investments through the full business cycle, with a focus on rigorous risk management.

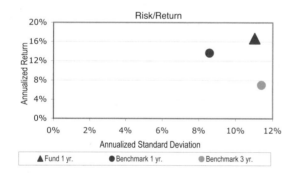

Rating: Not Rated

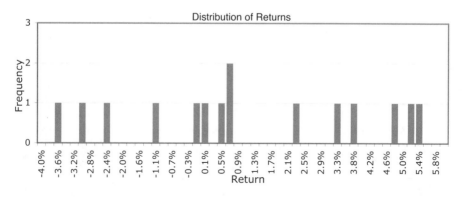

	1 yr.	3 yr.
Annualized rate of return	16.71%	
Annualized standard deviation	11.02%	
Percentage of negative months	25.00%	
Largest monthly drop	-3.71%	
Maximum drawdown	-6.62%	
Sharpe ratio	1.15	
Semideviation	6.92%	
Sortino ratio	1.84	
Jensen's alpha	5.67%	
Beta	0.73	
Up capture ratio	99.87%	
Down capture ratio	67.77%	
Omega -0%	274%	
Appraisal ratio	-4.86	
Average α over benchmark	0.24%	
Tracking error	2.55%	
Information ratio	9.49%	
Sterling ratio	1.92	
Treynor measure	0.17	
M² – Modigliani measure	0.25%	
Burke ratio	2.34	
Skewness	-36.23%	
Kurtosis	-122%	
Correlation to S&P/TSX	0.620	
R squared	0.384	
Benchmark: S&P/TSX		

TERMS AND CONDITIONS

Inception:	September 1, 2003
Style:	Security Selection
Sub-style:	N/A
Valuation:	Monthly
RRSP:	No
Management fee:	2.00%
Performance fee:	20.00%
High-water mark:	Yes
Hurdle rate:	N/A
NAV:	$109.41
Asset Size (million):	N/A
Maximum leverage:	N/A
Early red'n period:	N/A
Early red'n fee:	6.00%

PERFORMANCE (as of December 31, 2004)

	1 mo.	3 mo.	6 mo.
Funds	5.11%	10.58%	10.78%
S&P/TSX	2.40%	6.67%	8.41%
Van Global HF Index	1.50%	4.87%	5.48%

	1 yr.	2 yr.	3 yr.
Funds	16.71%		
S&P/TSX	13.66%	19.32%	6.99%
Van Global HF Index	7.79%	13.04%	8.40%

Year	Jan	Feb	Mar	Apr	May	Jun	Jul	Aug	Sep	Oct	Nov	Dec	Total
2004	3.63%	3.16%	0.33%	-3.71%	-3.02%	5.19%	-2.56%	0.64%	2.17%	0.49%	4.68%	5.11%	16.71%
2003										0.06%	-1.21%	-0.32%	-1.47%
2002													

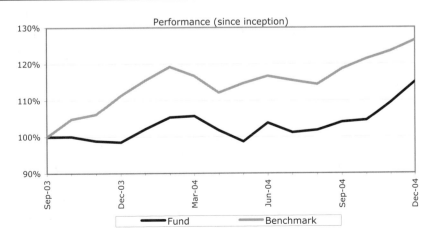

Performance (since inception)

FG LIMITED PARTNERSHIP

FUND SPONSOR COMPANY
Formula Growth Limited Partnership
Tel: 514-288-5136   Toll-Free: N/A
Fax: 514-844-4561   Web site: www.formulagrowth.ca

PORTFOLIO MANAGER(S)

Kimberley Holden, Randall W. Kelly, John Liddy, Anthony Staples

FUND DESCRIPTION

The investment objective of the Fund is to obtain long-term capital appreciation.

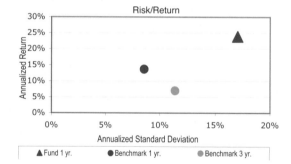

Rating: Not Rated

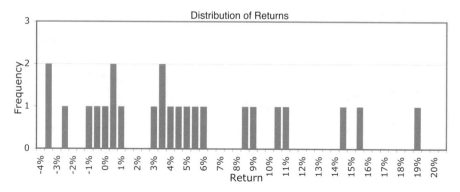

	1 yr.	3 yr.
Annualized rate of return	23.85%	
Annualized standard deviation	17.02%	
Percentage of negative months	41.67%	
Largest monthly drop	-3.95%	
Maximum drawdown	-9.04%	
Sharpe ratio	1.17	
Semideviation	6.64%	
Sortino ratio	2.99	
Jensen's alpha	12.10%	
Beta	0.80	
Up capture ratio	132.27%	
Down capture ratio	67.73%	
Omega -0%	321%	
Appraisal ratio	-5.74	
Average α over benchmark	0.80%	
Tracking error	4.42%	
Information ratio	18.18%	
Sterling ratio	2.20	
Treynor measure	0.25	
M² – Modigliani measure	0.36%	
Burke ratio	3.42	
Skewness	115.13%	
Kurtosis	188%	
Correlation to S&P/TSX	0.442	
R squared	0.195	
Benchmark: S&P/TSX		

TERMS AND CONDITIONS

Inception:	December 31, 2002
Style:	N/A
Sub-style:	N/A
Valuation:	Monthly
RRSP:	No
Management fee:	N/A
Performance fee:	N/A
High-water mark:	N/A
Hurdle rate:	N/A
NAV:	$260.57
Asset Size (million):	N/A
Maximum leverage:	N/A
Early red'n period:	N/A
Early red'n fee:	N/A

PERFORMANCE (as of December 31, 2004)

	1 mo.	3 mo.	6 mo.
Funds	5.07%	5.62%	0.02%
S&P/TSX	2.40%	6.67%	8.41%
Van Global HF Index	1.50%	4.87%	5.48%

	1 yr.	2 yr.	3 yr.
Funds	23.85%	63.05%	
S&P/TSX	13.66%	19.32%	6.99%
Van Global HF Index	7.79%	13.04%	8.40%

Year	Jan	Feb	Mar	Apr	May	Jun	Jul	Aug	Sep	Oct	Nov	Dec	Total
2004	13.65%	0.16%	-1.03%	0.88%	5.52%	3.25%	-3.92%	-1.24%	-0.20%	-3.95%	4.66%	5.07%	23.85%
2003	0.12%	-2.59%	8.56%	15.06%		8.03%	10.22%	18.13%	4.25%	3.73%	9.74%	3.00%	2.49%	114.66%
2002													

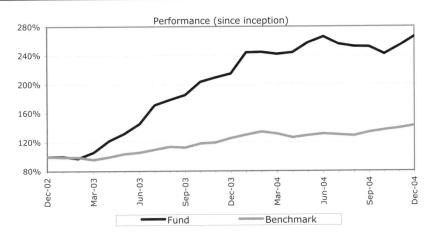

Performance (since inception)

THE FRIEDBERG CURRENCY FUND

FUND SPONSOR COMPANY
Friedberg Mercantile Group Ltd.
Tel: 416-364-1171   Toll-Free: 800-346-7761
Fax: 416-364-0572   Web site: www.friedberg.ca

PORTFOLIO MANAGER(S)

Albert D. Friedberg — Both the Trading Manager and FMG were founded by Mr. Friedberg, a recognized expert on foreign currencies and commodities, who was born in Lyon, France, raised in Uruguay, and educated at Johns Hopkins University and Columbia University, where he received an MBA in International Banking. Mr. Friedberg served as Chairman of the Toronto Futures Exchange from March, 1985 to June, 1988. Mr. Friedberg and his family indirectly beneficially own a controlling interest in the Trading Manager.

FUND DESCRIPTION

The investment objective of the Partnership is to achieve substantial gains in the long term through speculative trading of currency futures instruments under the management of the Trading Manager.

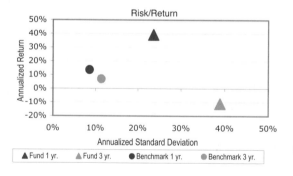

Rating:

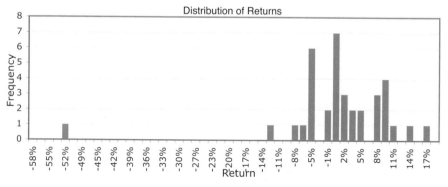

	1 yr.	3 yr.
Annualized rate of return	39.18%	-11.02%
Annualized standard deviation	23.63%	38.92%
Percentage of negative months	50.00%	52.78%
Largest monthly drop	-6.10%	-53.16%
Maximum drawdown	-11.24%	-55.33%
Sharpe ratio	1.49	-0.39
Semideviation	8.25%	40.95%
Sortino ratio	4.27	-0.37
Jensen's alpha	23.64%	-16.98%
Beta	1.19	0.65
Up capture ratio	198.27%	78.64%
Down capture ratio	60.63%	179.00%
Omega -0%	394%	96%
Appraisal ratio	-1.02	-0.37
Average α over benchmark	1.89%	-0.75%
Tracking error	6.05%	11.07%
Information ratio	31.29%	-6.75%
Sterling ratio	3.13	-0.27
Treynor measure	0.29	-0.23
M² – Modigliani measure	3.13%	-7.39%
Burke ratio	5.11	-0.26
Skewness	88.11%	-297.26%
Kurtosis	4%	1403%
Correlation to S&P/TSX	0.474	0.197
R squared	0.225	0.039
Benchmark: S&P/TSX		

TERMS AND CONDITIONS

Inception:	January 3, 1995
Style:	Directional Trading
Sub-style:	N/A
Valuation:	Daily
RRSP:	No
Management fee:	N/A
Performance fee:	N/A
High-water mark:	Yes
Hurdle rate:	0.00%
NAV:	$9.98
Asset Size (million):	$10.57
Maximum leverage:	N/A
Early red'n period:	24 mo.
Early red'n fee:	N/A

PERFORMANCE (as of December 31, 2004)

	1 mo.	3 mo.	6 mo.
Funds	9.78%	18.38%	11.06%
S&P/TSX	2.40%	6.67%	8.41%
Van Global HF Index	1.50%	4.87%	5.48%

	1 yr.	2 yr.	3 yr.
Funds	39.18%	18.38%	-11.02%
S&P/TSX	13.66%	19.32%	6.99%
Van Global HF Index	7.79%	13.04%	8.40%

Year	Jan	Feb	Mar	Apr	May	Jun	Jul	Aug	Sep	Oct	Nov	Dec	Total
2004	17.30%	9.12%	1.95%	-1.01%	-2.52%	-0.47%	0.56%	-6.10%	-0.64%	-1.50%	9.47%	9.78%	39.18%
2003	7.34%	1.56%	-5.54%	9.02%	7.67%	-0.60%	-4.91%	4.26%	-13.17%	4.76%	-6.16%	-0.96%	0.69%
2002	-53.16%	0.94%	-5.04%	-0.50%	8.75%	13.81%	-7.94%	-0.23%	-4.88%	-5.43%	2.81%	7.03%	-49.74%

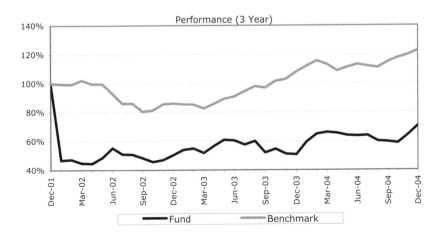

Performance (3 Year)

FRIEDBERG EQUITY-HEDGE FUND US$

FUND SPONSOR COMPANY
Friedberg Mercantile Group Ltd.
Tel: 416-364-1171   Toll-Free: 800-346-7761
Fax: 416-364-0572   Web site: www.friedberg.ca

PORTFOLIO MANAGER(S)

Albert D. Friedberg — Both the Trading Manager and FMG were founded by Mr. Friedberg, a recognized expert on foreign currencies and commodities, who was born in Lyon, France, raised in Uruguay, and educated at Johns Hopkins University and Columbia University, where he received an MBA in International Banking. Mr. Friedberg served as Chairman of the Toronto Futures Exchange from March, 1985 to June, 1988. Mr. Friedberg and his family indirectly beneficially own a controlling interest in the Trading Manager.

FUND DESCRIPTION

The investment objective of the Equity-Hedge Fund is to achieve capital appreciation.

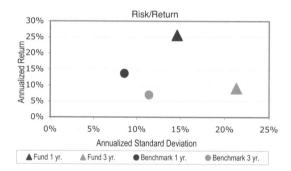

Rating:

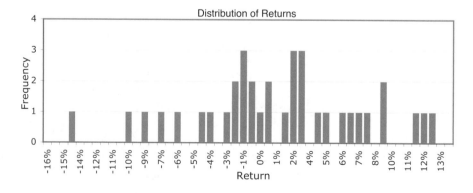

	1 yr.	3 yr.
Annualized rate of return	25.62%	9.07%
Annualized standard deviation	14.63%	21.33%
Percentage of negative months	33.33%	47.22%
Largest monthly drop	-4.56%	-14.19%
Maximum drawdown	-7.20%	-24.75%
Sharpe ratio	1.48	0.24
Semideviation	5.40%	13.98%
Sortino ratio	4.00	0.36
Jensen's alpha	12.97%	5.83%
Beta	0.90	-0.25
Up capture ratio	119.07%	5.09%
Down capture ratio	20.56%	-78.31%
Omega -0%	367%	147%
Appraisal ratio	-1.56	0.25
Average α over benchmark	0.90%	0.29%
Tracking error	3.46%	7.37%
Information ratio	25.94%	3.97%
Sterling ratio	3.00	0.20
Treynor measure	0.24	-0.20
M^2 – Modigliani measure	3.04%	-0.28%
Burke ratio	4.13	0.22
Skewness	86.03%	-21.51%
Kurtosis	164%	2%
Correlation to S&P/TSX	0.574	-0.139
R squared	0.329	0.019
Benchmark: S&P/TSX		

TERMS AND CONDITIONS

Inception:	January 5, 1998
Style:	Security Selection
Sub-style:	N/A
Valuation:	Daily
RRSP:	No
Management fee:	1.50%
Performance fee:	20.00%
High-water mark:	Yes
Hurdle rate:	0.00%
NAV:	$20.62
Asset Size (million):	$6.71
Maximum leverage:	N/A
Early red'n period:	N/A
Early red'n fee:	N/A

PERFORMANCE (as of December 31, 2004)

	1 mo.	3 mo.	6 mo.
Funds	-1.64%	7.33%	14.73%
S&P/TSX	2.40%	6.67%	8.41%
Van Global HF Index	1.50%	4.87%	5.48%

	1 yr.	2 yr.	3 yr.
Funds	25.62%	13.95%	9.07%
S&P/TSX	13.66%	19.32%	6.99%
Van Global HF Index	7.79%	13.04%	8.40%

Year	Jan	Feb	Mar	Apr	May	Jun	Jul	Aug	Sep	Oct	Nov	Dec	Total
2004	11.64%	2.89%	-1.19%	-4.56%	-1.59%	2.72%	2.19%	2.12%	2.43%	2.25%	6.71%	-1.64%	25.62%
2003	-1.67%	-4.20%	4.53%	-10.01%	6.31%	-2.06%	-2.55%	1.49%	8.96%	-0.94%	12.29%	-6.55%	3.36%
2002	0.39%	3.62%	-0.19%	7.49%	-0.08%	5.53%	-7.72%	-2.39%	8.58%	-14.19%	-8.94%	11.12%	-0.07%

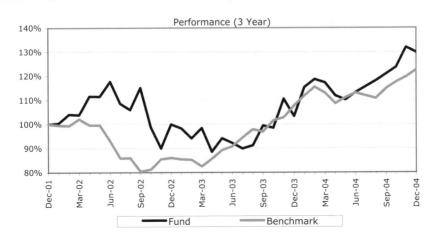

FRIEDBERG FUTURES FUND

FUND SPONSOR COMPANY

Friedberg Mercantile Group Ltd.
Tel: 416-364-1171   Toll-Free: 800-346-7761
Fax: 416-364-0572   Web site: www.friedberg.ca

PORTFOLIO MANAGER(S)

Albert D. Friedberg—Both the Trading Manager and FMG were founded by Mr. Friedberg, a recognized expert on foreign currencies and commodities, who was born in Lyon, France, raised in Uruguay, and educated at Johns Hopkins University and Columbia University, where he received an MBA in International Banking. Mr. Friedberg served as Chairman of the Toronto Futures Exchange from March, 1985 to June, 1988. Mr. Friedberg and his family indirectly beneficially own a controlling interest in the Trading Manager.

FUND DESCRIPTION

The investment objective of the Partnership is to achieve substantial gains through speculative trading in commodity futures investment and currency futures instruments. Commodity futures instruments include exchange traded commodity, interest rate, and stock index contracts. Currency Futures Instruments include exchange traded futures and options contracts and interbank forward and options contracts on any traded currency.

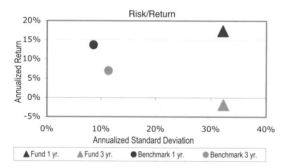

Rating: 🦔

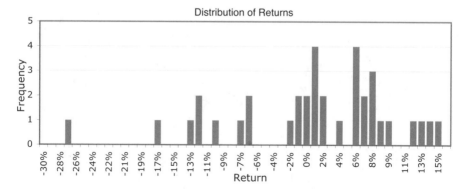

	1 yr.	3 yr.
Annualized rate of return	17.37%	-1.87%
Annualized standard deviation	32.18%	32.27%
Percentage of negative months	33.33%	38.89%
Largest monthly drop	-17.14%	-27.43%
Maximum drawdown	-29.51%	-31.82%
Sharpe ratio	0.42	-0.18
Semideviation	28.25%	27.05%
Sortino ratio	0.47	-0.22
Jensen's alpha	-2.51%	-6.47%
Beta	1.64	0.20
Up capture ratio	118.15%	11.25%
Down capture ratio	101.81%	41.84%
Omega -0%	165%	109%
Appraisal ratio	-0.69	-0.20
Average α over benchmark	0.65%	-0.32%
Tracking error	8.39%	9.65%
Information ratio	7.80%	-3.37%
Sterling ratio	0.45	-0.18
Treynor measure	0.08	-0.29
M² – Modigliani measure	-6.09%	-5.07%
Burke ratio	0.61	-0.14
Skewness	-97.10%	-93.59%
Kurtosis	59%	95%
Correlation to S&P/TSX	0.479	0.073
R squared	0.229	0.005
Benchmark: S&P/TSX		

TERMS AND CONDITIONS

Inception:	May 11, 1998
Style:	Directional Trading
Sub-style:	N/A
Valuation:	Daily
RRSP:	No
Management fee:	0.00%
Performance fee:	N/A
High-water mark:	N/A
Hurdle rate:	N/A
NAV:	$6.96
Asset Size (million):	$0.51
Maximum leverage:	N/A
Early red'n period:	N/A
Early red'n fee:	N/A

PERFORMANCE (as of December 31, 2004)

	1 mo.	3 mo.	6 mo.
Funds	1.47%	13.69%	22.98%
S&P/TSX	2.40%	6.67%	8.41%
Van Global HF Index	1.50%	4.87%	5.48%

	1 yr.	2 yr.	3 yr.
Funds	17.37%	1.02%	-1.87%
S&P/TSX	13.66%	19.32%	6.99%
Van Global HF Index	7.79%	13.04%	8.40%

Year	Jan	Feb	Mar	Apr	May	Jun	Jul	Aug	Sep	Oct	Nov	Dec	Total
2004	12.86%	13.23%	5.95%	-13.63%	-17.14%	-1.51%	0.64%	-0.01%	7.49%	5.08%	6.63%	1.47%	17.37%
2003	9.29%	0.23%	-13.08%	0.72%	5.30%	-7.27%	12.96%	8.35%	5.43%	-0.51%	-7.70%	1.69%	-13.05%
2002	-27.43%	0.90%	-6.88%	3.55%	14.23%	4.95%	-2.63%	6.75%	6.05%	-10.37%	-1.30%	12.17%	-7.41%

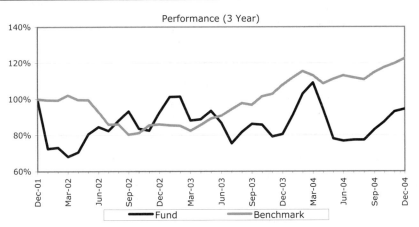

Performance (3 Year)

FRIEDBERG GLOBAL-MACRO HEDGE FUND (US$)

FUND SPONSOR COMPANY
Friedberg Mercantile Group Ltd.
Tel: 416-364-1171   Toll-Free: 800-346-7761
Fax: 416-364-0572   Web site: www.friedberg.ca

PORTFOLIO MANAGER(S)

Albert D. Friedberg — Both the Trading Manager and FMG were founded by Mr. Friedberg, a recognized expert on foreign currencies and commodities, who was born in Lyon, France, raised in Uruguay, and educated at Johns Hopkins University and Columbia University, where he received an MBA in International Banking. Mr. Friedberg served as Chairman of the Toronto Futures Exchange from March, 1985 to June, 1988. Mr. Friedberg and his family indirectly beneficially own a controlling interest in the Trading Manager.

FUND DESCRIPTION

The Fund is a fund of funds that allocates its assets among various funds (each an underlying fund) that employ a variety of strategies. The Fund's investments include, but are not limited to, funds managed by Friedberg Mercantile or companies related to it, or directly invested assets that follow the same trading strategies as the funds.

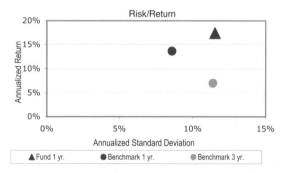

Rating: Not Rated

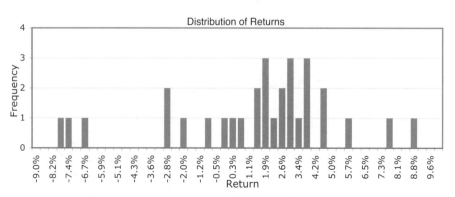

	1 yr.	3 yr.
Annualized rate of return	17.42%	
Annualized standard deviation	11.53%	
Percentage of negative months	16.67%	
Largest monthly drop	-7.93%	
Maximum drawdown	-8.89%	
Sharpe ratio	1.16	
Semideviation	15.64%	
Sortino ratio	0.86	
Jensen's alpha	13.32%	
Beta	0.04	
Up capture ratio	33.36%	
Down capture ratio	-111.75%	
Omega -0%	287%	
Appraisal ratio	1.22	
Average α over benchmark	0.81%	
Tracking error	4.24%	
Information ratio	19.18%	
Sterling ratio	1.51	
Treynor measure	3.71	
M² – Modigliani measure	8.16%	
Burke ratio	1.68	
Skewness	-223.28%	
Kurtosis	599%	
Correlation to S&P/TSX	0.661	
R squared	0.001	
Benchmark: MSCI World C$		

TERMS AND CONDITIONS

Inception:	June 1, 2002
Style:	Fund of Hedge Funds
Sub-style:	N/A
Valuation:	Daily
RRSP:	No
Management fee:	0.75%
Performance fee:	N/A
High-water mark:	No
Hurdle rate:	No
NAV:	$14.38
Asset Size (million):	$12.53
Maximum leverage:	N/A
Early red'n period:	N/A
Early red'n fee:	N/A

PERFORMANCE (as of December 31, 2004)

	1 mo.	3 mo.	6 mo.
Funds	3.02%	10.21%	15.62%
MSCI World C$	5.25%	6.76%	0.07%
Van Global HF Index	1.50%	4.87%	5.48%

	1 yr.	2 yr.	3 yr.
Funds	17.42%	16.00%	
MSCI World C$	6.85%	8.58%	-2.18%
Van Global HF Index	7.79%	13.04%	8.40%

Year	Jan	Feb	Mar	Apr	May	Jun	Jul	Aug	Sep	Oct	Nov	Dec	Total
2004	4.46%	3.73%	2.29%	-7.93%	-1.05%	0.58%	1.52%	1.42%	1.89%	2.58%	4.29%	3.02%	17.42%
2003	3.61%	2.94%	-2.97%	0.19%	8.70%	-2.90%	-7.51%	2.66%	5.36%	1.50%	1.68%	1.43%	14.60%
2002							-2.13%	3.42%	2.70%	-6.96%	-0.29%	7.38%	3.54%

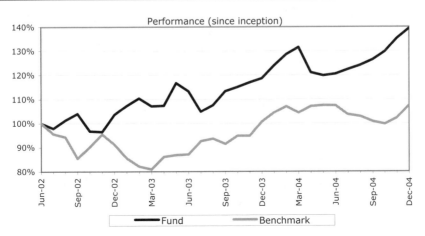

Performance (since inception)

— Fund   — Benchmark

FRONT STREET CANADIAN HEDGE FUND

FUND SPONSOR COMPANY
Front Street Investment Management Inc.
Tel: 416-364-1990   Toll-Free: 800-513-2832
Fax: 416-364-8893   Web site: www.frontstreetcapital.com

PORTFOLIO MANAGER(S)

Frank Mersch has more than 24 years' experience in the investment industry, including 11 years as an investment manager with Altamira Management Limited, where he was a shareholder, director, and Vice President. During that period, he was instrumental in building an organization with over 300 employees and approximately $17 billion of assets under management. At Altamira, Mr. Mersch managed and marketed private wealth, mutual funds, and pension funds, and frequently made appearances on *Wall Street Week*.

FUND DESCRIPTION

The Fund's investment objective is to provide holders of units with long-term capital growth primarily through the selection and strategic trading of both long and short positions in equity, debt, and derivative securities. The Fund's portfolio consists primarily of investments that generate capital gains, but also includes investments that generate income.

Rating: Not Rated

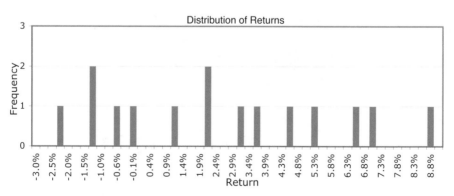

	1 yr.	3 yr.
Annualized rate of return	20.63%	
Annualized standard deviation	10.09%	
Percentage of negative months	41.67%	
Largest monthly drop	-2.46%	
Maximum drawdown	-3.72%	
Sharpe ratio	1.65	
Semideviation	4.17%	
Sortino ratio	3.99	
Jensen's alpha	9.99%	
Beta	0.69	
Up capture ratio	107.43%	
Down capture ratio	44.55%	
Omega -0%	416%	
Appraisal ratio	-2.44	
Average α over benchmark	0.51%	
Tracking error	2.32%	
Information ratio	22.06%	
Sterling ratio	4.48	
Treynor measure	0.24	
M² – Modigliani measure	4.51%	
Burke ratio	5.14	
Skewness	22.21%	
Kurtosis	-125%	
Correlation to S&P/TSX	0.639	
R squared	0.408	
Benchmark: S&P/TSX		

TERMS AND CONDITIONS

Inception:	September 30, 2003
Style:	Security selection
Sub-style:	Long bias
Valuation:	Weekly on Thursday
RRSP:	Yes
Management fee:	2.00%
Performance fee:	20.00%
High-water mark:	No
Hurdle rate:	6.00%
NAV:	$13.92
Asset Size (million):	$174.30
Maximum leverage:	N/A
Early red'n period:	N/A
Early red'n fee:	N/A

PERFORMANCE (as of December 31, 2004)

	1 mo.	3 mo.	6 mo.
Funds	3.41%	7.14%	7.79%
S&P/TSX	2.40%	6.67%	8.41%
Van Global HF Index	1.50%	4.87%	5.48%

	1 yr.	2 yr.	3 yr.
Funds	20.63%		
S&P/TSX	13.66%	19.32%	6.99%
Van Global HF Index	7.79%	13.04%	8.40%

Year	Jan	Feb	Mar	Apr	May	Jun	Jul	Aug	Sep	Oct	Nov	Dec	Total
2004	6.46%	3.03%	1.04%	-0.77%	-0.15%	1.92%	-2.46%	-1.29%	4.49%	-1.47%	5.16%	3.41%	20.63%
2003										6.81%	2.07%	8.62%	18.41%
2002													

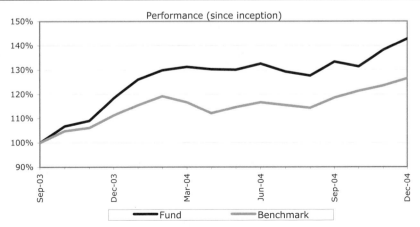

Performance (since inception)

Fund   Benchmark

FRONT STREET PERFORMANCE FUND

FUND SPONSOR COMPANY

Front Street Investment Management Inc.

Tel: 416-364-1990   Toll-Free: 800-513-2832

Fax: 416-364-8893   Web site: www.frontstreetcapital.com

PORTFOLIO MANAGER(S)

Frank Mersch has more than 24 years' experience in the investment industry, including 11 years as an investment manager with Altamira Management Limited where he was a shareholder, director, and Vice President. During that period, he was instrumental in building an organization with over 300 employees and approximately $17 billion of assets under management. At Altamira, Mr. Mersch managed and marketed private wealth, mutual funds, pension funds, and frequently made appearances on *Wall Street Week*.

FUND DESCRIPTION

The Fund's investment objective is to provide holders of units with long-term capital growth through selection and management of long and short positions in equity and debt securities and through strategic trading.

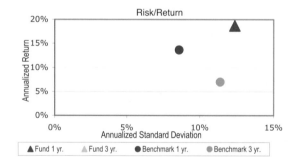

Rating: Not Rated

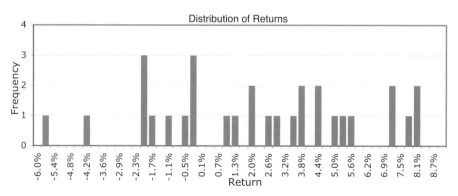

	1 yr.	3 yr.
Annualized rate of return	18.65%	
Annualized standard deviation	12.37%	
Percentage of negative months	41.67%	
Largest monthly drop	-4.37%	
Maximum drawdown	-6.42%	
Sharpe ratio	1.18	
Semideviation	6.28%	
Sortino ratio	2.33	
Jensen's alpha	5.52%	
Beta	0.95	
Up capture ratio	122.97%	
Down capture ratio	99.25%	
Omega -0%	280%	
Appraisal ratio	-1.05	
Average α over benchmark	0.39%	
Tracking error	2.49%	
Information ratio	15.75%	
Sterling ratio	2.28	
Treynor measure	0.15	
M² – Modigliani measure	0.52%	
Burke ratio	2.71	
Skewness	-4.01%	
Kurtosis	-114%	
Correlation to S&P/TSX	0.717	
R squared	0.514	
Benchmark: S&P/TSX		

TERMS AND CONDITIONS

Inception:	April 23, 2002
Style:	Security Selection
Sub-style:	Long Bias
Valuation:	Weekly on Thursday
RRSP:	Yes
Management fee:	2.00%
Performance fee:	20.00%
High-water mark:	No
Hurdle rate:	6.00%
NAV:	$28.95
Asset Size (million):	$59.00
Maximum leverage:	N/A
Early red'n period:	N/A
Early red'n fee:	N/A

PERFORMANCE (as of December 31, 2004)

	1 mo.	3 mo.	6 mo.
Funds	3.45%	6.13%	4.88%
S&P/TSX	2.40%	6.67%	8.41%
Van Global HF Index	1.50%	4.87%	5.48%

	1 yr.	2 yr.	3 yr.
Funds	18.65%	28.35%	
S&P/TSX	13.66%	19.32%	6.99%
Van Global HF Index	7.79%	13.04%	8.40%

Year	Jan	Feb	Mar	Apr	May	Jun	Jul	Aug	Sep	Oct	Nov	Dec	Total
2004	7.03%	4.24%	-0.21%	-1.18%	0.90%	1.92%	-4.37%	-2.15%	5.59%	-2.06%	4.75%	3.45%	18.65%
2003	-2.18%	1.14%	-1.72%	-0.44%	3.70%	2.57%	8.07%	6.93%	1.72%	7.50%	2.86%	3.74%	38.83%
2002							-5.85%	-0.79%	-0.22%	7.92%	5.27%	4.31%	10.45%

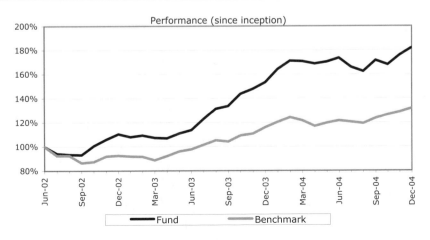

Performance (since inception)

GOODWOOD FUND CLASS A

FUND SPONSOR COMPANY
Goodwood Inc.
Tel: 416-203-2022   Toll-Free: 866-681-4393
Fax: 416 203-0732   Web site: www.goodwoodfunds.com

PORTFOLIO MANAGER(S)

The Fund is advised by **Peter Puccetti**, CFA and **Cam MacDonald**, CFA of Goodwood Inc, which is an asset management company based in Toronto, Canada. The Manager selects long and short positions on the basis of a "bottom up" security-specific approach. The portfolio is relatively concentrated and normally does not exceed 25 to 35 positions.

FUND DESCRIPTION

The Goodwood Fund is an open-ended long/short Canadian equity hedge fund. The objective is to maximize total return and reduce market risk through the purchase and short sale of primarily Canadian exchange listed securities. The portfolio has exhibited substantial returns with little correlation to the overall equity market direction.

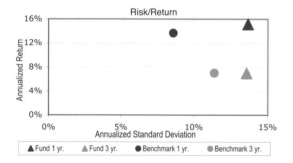

Rating:

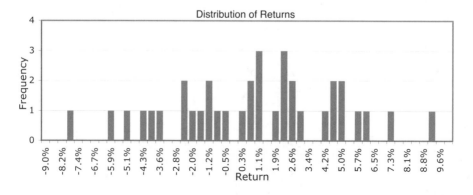

	1 yr.	3 yr.
Annualized rate of return	15.16%	6.97%
Annualized standard deviation	13.66%	13.56%
Percentage of negative months	25.00%	38.89%
Largest monthly drop	-6.08%	-8.07%
Maximum drawdown	-7.72%	-26.08%
Sharpe ratio	0.82	0.22
Semideviation	8.64%	8.35%
Sortino ratio	1.29	0.36
Jensen's alpha	8.75%	0.89%
Beta	0.25	0.69
Up capture ratio	70.78%	72.11%
Down capture ratio	14.25%	69.75%
Omega -0%	250%	150%
Appraisal ratio	0.88	0.10
Average α over benchmark	0.15%	0.02%
Tracking error	4.29%	3.27%
Information ratio	3.55%	0.59%
Sterling ratio	1.45	0.11
Treynor measure	0.45	0.04
M² – Modigliani measure	-2.65%	-0.50%
Burke ratio	1.65	0.20
Skewness	22.58%	-10.03%
Kurtosis	76%	-29%
Correlation to S&P/TSX	0.171	0.599
R squared	0.029	0.359
Benchmark: S&P/TSX		

TERMS AND CONDITIONS

Inception:	October 25, 1996
Style:	Security Selection
Sub-style:	Long Bias
Valuation:	Weekly on Friday
RRSP:	Yes
Management fee:	1.90%
Performance fee:	20.00%
High-water mark:	Yes
Hurdle rate:	10.00%
NAV:	$25.30
Asset Size (million):	$52.92
Maximum leverage:	100%
Early red'n period:	N/A
Early red'n fee:	N/A

PERFORMANCE (as of December 31, 2004)

	1 mo.	3 mo.	6 mo.
Funds	9.01%	20.49%	18.77%
S&P/TSX	2.40%	6.67%	8.41%
Van Global HF Index	1.50%	4.87%	5.48%

	1 yr.	2 yr.	3 yr.
Funds	15.16%	22.58%	6.97%
S&P/TSX	13.66%	19.32%	6.99%
Van Global HF Index	7.79%	13.04%	8.40%

Year	Jan	Feb	Mar	Apr	May	Jun	Jul	Aug	Sep	Oct	Nov	Dec	Total
2004	0.53%	1.95%	-1.29%	2.00%	-6.08%	0.04%	0.90%	-2.66%	0.36%	4.32%	5.95%	9.01%	15.16%
2003	2.28%	-4.33%	-5.40%	7.28%	4.53%	4.77%	2.67%	5.60%	-1.00%	4.04%	2.61%	4.72%	30.49%
2002	2.00%	-2.37%	1.55%	-0.82%	1.01%	-3.63%	-8.07%	-4.61%	-2.66%	1.03%	-1.49%	-1.78%	-18.54%

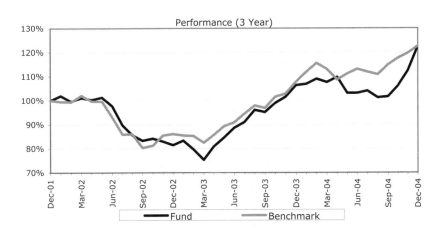

Performance (3 Year)

Fund   Benchmark

HILLSDALE CANADIAN AGGRESSIVE HEDGED

FUND SPONSOR COMPANY

Hillsdale Investment Management Inc.
Tel: 416-913-3900   Toll-Free: N/A
Fax: 416-913-3901   Web site: www.hillsdaleinv.com

PORTFOLIO MANAGER(S)

Chris Guthrie, CFA—In 1989, Chris became Portfolio Manager of CPM's Canadian Core Equity Fund and in 1993 was named Director, Client Service and Marketing for the firm, with responsibilities for the design and implementation of quantitative investment strategies.
Arun Kaul, CFA. Most recently Arun was at CPMS as an equity analyst, first covering the U.K., then Japan and U.S. equity markets. Starting in March 1996, Arun was co-manager of the firm's Canadian Growth Equity Fund.

FUND DESCRIPTION

The portfolio is constructed by taking long positions and partially offsetting them with short positions of Canadian corporations with market capitalization primarily in excess of $100 million. Its objective is to generate returns in excess of long-only Canadian equity investments over a three-year period with a low correlation to, and volatility equal to or less than, the S&P/TSX Composite Index.

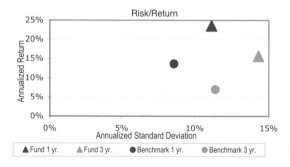

Rating:

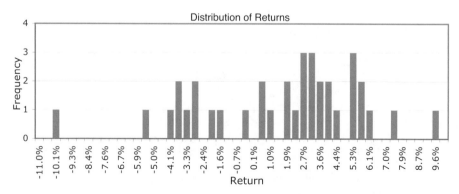

	1 yr.	3 yr.
Annualized rate of return	23.55%	15.67%
Annualized standard deviation	11.13%	14.30%
Percentage of negative months	25.00%	30.56%
Largest monthly drop	-5.64%	-10.41%
Maximum drawdown	-6.12%	-18.99%
Sharpe ratio	1.76	0.82
Semideviation	9.74%	10.21%
Sortino ratio	2.01	1.14
Jensen's alpha	10.11%	9.36%
Beta	0.98	0.77
Up capture ratio	129.60%	102.47%
Down capture ratio	64.90%	45.87%
Omega -0%	376%	210%
Appraisal ratio	-0.85	4.33
Average α over benchmark	0.72%	0.69%
Tracking error	1.83%	3.26%
Information ratio	39.54%	21.05%
Sterling ratio	3.19	0.61
Treynor measure	0.20	0.15
M² – Modigliani measure	5.43%	6.31%
Burke ratio	3.29	0.77
Skewness	-123.73%	-69.48%
Kurtosis	133%	48%
Correlation to S&P/TSX	0.823	0.635
R squared	0.677	0.403
Benchmark: S&P/TSX		

TERMS AND CONDITIONS

Inception:	December 31, 1999
Style:	Security Selection
Sub-style:	Long Bias
Valuation:	Weekly on Friday
RRSP:	Yes
Management fee:	2.87%
Performance fee:	20.00%
High-water mark:	Yes
Hurdle rate:	No
NAV:	$21.88
Asset Size (million):	$65.70
Maximum leverage:	200%
Early red'n period:	N/A
Early red'n fee:	N/A

PERFORMANCE (as of December 31, 2004)

	1 mo.	3 mo.	6 mo.
Funds	1.75%	10.59%	17.90%
S&P/TSX	2.40%	6.67%	8.41%
Van Global HF Index	1.50%	4.87%	5.48%

	1 yr.	2 yr.	3 yr.
Funds	23.55%	25.12%	15.67%
S&P/TSX	13.66%	19.32%	6.99%
Van Global HF Index	7.79%	13.04%	8.40%

Year	Jan	Feb	Mar	Apr	May	Jun	Jul	Aug	Sep	Oct	Nov	Dec	Total
2004	4.14%	3.58%	-0.51%	-5.64%	0.34%	3.14%	2.98%	-1.78%	5.39%	3.54%	4.98%	1.75%	23.55%
2003	2.38%	-3.64%	-3.07%	5.17%	0.98%	1.72%	7.05%	-2.21%	1.88%	9.27%	2.40%	2.79%	26.71%
2002	5.32%	3.87%	3.21%	0.42%	2.34%	-4.11%	-10.41%	5.77%	-4.30%	-3.07%	-3.89%	5.18%	-1.13%

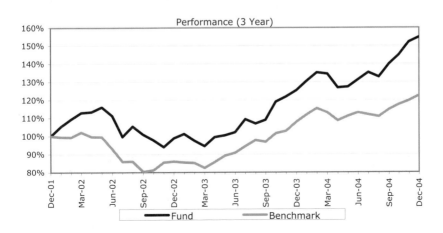

Performance (3 Year)

HILLSDALE CANADIAN MARKET NEUTRAL EQUITY

FUND SPONSOR COMPANY
Hillsdale Investment Management Inc.

Tel: 416-913-3900   Toll-Free: N/A
Fax: 416-913-3901   Web site: www.hillsdaleinv.com

PORTFOLIO MANAGER(S)

Chris Guthrie, CFA—In 1989, Chris became Portfolio Manager of CPM's Canadian Core Equity Fund and in 1993 was named Director, Client Service and Marketing for the firm, with responsibilities for the design and implementation of quantitative investment strategies.
Arun Kaul, CFA. Most recently Arun was at CPMS as an equity analyst, first covering the U.K., then Japan and U.S. equity markets. Starting in March 1996, Arun was co-manager of the firm's Canadian Growth Equity Fund.

FUND DESCRIPTION

The portfolio is constructed by taking long positions, and fully offsetting them with short positions, of Canadian corporations with market capitalization primarily in excess of $100 million. Its objective is to provide down market protection while generating equity-like returns, with substantially less volatility than equity markets.

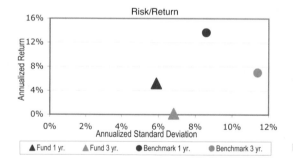

Rating: 🐚🐚

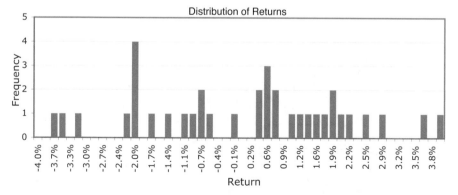

	1 yr.	3 yr.
Annualized rate of return	5.22%	0.17%
Annualized standard deviation	5.89%	6.84%
Percentage of negative months	25.00%	44.44%
Largest monthly drop	-3.79%	-3.79%
Maximum drawdown	-4.53%	-12.57%
Sharpe ratio	0.21	-0.56
Semideviation	5.78%	3.71%
Sortino ratio	0.21	-1.03
Jensen's alpha	-1.16%	-4.37%
Beta	0.25	0.18
Up capture ratio	26.14%	6.89%
Down capture ratio	10.33%	14.84%
Omega -0%	198%	104%
Appraisal ratio	-0.25	-0.64
Average α over benchmark	-0.66%	-0.59%
Tracking error	2.39%	3.28%
Information ratio	-27.67%	-17.85%
Sterling ratio	0.27	-0.30
Treynor measure	0.05	-0.22
M^2 – Modigliani measure	-7.88%	-9.38%
Burke ratio	0.31	-0.46
Skewness	-132.42%	-11.47%
Kurtosis	279%	-71%
Correlation to S&P/TSX	0.392	0.305
R squared	0.154	0.093
Benchmark: S&P/TSX		

TERMS AND CONDITIONS

Inception:	March 31, 2000
Style:	Security Selection
Sub-style:	No Bias
Valuation:	Weekly on Friday
RRSP:	Yes
Management fee:	2.81%
Performance fee:	20.00%
High-water mark:	N/A
Hurdle rate:	N/A
NAV:	$12.32
Asset Size (million):	$10.00
Maximum leverage:	150%
Early red'n period:	N/A
Early red'n fee:	N/A

PERFORMANCE (as of December 31, 2004)

	1 mo.	3 mo.	6 mo.
Funds	0.29%	3.96%	5.58%
S&P/TSX	2.40%	6.67%	8.41%
Van Global HF Index	1.50%	4.87%	5.48%

	1 yr.	2 yr.	3 yr.
Funds	5.22%	4.18%	0.17%
S&P/TSX	13.66%	19.32%	6.99%
Van Global HF Index	7.79%	13.04%	8.40%

Year	Jan	Feb	Mar	Apr	May	Jun	Jul	Aug	Sep	Oct	Nov	Dec	Total
2004	0.46%	1.38%	1.80%	-3.79%	-0.77%	0.68%	2.09%	-0.79%	0.28%	0.94%	2.70%	0.29%	5.22%
2003	1.41%	-2.05%	-1.55%	3.86%	-2.13%	-2.09%	0.72%	2.02%	-0.61%	3.54%	1.21%	-0.97%	3.15%
2002	1.76%	0.46%	-2.09%	0.44%	2.53%	-1.19%	-1.76%	-0.12%	-3.27%	-2.35%	-3.53%	1.67%	-7.40%

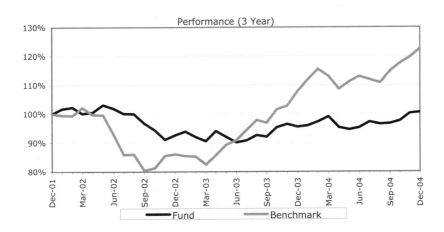

Performance (3 Year)

HILLSDALE US AGGRESSIVE HEDGED EQUITY A (US$)

FUND SPONSOR COMPANY

Hillsdale Investment Management Inc.

Tel: 416-913-3900   Toll-Free: N/A

Fax: 416-913-3901   Web site: www.hillsdaleinv.com

PORTFOLIO MANAGER(S)

Chris Guthrie, CFA—In 1989, Chris became Portfolio Manager of CPM's Canadian Core Equity Fund and in 1993 was named Director, Client Service and Marketing for the firm, with responsibilities for the design and implementation of quantitative investment strategies.

Arun Kaul, CFA. Most recently Arun was at CPMS as an equity analyst, first covering the U.K., then Japan and U.S. equity markets. Starting in March 1996, Arun was co-manager of the firm's Canadian Growth Equity Fund.

FUND DESCRIPTION

The portfolio is constructed by taking long positions, and partially offsetting them with short positions, of U.S. corporations with market capitalization primarily in excess of $500 million. Its objective is to generate returns in excess of long-only U.S. equity investments over a three-year period with a low correlation to, and volatility equal to or less than, the S&P 500 Composite Index.

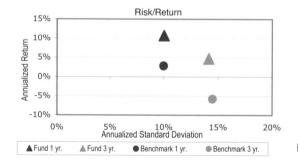

Rating: 🦔🦔

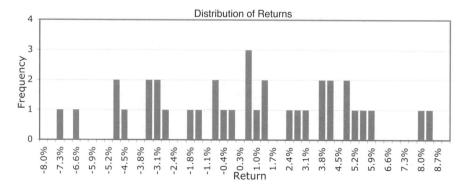

	1 yr.	3 yr.
Annualized rate of return	10.70%	4.68%
Annualized standard deviation	10.03%	14.13%
Percentage of negative months	41.67%	44.44%
Largest monthly drop	-3.58%	-7.51%
Maximum drawdown	-5.42%	-21.20%
Sharpe ratio	0.67	0.05
Semideviation	5.31%	8.27%
Sortino ratio	1.26	0.08
Jensen's alpha	6.98%	1.13%
Beta	0.23	0.05
Up capture ratio	67.12%	10.38%
Down capture ratio	5.69%	-13.92%
Omega -0%	211%	132%
Appraisal ratio	0.93	0.08
Average α over benchmark	0.62%	0.87%
Tracking error	3.53%	5.70%
Information ratio	17.55%	15.30%
Sterling ratio	1.24	0.03
Treynor measure	0.29	0.15
M^2 – Modigliani measure	7.87%	10.47%
Burke ratio	1.32	0.04
Skewness	-10.77%	-6.66%
Kurtosis	-142%	-74%
Correlation to S&P/TSX	0.762	0.340
R squared	0.065	0.002
Benchmark: S&P 500		

TERMS AND CONDITIONS

Inception:	July 31, 2000
Style:	Security Selection
Sub-style:	Long Bias
Valuation:	Weekly on Friday
RRSP:	No
Management fee:	2.77%
Performance fee:	20.00%
High-water mark:	N/A
Hurdle rate:	N/A
NAV:	$9.55
Asset Size (million):	$3.43
Maximum leverage:	200%
Early red'n period:	N/A
Early red'n fee:	N/A

PERFORMANCE (as of December 31, 2004)

	1 mo.	3 mo.	6 mo.
Funds	4.52%	7.44%	7.00%
S&P 500	4.80%	4.07%	-3.39%
Van Global HF Index	1.50%	4.87%	5.48%

	1 yr.	2 yr.	3 yr.
Funds	10.70%	14.60%	4.68%
S&P 500	2.81%	4.32%	-5.78%
Van Global HF Index	7.79%	13.04%	8.40%

Year	Jan	Feb	Mar	Apr	May	Jun	Jul	Aug	Sep	Oct	Nov	Dec	Total
2004	0.40%	3.77%	-0.27%	-3.58%	2.31%	0.93%	-2.00%	-2.82%	4.56%	-0.93%	3.77%	4.52%	10.70%
2003	0.44%	-0.61%	3.87%	0.56%	5.45%	5.71%	-3.47%	-0.97%	2.91%	4.90%	2.67%	-3.65%	18.63%
2002	8.30%	-1.59%	-7.51%	4.11%	-5.18%	-5.12%	-6.93%	7.89%	-4.74%	-3.38%	1.10%	1.24%	-12.66%

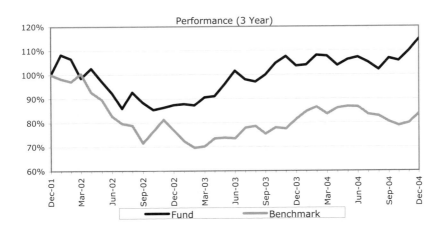

Performance (3 Year)

Fund   Benchmark

HORIZONS GLOBAL MACRO FUND

FUND SPONSOR COMPANY

Horizons Funds

Tel: 416-367-9333   Toll-Free: 800-665-1158
Fax: 416-601-1695   Web site: www.horizonsfunds.com

PORTFOLIO MANAGER(S)

Bradbrooke Capital Holdings

FUND DESCRIPTION

The investment objective of the Fund is to provide superior returns through investment in a diversified portfolio of securities and derivatives. One or more portfolio managers will be selected by the Fund Advisor to trade on behalf of the Fund. Each portfolio manager will be responsible for making and executing investment decisions for a portion of the Fund's investment portfolio. The aim of the portfolio manager selection process is for the Fund to achieve portfolio diversification and have the benefit of both systematic and discretionary management styles.

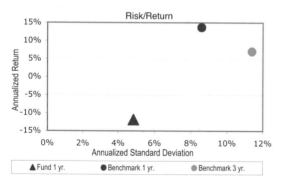

Rating: Not Rated

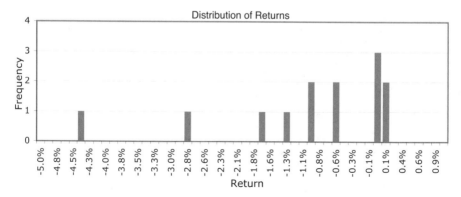

	1 yr.	3 yr.
Annualized rate of return	-11.86%	
Annualized standard deviation	4.84%	
Percentage of negative months	66.67%	
Largest monthly drop	-4.51%	
Maximum drawdown	-11.90%	
Sharpe ratio	-3.28	
Semideviation	5.20%	
Sortino ratio	-3.05	
Jensen's alpha	-14.30%	
Beta	-0.16	
Up capture ratio	-44.42%	
Down capture ratio	22.03%	
Omega -0%	1%	
Appraisal ratio	-4.89	
Average α over benchmark	-2.14%	
Tracking error	3.20%	
Information ratio	-66.74%	
Sterling ratio	-1.33	
Treynor measure	0.98	
M² – Modigliani measure	-37.80%	
Burke ratio	-2.71	
Skewness	-167.91%	
Kurtosis	266%	
Correlation to S&P/TSX	-0.312	
R squared	0.098	
Benchmark: S&P/TSX		

TERMS AND CONDITIONS

Inception:	November 21, 2003
Style:	Directional
Sub-style:	N/A
Valuation:	Daily
RRSP:	Yes
Management fee:	2.50%
Performance fee:	N/A
High-water mark:	N/A
Hurdle rate:	N/A
NAV:	$8.67
Asset Size (million):	$0.24
Maximum leverage:	N/A
Early red'n period:	N/A
Early red'n fee:	N/A

PERFORMANCE (as of December 31, 2004)

	1 mo.	3 mo.	6 mo.
Funds	0.01%	0.05%	-3.83%
S&P/TSX	2.40%	6.67%	8.41%
Van Global HF Index	1.50%	4.87%	5.48%

	1 yr.	2 yr.	3 yr.
Funds	-11.86%		
S&P/TSX	13.66%	19.32%	6.99%
Van Global HF Index	7.79%	13.04%	8.40%

Year	Jan	Feb	Mar	Apr	May	Jun	Jul	Aug	Sep	Oct	Nov	Dec	Total
2004	-0.64%	-1.05%	-0.70%	0.09%	-1.76%	-4.51%	-0.10%	-1.01%	-2.80%	0.03%	0.01%	0.01%	-11.86%
2003												-1.45%	-1.45%
2002													

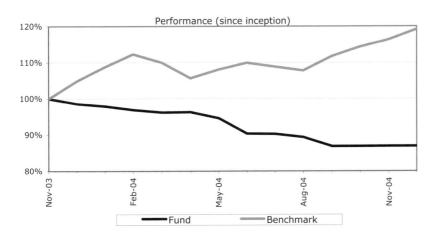

HORIZONS MONDIALE HEDGE FUND

FUND SPONSOR COMPANY

Horizons Funds
Tel: 416-367-9333   Toll-Free: 800-665-1158
Fax: 416-601-1695   Web site: www.horizonsfunds.com

PORTFOLIO MANAGER(S)

Mondiale Asset Mgmt. is a Vancouver-based company that has developed a unique and proprietary strategy for global investing. Founded in 1995, Mondiale is a Canadian leader in the development of hedging and risk management strategies for investors who want to reduce their dependence on a rising stock market.

FUND DESCRIPTION

The investment objective of the Fund is to provide a strategic alternative to traditional asset classes and meet the goals of capital preservation, diversification, and the production of consistent returns that are independent of the direction of global equity markets. Using only quantitative investment strategies both within and across multiple domestic and international markets, the Fund exploits emerging trends to generate returns while minimize the variability of returns. The fund's portfolio consists of a dynamic mix of currency, equity, and cash positions, each of which may be long, short, or neutral. Derivatives may be used to vary exposure to any of these sectors.

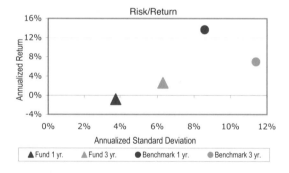

Rating: 🦔🦔🦔

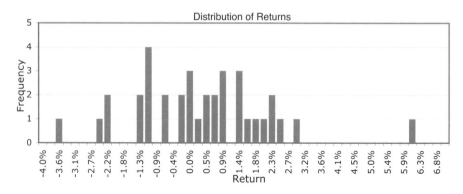

	1 yr.	3 yr.
Annualized rate of return	-0.79%	2.63%
Annualized standard deviation	3.76%	6.31%
Percentage of negative months	66.67%	47.22%
Largest monthly drop	-1.36%	-3.73%
Maximum drawdown	-5.12%	-6.30%
Sharpe ratio	-1.28	-0.22
Semideviation	1.63%	3.63%
Sortino ratio	-2.95	-0.38
Jensen's alpha	-5.06%	-0.35%
Beta	0.09	0.16
Up capture ratio	1.65%	23.61%
Down capture ratio	11.38%	17.50%
Omega -0%	86%	140%
Appraisal ratio	-1.32	-0.06
Average α over benchmark	-0.65%	0.34%
Tracking error	2.66%	3.77%
Information ratio	-24.34%	8.90%
Sterling ratio	-0.94	-0.22
Treynor measure	-0.51	-0.08
M^2 – Modigliani measure	-14.91%	3.13%
Burke ratio	-2.04	-0.21
Skewness	86.49%	54.02%
Kurtosis	21%	178%
Correlation to S&P/TSX	0.489	0.159
R squared	0.067	0.143
Benchmark: MSCI World C$		

TERMS AND CONDITIONS

Inception:	August 29, 1997
Style:	Directional Trading
Sub-style:	N/A
Valuation:	Daily
RRSP:	Yes
Management fee:	2.50%
Performance fee:	20.00%
High-water mark:	Yes
Hurdle rate:	0.00%
NAV:	$9.56
Asset Size (million):	$176.00
Maximum leverage:	150%
Early red'n period:	N/A
Early red'n fee:	N/A

PERFORMANCE (as of December 31, 2004)

	1 mo.	3 mo.	6 mo.
Funds	0.27%	4.08%	0.95%
MSCI World C$	5.25%	6.76%	0.07%
Van Global HF Index	1.50%	4.87%	5.48%

	1 yr.	2 yr.	3 yr.
Funds	-0.79%	4.35%	2.63%
MSCI World C$	6.85%	8.58%	-2.18%
Van Global HF Index	7.79%	13.04%	8.40%

Year	Jan	Feb	Mar	Apr	May	Jun	Jul	Aug	Sep	Oct	Nov	Dec	Total
2004	0.46%	-0.04%	-0.05%	-1.36%	-0.66%	-0.09%	-1.23%	-1.11%	-0.69%	2.12%	1.64%	0.27%	-0.79%
2003	-0.37%	-1.52%	0.12%	1.23%	2.48%	0.64%	0.89%	2.21%	-0.30%	1.25%	0.83%	1.98%	9.76%
2002	-1.11%	-1.19%	2.84%	-2.28%	-2.41%	1.52%	5.99%	0.81%	-2.55%	0.56%	1.23%	-3.73%	-0.73%

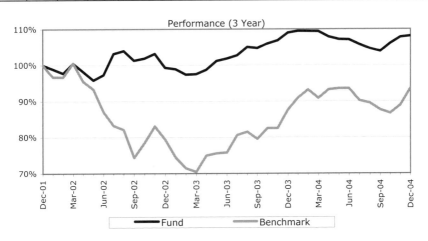

Performance (3 Year)

HORIZONS TACTICAL HEDGE FUND

FUND SPONSOR COMPANY

Horizons Funds
Tel: 416-367-9333   Toll-Free: 800-665-1158
Fax: 416-601-1695   Web site: www.horizonsfunds.com

PORTFOLIO MANAGER(S)

Cornerstone Trading
Quay Capital Management

FUND DESCRIPTION

The investment objective of the Fund is to provide superior returns through investment in a diversified portfolio of securities and derivatives. One or more portfolio managers will be selected by the Fund Advisor to trade on behalf of the Fund. Each portfolio manager will be responsible for making and executing investment decisions for a portion of the Fund's investment portfolio. The aim of the portfolio manager selection process is for the Fund to achieve portfolio diversification.

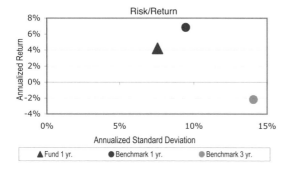

Risk/Return

▲ Fund 1 yr.   ● Benchmark 1 yr.   ● Benchmark 3 yr.   **Rating: Not Rated**

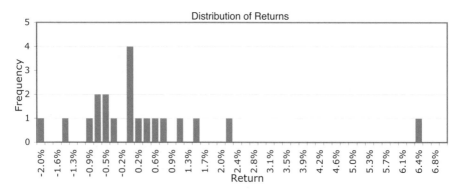

Distribution of Returns

	1 yr.	3 yr.
Annualized rate of return	4.21%	
Annualized standard deviation	7.54%	
Percentage of negative months	66.67%	
Largest monthly drop	-2.10%	
Maximum drawdown	-3.37%	
Sharpe ratio	0.03	
Semideviation	2.19%	
Sortino ratio	0.10	
Jensen's alpha	-0.28%	
Beta	0.17	
Up capture ratio	39.35%	
Down capture ratio	28.61%	
Omega -0%	173%	
Appraisal ratio	-0.04	
Average α over benchmark	-0.22%	
Tracking error	3.06%	
Information ratio	-7.25%	
Sterling ratio	0.06	
Treynor measure	0.01	
M² – Modigliani measure	-2.58%	
Burke ratio	0.08	
Skewness	201.66%	
Kurtosis	488%	
Correlation to S&P/TSX	-0.581	
R squared	0.057	
Benchmark: MSCI World C$		

TERMS AND CONDITIONS

Inception:	July 29, 2003
Style:	Directional Trading
Sub-style:	N/A
Valuation:	Daily
RRSP:	Yes
Management fee:	2.00%
Performance fee:	20.00%
High-water mark:	Yes
Hurdle rate:	0.00%
NAV:	$9.88
Asset Size (million):	$1.54
Maximum leverage:	200%
Early red'n period:	N/A
Early red'n fee:	N/A

PERFORMANCE (as of December 31, 2004)

	1 mo.	3 mo.	6 mo.
Funds	-0.16%	2.04%	1.01%
MSCI World C$	5.25%	6.76%	0.07%
Van Global HF Index	1.50%	4.87%	5.48%

	1 yr.	2 yr.	3 yr.
Funds	4.21%		
MSCI World C$	6.85%	8.58%	-2.18%
Van Global HF Index	7.79%	13.04%	8.40%

Year	Jan	Feb	Mar	Apr	May	Jun	Jul	Aug	Sep	Oct	Nov	Dec	Total
2004	-2.10%	-0.49%	-0.82%	6.27%	1.41%	-0.93%	-0.70%	0.49%	-0.79%	-0.02%	2.22%	-0.16%	4.21%
2003					0.00%	0.00%	0.12%	1.02%	-0.65%	-1.60%	0.27%	0.63%	-0.22%
2002													

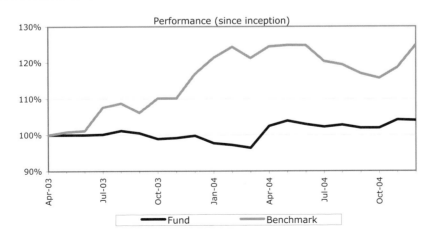

Performance (since inception)

IA MULTI-STRATEGY

FUND SPONSOR COMPANY
Industrial Alliance
Tel: 418-684-5182   Toll-Free: 800-463-6236
Fax: 418-684-5106   Web site: www.inalco.com

PORTFOLIO MANAGER(S)

Industrial Alliance Life
Industrial Alliance Insurance and Financial Services

FUND DESCRIPTION

To diligently follow an investment strategy that focuses on preservation of capital combined with yield-enhancing features of alternative investment strategies.

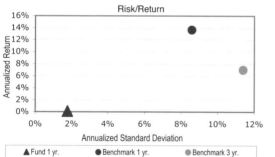

Rating: Not Rated

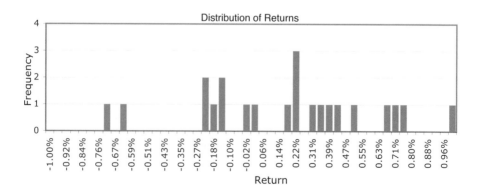

	1 yr.	3 yr.
Annualized rate of return	0.10%	
Annualized standard deviation	1.79%	
Percentage of negative months	58.33%	
Largest monthly drop	-0.73%	
Maximum drawdown	-2.20%	
Sharpe ratio	-2.19	
Semideviation	0.90%	
Sortino ratio	-4.32	
Jensen's alpha	-4.90%	
Beta	0.10	
Up capture ratio	7.62%	
Down capture ratio	21.19%	
Omega -0%	105%	
Appraisal ratio	-2.76	
Average α over benchmark	-1.09%	
Tracking error	2.24%	
Information ratio	-48.65%	
Sterling ratio	-1.77	
Treynor measure	-0.38	
M^2 – Modigliani measure	-28.44%	
Burke ratio	-3.70	
Skewness	88.22%	
Kurtosis	171%	
Correlation to S&P/TSX	0.539	
R squared	0.291	
Benchmark: S&P/TSX		

TERMS AND CONDITIONS

Inception:	January 6, 2003
Style:	Directional Trading
Sub-style:	N/A
Valuation:	Weekly on Friday
RRSP:	No
Management fee:	3.84%
Performance fee:	N/A
High-water mark:	N/A
Hurdle rate:	N/A
NAV:	$10.48
Asset Size (million):	$3.10
Maximum leverage:	N/A
Early red'n period:	N/A
Early red'n fee:	N/A

PERFORMANCE (as of December 31, 2004)

	1 mo.	3 mo.	6 mo.
Funds	0.35%	1.71%	0.55%
S&P/TSX	2.40%	6.67%	8.41%
Van Global HF Index	1.50%	4.87%	5.48%

	1 yr.	2 yr.	3 yr.
Funds	0.10%		
S&P/TSX	13.66%	19.32%	6.99%
Van Global HF Index	7.79%	13.04%	8.40%

Year	Jan	Feb	Mar	Apr	May	Jun	Jul	Aug	Sep	Oct	Nov	Dec	Total
2004	0.41%	0.22%	-0.05%	-0.64%	-0.25%	-0.15%	-0.73%	-0.24%	-0.17%	0.15%	1.21%	0.35%	0.10%
2003		0.20%	-0.20%	0.70%	0.99%	0.49%	0.00%	0.31%	0.73%	0.64%	0.19%	0.29%	4.42%
2002													

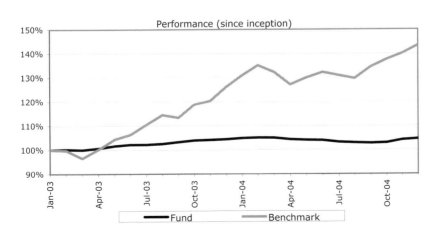

Performance (since inception)

J.C. CLARK PRESERVATION TRUST

FUND SPONSOR COMPANY
J.C. Clark Ltd.
Tel: 416-361-6144   Toll-Free: 866-480-0002
Fax: 416-361-0128   Web site: www.jcclark.com

PORTFOLIO MANAGER(S)

John Clark is the Chairman and CEO of J.C. Clark Ltd. He has over 25 years of investment experience and has been managing long/short investments since 1982. Prior to founding J.C. Clark Ltd. he was the Chairman and CEO of the wealth management firm Connor Clark & Company, one of Canada's largest wealth managers, with $2.5 billion in assets. He also co-founded pension manager Connor, Clark & Lunn, a premier pension fund manager with $14 billion in assets under management.

FUND DESCRIPTION

The objective of the Fund is to achieve consistent positive absolute returns on capital through long-short hedge investing. Based on extensive fundamental research, and subject to investment restrictions, the Fund invests primarily in U.S. and Canadian equities, focusing on buying high-quality companies trading at significant discounts to their intrinsic values and selling short businesses with weak fundamentals, poor or overly-promotional management, or aggressive accounting.

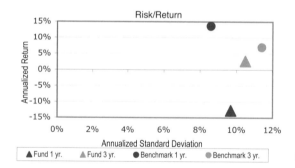

Rating:

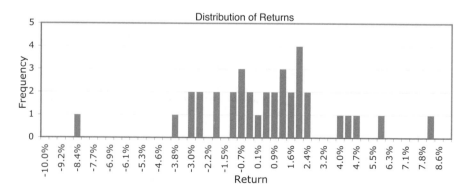

	1 yr.	3 yr.
Annualized rate of return	-12.77%	2.72%
Annualized standard deviation	9.69%	10.48%
Percentage of negative months	66.67%	44.44%
Largest monthly drop	-8.83%	-8.83%
Maximum drawdown	-14.73%	-14.73%
Sharpe ratio	-1.73	-0.12
Semideviation	12.01%	7.39%
Sortino ratio	-1.40	-0.17
Jensen's alpha	-15.38%	-0.89%
Beta	-0.14	-0.13
Up capture ratio	-50.23%	-11.23%
Down capture ratio	15.98%	-59.97%
Omega -0%	26%	127%
Appraisal ratio	-1.96	-0.08
Average α over benchmark	-2.20%	-0.35%
Tracking error	3.99%	4.78%
Information ratio	-55.06%	-7.31%
Sterling ratio	-1.14	-0.09
Treynor measure	1.17	0.10
M² – Modigliani measure	-24.52%	-4.38%
Burke ratio	-1.73	-0.11
Skewness	-209.52%	-21.71%
Kurtosis	555%	195%
Correlation to S&P/TSX	-0.138	-0.144
R squared	0.019	0.021
Benchmark: S&P/TSX		

TERMS AND CONDITIONS

Inception:	April 30, 1999
Style:	Security Selection
Sub-style:	Variable Bias
Valuation:	Monthly
RRSP:	Yes
Management fee:	2.00%
Performance fee:	20.00%
High-water mark:	Yes
Hurdle rate:	10.00%
NAV:	$274.22
Asset Size (million):	N/A
Maximum leverage:	N/A
Early red'n period:	N/A
Early red'n fee:	N/A

PERFORMANCE (as of December 31, 2004)

	1 mo.	3 mo.	6 mo.
Funds	-8.83%	-12.51%	-13.97%
S&P/TSX	2.40%	6.67%	8.41%
Van Global HF Index	1.50%	4.87%	5.48%

	1 yr.	2 yr.	3 yr.
Funds	-12.77%	-4.88%	2.72%
S&P/TSX	13.66%	19.32%	6.99%
Van Global HF Index	7.79%	13.04%	8.40%

Year	Jan	Feb	Mar	Apr	May	Jun	Jul	Aug	Sep	Oct	Nov	Dec	Total
2004	-0.87%	1.33%	0.51%	-0.48%	1.78%	-0.85%	0.89%	-2.14%	-0.40%	-1.10%	-2.97%	-8.83%	-12.77%
2003	0.53%	-3.90%	-0.28%	-3.32%	-0.73%	0.37%	3.93%	0.43%	-1.12%	1.80%	1.80%	4.50%	3.72%
2002	8.03%	4.04%	-3.26%	5.52%	1.77%	2.21%	1.38%	-2.22%	1.10%	-2.90%	1.04%	2.09%	19.80%

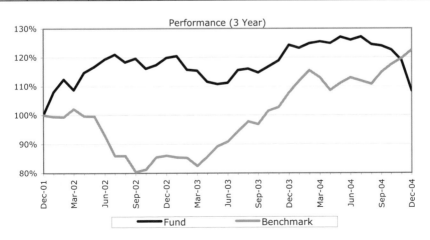

Performance (3 Year)

THE LOYALIST TRUST

FUND SPONSOR COMPANY
J.C. Clark Ltd.
Tel: 416-361-6144   Toll-Free: 866-480-0002
Fax: 416-361-0128   Web site: www.jcclark.com

PORTFOLIO MANAGER(S)

John Clark is the Chairman and CEO of J.C. Clark Ltd. He has over 15 years of investment experience and has been managing long/short investments since 1982. Prior to founding J.C. Clark Ltd. he was the Chairman and CEO of wealth management firm Connor Clark & Company, one of Canada's largest wealth managers, with $2.5 billion in assets. He also co-founded pension manager Connor, Clark & Lunn, a premier pension fund manager with $14 billion in assets under management.

FUND DESCRIPTION

The objective of the Fund is to achieve consistent positive absolute returns on capital through long-short hedge investing. Based on extensive fundamental research, and subject to investment restrictions, the Fund invests primarily in U.S. and Canadian equities, focusing on buying high-quality companies trading at significant discounts to their intrinsic values and selling short businesses with weak fundamentals, poor or overly-promotional management, or aggressive accounting.

Rating: Not Rated

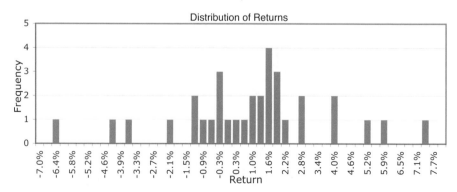

	1 yr.	3 yr.
Annualized rate of return	2.81%	
Annualized standard deviation	8.94%	
Percentage of negative months	41.67%	
Largest monthly drop	-6.60%	
Maximum drawdown	-7.27%	
Sharpe ratio	-0.13	
Semideviation	9.34%	
Sortino ratio	-0.13	
Jensen's alpha	-1.16%	
Beta	0.00	
Up capture ratio	-4.30%	
Down capture ratio	-49.47%	
Omega -0%	134%	
Appraisal ratio	-0.13	
Average α over benchmark	-0.84%	
Tracking error	3.58%	
Information ratio	-23.40%	
Sterling ratio	-0.16	
Treynor measure	3.71	
M² – Modigliani measure	-10.80%	
Burke ratio	-0.18	
Skewness	-167.57%	
Kurtosis	464%	
Correlation to S&P/TSX	-0.003	
R squared	0.000	
Benchmark: S&P/TSX		

TERMS AND CONDITIONS

Inception:	April 15, 2002
Style:	Security Selection
Sub-style:	Long/Short Equity
Valuation:	Monthly
RRSP:	No
Management fee:	2.00%
Performance fee:	20.00%
High-water mark:	Yes
Hurdle rate:	No
NAV:	$137.27
Asset Size (million):	$15.00
Maximum leverage:	N/A
Early red'n period:	N/A
Early red'n fee:	N/A

PERFORMANCE (as of December 31, 2004)

	1 mo.	3 mo.	6 mo.
Funds	-6.60%	-7.27%	-2.60%
S&P/TSX	2.40%	6.67%	8.41%
Van Global HF Index	1.50%	4.87%	5.48%

	1 yr.	2 yr.	3 yr.
Funds	2.81%	4.61%	
S&P/TSX	13.66%	19.32%	6.99%
Van Global HF Index	7.79%	13.04%	8.40%

Year	Jan	Feb	Mar	Apr	May	Jun	Jul	Aug	Sep	Oct	Nov	Dec	Total
2004	1.19%	4.02%	1.36%	-0.54%	0.76%	-1.27%	1.52%	1.47%	1.97%	-0.29%	-0.43%	-6.60%	2.81%
2003	1.06%	-3.89%	-0.68%	-1.23%	0.89%	0.35%	2.74%	1.61%	-0.93%	5.13%	1.76%	-0.26%	6.44%
2002				7.19%	5.85%	3.74%	-2.21%	1.48%	1.76%	-4.46%	0.61%	2.56%	17.16%

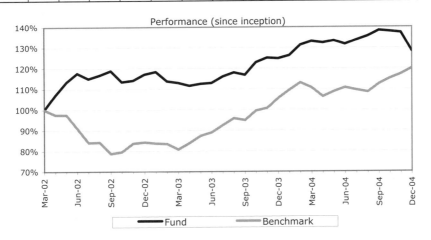

Performance (since inception)

LEEWARD BULL & BEAR FUND L.P.

FUND SPONSOR COMPANY
Leeward Hedge Funds Inc.
Tel: 416-482-0242   Toll-Free: 866-533-9273
Fax: 416-482-3067   Web site: www.leewardhedgefunds.ca

PORTFOLIO MANAGER(S)

Brendan Kyne graduated from McMaster University in Hamilton, Ontario in 1988 with a degree in Economics; in 1992 he earned the CFA designation. He founded Leeward Capital Management Inc. in May 2001 in order to provide Canadian investors with a low-risk hedge fund. Prior to starting his own firm, Brendan had accumulated over 14 years' experience in the money management field. He spent five years working at Driehaus Capital Management Inc. of Chicago.

FUND DESCRIPTION

The primary objective of the Partnership is to provide consistent positive returns on an annual basis. Great performance in 2003 within a short period followed by a below-par performance in 2004. Risk is definitely higher on this fund.

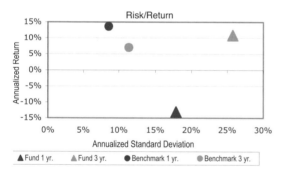

Rating:

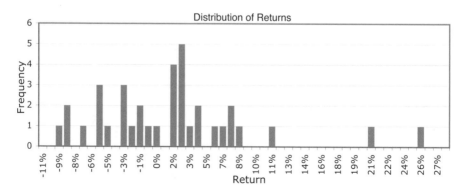

	1 yr.	3 yr.
Annualized rate of return	-13.11%	10.86%
Annualized standard deviation	17.87%	25.74%
Percentage of negative months	50.00%	44.44%
Largest monthly drop	-10.01%	-10.01%
Maximum drawdown	-25.83%	-25.83%
Sharpe ratio	-0.96	0.27
Semideviation	10.01%	10.18%
Sortino ratio	-1.71	0.67
Jensen's alpha	-29.78%	3.46%
Beta	1.31	1.14
Up capture ratio	67.40%	150.78%
Down capture ratio	320.14%	119.76%
Omega -0%	62%	153%
Appraisal ratio	-0.85	0.26
Average α over benchmark	-2.14%	0.50%
Tracking error	3.90%	6.38%
Information ratio	-54.94%	7.78%
Sterling ratio	-0.66	0.27
Treynor measure	-0.13	0.06
M² – Modigliani measure	-17.88%	0.04%
Burke ratio	-1.16	0.31
Skewness	-24.17%	133.86%
Kurtosis	-102%	298%
Correlation to S&P/TSX	0.688	0.518
R squared	0.473	0.268
Benchmark: S&P/TSX		

TERMS AND CONDITIONS

Inception:	June 29, 2001
Style:	Security Selection
Sub-style:	Variable Bias
Valuation:	Monthly
RRSP:	No
Management fee:	2.00%
Performance fee:	20.00%
High-water mark:	Yes
Hurdle rate:	10.00%
NAV:	$1,713.95
Asset Size (million):	$13.05
Maximum leverage:	100%
Early red'n period:	3 mo.
Early red'n fee:	N/A

PERFORMANCE (as of December 31, 2004)

	1 mo.	3 mo.	6 mo.
Funds	6.07%	14.10%	-1.51%
S&P/TSX	2.40%	6.67%	8.41%
Van Global HF Index	1.50%	4.87%	5.48%

	1 yr.	2 yr.	3 yr.
Funds	-13.11%	15.05%	10.86%
S&P/TSX	13.66%	19.32%	6.99%
Van Global HF Index	7.79%	13.04%	8.40%

Year	Jan	Feb	Mar	Apr	May	Jun	Jul	Aug	Sep	Oct	Nov	Dec	Total
2004	-2.20%	3.35%	-7.14%	-4.80%	-2.80%	1.57%	-10.01%	-5.56%	1.58%	1.86%	5.61%	6.07%	-13.11%
2003	-2.09%	1.19%	-6.07%	-0.23%	1.74%	7.64%	20.72%	25.41%	-3.57%	2.39%	-3.24%	3.59%	52.33%
2002	7.08%	-1.32%	-5.59%	2.23%	6.83%	-3.33%	-9.15%	11.24%	-9.04%	1.25%	2.38%	2.56%	2.94%

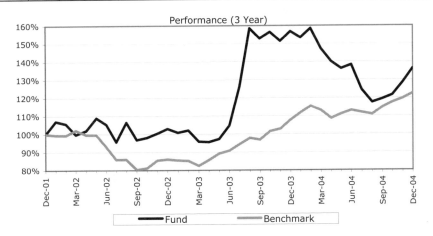

Performance (3 Year)

Fund   Benchmark

LAKE SHORE FINANCIAL ASSET ACCOUNT INC. US$

FUND SPONSOR COMPANY

Lake Shore Asset Management Inc.

Tel: 519-985-6676   Toll-Free: 866-544-1544

Fax: 519-985-6778   Web site: www.lakeshorefunds.com

PORTFOLIO MANAGER(S)

All assets are managed by **Lake Shore Asset Management Inc.,** a registered commodity trading adviser (CTA) with its head office in Chicago, Illinois. Lake Shore Asset Management is regulated by the Commodity Futures Exchange Commission and is a member of the National Futures Association.

FUND DESCRIPTION

The Lake Shore Alternative Financial Asset Account is not a fund, it is a separately managed account. All funds under management at Lake Shore are managed according to proprietary computerized trading models that include expert systems and neutral generated entries. Lake Shore trading has no market bias and endeavours to produce yield in any market environment.

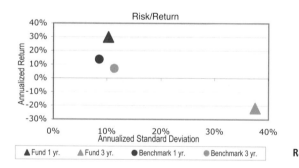

Rating:

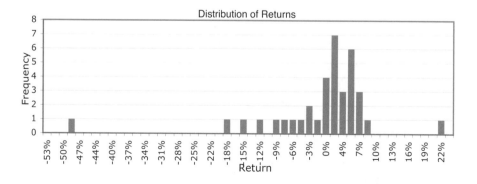

	1 yr.	3 yr.
Annualized rate of return	29.81%	-21.76%
Annualized standard deviation	10.28%	37.52%
Percentage of negative months	25.00%	36.11%
Largest monthly drop	-2.40%	-48.56%
Maximum drawdown	-2.40%	-75.24%
Sharpe ratio	2.51	-0.69
Semideviation	4.87%	45.88%
Sortino ratio	5.31	-0.56
Jensen's alpha	31.54%	-31.19%
Beta	-0.59	1.81
Up capture ratio	36.54%	1.81%
Down capture ratio	-252.98%	167.06%
Omega -0%	833%	66%
Appraisal ratio	1.13	-0.41
Average α over benchmark	1.14%	-1.91%
Tracking error	4.79%	9.37%
Information ratio	23.76%	-20.35%
Sterling ratio	10.76	-0.34
Treynor measure	-0.44	-0.14
M² – Modigliani measure	11.91%	-10.82%
Burke ratio	9.91	-0.44
Skewness	23.22%	-244.58%
Kurtosis	-93%	1019%
Correlation to S&P/TSX	-0.540	0.566
R squared	0.292	0.320
Benchmark: S&P/TSX		

TERMS AND CONDITIONS

Inception:	January 1, 1994
Style:	Directional Trading
Sub-style:	N/A
Valuation:	Weekly on Friday
RRSP:	No
Management fee:	N/A
Performance fee:	25.00%
High-water mark:	Yes
Hurdle rate:	N/A
NAV:	$12.72
Asset Size (million):	N/A
Maximum leverage:	N/A
Early red'n period:	N/A
Early red'n fee:	N/A

PERFORMANCE (as of December 31, 2004)

	1 mo.	3 mo.	6 mo.
Funds	2.33%	6.89%	16.88%
S&P/TSX	2.40%	6.67%	8.41%
Van Global HF Index	1.50%	4.87%	5.48%

	1 yr.	2 yr.	3 yr.
Funds	29.81%	26.10%	-21.76%
S&P/TSX	13.66%	19.32%	6.99%
Van Global HF Index	7.79%	13.04%	8.40%

Year	Jan	Feb	Mar	Apr	May	Jun	Jul	Aug	Sep	Oct	Nov	Dec	Total
2004	-0.97%	1.50%	5.71%	3.89%	0.91%	-0.29%	6.11%	2.68%	0.36%	7.02%	-2.40%	2.33%	29.81%
2003	0.92%	-3.22%	4.31%	3.98%	0.84%	3.09%	-4.74%	3.63%	1.77%	1.73%	3.92%	4.72%	22.48%
2002	1.99%	6.56%	-6.47%	-3.80%	0.33%	-12.50%	-48.56%	-9.52%	-19.39%	-16.45%	21.40%	-7.80%	-69.88%

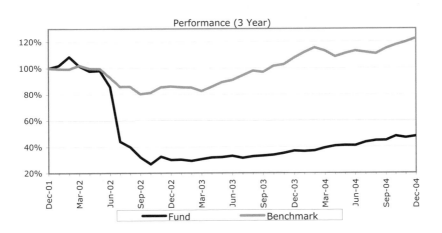

Performance (3 Year)

MACKENZIE ALTERNATIVE STRATEGIES FUND

FUND SPONSOR COMPANY

Mackenzie Financial Corporation

Tel: 416-922-5322   Toll-Free: 800-387-0780

Fax: 416-922-0399   Web site: www.mackenziefinancial.com

PORTFOLIO MANAGER(S)

Tremont Capital Management Corp.

Tremont Capital Management, Inc. is a global leader in the field of hedge fund investment management and research that has specialized in structuring and managing multi-manager, multi-strategy hedge fund portfolios since 1984.

FUND DESCRIPTION

The investment objective of the Fund is to achieve an attractive risk-adjusted return through the use of a multi-manager investment approach by investing with a variety of hedge fund managers.

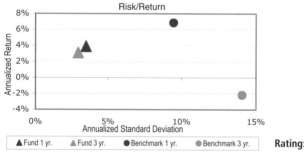

Rating:

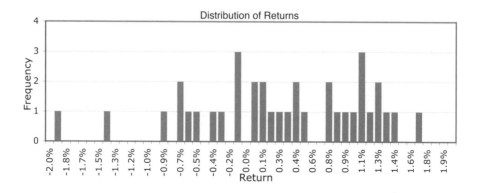

	1 yr.	3 yr.
Annualized rate of return	3.88%	3.11%
Annualized standard deviation	3.47%	2.93%
Percentage of negative months	41.67%	36.11%
Largest monthly drop	-1.93%	-1.93%
Maximum drawdown	-2.13%	-4.63%
Sharpe ratio	-0.03	-0.30
Semideviation	2.62%	2.02%
Sortino ratio	-0.04	-0.44
Jensen's alpha	-0.72%	-0.48%
Beta	0.21	0.07
Up capture ratio	21.91%	13.12%
Down capture ratio	0.99%	0.37%
Omega -0%	235%	212%
Appraisal ratio	-0.27	-0.18
Average α over benchmark	-0.26%	0.36%
Tracking error	2.23%	3.87%
Information ratio	-11.84%	9.35%
Sterling ratio	-0.05	-0.19
Treynor measure	-0.01	-0.14
M² – Modigliani measure	-3.16%	1.92%
Burke ratio	-0.06	-0.30
Skewness	-82.18%	-55.65%
Kurtosis	93%	-8%
Correlation to S&P/TSX	0.224	0.388
R squared	0.401	0.104
Benchmark: MSCI World C$		

TERMS AND CONDITIONS

Inception:	January 2, 2001
Style:	Multi Manager
Sub-style:	Security Selection
Valuation:	Daily
RRSP:	No
Management fee:	2.50%
Performance fee:	20.00%
High-water mark:	N/A
Hurdle rate:	0.00%
NAV:	$10.14
Asset Size (million):	$165.59
Maximum leverage:	N/A
Early red'n period:	N/A
Early red'n fee:	N/A

PERFORMANCE (as of December 31, 2004)

	1 mo.	3 mo.	6 mo.
Funds	1.08%	2.83%	1.89%
MSCI World C$	5.25%	6.76%	0.07%
Van Global HF Index	1.50%	4.87%	5.48%

	1 yr.	2 yr.	3 yr.
Funds	3.88%	6.11%	3.11%
MSCI World C$	6.85%	8.58%	-2.18%
Van Global HF Index	7.79%	13.04%	8.40%

Year	Jan	Feb	Mar	Apr	May	Jun	Jul	Aug	Sep	Oct	Nov	Dec	Total
2004	1.39%	1.32%	-0.01%	0.49%	-1.93%	0.72%	-0.57%	-0.18%	-0.17%	0.12%	1.60%	1.08%	3.88%
2003	1.24%	0.21%	0.45%	1.23%	1.08%	1.16%	0.37%	0.04%	0.93%	0.42%	0.18%	0.80%	8.39%
2002	-0.34%	-0.72%	0.73%	-0.70%	-0.67%	-0.93%	-0.45%	-0.19%	0.04%	-1.50%	1.00%	1.07%	-2.64%

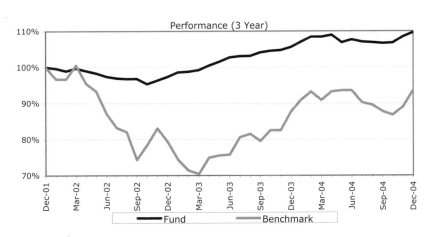

MAPLE KEY MARKET NEUTRAL L.P.

FUND SPONSOR COMPANY
Maple Financial Group Inc.
Tel: 416-350-8200   Toll-Free: N/A
Fax: 416-350-8222   Web site: www.maplefinancial.com

PORTFOLIO MANAGER(S)

Lucas Roffey joined Maple Financial in 2001. Mr. Roffey is part of the portfolio management team that manages Maple's various fund of funds products. The portfolio management team is responsible for quantitative and qualitative analysis of market neutral arbitrage strategies and hedge fund managers, allocation recommendations, and due diligence. Mr. Roffey has nine years of prior involvement in arbitrage investment strategies.

FUND DESCRIPTION

MAPLE KEY was designed to provide exposure to the market neutral asset class and to provide diversification among different market neutral strategies and managers. Market neutral funds selected by Maple employ a variety of strategies to hedge their exposure to the general direction of the equity and bond markets. The funds are selected to maximize the portfolio effect of enhancing returns without increasing risk and to create a portfolio that as a whole is market neutral and exhibits low volatility.

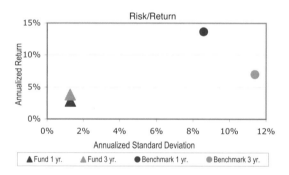

Rating:

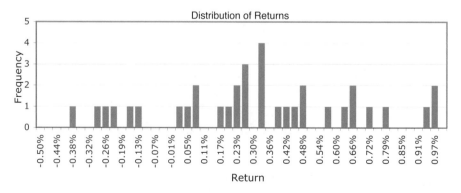

	1 yr.	3 yr.
Annualized rate of return	2.82%	3.83%
Annualized standard deviation	1.29%	1.29%
Percentage of negative months	25.00%	19.44%
Largest monthly drop	-0.31%	-0.38%
Maximum drawdown	-0.44%	-0.44%
Sharpe ratio	-0.91	-0.13
Semideviation	0.78%	0.79%
Sortino ratio	-1.52	-0.22
Jensen's alpha	-1.45%	-0.20%
Beta	0.03	0.01
Up capture ratio	9.75%	8.66%
Down capture ratio	-6.95%	-15.04%
Omega -0%	488%	839%
Appraisal ratio	-1.19	-0.16
Average α over benchmark	-0.87%	-0.30%
Tracking error	2.43%	3.28%
Information ratio	-35.69%	-9.26%
Sterling ratio	-2.68	-0.39
Treynor measure	-0.43	-0.22
M^2 – Modigliani measure	-17.50%	-4.52%
Burke ratio	-2.77	-0.27
Skewness	27.95%	8.25%
Kurtosis	-31%	-54%
Correlation to S&P/TSX	0.198	0.073
R squared	0.039	0.005
Benchmark: S&P/TSX		

TERMS AND CONDITIONS

Inception:	January 1, 1999
Style:	Fund of Hedge Funds
Sub-style:	N/A
Valuation:	Monthly
RRSP:	No
Management fee:	1.50%
Performance fee:	10.00%
High-water mark:	Yes
Hurdle rate:	0.00%
NAV:	$635.91
Asset Size (million):	N/A
Maximum leverage:	N/A
Early red'n period:	N/A
Early red'n fee:	N/A

PERFORMANCE (as of December 31, 2004)

	1 mo.	3 mo.	6 mo.
Funds	0.42%	1.05%	0.89%
S&P/TSX	2.40%	6.67%	8.41%
Van Global HF Index	1.50%	4.87%	5.48%

	1 yr.	2 yr.	3 yr.
Funds	2.82%	2.64%	3.83%
S&P/TSX	13.66%	19.32%	6.99%
Van Global HF Index	7.79%	13.04%	8.40%

Year	Jan	Feb	Mar	Apr	May	Jun	Jul	Aug	Sep	Oct	Nov	Dec	Total
2004	0.93%	0.72%	0.22%	0.31%	-0.31%	0.03%	0.25%	-0.24%	-0.17%	0.18%	0.45%	0.42%	2.82%
2003	0.96%	0.21%	-0.16%	0.07%	0.46%	0.06%	-0.26%	-0.01%	0.32%	0.24%	0.17%	0.38%	2.46%
2002	0.96%	0.30%	0.56%	0.62%	0.41%	-0.38%	0.24%	0.65%	0.64%	0.30%	0.77%	1.01%	6.24%

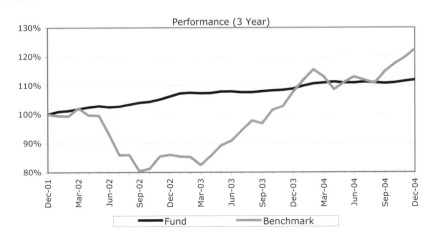

Performance (3 Year)

Fund — Benchmark

MONTRUSCO BOLTON FOCUS ABSOLUTE RETURN GLOBAL FUND

FUND SPONSOR COMPANY

Montrusco Bolton Investments

Tel: 514-282-2910   Toll-Free: N/A

Fax: 514-282-2973   Web site: www.hedgefunds.ca

PORTFOLIO MANAGER(S)

Frank Belvedere, Montrusco Bolton Investments

Eugenio Verzili, Focus Investment Group

FUND DESCRIPTION

The Montrusco Bolton Focus Absolute Return Global Fund seeks to achieve capital appreciation with low volatility. The Fund will invest in a diversified portfolio of alternative investment managers whose expertise varies by both strategy and geographical region. The Fund seeks to generate consistent absolute returns between 6 and 12% per annum.

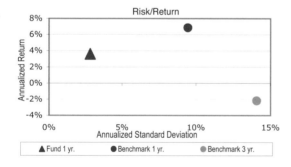

Rating: Not Rated

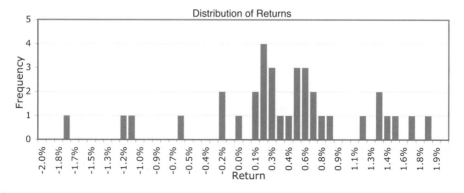

	1 yr.	3 yr.
Annualized rate of return	3.61%	
Annualized standard deviation	2.80%	
Percentage of negative months	33.33%	
Largest monthly drop	-1.14%	
Maximum drawdown	-1.77%	
Sharpe ratio	-0.14	
Semideviation	1.76%	
Sortino ratio	-0.22	
Jensen's alpha	-0.91%	
Beta	0.18	
Up capture ratio	20.16%	
Down capture ratio	0.52%	
Omega -0%	259%	
Appraisal ratio	-0.43	
Average α over benchmark	-0.29%	
Tracking error	2.26%	
Information ratio	-12.73%	
Sterling ratio	-0.22	
Treynor measure	-0.02	
M² – Modigliani measure	-4.16%	
Burke ratio	-0.29	
Skewness	-3.64%	
Kurtosis	-54%	
Correlation to S&P/TSX	0.444	
R squared	0.457	
Benchmark: MSCI World C$		

TERMS AND CONDITIONS

Inception:	February 1, 2002
Style:	Fund of Hedge Funds
Sub-style:	N/A
Valuation:	N/A
RRSP:	N/A
Management fee:	N/A
Performance fee:	N/A
High-water mark:	N/A
Hurdle rate:	N/A
NAV:	$113.79
Asset Size (million):	$175.00
Maximum leverage:	N/A
Early red'n period:	N/A
Early red'n fee:	N/A

PERFORMANCE (as of December 31, 2004)

	1 mo.	3 mo.	6 mo.
Funds	1.47%	3.03%	1.80%
MSCI World C$	5.25%	6.76%	0.07%
Van Global HF Index	1.50%	4.87%	5.48%

	1 yr.	2 yr.	3 yr.
Funds	3.61%	6.40%	
MSCI World C$	6.85%	8.58%	-2.18%
Van Global HF Index	7.79%	13.04%	8.40%

Year	Jan	Feb	Mar	Apr	May	Jun	Jul	Aug	Sep	Oct	Nov	Dec	Total
2004	1.31%	0.32%	0.52%	-0.23%	-0.62%	0.48%	-1.14%	-0.27%	0.21%	0.16%	1.38%	1.47%	3.61%
2003	0.58%	-0.06%	0.67%	1.28%	1.77%	0.16%	0.09%	0.75%	0.81%	1.63%	0.54%	0.68%	9.25%
2002		0.17%	0.61%	0.44%	0.21%	-1.22%	-1.77%	0.46%	0.10%	0.15%	1.13%	0.27%	0.52%

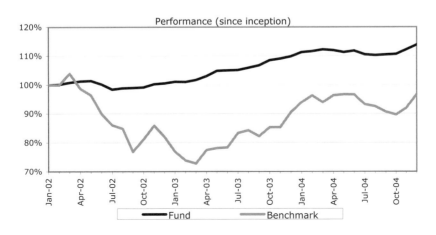

MOUNTAINVIEW OPPORTUNISTIC GROWTH FUND L.P.

FUND SPONSOR COMPANY

Felcom Management Corp.
Tel: 416-777-5189   Toll-Free: N/A
Fax: 416-226-3911   Web site: www.gcg.ca

PORTFOLIO MANAGER(S)

Andrew Ecclestone has 14 years of investment industry experience. He began his career with an independent venture capital firm in 1988. In 1991 he joined the Independent Order of Foresters where he was hired as the Investment Administration Officer responsible for upgrading all investment related systems and managing the investment administration staff. In 1993, he assumed the portfolio management responsibilities for a US$50 million venture capital portfolio.

FUND DESCRIPTION

The objective of the Fund is to achieve risk-adjusted positive annual returns. The Fund's assets are primarily invested in equities of small and mid-cap Canadian companies that trade on North American stock exchanges, including, but not limited to, the Toronto Stock Exchange, TSX Venture Exchange, New York Stock Exchange, American Stock Exchange, and NASDAQ.

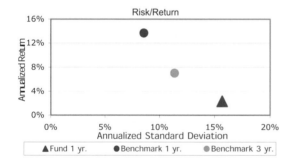

Rating: Not Rated

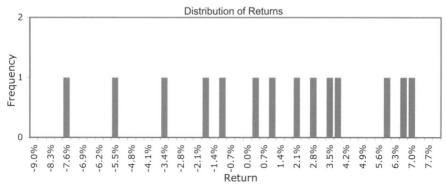

	1 yr.	3 yr.
Annualized rate of return	2.31%	
Annualized standard deviation	15.68%	
Percentage of negative months	41.67%	
Largest monthly drop	-7.74%	
Maximum drawdown	-18.50%	
Sharpe ratio	-0.11	
Semideviation	10.23%	
Sortino ratio	-0.17	
Jensen's alpha	-12.98%	
Beta	1.17	
Up capture ratio	80.56%	
Down capture ratio	177.90%	
Omega -0%	117%	
Appraisal ratio	-1.00	
Average α over benchmark	-0.82%	
Tracking error	3.31%	
Information ratio	-24.65%	
Sterling ratio	-0.09	
Treynor measure	-0.01	
M^2 – Modigliani measure	-10.59%	
Burke ratio	-0.16	
Skewness	-22.96%	
Kurtosis	-60%	
Correlation to S&P/TSX	0.698	
R squared	0.488	
Benchmark: S&P/TSX		

TERMS AND CONDITIONS

Inception:	November 1, 2002
Style:	Equity L/S
Sub-style:	N/A
Valuation:	Weekly on Friday
RRSP:	No
Management fee:	2.25%
Performance fee:	20.00%
High-water mark:	No
Hurdle rate:	10.00%
NAV:	$19.18
Asset Size (million):	N/A
Maximum leverage:	N/A
Early red'n period:	N/A
Early red'n fee:	N/A

PERFORMANCE (as of December 31, 2004)

	1 mo.	3 mo.	6 mo.
Funds	6.43%	11.54%	4.89%
S&P/TSX	2.40%	6.67%	8.41%
Van Global HF Index	1.50%	4.87%	5.48%

	1 yr.	2 yr.	3 yr.
Funds	2.31%		
S&P/TSX	13.66%	19.32%	6.99%
Van Global HF Index	7.79%	13.04%	8.40%

Year	Jan	Feb	Mar	Apr	May	Jun	Jul	Aug	Sep	Oct	Nov	Dec	Total
2004	6.92%	1.86%	0.14%	-5.57%	-1.73%	-3.63%	-7.74%	-1.22%	3.18%	3.71%	1.05%	6.43%	2.31%
2003											5.75%	2.69%	8.59%
2002													

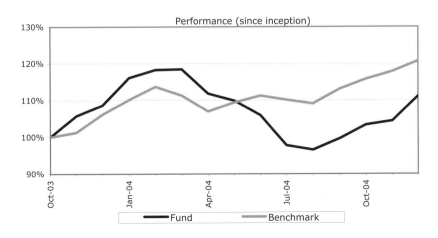

Performance (since inception)

NAVIGATOR COMPASS LONG/SHORT FUND

FUND SPONSOR COMPANY

Navigator Capital Management Inc.

Tel: 416-644-8312   Toll-Free: N/A

Fax: 416-644-8313   Web site: www.navcap.com

PORTFOLIO MANAGER(S)

James Darcel oversees investments and risk management for the Fund. Jim brings with him 18 years of capital markets experience and knowledge. Jim's proficiencies include stock index arbitrage, interest rate modelling, currency hedging and portfolio risk management, as well as other quantitative and fundamentally based trading strategies. Jim's most recent experience included employment as a Financial Analyst with Manitoba Public Insurance from May 2002 to October 2002.

FUND DESCRIPTION

To achieve an above-average absolute portfolio return.

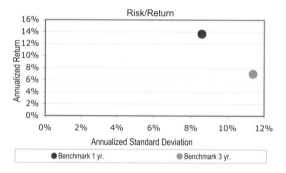

Rating: Not Rated

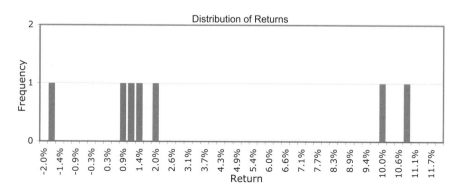

	1 yr.	3 yr.
Annualized rate of return		
Annualized standard deviation		
Percentage of negative months		
Largest monthly drop		
Maximum drawdown		
Sharpe ratio		
Semideviation		
Sortino ratio		
Jensen's alpha		
Beta		
Up capture ratio		
Down capture ratio		
Omega -0%		
Appraisal ratio		
Average α over benchmark		
Tracking error		
Information ratio		
Sterling ratio		
Treynor measure		
M² – Modigliani measure		
Burke ratio		
Skewness		
Kurtosis		
Correlation to S&P/TSX		
R squared		
Benchmark: S&P/TSX		

TERMS AND CONDITIONS

Inception:	May 3, 2004
Style:	Enhanced Equity
Sub-style:	Equity
Valuation:	Monthly
RRSP:	No
Management fee:	1.95%
Performance fee:	20.00%
High-water mark:	No
Hurdle rate:	4.00%
NAV:	$12.69
Asset Size (million):	$5.79
Maximum leverage:	N/A
Early red'n period:	1 mo.
Early red'n fee:	N/A

PERFORMANCE (as of December 31, 2004)

	1 mo.	3 mo.	6 mo.
Funds	9.78%	23.92%	23.78%
S&P/TSX	2.40%	6.67%	8.41%
Van Global HF Index	1.50%	4.87%	5.48%

	1 yr.	2 yr.	3 yr.
Funds			
S&P/TSX	13.66%	19.32%	6.99%
Van Global HF Index	7.79%	13.04%	8.40%

Year	Jan	Feb	Mar	Apr	May	Jun	Jul	Aug	Sep	Oct	Nov	Dec	Total
2004						1.31%	0.77%	-1.92%	1.06%	1.85%	10.83%	9.78%	25.41%
2003													
2002													

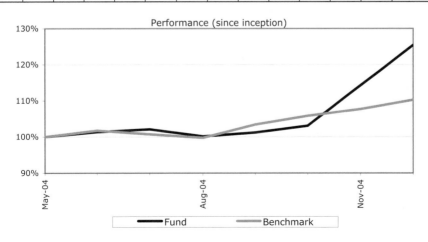

Performance (since inception)

Fund — Benchmark

NL GLOBAL TRADING

FUND SPONSOR COMPANY
Norshield Asset Management (Canada) Ltd.
Tel: 416-598-2122   Toll-Free: 800-268-8882
Fax: N/A   Web site: www.norshield.com

PORTFOLIO MANAGER(S)

In 1984, the **Norshield Financial Group**, under the leadership of John Xanthoudakis, commenced operations. Norshield's reputation is built on providing dynamic, timely, and professional alternative investment advice and services aimed at consistently generating superior risk-adjusted returns irrespective of market conditions.

FUND DESCRIPTION

To achieve long-term capital appreciation with yield enhancing features of alternative investment strategies.

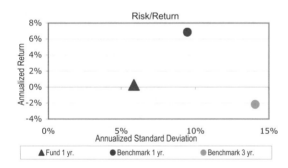

Rating: Not Rated

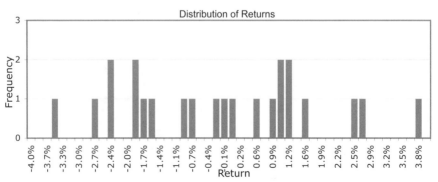

	1 yr.	3 yr.
Annualized rate of return	0.28%	
Annualized standard deviation	5.84%	
Percentage of negative months	58.33%	
Largest monthly drop	-2.01%	
Maximum drawdown	-6.16%	
Sharpe ratio	-0.64	
Semideviation	2.83%	
Sortino ratio	-1.31	
Jensen's alpha	-4.34%	
Beta	0.22	
Up capture ratio	15.96%	
Down capture ratio	26.58%	
Omega -0%	106%	
Appraisal ratio	-0.75	
Average α over benchmark	-0.55%	
Tracking error	2.60%	
Information ratio	-21.19%	
Sterling ratio	-0.60	
Treynor measure	-0.17	
M^2 – Modigliani measure	-8.87%	
Burke ratio	-1.06	
Skewness	79.83%	
Kurtosis	83%	
Correlation to S&P/TSX	0.521	
R squared	0.147	
Benchmark: MSCI World C$		

TERMS AND CONDITIONS

Inception:	January 20, 2003
Style:	Directional
Sub-style:	N/A
Valuation:	Weekly on Monday
RRSP:	NO
Management fee:	3.91%
Performance fee:	N/A
High-water mark:	N/A
Hurdle rate:	N/A
NAV:	$9.41
Asset Size (million):	$8.09
Maximum leverage:	N/A
Early red'n period:	N/A
Early red'n fee:	N/A

PERFORMANCE (as of December 31, 2004)

	1 mo.	3 mo.	6 mo.
Funds	1.39%	6.25%	3.56%
MSCI World C$	5.25%	6.76%	0.07%
Van Global HF Index	1.50%	4.87%	5.48%

	1 yr.	2 yr.	3 yr.
Funds	0.28%		
MSCI World C$	6.85%	8.58%	-2.18%
Van Global HF Index	7.79%	13.04%	8.40%

Year	Jan	Feb	Mar	Apr	May	Jun	Jul	Aug	Sep	Oct	Nov	Dec	Total
2004	-0.23%	0.81%	-2.01%	-1.89%	-0.90%	1.06%	-0.01%	-1.78%	-0.75%	0.96%	3.80%	1.39%	0.28%
2003		-2.47%	-2.48%	-3.66%	2.42%	-1.57%	2.59%	-2.76%	0.52%	0.91%	-0.31%	1.11%	-5.77%
2002													

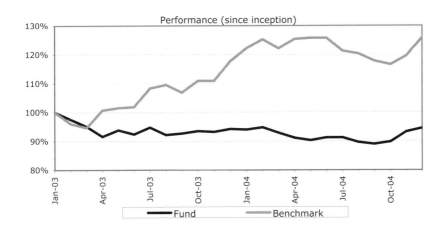

Performance (since inception)

NORTHERN RIVERS INNOVATION FUND L.P.

FUND SPONSOR COMPANY

Northern Rivers Capital Management Inc.
Tel: 416-597-1095   Toll-Free: N/A
Fax: 416-597-1202   Web site: www.deltaonecapital.com

PORTFOLIO MANAGER(S)

Hugh Cleland has a Bachelor of Arts (Honors, 1992/97) from Harvard University. After graduating from Harvard, Mr. Cleland worked in the Research Department at Midland Walwyn Capital (now Merrill Lynch Canada) as Research Associate to the Senior Telecommunications Services Analyst. From March 1998 to March 2001, he worked at Interward Capital Corporation. Mr. Cleland earned his CFA designation in 2001.

FUND DESCRIPTION

The NRIF is a specialty fund whose primary objective is to maximize absolute returns on investments through securities selection and asset allocation, while using hedging activities and asset allocation to manage market risk. The Fund focuses on achieving growth of capital through superior securities selection.

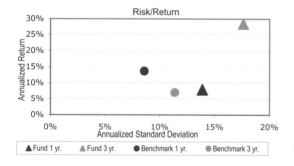

Rating:

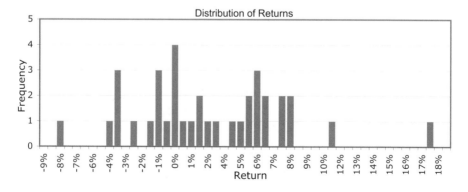

	1 yr.	3 yr.
Annualized rate of return	7.95%	28.44%
Annualized standard deviation	13.90%	17.63%
Percentage of negative months	50.00%	38.89%
Largest monthly drop	-4.79%	-8.15%
Maximum drawdown	-11.19%	-12.17%
Sharpe ratio	0.28	1.39
Semideviation	6.73%	8.50%
Sortino ratio	0.59	2.87
Jensen's alpha	-3.28%	21.85%
Beta	0.75	0.87
Up capture ratio	82.56%	136.69%
Down capture ratio	121.24%	-5.83%
Omega -0%	158%	327%
Appraisal ratio	-0.41	-3.12
Average α over benchmark	-0.39%	1.61%
Tracking error	3.49%	4.18%
Information ratio	-11.11%	38.58%
Sterling ratio	0.35	2.01
Treynor measure	0.05	0.28
M² – Modigliani measure	-7.22%	12.81%
Burke ratio	0.55	1.96
Skewness	39.25%	57.81%
Kurtosis	-87%	105%
Correlation to S&P/TSX	0.505	0.576
R squared	0.255	0.332
Benchmark: S&P/TSX		

TERMS AND CONDITIONS

Inception:	May 8, 2001
Style:	Security Selection
Sub-style:	N/A
Valuation:	Monthly
RRSP:	No
Management fee:	1.00%
Performance fee:	20.00%
High-water mark:	Yes
Hurdle rate:	8.00%
NAV:	$2,365
Asset Size (million):	$38.10
Maximum leverage:	N/A
Early red'n period:	N/A
Early red'n fee:	N/A

PERFORMANCE (as of December 31, 2004)

	1 mo.	3 mo.	6 mo.
Funds	1.34%	8.86%	1.80%
S&P/TSX	2.40%	6.67%	8.41%
Van Global HF Index	1.50%	4.87%	5.48%

	1 yr.	2 yr.	3 yr.
Funds	7.95%	37.53%	28.44%
S&P/TSX	13.66%	19.32%	6.99%
Van Global HF Index	7.79%	13.04%	8.40%

Year	Jan	Feb	Mar	Apr	May	Jun	Jul	Aug	Sep	Oct	Nov	Dec	Total
2004	5.12%	5.80%	-1.79%	-0.99%	-4.79%	2.99%	-2.84%	-4.13%	0.40%	-0.32%	7.76%	1.34%	7.95%
2003	3.92%	-1.31%	-4.05%	2.23%	5.13%	6.12%	10.45%	17.63%	7.46%	5.67%	-0.38%	6.22%	75.21%
2002	8.00%	4.15%	-0.31%	1.31%	7.21%	-3.92%	-8.15%	0.93%	-1.39%	0.10%	5.72%	-1.05%	12.03%

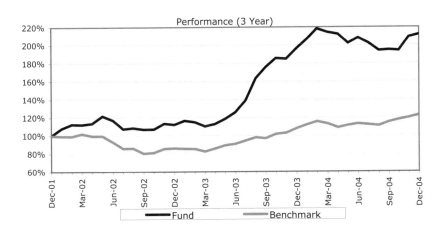

Performance (3 Year)

— Fund   — Benchmark

OLYMPUS UNITED GLOBAL TRADING FUND

FUND SPONSOR COMPANY
Olympus United Group Inc.
Tel: 416-203-2118   Toll-Free: 866-554-9994
Fax: 416-203-0721   Web site: www.olympusfunds.com

PORTFOLIO MANAGER(S)

In 1984, the **Norshield Financial Group**, under the leadership of John Xanthoudakis, commenced operations. Norshield's reputation is built on providing dynamic, timely, and professional alternative investment advice and services aimed at consistently generating superior risk-adjusted returns irrespective of market conditions.

FUND DESCRIPTION

The investment process combines both top-down and bottom-up styles. It consists of three alternative investment styles across five different managers, with a targeted return in the range of 15–20% and an annualized volatility of 5–10%. The portfolio for the Global Trading Fund will contain the following trading styles: currency trading, short-term opportunistic, managed futures, high-yield, and tactical trading.

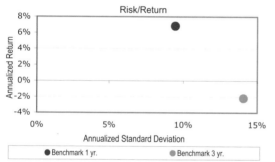

Rating: Not Rated

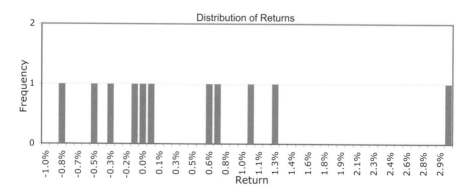

	1 yr.	3 yr.
Annualized rate of return		
Annualized standard deviation		
Percentage of negative months		
Largest monthly drop		
Maximum drawdown		
Sharpe ratio		
Semideviation		
Sortino ratio		
Jensen's alpha		
Beta		
Up capture ratio		
Down capture ratio		
Omega -0%		
Appraisal ratio		
Average α over benchmark		
Tracking error		
Information ratio		
Sterling ratio		
Treynor measure		
M² – Modigliani measure		
Burke ratio		
Skewness		
Kurtosis		
Correlation to S&P/TSX		
R squared		
Benchmark: MSCI World C$		

TERMS AND CONDITIONS

Inception:	January 4, 2004
Style:	Fund of Hedge Funds
Sub-style:	N/A
Valuation:	Monthly
RRSP:	No
Management fee:	1.75%
Performance fee:	10.00%
High-water mark:	Yes
Hurdle rate:	0.00%
NAV:	$12.42
Asset Size (million):	$3.87
Maximum leverage:	N/A
Early red'n period:	N/A
Early red'n fee:	N/A

PERFORMANCE (as of December 31, 2004)

	1 mo.	3 mo.	6 mo.
Funds	1.28%	5.28%	5.29%
MSCI World C$	5.25%	6.76%	0.07%
Van Global HF Index	1.50%	4.87%	5.48%

	1 yr.	2 yr.	3 yr.
Funds			
MSCI World C$	6.85%	8.58%	-2.18%
Van Global HF Index	7.79%	13.04%	8.40%

Year	Jan	Feb	Mar	Apr	May	Jun	Jul	Aug	Sep	Oct	Nov	Dec	Total
2004		0.04%	-0.90%	-0.04%	-0.35%	0.57%	0.71%	-0.52%	-0.17%	0.99%	2.93%	1.28%	4.58%
2003													
2002													

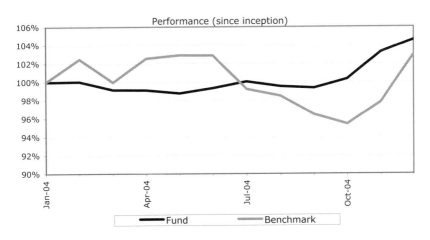

Performance (since inception)

Fund   Benchmark

OLYMPUS UNITED MULTI-ASSET FUND

FUND SPONSOR COMPANY

Norshield Asset Management (Canada)

Tel: 416-203-2118   Toll-Free: 866-554-9994

Fax: 416-203-0721   Web site: www.olympusfunds.com

PORTFOLIO MANAGER(S)

In 1984, the **Norshield Financial Group**, under the leadership of John Xanthoudakis, commenced operations. Norshield's reputation is built on providing dynamic, timely, and professional alternative investment advice and services aimed at consistently generating superior risk-adjusted returns irrespective of market conditions.

FUND DESCRIPTION

The Fund's investment objective is to deliver a return on investment that is above the average for fixed income investments while comparable with equity fund investments, and to do so in a manner with lower volatility and more consistent month-over-month performance than would normally be expected from investments with similarly targeted returns.

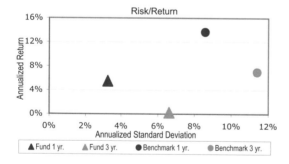

Rating: Not Rated

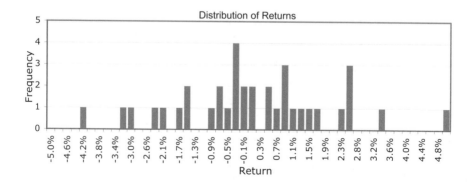

	1 yr.	3 yr.
Annualized rate of return	5.52%	0.24%
Annualized standard deviation	3.25%	6.63%
Percentage of negative months	33.33%	52.78%
Largest monthly drop	-0.84%	-4.20%
Maximum drawdown	-1.74%	-18.81%
Sharpe ratio	0.47	-0.57
Semideviation	1.57%	4.19%
Sortino ratio	0.96	-0.90
Jensen's alpha	1.55%	-3.47%
Beta	0.00	-0.09
Up capture ratio	17.24%	1.78%
Down capture ratio	-18.69%	2.10%
Omega -0%	408%	105%
Appraisal ratio	0.47	-0.52
Average α over benchmark	-0.65%	-0.58%
Tracking error	2.66%	4.07%
Information ratio	-24.37%	-14.25%
Sterling ratio	0.87	-0.20
Treynor measure	-3.89	0.40
M² – Modigliani measure	-5.65%	-9.45%
Burke ratio	1.38	-0.48
Skewness	75.53%	10.34%
Kurtosis	60%	26%
Correlation to S&P/TSX	-0.011	-0.166
R squared	0.000	0.027
Benchmark: S&P/TSX		

TERMS AND CONDITIONS

Inception:	January 1, 1994
Style:	Directional
Sub-style:	Equity
Valuation:	Weekly
RRSP:	No
Management fee:	1.75%
Performance fee:	10.00%
High-water mark:	Yes
Hurdle rate:	0.00%
NAV:	$11.57
Asset Size (million):	$4.55
Maximum leverage:	N/A
Early red'n period:	N/A
Early red'n fee:	N/A

PERFORMANCE (as of December 31, 2004)

	1 mo.	3 mo.	6 mo.
Funds	0.95%	2.15%	1.21%
S&P/TSX	2.40%	6.67%	8.41%
Van Global HF Index	1.50%	4.87%	5.48%

	1 yr.	2 yr.	3 yr.
Funds	5.52%	-1.69%	0.24%
S&P/TSX	13.66%	19.32%	6.99%
Van Global HF Index	7.79%	13.04%	8.40%

Year	Jan	Feb	Mar	Apr	May	Jun	Jul	Aug	Sep	Oct	Nov	Dec	Total
2004	2.46%	0.32%	0.65%	1.62%	-0.84%	0.01%	-0.70%	-0.11%	-0.12%	0.32%	0.87%	0.95%	5.52%
2003	-3.24%	-4.20%	-0.98%	-2.28%	-2.40%	-1.85%	-0.85%	-3.01%	2.54%	0.89%	4.80%	2.25%	-8.40%
2002	-0.38%	1.15%	1.48%	-0.39%	-1.61%	2.41%	3.35%	-0.07%	-0.47%	-0.47%	0.91%	-1.65%	4.22%

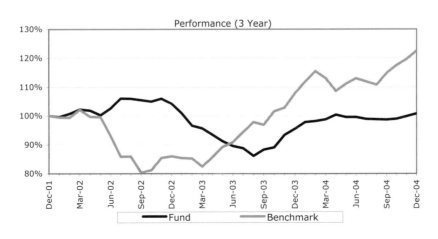

Performance (3 Year)

OLYMPUS UNITED TACTICAL TRADING FUND

FUND SPONSOR COMPANY
Olympus United Group Inc.
Tel: 416-203-2118   Toll-Free: 866-554-9994
Fax: 416-203-0721   Web site: www.olympusfunds.com

PORTFOLIO MANAGER(S)

In 1984, the **Norshield Financial Group**, under the leadership of John Xanthoudakis, commenced operations. Norshield's reputation was, from inception, built on providing dynamic, timely, and professional alternative investment advice and services aimed at consistently generating superior risk-adjusted returns irrespective of market conditions.

FUND DESCRIPTION

The Fund's investment objective is to delivery a return on investment that is above the average for fixed income investments while comparable with equity fund investments, and to do so in a manner with lower volatility and more consistent month-over-month performance than would normally be expected from investments with similarly targeted returns.

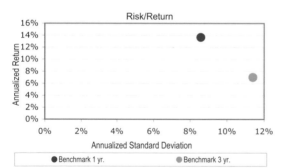

Rating: Not Rated

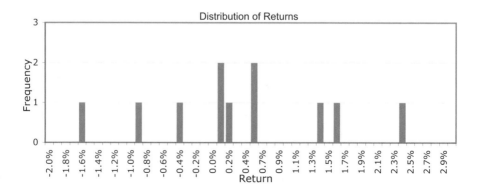

	1 yr.	3 yr.
Annualized rate of return		
Annualized standard deviation		
Percentage of negative months		
Largest monthly drop		
Maximum drawdown		
Sharpe ratio		
Semideviation		
Sortino ratio		
Jensen's alpha		
Beta		
Up capture ratio		
Down capture ratio		
Omega -0%		
Appraisal ratio		
Average α over benchmark		
Tracking error		
Information ratio		
Sterling ratio		
Treynor measure		
M² – Modigliani measure		
Burke ratio		
Skewness		
Kurtosis		
Correlation to S&P/TSX		
R squared		
Benchmark: S&P/TSX		

TERMS AND CONDITIONS

Inception:	January 4, 2004
Style:	Directional Trading
Sub-style:	N/A
Valuation:	Weekly
RRSP:	No
Management fee:	1.75%
Performance fee:	10.00%
High-water mark:	Yes
Hurdle rate:	0.00%
NAV:	$7.76
Asset Size (million):	$10.54
Maximum leverage:	N/A
Early red'n period:	N/A
Early red'n fee:	N/A

PERFORMANCE (as of December 31, 2004)

	1 mo.	3 mo.	6 mo.
Funds	1.30%	5.19%	4.85%
S&P/TSX	2.40%	6.67%	8.41%
Van Global HF Index	1.50%	4.87%	5.48%

	1 yr.	2 yr.	3 yr.
Funds			
S&P/TSX	13.66%	19.32%	6.99%
Van Global HF Index	7.79%	13.04%	8.40%

Year	Jan	Feb	Mar	Apr	May	Jun	Jul	Aug	Sep	Oct	Nov	Dec	Total
2004		-0.46%	0.46%	-1.65%	0.16%	0.07%	-0.91%	0.08%	0.51%	1.48%	2.32%	1.30%	3.36%
2003													
2002													

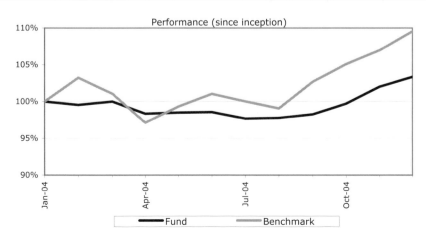

Performance (since inception)

OLYMPUS UNITED UNIVEST II FUND

FUND SPONSOR COMPANY
Olympus United Group Inc.
Tel: 416-203-2118   Toll-Free: 866-554-9994
Fax: 416-203-0721   Web site: www.olympusfunds.com

PORTFOLIO MANAGER(S)

In 1984, the **Norshield Financial Group**, under the leadership of John Xanthoudakis, commenced operations. Norshield's reputation is built on providing dynamic, timely and professional alternative investment advice and services aimed at consistently generating superior risk-adjusted returns irrespective of market conditions.

FUND DESCRIPTION

The Fund's investment objective is to provide a superior yield while maintaining a low degree of volatility and correlation relative to major global markets. The Fund will attempt to achieve this objective through allocation of assets to both traditional and non-traditional strategies. The fund's performance has been different from Univest's earlier experience from the 1990s, nevertheless the fund has never lost in any four-month period and has very low risk.

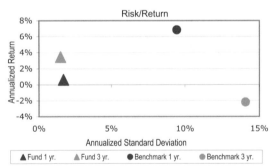

Rating: Not Rated

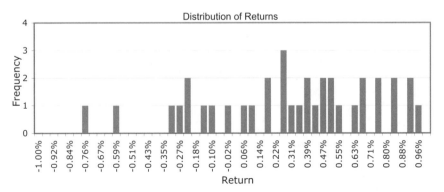

	1 yr.	3 yr.
Annualized rate of return	0.61%	3.45%
Annualized standard deviation	1.70%	1.50%
Percentage of negative months	41.67%	25.00%
Largest monthly drop	-0.78%	-0.78%
Maximum drawdown	-1.82%	-1.82%
Sharpe ratio	-2.00	-0.37
Semideviation	1.02%	1.08%
Sortino ratio	-3.32	-0.51
Jensen's alpha	-3.62%	-0.51%
Beta	0.08	0.01
Up capture ratio	8.02%	8.83%
Down capture ratio	8.73%	-8.29%
Omega -0%	130%	460%
Appraisal ratio	-2.19	-0.35
Average α over benchmark	-0.54%	0.39%
Tracking error	2.53%	4.06%
Information ratio	-21.17%	9.54%
Sterling ratio	-1.86	-0.30
Treynor measure	-0.43	-0.86
M^2 – Modigliani measure	-21.75%	1.02%
Burke ratio	-3.10	-0.47
Skewness	-19.59%	-55.93%
Kurtosis	-58%	-16%
Correlation to S&P/TSX	0.648	0.200
R squared	0.233	0.004
Benchmark: MSCI World C$		

TERMS AND CONDITIONS

Inception:	December 22, 2000
Style:	Fund of Hedge Funds
Sub-style:	N/A
Valuation:	Weekly
RRSP:	No
Management fee:	1.75%
Performance fee:	10.00%
High-water mark:	N/A
Hurdle rate:	N/A
NAV:	$12.07
Asset Size (million):	$115.85
Maximum leverage:	N/A
Early red'n period:	N/A
Early red'n fee:	N/A

PERFORMANCE (as of December 31, 2004)

	1 mo.	3 mo.	6 mo.
Funds	0.73%	1.89%	0.91%
MSCI World C$	5.25%	6.76%	0.07%
Van Global HF Index	1.50%	4.87%	5.48%

	1 yr.	2 yr.	3 yr.
Funds	0.61%	2.34%	3.45%
MSCI World C$	6.85%	8.58%	-2.18%
Van Global HF Index	7.79%	13.04%	8.40%

Year	Jan	Feb	Mar	Apr	May	Jun	Jul	Aug	Sep	Oct	Nov	Dec	Total
2004	0.32%	0.17%	0.09%	-0.78%	0.23%	-0.32%	-0.63%	-0.29%	-0.04%	0.35%	0.80%	0.73%	0.61%
2003	0.25%	-0.14%	-0.23%	0.41%	0.91%	0.27%	0.06%	0.38%	0.53%	0.61%	0.50%	0.48%	4.09%
2002	0.90%	-0.18%	0.67%	0.25%	0.43%	0.83%	0.73%	0.45%	0.17%	-0.24%	0.93%	0.64%	5.72%

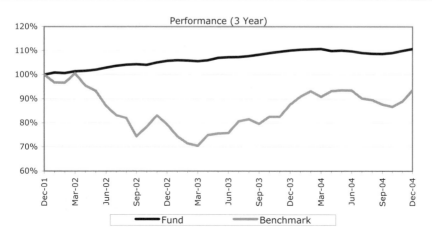

Performance (3 Year)

ONE FINANCIAL GUARANTEED ABSOLUTE RETURN NOTES

FUND SPONSOR COMPANY
ONE Financial Corporation
Tel: 416-360-7888   Toll-Free: 866-360-7888
Fax: 416-360-8947   Web site: www.one-financial.ca

PORTFOLIO MANAGER(S)

Alliance Capital; Forest Investment Associates; PanAgora Asset Management; Thames River Kingsway;
Weiss, Peck & Greer, LLC

FUND DESCRIPTION

The Fund is 100% guaranteed principal by Société Générale. It has a medium term to maturity of approximately six years.
It is a low-correlation alternative to traditional equity or fixed income investments, designed for the potential to achieve
positive performance in all stock market environments. The Fund has access to experienced hedge fund managers
through Société Générale's Lyxor program.

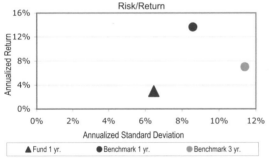

Rating: Not Rated

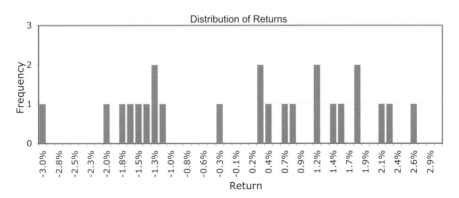

	1 yr.	3 yr.
Annualized rate of return	2.98%	
Annualized standard deviation	6.46%	
Percentage of negative months	41.67%	
Largest monthly drop	-3.14%	
Maximum drawdown	-7.56%	
Sharpe ratio	-0.16	
Semideviation	3.54%	
Sortino ratio	-0.29	
Jensen's alpha	-1.49%	
Beta	0.16	
Up capture ratio	16.01%	
Down capture ratio	-0.71%	
Omega -0%	139%	
Appraisal ratio	-0.25	
Average α over benchmark	-0.33%	
Tracking error	2.88%	
Information ratio	-11.35%	
Sterling ratio	-0.14	
Treynor measure	-0.06	
M² – Modigliani measure	-4.34%	
Burke ratio	-0.25	
Skewness	-40.56%	
Kurtosis	-79%	
Correlation to S&P/TSX	0.473	
R squared	0.068	
Benchmark: MSCI World C$		

TERMS AND CONDITIONS

Inception:	October 11, 2002
Style:	Multi Manager
Sub-style:	N/A
Valuation:	Weekly on Friday
RRSP:	Yes
Management fee:	2.75%
Performance fee:	N/A
High-water mark:	N/A
Hurdle rate:	N/A
NAV:	$10.07
Asset Size (million):	N/A
Maximum leverage:	N/A
Early red'n period:	N/A
Early red'n fee:	N/A

PERFORMANCE (as of December 31, 2004)

	1 mo.	3 mo.	6 mo.
Funds	1.06%	2.93%	3.57%
MSCI World C$	5.25%	6.76%	0.07%
Van Global HF Index	1.50%	4.87%	5.48%

	1 yr.	2 yr.	3 yr.
Funds	2.98%	2.36%	
MSCI World C$	6.85%	8.58%	-2.18%
Van Global HF Index	7.79%	13.04%	8.40%

Year	Jan	Feb	Mar	Apr	May	Jun	Jul	Aug	Sep	Oct	Nov	Dec	Total
2004	3.03%	1.66%	1.49%	-3.14%	-1.78%	-1.68%	-1.17%	1.06%	0.75%	-0.34%	2.19%	1.06%	2.98%
2003	-1.48%	0.58%	-1.61%	1.36%	2.58%	0.24%	-1.39%	-2.11%	3.09%	-1.38%	0.36%	1.66%	1.74%
2002											0.23%	2.14%	2.38%

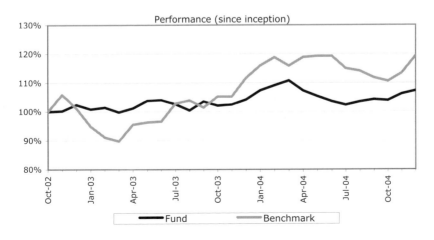

Performance (since inception)

Fund — Benchmark

ONE FINANCIAL MSCI HEDGE INVEST INDEX NOTES SERIES 1

FUND SPONSOR COMPANY

ONE Financial Corporation
Tel: 416-360-7888   Toll-Free: 866-360-7888
Fax: 416-360-8947   Web site: www.one-financial.ca

PORTFOLIO MANAGER(S)

ONE Financial

FUND DESCRIPTION

100% original principal guarantee at maturity plus exposure to the MSCI Hedge Invest Index. This index consists of a diverse sample of hedge funds that represent a broad range of hedge fund strategies and have weekly liquidity. As of December 2004, the index contained 120 funds in 11 investment processes and 24 strategies. The number of funds in the index is expected to increase over time.

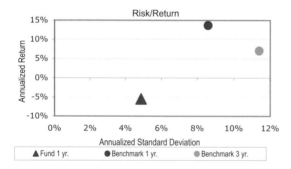

Rating: Not Rated

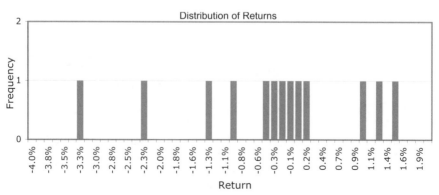

	1 yr.	3 yr.
Annualized rate of return	-5.51%	
Annualized standard deviation	4.87%	
Percentage of negative months	66.67%	
Largest monthly drop	-3.33%	
Maximum drawdown	-8.58%	
Sharpe ratio	-1.95	
Semideviation	3.87%	
Sortino ratio	-2.45	
Jensen's alpha	-9.14%	
Beta	-0.13	
Up capture ratio	-34.03%	
Down capture ratio	-7.52%	
Omega -0%	40%	
Appraisal ratio	-2.19	
Average α over benchmark	-1.05%	
Tracking error	3.39%	
Information ratio	-30.93%	
Sterling ratio	-1.11	
Treynor measure	0.75	
M² – Modigliani measure	-21.30%	
Burke ratio	-2.14	
Skewness	-62.68%	
Kurtosis	26%	
Correlation to S&P/TSX	0.179	
R squared	0.073	
Benchmark: MSCI World C$		

TERMS AND CONDITIONS

Inception:	November 6, 2003
Style:	Fund of Funds
Sub-style:	Guaranteed Note
Valuation:	Weekly on Friday
RRSP:	Yes
Management fee:	1.50%
Performance fee:	0.00%
High-water mark:	No
Hurdle rate:	No
NAV:	$9.49
Asset Size (million):	N/A
Maximum leverage:	N/A
Early red'n period:	N/A
Early red'n fee:	N/A

PERFORMANCE (as of December 31, 2004)

	1 mo.	3 mo.	6 mo.
Funds	-0.10%	0.75%	3.36%
MSCI World C$	5.25%	6.76%	0.07%
Van Global HF Index	1.50%	4.87%	5.48%

	1 yr.	2 yr.	3 yr.
Funds	-5.51%		
MSCI World C$	6.85%	8.58%	-2.18%
Van Global HF Index	7.79%	13.04%	8.40%

Year	Jan	Feb	Mar	Apr	May	Jun	Jul	Aug	Sep	Oct	Nov	Dec	Total
2004	-0.33%	-1.37%	-0.57%	-3.33%	-2.32%	-0.94%	0.94%	1.51%	0.13%	-0.32%	1.17%	-0.10%	-5.51%
2003												0.04%	0.04%
2002													

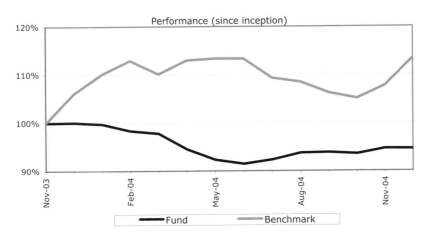

Performance (since inception)

Legend: —— Fund   —— Benchmark

PERFORMANCE MARKET HEDGE FUND

FUND SPONSOR COMPANY

Performance Group GenPar Ltd.

Tel: 416-967-5522   Toll-Free: N/A
Fax: 416-967-5755   Web site: www.performance-group.ca

PORTFOLIO MANAGER(S)

Rocco Marcello has worked in the securities industry for over 40 years. He is a former vice-chairman of the Toronto Stock Exchange and a former director of the Investment Dealers Association.

FUND DESCRIPTION

Consistent monthly returns with low volatility.

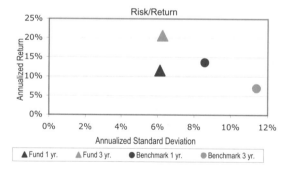

Rating:

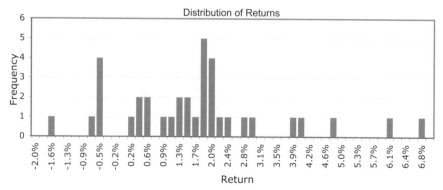

	1 yr.	3 yr.
Annualized rate of return	11.56%	20.62%
Annualized standard deviation	6.12%	6.26%
Percentage of negative months	33.33%	16.67%
Largest monthly drop	-1.77%	-1.77%
Maximum drawdown	-2.94%	-2.94%
Sharpe ratio	1.23	2.65
Semideviation	2.76%	3.31%
Sortino ratio	2.74	5.03
Jensen's alpha	2.09%	15.60%
Beta	0.57	0.34
Up capture ratio	67.95%	82.32%
Down capture ratio	46.95%	-19.97%
Omega -0%	402%	1238%
Appraisal ratio	-4.88	-20.35
Average α over benchmark	-0.17%	0.97%
Tracking error	1.29%	2.55%
Information ratio	-13.21%	38.12%
Sterling ratio	2.58	5.66
Treynor measure	0.13	0.49
M² – Modigliani measure	0.95%	27.25%
Burke ratio	3.62	7.24
Skewness	54.21%	85.46%
Kurtosis	51%	135%
Correlation to S&P/TSX	0.867	0.638
R squared	0.752	0.407
Benchmark: S&P/TSX		

TERMS AND CONDITIONS

Inception:	July 31, 2000
Style:	Non-directional
Sub-style:	N/A
Valuation:	Monthly
RRSP:	No
Management fee:	N/A
Performance fee:	N/A
High-water mark:	N/A
Hurdle rate:	N/A
NAV:	$2,027.42
Asset Size (million):	$70.00
Maximum leverage:	N/A
Early red'n period:	N/A
Early red'n fee:	N/A

PERFORMANCE (as of December 31, 2004)

	1 mo.	3 mo.	6 mo.
Funds	1.52%	5.55%	6.12%
S&P/TSX	2.40%	6.67%	8.41%
Van Global HF Index	1.50%	4.87%	5.48%

	1 yr.	2 yr.	3 yr.
Funds	11.56%	24.15%	20.62%
S&P/TSX	13.66%	19.32%	6.99%
Van Global HF Index	7.79%	13.04%	8.40%

Year	Jan	Feb	Mar	Apr	May	Jun	Jul	Aug	Sep	Oct	Nov	Dec	Total
2004	4.72%	2.12%	-0.66%	-1.77%	0.42%	0.32%	-0.62%	-0.65%	1.83%	2.00%	1.94%	1.52%	11.56%
2003	1.49%	1.22%	1.14%	1.84%	1.43%	0.97%	5.93%	3.72%	1.84%	6.71%	2.78%	3.90%	38.16%
2002	0.94%	2.03%	1.78%	0.31%	0.50%	-0.77%	-0.57%	2.30%	1.81%	2.65%	1.98%	0.17%	13.86%

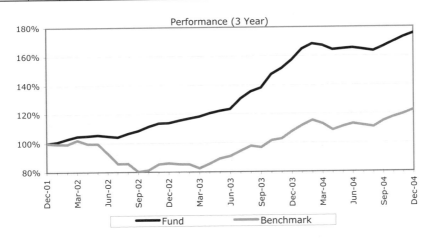

Performance (3 Year)

— Fund   — Benchmark

PESCARA FUND OF FUNDS

FUND SPONSOR COMPANY
Pescara Partners Inc.
Tel: 905-502-8738   Toll-Free: N/A
Fax: 905-502-9504   Web site: www.pescara.ca

PORTFOLIO MANAGER(S)

Pescara has retained Felcom Management Corp. of Toronto to provide investment advice on the selection of hedge fund managers and for the fund's asset allocation strategy. In order to diversify risks, Felcom will allocate the Fund's assets to various hedge fund managers using quantitative and qualitative methodologies. Additionally, Felcom's Alternative Strategy Committee will continuously monitor the performance of the Fund and when it deems it appropriate, make changes to the mix of the managers.

FUND DESCRIPTION

The investment objective of the Fund is to earn a positive risk-adjusted return on capital in each year (an absolute return) that is uncorrelated with major equity and fixed income markets. The Fund will attempt to achieve its objective by allocating the Fund's investments among a variety of Underlying Funds with differing investment strategies.

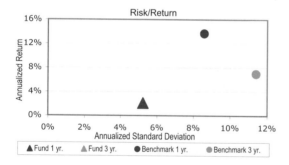

Rating: Not Rated

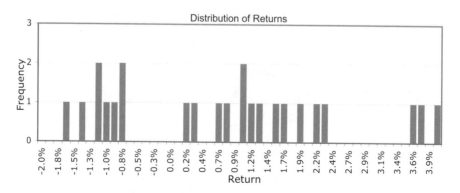

	1 yr.	3 yr.
Annualized rate of return	2.07%	
Annualized standard deviation	5.23%	
Percentage of negative months	50.00%	
Largest monthly drop	-1.68%	
Maximum drawdown	-7.02%	
Sharpe ratio	-0.37	
Semideviation	1.05%	
Sortino ratio	-1.83	
Jensen's alpha	-6.10%	
Beta	0.43	
Up capture ratio	31.80%	
Down capture ratio	63.68%	
Omega -0%	130%	
Appraisal ratio	-1.41	
Average α over benchmark	-0.92%	
Tracking error	1.62%	
Information ratio	-56.62%	
Sterling ratio	-0.27	
Treynor measure	-0.04	
M^2 – Modigliani measure	-12.82%	
Burke ratio	-0.64	
Skewness	13.99%	
Kurtosis	-196%	
Correlation to S&P/TSX	0.773	
R squared	0.598	
Benchmark: S&P/TSX		

TERMS AND CONDITIONS

Inception:	December 6, 2002
Style:	Fund of Hedge Funds
Sub-style:	N/A
Valuation:	Weekly on Friday
RRSP:	No
Management fee:	1.65%
Performance fee:	10.00%
High-water mark:	Yes
Hurdle rate:	N/A
NAV:	$11.73
Asset Size (million):	$19.96
Maximum leverage:	N/A
Early red'n period:	N/A
Early red'n fee:	N/A

PERFORMANCE (as of December 31, 2004)

	1 mo.	3 mo.	6 mo.
Funds	2.07%	4.41%	3.16%
S&P/TSX	2.40%	6.67%	8.41%
Van Global HF Index	1.50%	4.87%	5.48%

	1 yr.	2 yr.	3 yr.
Funds	2.07%	8.95%	
S&P/TSX	13.66%	19.32%	6.99%
Van Global HF Index	7.79%	13.04%	8.40%

Year	Jan	Feb	Mar	Apr	May	Jun	Jul	Aug	Sep	Oct	Nov	Dec	Total
2004	2.28%	1.64%	-1.04%	-1.68%	-1.01%	-1.18%	-1.45%	-0.87%	1.14%	0.79%	1.49%	2.07%	2.07%
2003	1.89%	-0.83%	-1.17%	0.11%	1.01%	0.98%	3.62%	4.00%	0.59%	3.69%	1.19%	0.26%	16.28%
2002													

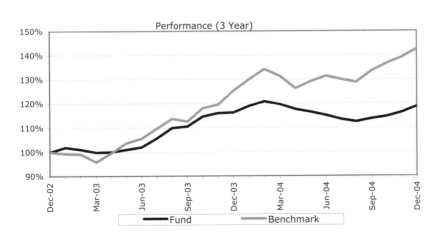

Performance (3 Year)

KING & VICTORIA RSP FUND CLASS A UNITS

FUND SPONSOR COMPANY

Equilibrium Capital Management Inc.

Tel: 416-603-1455   Toll-Free: N/A

Fax: 416-603-0363   Web site: N/A

PORTFOLIO MANAGER(S)

Equilibrium Capital Management Inc.

FUND DESCRIPTION

The objective of the Fund is to provide positive absolute returns with a focus on capital preservation. Assets are managed opportunistically, utilizing a multi-strategy approach including capital structure arbitrage, long/short bonds and equities, as well as investing in distressed securities. The Fund's investment universe is Canada and the United States and includes corporate bonds, bank debt, preferred and common shares.

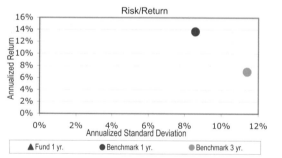

Rating: Not Rated

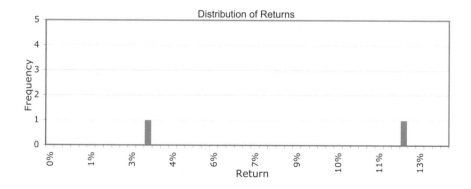

	1 yr.	3 yr.
Annualized rate of return		
Annualized standard deviation		
Percentage of negative months		
Largest monthly drop		
Maximum drawdown		
Sharpe ratio		
Semideviation		
Sortino ratio		
Jensen's alpha		
Beta		
Up capture ratio		
Down capture ratio		
Omega -0%		
Appraisal ratio		
Average α over benchmark		
Tracking error		
Information ratio		
Sterling ratio		
Treynor measure		
M^2 – Modigliani measure		
Burke ratio		
Skewness		
Kurtosis		
Correlation to S&P/TSX		
R squared		
Benchmark: S&P/TSX		

TERMS AND CONDITIONS

Inception:	October 29, 2004
Style:	Multi Manager
Sub-style:	N/A
Valuation:	Monthly
RRSP:	Yes
Management fee:	N/A
Performance fee:	N/A
High-water mark:	N/A
Hurdle rate:	N/A
NAV:	$11.64
Asset Size (million):	N/A
Maximum leverage:	N/A
Early red'n period:	N/A
Early red'n fee:	N/A

PERFORMANCE (as of December 31, 2004)

	1 mo.	3 mo.	6 mo.
Funds	3.51%		
S&P/TSX	2.40%	6.67%	8.41%
Van Global HF Index	1.50%	4.87%	5.48%

	1 yr.	2 yr.	3 yr.
Funds			
S&P/TSX	13.66%	19.32%	6.99%
Van Global HF Index	7.79%	13.04%	8.40%

Year	Jan	Feb	Mar	Apr	May	Jun	Jul	Aug	Sep	Oct	Nov	Dec	Total
2004											12.49%	3.51%	16.44%
2003													
2002													

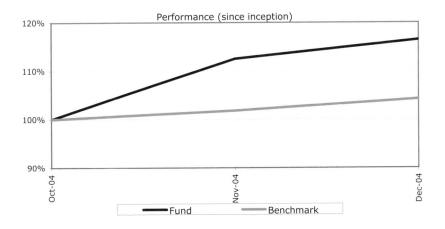

Performance (since inception)

Fund   Benchmark

NL MULTI-STRATEGY

FUND SPONSOR COMPANY
Northshield Asset Management (Canada) Ltd.
Tel: 416-598-2122   Toll-Free: 800-268-8882
Fax: N/A   Web site: www.norshield.com

PORTFOLIO MANAGER(S)

In 1984, the **Norshield Financial Group**, under the leadership of John Xanthoudakis, commenced operations. Norshield's reputation is built on providing dynamic, timely and professional alternative investment advice and services aimed at consistently generating superior risk-adjusted returns irrespective of market conditions.

FUND DESCRIPTION

The Fund's objective is to diligently follow an investment strategy that focuses on preservation of capital combined with yield enhancing features of alternative investment strategies.

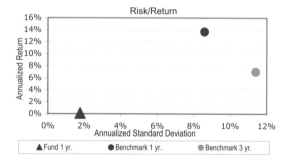

Rating: Not Rated

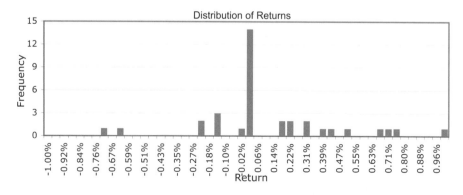

	1 yr.	3 yr.
Annualized rate of return	0.10%	
Annualized standard deviation	1.79%	
Percentage of negative months	58.33%	
Largest monthly drop	-0.73%	
Maximum drawdown	-2.20%	
Sharpe ratio	-2.19	
Semideviation	0.90%	
Sortino ratio	-4.32	
Jensen's alpha	-4.17%	
Beta	0.09	
Up capture ratio	7.13%	
Down capture ratio	12.35%	
Omega -0%	105%	
Appraisal ratio	-2.35	
Average α over benchmark	-0.58%	
Tracking error	2.49%	
Information ratio	-23.19%	
Sterling ratio	-1.77	
Treynor measure	-0.42	
M^2 – Modigliani measure	-23.53%	
Burke ratio	-3.70	
Skewness	88.22%	
Kurtosis	171%	
Correlation to S&P/TSX	0.539	
R squared	0.285	
Benchmark: MSCI World C$		

TERMS AND CONDITIONS

Inception:	January 6, 2003
Style:	Fund of Hedge Funds
Sub-style:	N/A
Valuation:	Weekly on Monday
RRSP:	No
Management fee:	3.91%
Performance fee:	N/A
High-water mark:	N/A
Hurdle rate:	N/A
NAV:	$10.47
Asset Size (million):	$56.13
Maximum leverage:	N/A
Early red'n period:	N/A
Early red'n fee:	N/A

PERFORMANCE (as of December 31, 2004)

	1 mo.	3 mo.	6 mo.
Funds	0.35%	1.71%	0.55%
S&P/TSX	5.25%	6.76%	0.07%
Van Global HF Index	1.50%	4.87%	5.48%

	1 yr.	2 yr.	3 yr.
Funds	0.10%		
S&P/TSX	6.85%		
Van Global HF Index	7.79%		

Year	Jan	Feb	Mar	Apr	May	Jun	Jul	Aug	Sep	Oct	Nov	Dec	Total
2004	0.41%	0.22%	-0.05%	-0.64%	-0.25%	-0.15%	-0.73%	-0.24%	-0.17%	0.15%	1.21%	0.35%	0.10%
2003		0.15%	-0.17%	0.71%	0.97%	0.49%	0.01%	0.29%	0.73%	0.64%	0.19%	0.29%	4.38%
2002													

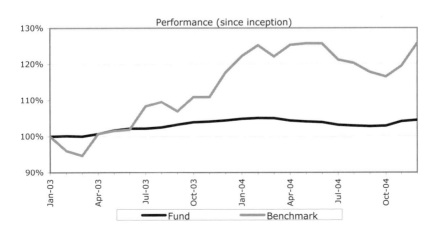

PRO-HEDGE ELITE FUND

FUND SPONSOR COMPANY
Pro-Hedge Elite Fund Management Inc.
Tel: 905-273-7788   Toll-Free: 877-566-5145
Fax: 905-803-3192   Web site: www.pro-hedge.com

PORTFOLIO MANAGER(S)

Dennis Heskel, (Mansur Capital Corporation);
Eric Sprott, CA (Sprott Asset Management Inc.);
Frank Mersch, BA, CFA (Front Street Capital);
Gene M. Vollendorf, CFA (Savoy Capital Management Ltd.);
Jim Goar, MBA, CFA (O'Donnell Asset Management Inc.)

FUND DESCRIPTION

The investment objective of the Fund is to earn a positve risk-adjusted return on capital in each year (an absolute return) that is uncorrelated with major equity and fixed income markets. The Fund will attempt to achieve its objective by allocating its investments among a variety of underlying funds with differing strategies.

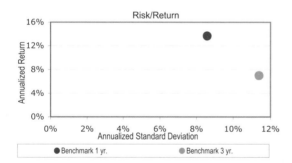

Rating: Not Rated

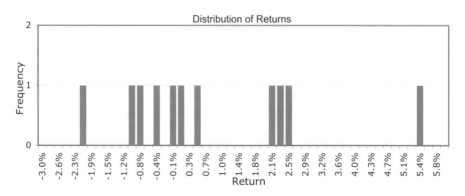

	1 yr.	3 yr.
Annualized rate of return		
Annualized standard deviation		
Percentage of negative months		
Largest monthly drop		
Maximum drawdown		
Sharpe ratio		
Semideviation		
Sortino ratio		
Jensen's alpha		
Beta		
Up capture ratio		
Down capture ratio		
Omega -0%		
Appraisal ratio		
Average α over benchmark		
Tracking error		
Information ratio		
Sterling ratio		
Treynor measure		
M^2 – Modigliani measure		
Burke ratio		
Skewness		
Kurtosis		
Correlation to S&P/TSX		
R squared		
Benchmark: S&P/TSX		

TERMS AND CONDITIONS

Inception:	February 1, 2004
Style:	Multi Manager
Sub-style:	N/A
Valuation:	Monthly
RRSP:	No
Management fee:	1.50%
Performance fee:	10.00%
High-water mark:	Yes
Hurdle rate:	N/A
NAV:	$10.79
Asset Size (million):	$3.33
Maximum leverage:	N/A
Early red'n period:	N/A
Early red'n fee:	N/A

PERFORMANCE (as of December 31, 2004)

	1 mo.	3 mo.	6 mo.
Funds	2.07%	7.03%	8.10%
S&P/TSX	2.40%	6.67%	8.41%
Van Global HF Index	1.50%	4.87%	5.48%

	1 yr.	2 yr.	3 yr.
Funds			
S&P/TSX	13.66%	19.32%	6.99%
Van Global HF Index	7.79%	13.04%	8.40%

Year	Jan	Feb	Mar	Apr	May	Jun	Jul	Aug	Sep	Oct	Nov	Dec	Total
2004		2.35%	0.10%	0.35%	-2.11%	-0.85%	-0.07%	-1.14%	2.24%	-0.47%	5.35%	2.07%	7.87%
2003													
2002													

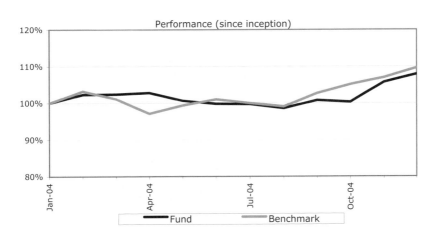

Performance (since inception)

PRO-HEDGE PROTECTED NOTES SERIES 1

FUND SPONSOR COMPANY
Pro-Hedge Funds Inc.
Tel: 905-273-7788   Toll-Free: 877-566-5145
Fax: 905-803-3192   Web site: www.pro-hedge.com

PORTFOLIO MANAGER(S)

John Xanthoudakis started his first operations in 1984 under the trade name "Norshield" and established his firm as a successful managed futures manager, and throughout the latter half of the decade developed a proprietary "tactical market trading" model.

FUND DESCRIPTION

Exclusive opportunity to invest in a principal guaranteed note, the return on which is linked to the Univest Ltd. Fund, ranked in the top five by several leading international ranking systems for alternative investment managers on a risk-adjusted basis

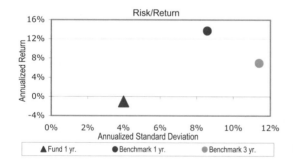

Risk/Return

▲ Fund 1 yr.   ● Benchmark 1 yr.   ● Benchmark 3 yr.   **Rating: Not Rated**

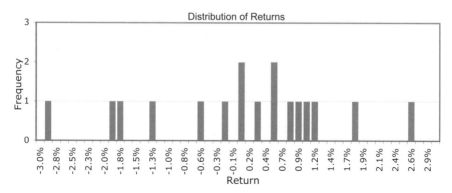

Distribution of Returns

	1 yr.	3 yr.
Annualized rate of return	-1.03%	
Annualized standard deviation	4.01%	
Percentage of negative months	41.67%	
Largest monthly drop	-2.99%	
Maximum drawdown	-5.14%	
Sharpe ratio	-1.26	
Semideviation	4.23%	
Sortino ratio	-1.19	
Jensen's alpha	-7.35%	
Beta	0.24	
Up capture ratio	4.82%	
Down capture ratio	27.40%	
Omega -0%	82%	
Appraisal ratio	-1.73	
Average α over benchmark	-1.18%	
Tracking error	2.07%	
Information ratio	-57.19%	
Sterling ratio	-0.98	
Treynor measure	-0.21	
M² – Modigliani measure	-20.45%	
Burke ratio	-1.50	
Skewness	-162.39%	
Kurtosis	290%	
Correlation to S&P/TSX	0.562	
R squared	0.315	
Benchmark: S&P/TSX		

TERMS AND CONDITIONS

Inception:	July 18, 2003
Style:	Fund of Hedge Funds
Sub-style:	Princ. Guaranteed Note
Valuation:	Weekly on Friday
RRSP:	Yes
Management fee:	1.80%
Performance fee:	5.00%
High-water mark:	N/A
Hurdle rate:	N/A
NAV:	$99.85
Asset Size (million):	N/A
Maximum leverage:	N/A
Early red'n period:	N/A
Early red'n fee:	N/A

PERFORMANCE (as of December 31, 2004)

	1 mo.	3 mo.	6 mo.
Funds	0.30%	1.07%	3.13%
S&P/TSX	2.40%	6.67%	8.41%
Van Global HF Index	1.50%	4.87%	5.48%

	1 yr.	2 yr.	3 yr.
Funds	-1.03%		
S&P/TSX	13.66%	19.32%	6.99%
Van Global HF Index	7.79%	13.04%	8.40%

Year	Jan	Feb	Mar	Apr	May	Jun	Jul	Aug	Sep	Oct	Nov	Dec	Total
2004	0.47%	0.70%	-0.21%	-2.99%	-0.66%	-1.37%	0.02%	1.08%	0.92%	-0.05%	0.82%	0.30%	-1.03%
2003								-1.95%	2.54%	-1.88%	0.47%	1.67%	0.76%
2002													

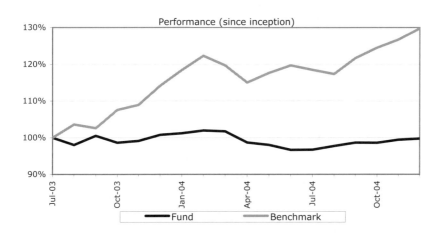

Performance (since inception)

R LEVERAGED CAPITAL HOLDINGS FUND

FUND SPONSOR COMPANY

Industrial Alliance Fund Mgmt. Inc.

Tel: 416-865-5628   Toll-Free: 877-876-6989

Fax: 416-865-5945   Web site: www.blc-rothschild.com

PORTFOLIO MANAGER(S)

Leveraged Capital Holdings NV

R Funds (BLC-Rothschild) Leveraged Holdings NV is registered in Curacan, Netherlands.

FUND DESCRIPTION

To achieve long-term risk-adjusted capital appreciation through a variety of hedge funds and hedge fund managers while managing risk and reducing volatility.

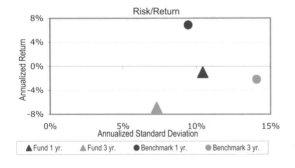

Rating: 🦔🦔

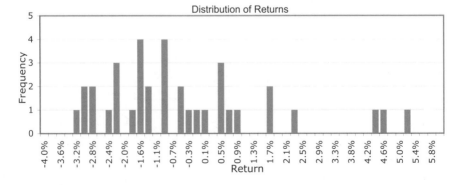

	1 yr.	3 yr.
Annualized rate of return	-1.01%	-6.88%
Annualized standard deviation	10.43%	7.28%
Percentage of negative months	66.67%	69.44%
Largest monthly drop	-3.00%	-3.30%
Maximum drawdown	-13.12%	-23.17%
Sharpe ratio	-0.48	-1.49
Semideviation	3.56%	2.81%
Sortino ratio	-1.41	-3.87
Jensen's alpha	-7.27%	-9.77%
Beta	0.79	0.18
Up capture ratio	58.67%	5.99%
Down capture ratio	110.06%	48.89%
Omega -0%	97%	51%
Appraisal ratio	-0.65	-1.15
Average α over benchmark	-0.63%	-0.47%
Tracking error	1.90%	3.85%
Information ratio	-33.14%	-12.16%
Sterling ratio	-0.38	-0.47
Treynor measure	-0.06	-0.60
M² – Modigliani measure	-7.39%	-14.85%
Burke ratio	-0.84	-1.14
Skewness	86.46%	117.48%
Kurtosis	-82%	113%
Correlation to S&P/TSX	0.064	0.092
R squared	0.615	0.128
Benchmark: MSCI World C$		

TERMS AND CONDITIONS

Inception:	September 10, 2001
Style:	Fund of Hedge Funds
Sub-style:	N/A
Valuation:	Weekly on Friday
RRSP:	No
Management fee:	2.25%
Performance fee:	N/A
High-water mark:	N/A
Hurdle rate:	N/A
NAV:	$82.23
Asset Size (million):	$8.34
Maximum leverage:	N/A
Early red'n period:	N/A
Early red'n fee:	N/A

PERFORMANCE (as of December 31, 2004)

	1 mo.	3 mo.	6 mo.
Funds	5.09%	0.07%	-6.04%
MSCI World C$	5.25%	6.76%	0.07%
Van Global HF Index	1.50%	4.87%	5.48%

	1 yr.	2 yr.	3 yr.
Funds	-1.01%	-5.04%	-6.88%
MSCI World C$	6.85%	8.58%	-2.18%
Van Global HF Index	7.79%	13.04%	8.40%

Year	Jan	Feb	Mar	Apr	May	Jun	Jul	Aug	Sep	Oct	Nov	Dec	Total
2004	4.44%	0.72%	-1.13%	4.25%	-2.18%	-0.67%	-2.96%	-2.80%	-0.46%	-3.00%	-1.83%	5.09%	-1.01%
2003	-0.96%	-2.51%	-1.36%	-1.65%	-1.71%	0.42%	1.53%	-0.10%	-1.08%	-2.25%	-1.70%	2.20%	-8.91%
2002	-0.65%	-2.36%	0.39%	-3.07%	-1.40%	-3.30%	1.61%	-0.29%	0.64%	-1.67%	-1.08%	0.31%	-10.45%

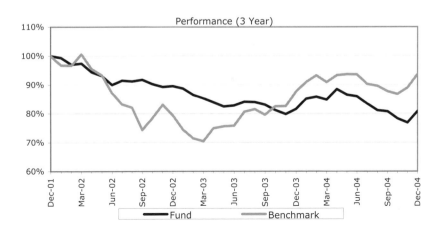

Performance (3 Year)

Fund — Benchmark

REDWOOD LONG/SHORT CANADIAN GROWTH FUND

FUND SPONSOR COMPANY
Redwood Asset Management
Tel: 416-368-8898   Toll-Free: N/A
Fax: 416-368-1608   Web site: www.redwoodasset.com

PORTFOLIO MANAGER(S)

Gene Vollendorf has over 10 years of experience in fundamental credit and security research. When President of Savoy Capital Management, he was responsible for investment policy and strategic decisions, and while employed at Bissett, was responsible for the development, management, and repositioning of a $500 million small cap program.

FUND DESCRIPTION

The Fund's investment objective is to maximize absolute returns on investments. The Fund intends to accomplish its set objective by taking a growth-oriented fundamental research approach to identifying compelling long and short investments. Investments in equity, debt and other securities of issuers primarily in Canada and the United States will be considered. A variety of hedging strategies will be deployed to enhance returns, reduce risk, or both.

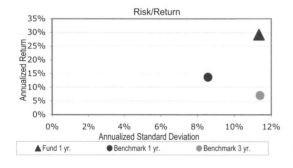

Rating: Not Rated

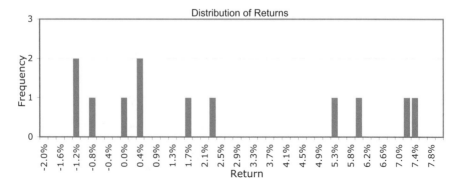

	1 yr.	3 yr.
Annualized rate of return	29.16%	
Annualized standard deviation	11.34%	
Percentage of negative months	33.33%	
Largest monthly drop	-1.37%	
Maximum drawdown	-3.20%	
Sharpe ratio	2.22	
Semideviation	3.80%	
Sortino ratio	6.61	
Jensen's alpha	19.74%	
Beta	0.56	
Up capture ratio	119.13%	
Down capture ratio	-14.98%	
Omega -0%	837%	
Appraisal ratio	-3.92	
Average α over benchmark	1.10%	
Tracking error	3.05%	
Information ratio	36.08%	
Sterling ratio	7.87	
Treynor measure	0.45	
M² – Modigliani measure	9.40%	
Burke ratio	12.09	
Skewness	55.57%	
Kurtosis	-139%	
Correlation to S&P/TSX	0.464	
R squared	0.215	
Benchmark: S&P/TSX		

TERMS AND CONDITIONS

Inception:	December 12, 2003
Style:	Security Selection
Sub-style:	N/A
Valuation:	Weekly on Friday
RRSP:	Yes
Management fee:	2.50%
Performance fee:	20.00%
High-water mark:	Yes
Hurdle rate:	N/A
NAV:	$12.73
Asset Size (million):	$39.90
Maximum leverage:	N/A
Early red'n period:	N/A
Early red'n fee:	N/A

PERFORMANCE (as of December 31, 2004)

	1 mo.	3 mo.	6 mo.
Funds	7.28%	13.94%	14.66%
S&P/TSX	2.40%	6.67%	8.41%
Van Global HF Index	1.50%	4.87%	5.48%

	1 yr.	2 yr.	3 yr.
Funds	29.16%		
S&P/TSX	13.66%	19.32%	6.99%
Van Global HF Index	7.79%	13.04%	8.40%

Year	Jan	Feb	Mar	Apr	May	Jun	Jul	Aug	Sep	Oct	Nov	Dec	Total
2004	7.09%	5.20%	2.24%	-0.04%	-0.90%	-1.28%	0.36%	-1.37%	1.67%	0.41%	5.78%	7.28%	29.16%
2003													
2002													

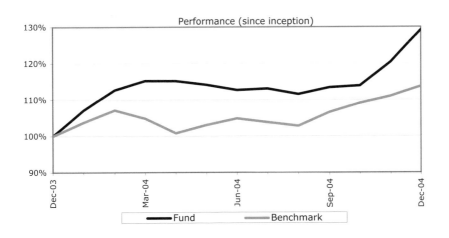

Performance (since inception)

Fund   Benchmark

REDWOOD LONG/SHORT VALUE FUND L.P.

FUND SPONSOR COMPANY

GrowthQuest Capital Inc.

Tel: 416-368-8898   Toll-Free: N/A

Fax: 416-368-1608   Web site: www.redwoodasset.com

PORTFOLIO MANAGER(S)

George Leon, who is President and a director of GrowthQuest Capital Inc., began his investment career in 1976 at Leon's Furniture Limited, where as a senior officer, he founded and managed the Leon's Furniture Deferred Profit Sharing Plan. Since 1986, he has successfully managed the private assets of the George Leon Family Trust in addition to the assets of other family members. In 1998, George founded GrowthQuest Capital Inc. to provide the same asset management services to non-family members.

FUND DESCRIPTION

The Fund's investment objective is to maximize absolute returns on investments. The Fund intends to accomplish its set objective by taking a value approach to making investments through both long and short positions and option strategies.

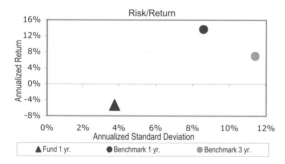

Rating: Not Rated

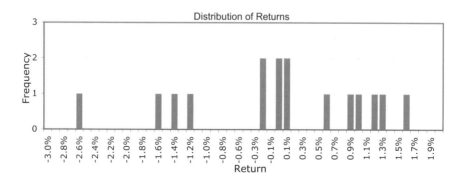

	1 yr.	3 yr.
Annualized rate of return	-5.27%	
Annualized standard deviation	3.76%	
Percentage of negative months	75.00%	
Largest monthly drop	-2.67%	
Maximum drawdown	-6.92%	
Sharpe ratio	-2.47	
Semideviation	2.28%	
Sortino ratio	-4.07	
Jensen's alpha	-8.78%	
Beta	-0.05	
Up capture ratio	-18.04%	
Down capture ratio	14.48%	
Omega -0%	30%	
Appraisal ratio	-2.51	
Average α over benchmark	-1.55%	
Tracking error	2.83%	
Information ratio	-54.61%	
Sterling ratio	-1.34	
Treynor measure	1.82	
M² – Modigliani measure	-30.83%	
Burke ratio	-2.53	
Skewness	-69.12%	
Kurtosis	-2%	
Correlation to S&P/TSX	-0.127	
R squared	0.016	
Benchmark: S&P/TSX		

TERMS AND CONDITIONS

Inception:	September 26, 2003
Style:	Security Selection
Sub-style:	N/A
Valuation:	Weekly on Friday
RRSP:	No
Management fee:	2.50%
Performance fee:	20.00%
High-water mark:	N/A
Hurdle rate:	N/A
NAV:	$9.84
Asset Size (million):	$8.00
Maximum leverage:	0%
Early red'n period:	N/A
Early red'n fee:	N/A

PERFORMANCE (as of December 31, 2004)

	1 mo.	3 mo.	6 mo.
Funds	0.96%	-1.03%	-3.98%
S&P/TSX	2.40%	6.67%	8.41%
Van Global HF Index	1.50%	4.87%	5.48%

	1 yr.	2 yr.	3 yr.
Funds	-5.27%		
S&P/TSX	13.66%	19.32%	6.99%
Van Global HF Index	7.79%	13.04%	8.40%

Year	Jan	Feb	Mar	Apr	May	Jun	Jul	Aug	Sep	Oct	Nov	Dec	Total
2004	0.81%	-0.07%	-1.37%	0.57%	-0.07%	-1.20%	-0.30%	-0.02%	-2.67%	-0.31%	-1.67%	0.96%	-5.27%
2003									0.00%	1.10%	1.23%	1.51%	3.88%
2002													

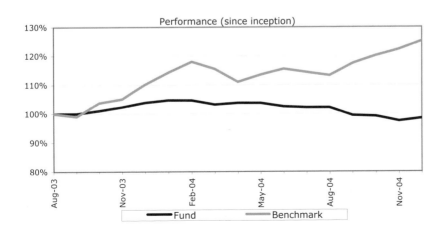

Performance (since inception)

REFCO ASSISTED FUTURES TRUST MERREL GROUP B

FUND SPONSOR COMPANY
Refco Futures (Canada) Ltd.
Tel: 416-862-7000   Toll-Free: 800-268-9294
Fax: 416-862-0576   Web site: www.refco.ca

PORTFOLIO MANAGER(S)

Refco Group Ltd., LLC is the world's largest non-bank futures commission merchant, with more than US$4.0 billion in global client equity and over $20.0 billion US in total assets. Refco is the world's dominant futures commission merchant (FCM), servicing in excess of 250,000 client accounts and clearing more contracts than any other FCM globally.

FUND DESCRIPTION

RAFT isn't one mechanical trading system, but a pool of some of the most respected systems available today, integrated to give maximum diversification and performance. Refco developed RAFT to provide sophisticated investors access to a portfolio of futures contracts using a number of mechanical systems developed by third parties.

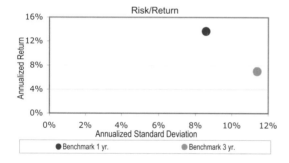

Rating: Not Rated

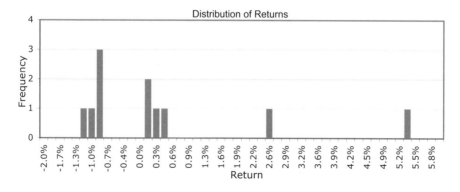

	1 yr.	3 yr.
Annualized rate of return		
Annualized standard deviation		
Percentage of negative months		
Largest monthly drop		
Maximum drawdown		
Sharpe ratio		
Semideviation		
Sortino ratio		
Jensen's alpha		
Beta		
Up capture ratio		
Down capture ratio		
Omega -0%		
Appraisal ratio		
Average α over benchmark		
Tracking error		
Information ratio		
Sterling ratio		
Treynor measure		
M² – Modigliani measure		
Burke ratio		
Skewness		
Kurtosis		
Correlation to S&P/TSX		
R squared		
Benchmark: S&P/TSX		

TERMS AND CONDITIONS

Inception:	January 31, 2004
Style:	Directional
Sub-style:	N/A
Valuation:	Monthly
RRSP:	No
Management fee:	N/A
Performance fee:	N/A
High-water mark:	N/A
Hurdle rate:	N/A
NAV:	$10.28
Asset Size (million):	N/A
Maximum leverage:	N/A
Early red'n period:	N/A
Early red'n fee:	N/A

PERFORMANCE (as of December 31, 2004)

	1 mo.	3 mo.	6 mo.
Funds	-1.31%	2.82%	4.19%
S&P/TSX	2.40%	6.67%	8.41%
Van Global HF Index	1.50%	4.87%	5.48%

	1 yr.	2 yr.	3 yr.
Funds			
S&P/TSX	13.66%	19.32%	6.99%
Van Global HF Index	7.79%	13.04%	8.40%

Year	Jan	Feb	Mar	Apr	May	Jun	Jul	Aug	Sep	Oct	Nov	Dec	Total
2004		0.00%	-0.96%	0.31%	0.19%	-0.89%	-0.02%	-1.07%	2.44%	5.20%	-0.97%	-1.31%	2.78%
2003													
2002													

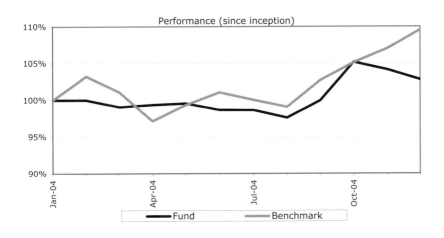

Performance (since inception)

SCIVEST CONSERVATIVE MARKET NEUTRAL EQUITY FUND

FUND SPONSOR COMPANY

SciVest Capital Management Company

Tel: 416-304-6800   Toll-Free: 866-599-2400

Fax: 416-304-6832   Web site: www.scivest.com

PORTFOLIO MANAGER(S)

Dr. John J. Schmitz earned a Doctorate of Philosophy (PhD) in Business Administration specializing in Finance from the Richard Ivey School of Business at the University of Western Ontario in 1997. During his PhD studies and research, he spent a considerable amount of time consulting to various corporations and investment funds through his consulting company John J. Schmitz & Associates.

FUND DESCRIPTION

The objective of the Fund is to produce consistent long-term growth through capital appreciation, while maintaining volatility of returns, risk less than broad-based equity indices and minimal exposure to the general movements of the equity markets.

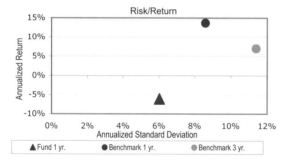

Rating: Not Rated

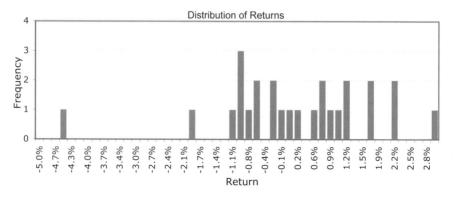

	1 yr.	3 yr.
Annualized rate of return	-6.11%	
Annualized standard deviation	6.03%	
Percentage of negative months	66.67%	
Largest monthly drop	-4.62%	
Maximum drawdown	-8.02%	
Sharpe ratio	-1.67	
Semideviation	5.09%	
Sortino ratio	-1.98	
Jensen's alpha	-12.98%	
Beta	0.30	
Up capture ratio	4.73%	
Down capture ratio	91.72%	
Omega -0%	44%	
Appraisal ratio	-1.65	
Average α over benchmark	-1.61%	
Tracking error	2.28%	
Information ratio	-70.68%	
Sterling ratio	-1.26	
Treynor measure	-0.34	
M² – Modigliani measure	-24.04%	
Burke ratio	-1.87	
Skewness	-94.28%	
Kurtosis	199%	
Correlation to S&P/TSX	0.462	
R squared	0.214	
Benchmark: S&P/TSX		

TERMS AND CONDITIONS

Inception:	October 11, 2002
Style:	Security Selection
Sub-style:	No Bias
Valuation:	Weekly on Friday
RRSP:	No
Management fee:	2.50%
Performance fee:	20.00%
High-water mark:	Yes
Hurdle rate:	0.00%
NAV:	$87.28
Asset Size (million):	N/A
Maximum leverage:	N/A
Early red'n period:	N/A
Early red'n fee:	N/A

PERFORMANCE (as of December 31, 2004)

	1 mo.	3 mo.	6 mo.
Funds	-0.75%	0.19%	-4.11%
S&P/TSX	2.40%	6.67%	8.41%
Van Global HF Index	1.50%	4.87%	5.48%

	1 yr.	2 yr.	3 yr.
Funds	-6.11%	0.57%	
S&P/TSX	13.66%	19.32%	6.99%
Van Global HF Index	7.79%	13.04%	8.40%

Year	Jan	Feb	Mar	Apr	May	Jun	Jul	Aug	Sep	Oct	Nov	Dec	Total
2004	-0.39%	1.17%	-1.07%	-1.98%	-0.96%	1.18%	0.42%	-4.62%	-0.08%	-1.09%	2.07%	-0.75%	-6.11%
2003	2.86%	-0.20%	-0.67%	2.15%	0.59%	-0.78%	-0.36%	-0.93%	1.55%	0.70%	1.61%	1.02%	7.71%
2002											0.22%	0.80%	1.02%

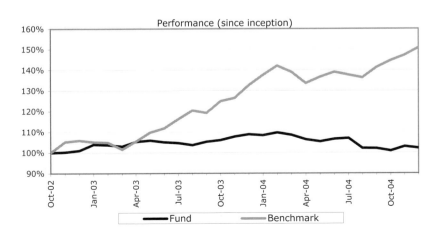

Performance (since inception)

SCIVEST ENHANCED MARKET NEUTRAL EQUITY FUND

FUND SPONSOR COMPANY

SciVest Capital Management Company

Tel: 416-304-6800   Toll-Free: 866-599-2400

Fax: 416-304-6832   Web site: www.scivest.com

PORTFOLIO MANAGER(S)

Dr. John J. Schmitz earned a Doctorate of Philosophy (PhD) in Business Administration specializing in Finance from the Richard Ivey School of Business at the University of Western Ontario in 1997. During his PhD studies and research, he spent a considerable amount of time consulting to various corporations and investment funds through his consulting company John J. Schmitz & Associates.

FUND DESCRIPTION

The objective of the Fund is to produce consistent long-term growth through capital appreciation, while maintaining volatility of returns, risk less than broad-based equity indices and minimal exposure to the general movements of the equity markets.

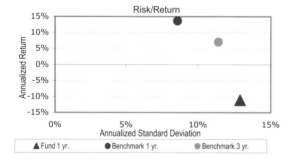

Rating: Not Rated

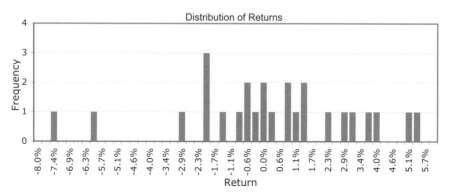

	1 yr.	3 yr.
Annualized rate of return	-11.11%	
Annualized standard deviation	12.89%	
Percentage of negative months	58.33%	
Largest monthly drop	-7.50%	
Maximum drawdown	-15.21%	
Sharpe ratio	-1.17	
Semideviation	8.34%	
Sortino ratio	-1.81	
Jensen's alpha	-21.32%	
Beta	0.64	
Up capture ratio	8.74%	
Down capture ratio	165.70%	
Omega -0%	54%	
Appraisal ratio	-1.06	
Average α over benchmark	-2.01%	
Tracking error	3.37%	
Information ratio	-59.71%	
Sterling ratio	-0.99	
Treynor measure	-0.23	
M² – Modigliani measure	-19.72%	
Burke ratio	-1.39	
Skewness	-24.14%	
Kurtosis	-37%	
Correlation to S&P/TSX	0.468	
R squared	0.219	
Benchmark: S&P/TSX		

TERMS AND CONDITIONS

Inception:	October 11, 2002
Style:	Security Selection
Sub-style:	No Bias
Valuation:	Weekly on Friday
RRSP:	No
Management fee:	2.50%
Performance fee:	20.00%
High-water mark:	Yes
Hurdle rate:	0.00%
NAV:	$99.81
Asset Size (million):	N/A
Maximum leverage:	N/A
Early red'n period:	N/A
Early red'n fee:	N/A

PERFORMANCE (as of December 31, 2004)

	1 mo.	3 mo.	6 mo.
Funds	-2.04%	-0.19%	-5.74%
S&P/TSX	2.40%	6.67%	8.41%
Van Global HF Index	1.50%	4.87%	5.48%

	1 yr.	2 yr.	3 yr.
Funds	-11.11%	0.37%	
S&P/TSX	13.66%	19.32%	6.99%
Van Global HF Index	7.79%	13.04%	8.40%

Year	Jan	Feb	Mar	Apr	May	Jun	Jul	Aug	Sep	Oct	Nov	Dec	Total
2004	1.02%	0.83%	-2.16%	-6.25%	-2.08%	3.09%	2.69%	-7.50%	-0.58%	-3.04%	5.08%	-2.04%	-11.11%
2003	3.82%	-0.11%	-0.69%	1.24%	3.55%	-0.47%	-0.89%	-1.45%	5.15%	0.00%	2.01%	0.69%	13.34%
2002											0.17%	1.33%	1.50%

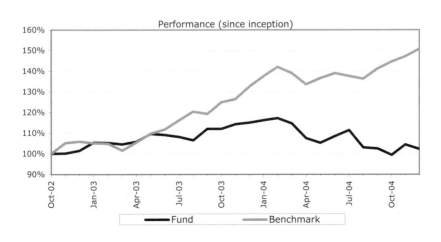

Performance (since inception)

SCIVEST MARKET NEUTRAL EQUITY FUND

FUND SPONSOR COMPANY
SciVest Capital Management Company
Tel: 416-304-6800   Toll-Free: 866-599-2400
Fax: 416-304-6832   Web site: www.scivest.com

PORTFOLIO MANAGER(S)

Dr. John J. Schmitz earned a Doctorate of Philosophy (PhD) in Business Administration specializing in Finance from the Richard Ivey School of Business at the University of Western Ontario in 1997. During his PhD studies and research, he spent a considerable amount of time consulting to various corporations and investment funds through his consulting company John J. Schmitz & Associates.

FUND DESCRIPTION

The investment objective of the Fund is to provide consistent long-term growth through capital appreciation, while maintaining minimal exposure to general movement in the equity markets.

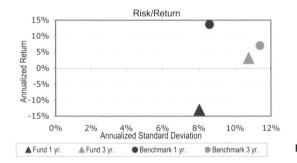

Rating:

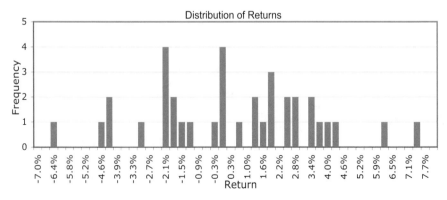

	1 yr.	3 yr.
Annualized rate of return	-13.05%	3.13%
Annualized standard deviation	8.02%	10.75%
Percentage of negative months	66.67%	47.22%
Largest monthly drop	-4.77%	-6.40%
Maximum drawdown	-14.09%	-14.09%
Sharpe ratio	-2.12	-0.08
Semideviation	4.39%	6.31%
Sortino ratio	-3.88	-0.14
Jensen's alpha	-20.98%	-0.76%
Beta	0.41	-0.04
Up capture ratio	-12.71%	5.35%
Down capture ratio	133.87%	-16.53%
Omega -0%	30%	127%
Appraisal ratio	-1.57	-0.07
Average α over benchmark	-2.23%	-0.31%
Tracking error	2.46%	4.61%
Information ratio	-90.80%	-6.82%
Sterling ratio	-1.21	-0.06
Treynor measure	-0.42	0.24
M² – Modigliani measure	-27.91%	-3.92%
Burke ratio	-2.15	-0.07
Skewness	7.49%	1.32%
Kurtosis	-74%	-21%
Correlation to S&P/TSX	0.475	-0.039
R squared	0.226	0.002
Benchmark: S&P/TSX		

TERMS AND CONDITIONS

Inception:	May 1, 2001
Style:	Security Selection
Sub-style:	No Bias
Valuation:	Daily
RRSP:	Yes
Management fee:	2.50%
Performance fee:	20.00%
High-water mark:	Yes
Hurdle rate:	0.00%
NAV:	$94.03
Asset Size (million):	N/A
Maximum leverage:	N/A
Early red'n period:	N/A
Early red'n fee:	N/A

PERFORMANCE (as of December 31, 2004)

	1 mo.	3 mo.	6 mo.
Funds	-1.48%	-0.93%	-5.00%
S&P/TSX	2.40%	6.67%	8.41%
Van Global HF Index	1.50%	4.87%	5.48%

	1 yr.	2 yr.	3 yr.
Funds	-13.05%	-1.07%	3.13%
S&P/TSX	13.66%	19.32%	6.99%
Van Global HF Index	7.79%	13.04%	8.40%

Year	Jan	Feb	Mar	Apr	May	Jun	Jul	Aug	Sep	Oct	Nov	Dec	Total
2004	-2.24%	1.04%	-2.09%	-4.77%	-2.25%	1.66%	0.48%	-4.36%	-0.21%	-2.11%	2.73%	-1.48%	-13.05%
2003	3.82%	1.07%	-0.40%	1.78%	1.39%	-1.62%	-0.03%	-1.90%	2.48%	0.03%	3.11%	2.33%	12.55%
2002	7.33%	-2.37%	4.25%	-0.14%	2.61%	1.72%	-3.14%	3.13%	3.65%	-4.32%	-6.40%	6.16%	12.07%

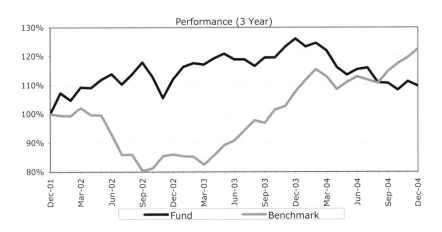

Performance (3 Year)

SCIVEST NORTH AMERICAN LONG/SHORT EQUITY FUND

FUND SPONSOR COMPANY

SciVest Capital Management Company

Tel: 416-304-6800   Toll-Free: 866-599-2400

Fax: 416-304-6832   Web site: www.scivest.com

PORTFOLIO MANAGER(S)

Dr. John J. Schmitz earned a Doctorate of Philosophy (PhD) in Business Administration specializing in Finance from the Richard Ivey School of Business at the University of Western Ontario in 1997. During his PhD studies and research, he spent a considerable amount of time consulting to various corporations and investment funds through his consulting company John J. Schmitz & Associates.

FUND DESCRIPTION

The objective of the Fund is to produce consistent long-term growth through capital appreciation, while maintaining minimal exposure to general movement in the equity markets. The Fund will hold a portfolio consisting of three segments: 1) cash and money market instruments; 2) long positions in equities; and 3) short positions in equities. These segments are combined in such a manner that the Fund's returns are not expected to be correlated with the returns of the equity markets.

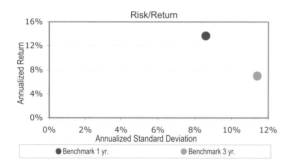

Rating: Not Rated

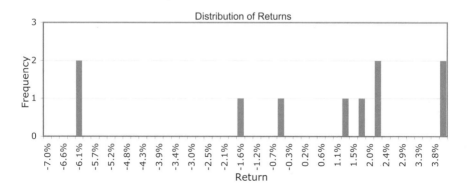

	1 yr.	3 yr.
Annualized rate of return		
Annualized standard deviation		
Percentage of negative months		
Largest monthly drop		
Maximum drawdown		
Sharpe ratio		
Semideviation		
Sortino ratio		
Jensen's alpha		
Beta		
Up capture ratio		
Down capture ratio		
Omega -0%		
Appraisal ratio		
Average α over benchmark		
Tracking error		
Information ratio		
Sterling ratio		
Treynor measure		
M² – Modigliani measure		
Burke ratio		
Skewness		
Kurtosis		
Correlation to S&P/TSX		
R squared		
Benchmark: S&P 500		

TERMS AND CONDITIONS

Inception:	February 27, 2004
Style:	Security Selection
Sub-style:	Long Bias
Valuation:	Weekly on Friday
RRSP:	No
Management fee:	2.50%
Performance fee:	20.00%
High-water mark:	Yes
Hurdle rate:	0.00%
NAV:	$99.82
Asset Size (million):	N/A
Maximum leverage:	N/A
Early red'n period:	N/A
Early red'n fee:	N/A

PERFORMANCE (as of December 31, 2004)

	1 mo.	3 mo.	6 mo.
Funds	1.74%	3.91%	0.68%
S&P 500	4.80%	4.07%	-3.39%
Van Global HF Index	1.50%	4.87%	5.48%

	1 yr.	2 yr.	3 yr.
Funds			
S&P 500	2.81%	4.32%	-5.78%
Van Global HF Index	7.79%	13.04%	8.40%

Year	Jan	Feb	Mar	Apr	May	Jun	Jul	Aug	Sep	Oct	Nov	Dec	Total
2004			-0.55%	-6.16%	2.10%	3.91%	2.04%	-6.27%	1.30%	-1.79%	4.00%	1.74%	-0.32%
2003													
2002													

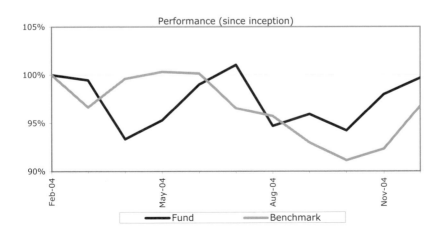

Performance (since inception)

SCIVEST US EQUITY INDEX PLUS FUND

FUND SPONSOR COMPANY

SciVest Capital Management Company

Tel: 416-304-6800   Toll-Free: 866-599-2400
Fax: 416-304-6832   Web site: www.scivest.com

PORTFOLIO MANAGER(S)

Dr. John J. Schmitz earned a Doctorate of Philosophy (PhD) in Business Administration specializing in Finance from the Richard Ivey School of Business at the University of Western Ontario in 1997. During his PhD studies and research, he spent a considerable amount of time consulting to various corporations and investment funds through his consulting company John J. Schmitz & Associates.

FUND DESCRIPTION

The objective of the Fund is to produce consistent long-term growth through capital appreciation in excess of the Standard and Poor's 500 Index, while maintaining full exposure to the general movements in the S&P 500 Index.

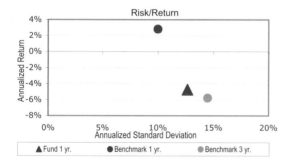

Rating: Not Rated

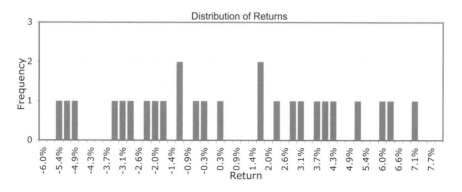

	1 yr.	3 yr.
Annualized rate of return	-4.72%	
Annualized standard deviation	12.65%	
Percentage of negative months	58.33%	
Largest monthly drop	-5.31%	
Maximum drawdown	-18.15%	
Sharpe ratio	-0.69	
Semideviation	6.50%	
Sortino ratio	-1.34	
Jensen's alpha	-7.62%	
Beta	0.92	
Up capture ratio	85.32%	
Down capture ratio	138.14%	
Omega -0%	81%	
Appraisal ratio	-0.45	
Average α over benchmark	-0.61%	
Tracking error	2.21%	
Information ratio	-27.60%	
Sterling ratio	-0.48	
Treynor measure	-0.09	
M² – Modigliani measure	-5.70%	
Burke ratio	-0.95	
Skewness	6.68%	
Kurtosis	-155%	
Correlation to S&P/TSX	0.478	
R squared	0.633	
Benchmark: S&P 500		

TERMS AND CONDITIONS

Inception:	October 11, 2002
Style:	Security Selection
Sub-style:	Long Bias
Valuation:	Weekly on Friday
RRSP:	No
Management fee:	2.50%
Performance fee:	20.00%
High-water mark:	N/A
Hurdle rate:	N/A
NAV:	$107.29
Asset Size (million):	$3.20
Maximum leverage:	N/A
Early red'n period:	N/A
Early red'n fee:	N/A

PERFORMANCE (as of December 31, 2004)

	1 mo.	3 mo.	6 mo.
Funds	3.05%	3.51%	-7.43%
S&P 500	4.80%	4.07%	-3.39%
Van Global HF Index	1.50%	4.87%	5.48%

	1 yr.	2 yr.	3 yr.
Funds	-4.72%	4.59%	
S&P 500	2.81%	4.32%	-5.78%
Van Global HF Index	7.79%	13.04%	8.40%

Year	Jan	Feb	Mar	Apr	May	Jun	Jul	Aug	Sep	Oct	Nov	Dec	Total
2004	4.88%	3.61%	-5.14%	-0.34%	-1.23%	1.44%	-2.19%	-5.31%	-3.44%	-3.37%	3.95%	3.05%	-4.72%
2003	-1.82%	-3.09%	0.17%	6.96%	1.65%	-1.28%	5.95%	-0.80%	-2.33%	2.82%	2.14%	4.11%	14.81%
2002											6.08%	-5.46%	0.29%

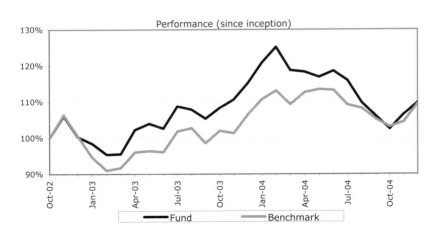

Performance (since inception)

Fund — Benchmark

SEI FUTURES INDEX FUND—O CLASS

FUND SPONSOR COMPANY

SEI Investments

Tel: 416-777-9700   Toll-Free: N/A
Fax: 416-777-9093   Web site: www.seic.ca

PORTFOLIO MANAGER(S)

SEI Investments

FUND DESCRIPTION

The fundamental investment objective of Futures Index Fund is to achieve long-term capital appreciation through unleveraged investments exclusively in the futures contracts that compose the MLM Index.

Rating: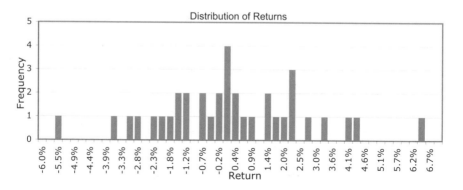

	1 yr.	3 yr.
Annualized rate of return	-1.31%	0.56%
Annualized standard deviation	10.45%	8.28%
Percentage of negative months	58.33%	47.22%
Largest monthly drop	-3.65%	-5.61%
Maximum drawdown	-8.66%	-8.66%
Sharpe ratio	-0.51	-0.42
Semideviation	3.74%	5.13%
Sortino ratio	-1.42	-0.67
Jensen's alpha	-9.23%	-3.66%
Beta	0.41	0.07
Up capture ratio	10.15%	3.60%
Down capture ratio	46.14%	3.56%
Omega -0%	94%	109%
Appraisal ratio	-0.84	-0.44
Average α over benchmark	-1.17%	-0.54%
Tracking error	3.13%	3.86%
Information ratio	-37.38%	-14.08%
Sterling ratio	-0.61	-0.40
Treynor measure	-0.13	-0.47
M² – Modigliani measure	-14.02%	-7.73%
Burke ratio	-0.87	-0.36
Skewness	97.34%	17.90%
Kurtosis	27%	59%
Correlation to S&P/TSX	0.364	0.103
R squared	0.133	0.011
Benchmark: S&P/TSX		

TERMS AND CONDITIONS

Inception:	December 15, 2000
Style:	Directional Trading
Sub-style:	N/A
Valuation:	Daily
RRSP:	Yes
Management fee:	N/A
Performance fee:	N/A
High-water mark:	N/A
Hurdle rate:	N/A
NAV:	$10.55
Asset Size (million):	$49.36
Maximum leverage:	N/A
Early red'n period:	N/A
Early red'n fee:	N/A

PERFORMANCE (as of December 31, 2004)

	1 mo.	3 mo.	6 mo.
Funds	-2.01%	-5.56%	-2.96%
S&P/TSX	2.40%	6.67%	8.41%
Van Global HF Index	1.50%	4.87%	5.48%

	1 yr.	2 yr.	3 yr.
Funds	-1.31%	1.89%	0.56%
S&P/TSX	13.66%	19.32%	6.99%
Van Global HF Index	7.79%	13.04%	8.40%

Year	Jan	Feb	Mar	Apr	May	Jun	Jul	Aug	Sep	Oct	Nov	Dec	Total
2004	1.24%	4.14%	2.10%	-2.32%	-1.68%	-1.63%	-0.30%	-3.04%	6.28%	-3.65%	0.02%	-2.01%	-1.31%
2003	3.12%	2.10%	-2.27%	-0.10%	0.33%	-0.81%	-3.31%	0.49%	-1.32%	3.85%	1.28%	1.97%	5.20%
2002	0.78%	-0.41%	-5.61%	0.26%	-0.86%	0.07%	-0.59%	1.47%	1.75%	-1.31%	0.08%	2.53%	-2.05%

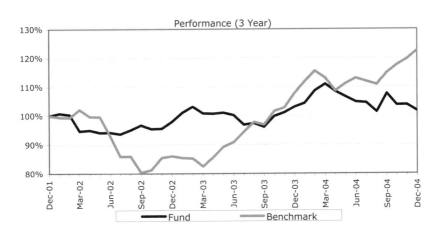

Performance (3 Year)

SKYLON GLOBAL RESOURCE SPLIT CORP.

FUND SPONSOR COMPANY

Skylon Global Resource Split Corp.
Tel: 416-681-8894   Toll-Free: 800-822-0245
Fax: 416-364-2969   Web site: www.skyloncapital.com

PORTFOLIO MANAGER(S)

Eric Bushell, Senior VP, Portfolio Management and CIO of the Signature Funds Group of CI Funds, has 10 years of investment industry experience.

Robert Lyon is VP, Portfolio Management with CI Mutual Funds Inc., where he manages all of the investment advisor's dedicated natural resource and energy funds. He has over 14 years of investment industry experience.

James J. Dutkiewicz, VP, Portfolio Management at CI Mutual Funds Inc., has 11 years of experience in analyzing and trading bonds.

Paul E. Simon, is Investment Analyst, Portfolio Management at CI Mutual Funds Inc.

FUND DESCRIPTION

The Company's investment objectives are to provide holders of preferred shares with fixed, cumulative, preferential, quarterly cash distributions in the amount of $0.13125 per preferred share, representing a yield on the issue price of the preferred shares of 5.25% per annum; and to return the original issue price of $10.00 to holders of preferred shares at the time of redemption of such shares on June 30, 2009 (the "Termination Date").

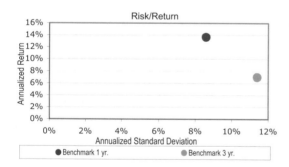

Rating: Not Rated

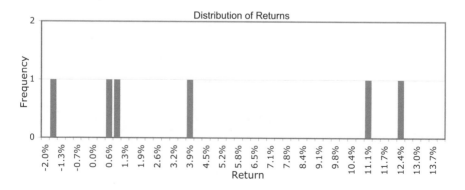

	1 yr.	3 yr.
Annualized rate of return		
Annualized standard deviation		
Percentage of negative months		
Largest monthly drop		
Maximum drawdown		
Sharpe ratio		
Semideviation		
Sortino ratio		
Jensen's alpha		
Beta		
Up capture ratio		
Down capture ratio		
Omega -0%		
Appraisal ratio		
Average α over benchmark		
Tracking error		
Information ratio		
Sterling ratio		
Treynor measure		
M² – Modigliani measure		
Burke ratio		
Skewness		
Kurtosis		
Correlation to S&P/TSX		
R squared		
Benchmark: S&P/TSX		

TERMS AND CONDITIONS

Inception:	April 30, 2004
Style:	N/A
Sub-style:	N/A
Valuation:	Daily
RRSP:	No
Management fee:	N/A
Performance fee:	N/A
High-water mark:	N/A
Hurdle rate:	N/A
NAV:	$16.70
Asset Size (million):	$42.30
Maximum leverage:	N/A
Early red'n period:	N/A
Early red'n fee:	N/A

PERFORMANCE (as of December 31, 2004)

	1 mo.	3 mo.	6 mo.
Funds	0.81%	9.94%	28.62%
S&P/TSX	2.40%	6.67%	8.41%
Van Global HF Index	1.50%	4.87%	5.48%

	1 yr.	2 yr.	3 yr.
Funds			
S&P/TSX	13.66%	19.32%	6.99%
Van Global HF Index	7.79%	13.04%	8.40%

Year	Jan	Feb	Mar	Apr	May	Jun	Jul	Aug	Sep	Oct	Nov	Dec	Total
2004							3.61%	0.57%	12.29%	-1.76%	11.01%	0.81%	28.62%
2003													
2002													

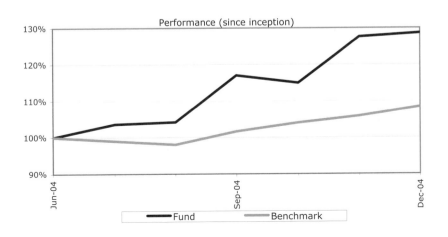

Performance (since inception)

— Fund — Benchmark

SPROTT BULL/BEAR RSP FUND

FUND SPONSOR COMPANY
Sprott Asset Management Inc.
Tel: 416-943-6707   Toll-Free: 866-299-9906
Fax: 416-362-4928   Web site: www.sprott.com

PORTFOLIO MANAGER(S)

Anne Spork, CIM, joined Sprott Securities Ltd. in 1981. Over the past 20 years, Anne has directly participated in all aspects of sales and trading functions of the Institutional Equities Department. Eric Sprott has accumulated over 34 years of experience in the investment industry. In 1981, he founded Sprott Securities Inc. Jean-François Tardif has accumulated over 11 years of experience in the investment industry.

FUND DESCRIPTION

The objective of the Fund is to maximize absolute returns on investments. The Fund intends to accomplish its set objective through superior securities selection by taking both long and short investment positions.

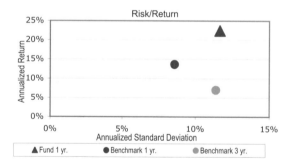

Rating: Not Rated

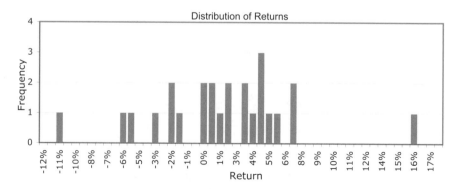

	1 yr.	3 yr.
Annualized rate of return	22.42%	
Annualized standard deviation	11.66%	
Percentage of negative months	41.67%	
Largest monthly drop	-2.51%	
Maximum drawdown	-4.31%	
Sharpe ratio	1.58	
Semideviation	5.39%	
Sortino ratio	3.41	
Jensen's alpha	17.48%	
Beta	0.10	
Up capture ratio	57.42%	
Down capture ratio	-103.12%	
Omega -0%	396%	
Appraisal ratio	1.84	
Average α over benchmark	0.65%	
Tracking error	4.02%	
Information ratio	16.17%	
Sterling ratio	4.27	
Treynor measure	1.89	
M² – Modigliani measure	3.91%	
Burke ratio	4.79	
Skewness	28.82%	
Kurtosis	-131%	
Correlation to S&P/TSX	0.078	
R squared	0.006	
Benchmark: S&P/TSX		

TERMS AND CONDITIONS

Inception:	November 12, 2002
Style:	Security Selection
Sub-style:	Variable Bias
Valuation:	Monthly
RRSP:	Yes
Management fee:	2.50%
Performance fee:	20.00%
High-water mark:	Yes
Hurdle rate:	0.00%
NAV:	$6.17
Asset Size (million):	$46.06
Maximum leverage:	N/A
Early red'n period:	6 mo.
Early red'n fee:	N/A

PERFORMANCE (as of December 31, 2004)

	1 mo.	3 mo.	6 mo.
Funds	-2.22%	4.22%	15.76%
S&P/TSX	2.40%	6.67%	8.41%
Van Global HF Index	1.50%	4.87%	5.48%

	1 yr.	2 yr.	3 yr.
Funds	22.42%	8.30%	
S&P/TSX	13.66%	19.32%	6.99%
Van Global HF Index	7.79%	13.04%	8.40%

Year	Jan	Feb	Mar	Apr	May	Jun	Jul	Aug	Sep	Oct	Nov	Dec	Total
2004	1.59%	4.69%	3.17%	0.72%	-2.51%	-1.84%	4.32%	-0.36%	6.86%	-0.17%	6.77%	-2.22%	22.42%
2003	0.57%	1.10%	-6.14%	-10.96%	-5.82%	-3.80%	3.95%	5.70%	3.60%	4.34%	2.70%	2.02%	-4.18%
2002												15.96%	15.96%

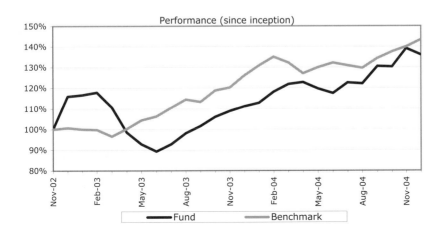

Performance (since inception)

SPROTT HEDGE FUND L.P.

FUND SPONSOR COMPANY
Sprott Asset Management Inc.
Tel: 416-943-6707   Toll-Free: 866-299-9906
Fax: 416-362-4928   Web site: www.sprott.com

PORTFOLIO MANAGER(S)

Anne Spork, CIM. After completing her bachelor's degree in Business Administration, majoring in International Finance, Anne entered the investment industry. Shortly after its formation in 1981, Anne joined Sprott Securities Ltd. and has been instrumental in helping the firm become one of the most successful brokerage firms in Canada. Over the past 20 years Anne has directly participated in all aspects of sales and trading functions of the Institutional Equities Department.
Eric Sprott has accumulated over 34 years of experience in the investment industry. After completing his undergraduate degree at Carleton University and earning his designation as a chartered accountant, Eric entered the investment industry as a research analyst at Merrill Lynch. In 1981, he founded Sprott Securities Inc. (SSI), which has become one of Canada's largest independently owned institutional brokerage firms.
Jean-Francois Tardif has accumulated over 11 years of experience in the investment industry. After spending almost one year at Desjardins Securities as a financial advisor, Jean-Francois joined a small Canadian firm that specialized in small capitalization stocks. For 3 years, Jean-Francois participated in all small capitalization equity buying and selling decisions, fostered substantial asset growth of the firm and obtained superior performance for investors.

FUND DESCRIPTION

The objective of the Partnership is to maximize absolute returns on investments while attempting to mitigate market risk. The Partnership intends to accomplish its set objective through superior securities selection by taking both long and short investment positions. This partnership is performing very well, although its risk is on the higher side.

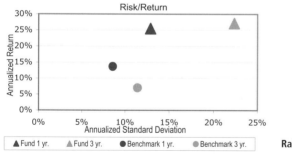

Rating:

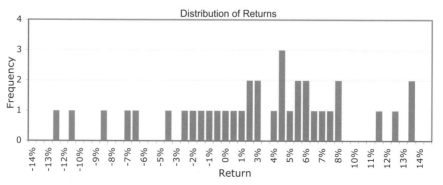

	1 yr.	3 yr.
Annualized rate of return	25.50%	27.18%
Annualized standard deviation	12.85%	22.32%
Percentage of negative months	33.33%	30.56%
Largest monthly drop	-3.17%	-12.56%
Maximum drawdown	-5.44%	-31.81%
Sharpe ratio	1.67	1.04
Semideviation	6.42%	16.05%
Sortino ratio	3.35	1.44
Jensen's alpha	21.08%	24.24%
Beta	0.04	-0.36
Up capture ratio	60.68%	15.68%
Down capture ratio	-128.68%	-262.69%
Omega -0%	391%	234%
Appraisal ratio	1.80	0.76
Average α over benchmark	0.87%	1.61%
Tracking error	4.40%	7.76%
Information ratio	19.84%	20.70%
Sterling ratio	3.95	0.73
Treynor measure	4.92	-0.65
M^2 – Modigliani measure	4.71%	8.84%
Burke ratio	4.85	1.04
Skewness	15.05%	-41.70%
Kurtosis	-142%	-4%
Correlation to S&P/TSX	0.032	-0.187
R squared	0.001	0.035
Benchmark: S&P/TSX		

TERMS AND CONDITIONS

Inception:	November 7, 2000
Style:	Security Selection
Sub-style:	Variable Bias
Valuation:	Monthly
RRSP:	No
Management fee:	2.00%
Performance fee:	20.00%
High-water mark:	Yes
Hurdle rate:	10.00%
NAV:	$35.97
Asset Size (million):	$409.63
Maximum leverage:	N/A
Early red'n period:	6 mo.
Early red'n fee:	N/A

PERFORMANCE (as of December 31, 2004)

	1 mo.	3 mo.	6 mo.
Funds	-1.91%	5.02%	18.21%
S&P/TSX	2.40%	6.67%	8.41%
Van Global HF Index	1.50%	4.87%	5.48%

	1 yr.	2 yr.	3 yr.
Funds	25.50%	8.74%	27.18%
S&P/TSX	13.66%	19.32%	6.99%
Van Global HF Index	7.79%	13.04%	8.40%

Year	Jan	Feb	Mar	Apr	May	Jun	Jul	Aug	Sep	Oct	Nov	Dec	Total
2004	1.57%	5.19%	3.63%	1.42%	-3.17%	-2.34%	5.42%	-0.72%	7.54%	0.15%	6.91%	-1.91%	25.50%
2003	0.79%	1.34%	-6.44%	-12.56%	-7.28%	-3.95%	5.57%	5.94%	3.87%	4.26%	2.33%	2.14%	-5.79%
2002	12.33%	13.37%	8.21%	11.44%	8.15%	-1.24%	4.12%	4.69%	6.21%	-11.06%	-9.04%	13.25%	73.96%

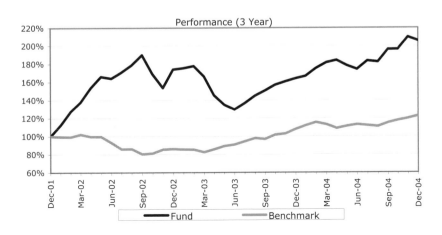

Performance (3 Year)

Fund — Benchmark

SPROTT OPPORTUNITIES HEDGE FUND L.P.

FUND SPONSOR COMPANY
Sprott Asset Management Inc.
Tel: 416-943-6707   Toll-Free: 866-299-9906
Fax: 416-362-4928   Web site: www.sprott.com

PORTFOLIO MANAGER(S)

Jean-François Tardif has accumulated over 11 years of experience in the investment industry. After spending almost one year at Desjardins Securities as a financial adviser, Jean-François joined a small Canadian firm that specialized in small capitalization stocks. For three years, Jean-François participated in all small capitalization equity buying and selling decisions, fostered substantial asset growth of the firm, and obtained superior performance for investors.

FUND DESCRIPTION

The objective of the Partnership is to provide limited partners with long-term capital growth and fundamental securities selection by taking both long and short investment positions in equity, and debt, and through strategic trading. The Partnership's portfolio will consist primarily of securities that generate capital gains, but will also include investments that generate income.

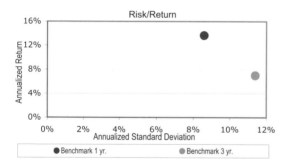

Rating: Not Rated

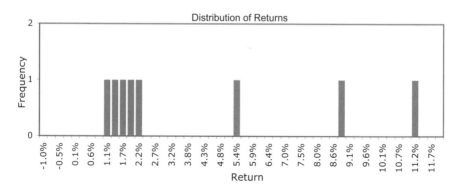

	1 yr.	3 yr.
Annualized rate of return		
Annualized standard deviation		
Percentage of negative months		
Largest monthly drop		
Maximum drawdown		
Sharpe ratio		
Semideviation		
Sortino ratio		
Jensen's alpha		
Beta		
Up capture ratio		
Down capture ratio		
Omega -0%		
Appraisal ratio		
Average α over benchmark		
Tracking error		
Information ratio		
Sterling ratio		
Treynor measure		
M² – Modigliani measure		
Burke ratio		
Skewness		
Kurtosis		
Correlation to S&P/TSX		
R squared		
Benchmark: S&P/TSX		

TERMS AND CONDITIONS

Inception:	April 7, 2004
Style:	N/A
Sub-style:	N/A
Valuation:	Monthly
RRSP:	No
Management fee:	2.00%
Performance fee:	20.00%
High-water mark:	N/A
Hurdle rate:	N/A
NAV:	$13.72
Asset Size (million):	$27.95
Maximum leverage:	N/A
Early red'n period:	N/A
Early red'n fee:	N/A

PERFORMANCE (as of December 31, 2004)

	1 mo.	3 mo.	6 mo.
Funds	5.20%	16.16%	32.93%
S&P/TSX	2.40%	6.67%	8.41%
Van Global HF Index	1.50%	4.87%	5.48%

	1 yr.	2 yr.	3 yr.
Funds			
S&P/TSX	13.66%	19.32%	6.99%
Van Global HF Index	7.79%	13.04%	8.40%

Year	Jan	Feb	Mar	Apr	May	Jun	Jul	Aug	Sep	Oct	Nov	Dec	Total
2004					1.85%	1.38%	0.87%	2.11%	11.10%	1.52%	8.76%	5.20%	37.25%
2003													
2002													

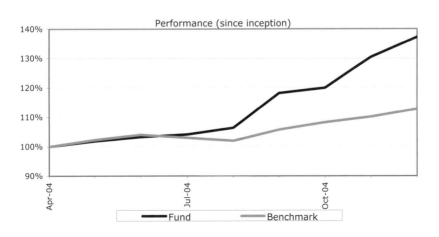

Performance (since inception)

Fund — Benchmark

STONESTREET L.P.

FUND SPONSOR COMPANY

Stonestreet L.P.

Tel: 416-867-6059   Toll-Free: N/A

Fax: N/A   Web site: www.stonestreetlp.com

PORTFOLIO MANAGER(S)

Michael Finkelstein C.A., Elizabeth Leonard CFA, Hartley Zwingerman C.A.

Stonestreet is a leader in alternative investment management, offering an aggressive and mathematically disciplined approach to investment management.

FUND DESCRIPTION

The Partnership's objectives are to seek a high rate of short- to medium-term capital appreciation, primarily through investing in securities of U.S. issuers issued pursuant to Regulation D under the *Securities Act of 1933*, convertible debentures and preferred shares, and other equity securities.

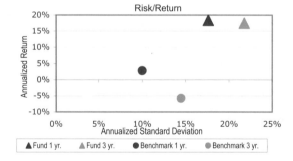

Rating:

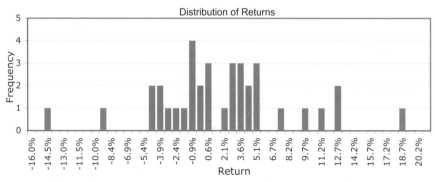

	1 yr.	3 yr.
Annualized rate of return	18.38%	17.49%
Annualized standard deviation	17.62%	21.75%
Percentage of negative months	50.00%	41.67%
Largest monthly drop	-5.04%	-14.56%
Maximum drawdown	-10.94%	-26.39%
Sharpe ratio	0.82	0.62
Semideviation	6.62%	13.13%
Sortino ratio	2.17	1.03
Jensen's alpha	15.54%	17.00%
Beta	0.98	0.36
Up capture ratio	150.51%	90.27%
Down capture ratio	47.97%	0.24%
Omega -0%	233%	198%
Appraisal ratio	-38.89	1.10
Average α over benchmark	1.26%	1.95%
Tracking error	4.05%	6.63%
Information ratio	31.14%	29.40%
Sterling ratio	1.31	0.51
Treynor measure	0.15	0.37
M² – Modigliani measure	9.34%	18.75%
Burke ratio	2.03	0.66
Skewness	88.43%	25.88%
Kurtosis	44%	136%
Correlation to S&P/TSX	0.165	0.341
R squared	0.368	0.061
Benchmark: S&P 500		

TERMS AND CONDITIONS

Inception:	December 1, 2000
Style:	Security Selection
Sub-style:	N/A
Valuation:	Monthly
RRSP:	No
Management fee:	1.50%
Performance fee:	25.00%
High-water mark:	Yes
Hurdle rate:	6.00%
NAV:	N/A
Asset Size (million):	$25.10
Maximum leverage:	N/A
Early red'n period:	6 mo.
Early red'n fee:	N/A

PERFORMANCE (as of December 31, 2004)

	1 mo.	3 mo.	6 mo.
Funds	12.00%	8.35%	8.01%
S&P 500	4.80%	4.07%	-3.39%
Van Global HF Index	1.50%	4.87%	5.48%

	1 yr.	2 yr.	3 yr.
Funds	18.38%	20.57%	17.49%
S&P 500	2.81%	4.32%	-5.78%
Van Global HF Index	7.79%	13.04%	8.40%

Year	Jan	Feb	Mar	Apr	May	Jun	Jul	Aug	Sep	Oct	Nov	Dec	Total
2004	9.30%	2.46%	4.02%	-1.11%	-0.50%	-4.38%	-1.13%	2.51%	-1.65%	-5.04%	1.88%	12.00%	18.38%
2003	-3.24%	-14.56%	-9.39%	0.24%	4.18%	2.99%	3.61%	10.67%	18.70%	6.80%	4.77%	0.08%	22.80%
2002	3.54%	-0.45%	4.85%	4.86%	0.17%	-0.90%	-1.87%	-2.87%	-4.08%	-5.33%	12.17%	2.14%	11.55%

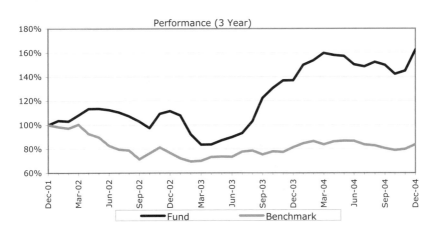

Performance (3 Year)

THALES TA3—CAMPBELL 'A' C$

FUND SPONSOR COMPANY

Thales Alternative Investments Inc.
Tel: 416-955-0710   Toll-Free: N/A
Fax: 416-862-0576   Web site: www.thales.ca

PORTFOLIO MANAGER(S)

Mesirow Advanced Strategies, Inc., Campbell & Company, Inc., Thales Alternative Investments Inc.

FUND DESCRIPTION

TA3 takes the concept of "balanced" to another level for Canadians, because it increases diversification through exposure to different asset classes and management styles. The diversification provided through investments in several managers seeks to generate low volatility returns and perform in both bull and bear markets.

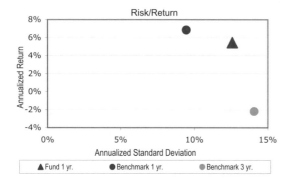

Rating: Not Rated

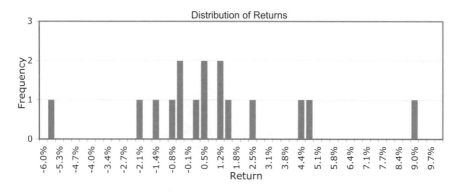

	1 yr.	3 yr.
Annualized rate of return	5.45%	
Annualized standard deviation	12.58%	
Percentage of negative months	41.67%	
Largest monthly drop	-5.75%	
Maximum drawdown	-11.01%	
Sharpe ratio	0.12	
Semideviation	7.16%	
Sortino ratio	0.20	
Jensen's alpha	0.64%	
Beta	0.28	
Up capture ratio	46.51%	
Down capture ratio	28.91%	
Omega -0%	153%	
Appraisal ratio	0.06	
Average α over benchmark	-0.09%	
Tracking error	4.01%	
Information ratio	-2.12%	
Sterling ratio	0.13	
Treynor measure	0.05	
M² – Modigliani measure	-1.76%	
Burke ratio	0.22	
Skewness	87.78%	
Kurtosis	221%	
Correlation to S&P/TSX	0.551	
R squared	0.054	
Benchmark: MSCI World C$		

TERMS AND CONDITIONS

Inception:	August 31, 2003
Style:	Fund of Hedge Funds
Sub-style:	N/A
Valuation:	Monthly
RRSP:	No
Management fee:	N/A
Performance fee:	N/A
High-water mark:	N/A
Hurdle rate:	N/A
NAV:	$113.72
Asset Size (million):	N/A
Maximum leverage:	N/A
Early red'n period:	N/A
Early red'n fee:	N/A

PERFORMANCE (as of December 31, 2004)

	1 mo.	3 mo.	6 mo.
Funds	1.50%	7.26%	4.76%
MSCI World C$	5.25%	6.76%	0.07%
Van Global HF Index	1.50%	4.87%	5.48%

	1 yr.	2 yr.	3 yr.
Funds	5.45%		
MSCI World C$	6.85%	8.58%	-2.18%
Van Global HF Index	7.79%	13.04%	8.40%

Year	Jan	Feb	Mar	Apr	May	Jun	Jul	Aug	Sep	Oct	Nov	Dec	Total
2004	0.44%	8.90%	0.96%	-5.75%	-1.02%	-2.30%	-0.73%	-1.66%	0.04%	0.92%	4.71%	1.50%	5.45%
2003									0.49%	2.22%	-0.70%	4.32%	6.40%
2002													

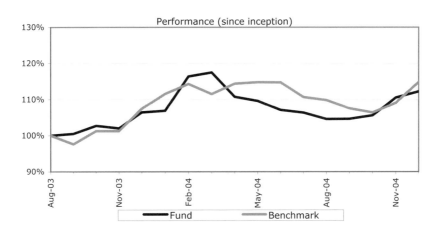

Performance (since inception)

— Fund   — Benchmark

THALES TA3—SAFEGUARD C$

FUND SPONSOR COMPANY

Thales Alternative Investments Inc.

Tel: 416-955-0710   Toll-Free: N/A

Fax: 416-862-0576   Web site: www.thales.ca

PORTFOLIO MANAGER(S)

Mesirow Advanced Strategies, Inc., Campbell & Company, Inc., Thales Alternative Investments Inc.

FUND DESCRIPTION

TA3 takes the concept of "balanced" to another level for Canadians, because it increases diversification through exposure to different asset classes and management styles. The diversification provided through investments in several managers seeks to generate low volatility returns and perform in both bull and bear markets.

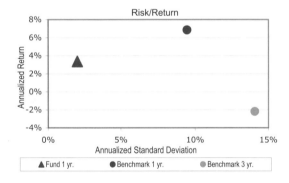

Rating: Not Rated

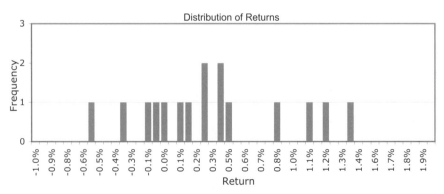

	1 yr.	3 yr.
Annualized rate of return	3.36%	
Annualized standard deviation	2.01%	
Percentage of negative months	33.33%	
Largest monthly drop	-0.62%	
Maximum drawdown	-1.12%	
Sharpe ratio	-0.32	
Semideviation	1.04%	
Sortino ratio	-0.61	
Jensen's alpha	-0.94%	
Beta	0.10	
Up capture ratio	17.69%	
Down capture ratio	-1.48%	
Omega -0%	375%	
Appraisal ratio	-0.56	
Average α over benchmark	-0.31%	
Tracking error	2.47%	
Information ratio	-12.55%	
Sterling ratio	-0.57	
Treynor measure	-0.06	
M² – Modigliani measure	-5.85%	
Burke ratio	-0.87	
Skewness	48.05%	
Kurtosis	-17%	
Correlation to S&P/TSX	0.407	
R squared	0.288	
Benchmark: MSCI World C$		

TERMS AND CONDITIONS

Inception:	August 31, 2003
Style:	Fund of Hedge Funds
Sub-style:	N/A
Valuation:	Monthly
RRSP:	No
Management fee:	N/A
Performance fee:	N/A
High-water mark:	N/A
Hurdle rate:	N/A
NAV:	$104.89
Asset Size (million):	N/A
Maximum leverage:	N/A
Early red'n period:	N/A
Early red'n fee:	N/A

PERFORMANCE (as of December 31, 2004)

	1 mo.	3 mo.	6 mo.
Funds	1.38%	1.99%	2.54%
MSCI World C$	5.25%	6.76%	0.07%
Van Global HF Index	1.50%	4.87%	5.48%

	1 yr.	2 yr.	3 yr.
Funds	3.36%		
MSCI World C$	6.85%	8.58%	-2.18%
Van Global HF Index	7.79%	13.04%	8.40%

Year	Jan	Feb	Mar	Apr	May	Jun	Jul	Aug	Sep	Oct	Nov	Dec	Total
2004	0.78%	1.07%	0.08%	-0.17%	-0.33%	-0.62%	0.39%	-0.09%	0.24%	0.15%	0.46%	1.38%	3.36%
2003									-0.06%	1.19%	0.37%	0.25%	1.75%
2002													

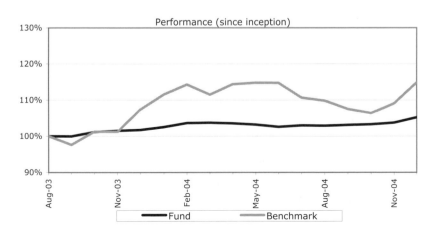

Performance (since inception)

THALES BNP—MESIROW NOTES SERIES 2

FUND SPONSOR COMPANY
Thales Alternative Investments Inc.
Tel: 416-955-0710   Toll-Free: N/A
Fax: 416-862-0576   Web site: www.thales.ca

PORTFOLIO MANAGER(S)

Mesirow Advanced Strategies, Inc. is one of the largest managers of fund of hedge funds in the world, with over 20 years' experience and over US$5 billion under management.

FUND DESCRIPTION

The investment manager utilizes a multi-strategy, multi-manager, diversified investment approach on behalf of the Fund, with the objective of generating consistent and superior rates of return while maintaining a low level of volatility. The investment program includes 1) identification, evaluation, and selection of investment strategies; 2) identification evaluation, and selection of managers; and 3) allocation and re-allocation of assets among strategies and managers.

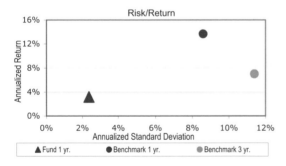

Rating: Not Rated

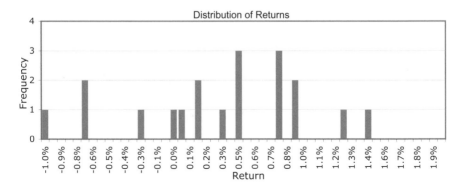

	1 yr.	3 yr.
Annualized rate of return	3.17%	
Annualized standard deviation	2.37%	
Percentage of negative months	33.33%	
Largest monthly drop	-0.75%	
Maximum drawdown	-1.36%	
Sharpe ratio	-0.35	
Semideviation	1.32%	
Sortino ratio	-0.63	
Jensen's alpha	-1.95%	
Beta	0.12	
Up capture ratio	16.29%	
Down capture ratio	7.59%	
Omega -0%	277%	
Appraisal ratio	-0.98	
Average α over benchmark	-0.84%	
Tracking error	2.25%	
Information ratio	-37.29%	
Sterling ratio	-0.61	
Treynor measure	-0.07	
M^2 – Modigliani measure	-12.66%	
Burke ratio	-0.78	
Skewness	18.36%	
Kurtosis	-52%	
Correlation to S&P/TSX	0.462	
R squared	0.213	
Benchmark: S&P/TSX		

TERMS AND CONDITIONS

Inception:	May 31, 2003
Style:	Fund of Hedge Funds
Sub-style:	Note
Valuation:	Monthly
RRSP:	No
Management fee:	N/A
Performance fee:	N/A
High-water mark:	N/A
Hurdle rate:	N/A
NAV:	$10.57
Asset Size (million):	N/A
Maximum leverage:	N/A
Early red'n period:	N/A
Early red'n fee:	N/A

PERFORMANCE (as of December 31, 2004)

	1 mo.	3 mo.	6 mo.
Funds	1.43%	2.73%	2.53%
S&P/TSX	2.40%	6.67%	8.41%
Van Global HF Index	1.50%	4.87%	5.48%

	1 yr.	2 yr.	3 yr.
Funds	3.17%		
S&P/TSX	13.66%	19.32%	6.99%
Van Global HF Index	7.79%	13.04%	8.40%

Year	Jan	Feb	Mar	Apr	May	Jun	Jul	Aug	Sep	Oct	Nov	Dec	Total
2004	1.22%	0.42%	0.02%	-0.27%	-0.70%	-0.06%	0.42%	-0.75%	0.15%	0.43%	0.85%	1.43%	3.17%
2003						0.14%	0.75%	-1.19%	0.76%	0.77%	0.87%	0.30%	2.41%
2002													

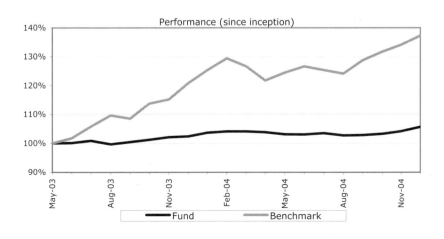

Performance (since inception)

TRANS IMS GLOBAL MARKET NEUTRAL FUND

FUND SPONSOR COMPANY

Transamerica Life Canada

Tel: 866-209-9253   Toll-Free: 866-209-9253
Fax: N/A   Web site: www.transamerica.ca

PORTFOLIO MANAGER(S)

David Patterson founded Newcastle Capital Management Inc. in January of 1989. Immediately prior to establishing the firm, he was President of Security Pacific Futures Inc. in Chicago, Illinois and at the same time, Director of Futures and Options for Burns Fry Limited in Toronto.

FUND DESCRIPTION

The investment objective of this Fund is long-term accumulation of capital through appreciation and reinvestment of net income.

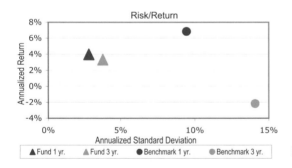

Rating:

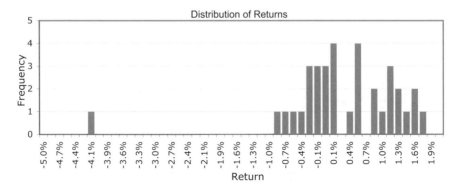

	1 yr.	3 yr.
Annualized rate of return	3.99%	3.33%
Annualized standard deviation	2.80%	3.77%
Percentage of negative months	33.33%	30.56%
Largest monthly drop	-0.86%	-4.23%
Maximum drawdown	-1.96%	-4.51%
Sharpe ratio	0.00	-0.18
Semideviation	1.46%	3.40%
Sortino ratio	-0.01	-0.20
Jensen's alpha	-0.63%	-0.24%
Beta	0.22	0.07
Up capture ratio	26.43%	15.47%
Down capture ratio	8.14%	2.42%
Omega -0%	293%	212%
Appraisal ratio	-0.33	-0.07
Average α over benchmark	-0.26%	0.38%
Tracking error	2.14%	3.91%
Information ratio	-12.06%	9.77%
Sterling ratio	-0.01	-0.15
Treynor measure	0.00	-0.10
M² – Modigliani measure	-2.89%	3.67%
Burke ratio	-0.01	-0.15
Skewness	21.38%	-186.85%
Kurtosis	-102%	745%
Correlation to S&P/TSX	0.164	0.239
R squared	0.637	0.073
Benchmark: MSCI World C$		

TERMS AND CONDITIONS

Inception:	October 31, 1994
Style:	Non-Directional
Sub-style:	Equity
Valuation:	Daily
RRSP:	Yes
Management fee:	2.25%
Performance fee:	N/A
High-water mark:	N/A
Hurdle rate:	N/A
NAV:	$7.96
Asset Size (million):	$22.73
Maximum leverage:	N/A
Early red'n period:	N/A
Early red'n fee:	N/A

PERFORMANCE (as of December 31, 2004)

	1 mo.	3 mo.	6 mo.
Funds	1.70%	2.81%	1.59%
MSCI World C$	5.25%	6.76%	0.07%
Van Global HF Index	1.50%	4.87%	5.48%

	1 yr.	2 yr.	3 yr.
Funds	3.99%	5.19%	3.33%
MSCI World C$	6.85%	8.58%	-2.18%
Van Global HF Index	7.79%	13.04%	8.40%

Year	Jan	Feb	Mar	Apr	May	Jun	Jul	Aug	Sep	Oct	Nov	Dec	Total
2004	1.22%	1.12%	0.33%	0.46%	-0.86%	0.08%	-0.26%	-0.25%	-0.69%	0.00%	1.10%	1.70%	3.99%
2003	0.00%	2.04%	0.09%	0.74%	1.02%	1.00%	-0.42%	-0.77%	0.76%	1.24%	0.52%	0.05%	6.41%
2002	-4.23%	-0.30%	1.43%	0.49%	0.51%	-0.25%	-0.42%	-0.52%	0.05%	0.00%	1.52%	1.56%	-0.30%

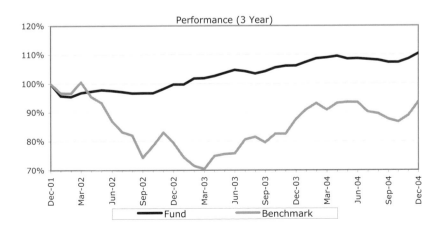

Performance (3 Year)

Fund — Benchmark

TREMONT CORE DIVERSIFIED FUND CLASS A

FUND SPONSOR COMPANY
Tremont Capital Management Corp.
Tel: 416-360-3395   Toll-Free: 888-263-8573
Fax: 416-360-3399   Web site: www.tremont.ca

PORTFOLIO MANAGER(S)

Tremont Capital Management Corp. is the Canadian subsidiary of Tremont Capital Management, Inc. ("Tremont"). Founded in 1984, Tremont is an acknowledged global leader in innovative hedge fund investment products and advisory services, supported by the world's premier research and information network. Tremont oversees US$8.1 billion in hedge fund of fund assets. Tremont is an affiliate of OppenheimerFunds, Inc., one of the largest asset management firms in the United States.

FUND DESCRIPTION

The Tremont Core Diversified Fund is an actively managed fund of hedge funds employing Tremont's "core diversified" investment strategy. This diversified, opportunistic, and institutional approach recognizes that hedge fund strategies move into and out of favour as economic conditions, strategy specific factors, and supply and demand change over time. The Fund invests in complementary strategies, including long/short equity, convertible arbitrage, equity market neutral, event driven, and global macro.

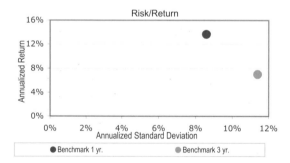

Rating: Not Rated

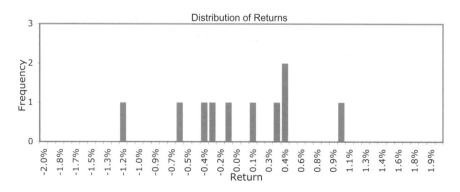

	1 yr.	3 yr.
Annualized rate of return		
Annualized standard deviation		
Percentage of negative months		
Largest monthly drop		
Maximum drawdown		
Sharpe ratio		
Semideviation		
Sortino ratio		
Jensen's alpha		
Beta		
Up capture ratio		
Down capture ratio		
Omega -0%		
Appraisal ratio		
Average α over benchmark		
Tracking error		
Information ratio		
Sterling ratio		
Treynor measure		
M² – Modigliani measure		
Burke ratio		
Skewness		
Kurtosis		
Correlation to S&P/TSX		
R squared		
Benchmark: S&P/TSX		

TERMS AND CONDITIONS

Inception:	January 30, 2004
Style:	Directional Trading
Sub-style:	N/A
Valuation:	Monthly
RRSP:	No
Management fee:	1.20%
Performance fee:	18.00%
High-water mark:	Yes
Hurdle rate:	N/A
NAV:	$93.07
Asset Size (million):	$35.84
Maximum leverage:	N/A
Early red'n period:	N/A
Early red'n fee:	N/A

PERFORMANCE (as of December 31, 2004)

	1 mo.	3 mo.	6 mo.
Funds	0.38%	3.48%	1.24%
S&P/TSX	2.40%	6.67%	8.41%
Van Global HF Index	1.50%	4.87%	5.48%

	1 yr.	2 yr.	3 yr.
Funds			
S&P/TSX	13.66%	19.32%	6.99%
Van Global HF Index	7.79%	13.04%	8.40%

Year	Jan	Feb	Mar	Apr	May	Jun	Jul	Aug	Sep	Oct	Nov	Dec	Total
2004		-0.17%	0.29%	0.37%	-0.43%	0.05%	-1.23%	-0.34%	-0.62%	1.01%	2.07%	0.38%	1.35%
2003													
2002													

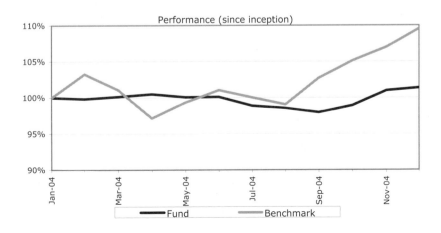

Performance (since inception)

BDC MANAGED FUTURES NOTES, SERIES N–2

FUND SPONSOR COMPANY

Tricycle Asset Management Corp.

Tel: 416-440-7990   Toll-Free: 877-747-2992
Fax: 416-440-7989   Web site: www.3-wheeler.com

PORTFOLIO MANAGER(S)

Rob Bourgeois is responsible for overall operations and product development. Rob has held senior management positions for Nesbitt Burns Inc. in domestic and non-North American Fixed Income, as well as Debt Capital Markets.
Fred Hirshfeld is responsible for marketing, implementation, and overall risk evaluation. For two decades, he has held senior positions in commodities, futures, and money management.
Jan Holland is responsible for research, structuring, marketing, and implementation.

FUND DESCRIPTION

Managed futures are defined as the investing in futures contracts by professional futures traders who trade in global commodities and futures markets, as either buyers or sellers of real assets such as wheat, corn, gold, crude oil, and natural gas, as well as financial assets such as government bonds and currencies. BDC Managed Futures Notes provide a way for individual investors to take advantage of potential returns of the futures market without risking loss of their capital investment.

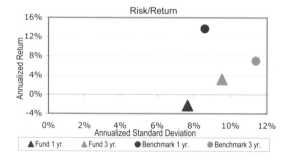

Rating:

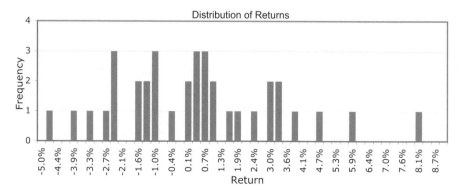

	1 yr.	3 yr.
Annualized rate of return	-2.30%	3.18%
Annualized standard deviation	7.64%	9.53%
Percentage of negative months	41.67%	41.67%
Largest monthly drop	-4.80%	-4.80%
Maximum drawdown	-9.89%	-10.97%
Sharpe ratio	-0.82	-0.09
Semideviation	5.78%	4.86%
Sortino ratio	-1.09	-0.17
Jensen's alpha	-10.39%	-0.23%
Beta	0.42	-0.20
Up capture ratio	13.53%	2.41%
Down capture ratio	67.87%	-24.66%
Omega -0%	81%	133%
Appraisal ratio	-1.21	-0.02
Average α over benchmark	-1.27%	-0.32%
Tracking error	2.31%	4.77%
Information ratio	-55.11%	-6.72%
Sterling ratio	-0.64	-0.07
Treynor measure	-0.15	0.04
M² – Modigliani measure	-16.73%	-3.97%
Burke ratio	-1.07	-0.09
Skewness	-59.61%	59.65%
Kurtosis	48%	56%
Correlation to S&P/TSX	0.520	-0.241
R squared	0.271	0.058
Benchmark: S&P/TSX		

TERMS AND CONDITIONS

Inception:	August 30, 2000
Style:	Directional Trading
Sub-style:	Note
Valuation:	Daily
RRSP:	Yes
Management fee:	4.50%
Performance fee:	10.00%
High-water mark:	No
Hurdle rate:	0.00%
NAV:	$124.69
Asset Size (million):	$10.00
Maximum leverage:	N/A
Early red'n period:	N/A
Early red'n fee:	N/A

PERFORMANCE (as of December 31, 2004)

	1 mo.	3 mo.	6 mo.
Funds	0.41%	4.78%	4.42%
S&P/TSX	2.40%	6.67%	8.41%
Van Global HF Index	1.50%	4.87%	5.48%

	1 yr.	2 yr.	3 yr.
Funds	-2.30%	-2.31%	3.18%
S&P/TSX	13.66%	19.32%	6.99%
Van Global HF Index	7.79%	13.04%	8.40%

Year	Jan	Feb	Mar	Apr	May	Jun	Jul	Aug	Sep	Oct	Nov	Dec	Total
2004	-0.60%	2.85%	0.52%	-4.80%	-1.71%	-2.70%	-1.04%	0.03%	0.68%	1.46%	2.85%	0.41%	-2.30%
2003	0.21%	0.79%	-3.34%	0.41%	3.63%	-2.47%	-1.38%	0.73%	-1.03%	1.57%	-1.73%	0.45%	-2.33%
2002	0.06%	-2.52%	-4.00%	-1.00%	4.57%	7.95%	5.66%	3.05%	2.26%	-2.85%	-1.40%	3.15%	15.10%

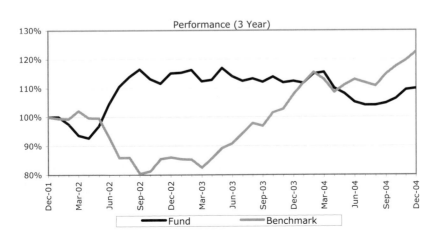

Performance (3 Year)

VERACITY CAPITAL PARTNERS L.P.

FUND SPONSOR COMPANY
Veracity Capital Partners L.P.
Tel: 416-777-6749   Toll-Free: N/A
Fax: 416-777-6784   Web site: www.veracitycapital.com

PORTFOLIO MANAGER(S)

Veracity Capital Partners L.P.

FUND DESCRIPTION

The investment objective of the Partnership is to create and maintain a portfolio of long and short investment security positions primarily in Canada and the United States in order to achieve superior rates of return on invested capital.

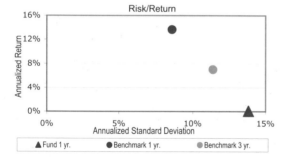

Rating: Not Rated

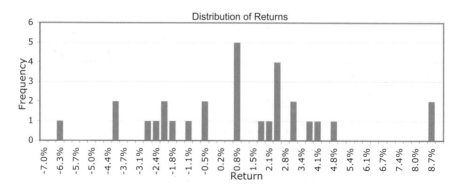

	1 yr.	3 yr.
Annualized rate of return	0.06%	
Annualized standard deviation	13.82%	
Percentage of negative months	41.67%	
Largest monthly drop	-6.56%	
Maximum drawdown	-16.06%	
Sharpe ratio	-0.28	
Semideviation	6.40%	
Sortino ratio	-0.62	
Jensen's alpha	-13.80%	
Beta	1.02	
Up capture ratio	74.05%	
Down capture ratio	188.23%	
Omega -0%	105%	
Appraisal ratio	-1.00	
Average α over benchmark	-1.02%	
Tracking error	2.89%	
Information ratio	-35.36%	
Sterling ratio	-0.25	
Treynor measure	-0.04	
M² – Modigliani measure	-12.10%	
Burke ratio	-0.45	
Skewness	40.80%	
Kurtosis	60%	
Correlation to S&P/TSX	0.692	
R squared	0.479	
Benchmark: S&P/TSX		

TERMS AND CONDITIONS

Inception:	July 31, 2002
Style:	Enhanced Equity
Sub-style:	Equity
Valuation:	Monthly
RRSP:	No
Management fee:	1.90%
Performance fee:	20.00%
High-water mark:	Yes
Hurdle rate:	N/A
NAV:	$29,812.00
Asset Size (million):	N/A
Maximum leverage:	N/A
Early red'n period:	N/A
Early red'n fee:	N/A

PERFORMANCE (as of December 31, 2004)

	1 mo.	3 mo.	6 mo.
Funds	3.65%	12.97%	7.80%
S&P/TSX	2.40%	6.67%	8.41%
Van Global HF Index	1.50%	4.87%	5.48%

	1 yr.	2 yr.	3 yr.
Funds	0.06%	13.68%	
S&P/TSX	13.66%	19.32%	6.99%
Van Global HF Index	7.79%	13.04%	8.40%

Year	Jan	Feb	Mar	Apr	May	Jun	Jul	Aug	Sep	Oct	Nov	Dec	Total
2004	0.57%	2.43%	-1.92%	-6.56%	-2.48%	0.82%	-4.10%	-2.86%	2.43%	0.53%	8.42%	3.65%	0.06%
2003	4.56%	-0.47%	-1.15%	3.89%	2.29%	-2.14%	0.58%	2.46%	1.77%	8.57%	3.06%	2.87%	29.15%
2002								0.78%	-4.35%	2.08%	-2.29%	-0.53%	-4.36%

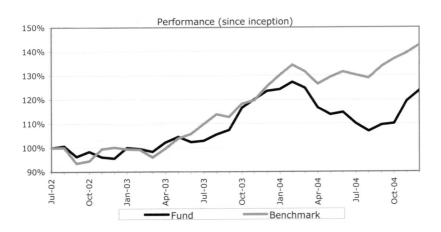

Performance (since inception)

Fund   Benchmark

VERTEX FUND

FUND SPONSOR COMPANY
Vertex Asset Management
Tel: 604-681-5787   Toll-Free: 888-432-5350
Fax: 604-681-5146   Web site: www.vertexone.com

PORTFOLIO MANAGER(S)

Vertex was founded in 1997. The firm manages $150 million in assets for individuals, pension funds, and trusts. The portfolio managers previously had a long history with very large bank-owned investment counsellors. Vertex One applies an investment management system using two funds to provide a superior risk return tradeoff.

FUND DESCRIPTION

The Fund's objective is to maximize pretax return for its unit holders. Good performance and reasonable risk.

Risk/Return

Rating: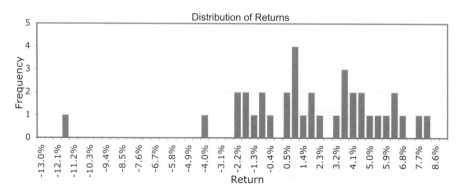

Distribution of Returns

	1 yr.	3 yr.
Annualized rate of return	20.20%	20.42%
Annualized standard deviation	11.00%	13.39%
Percentage of negative months	25.00%	27.78%
Largest monthly drop	-4.11%	-11.93%
Maximum drawdown	-5.35%	-14.32%
Sharpe ratio	1.47	1.23
Semideviation	6.25%	10.53%
Sortino ratio	2.59	1.56
Jensen's alpha	9.34%	14.00%
Beta	0.71	0.81
Up capture ratio	94.46%	125.03%
Down capture ratio	18.42%	38.57%
Omega -0%	423%	303%
Appraisal ratio	-2.79	-4.45
Average α over benchmark	0.49%	1.02%
Tracking error	2.59%	2.78%
Information ratio	18.91%	36.53%
Sterling ratio	3.03	1.15
Treynor measure	0.23	0.20
M^2 – Modigliani measure	2.99%	10.98%
Burke ratio	3.73	1.21
Skewness	28.25%	-106.43%
Kurtosis	20%	294%
Correlation to S&P/TSX	0.605	0.709
R squared	0.366	0.503
Benchmark: S&P/TSX		

TERMS AND CONDITIONS

Inception:	February 6, 1998
Style:	Security Selection
Sub-style:	N/A
Valuation:	Monthly
RRSP:	No
Management fee:	1.00%
Performance fee:	20.00%
High-water mark:	N/A
Hurdle rate:	N/A
NAV:	$40.13
Asset Size (million):	$218.16
Maximum leverage:	115%
Early red'n period:	1 mo.
Early red'n fee:	N/A

PERFORMANCE (as of December 31, 2004)

	1 mo.	3 mo.	6 mo.
Funds	0.81%	7.39%	18.10%
S&P/TSX	2.40%	6.67%	8.41%
Van Global HF Index	1.50%	4.87%	5.48%

	1 yr.	2 yr.	3 yr.
Funds	20.20%	33.79%	20.42%
S&P/TSX	13.66%	19.32%	6.99%
Van Global HF Index	7.79%	13.04%	8.40%

Year	Jan	Feb	Mar	Apr	May	Jun	Jul	Aug	Sep	Oct	Nov	Dec	Total
2004	1.45%	4.80%	0.49%	-4.11%	-1.29%	0.65%	2.81%	-0.50%	7.51%	0.92%	5.55%	0.81%	20.20%
2003	1.61%	0.08%	-2.37%	3.21%	6.66%	3.29%	3.77%	6.06%	0.32%	6.08%	4.32%	7.96%	48.91%
2002	1.82%	0.96%	3.26%	-2.13%	4.23%	-2.23%	-11.93%	4.01%	-0.94%	-1.54%	-1.90%	5.16%	-2.44%

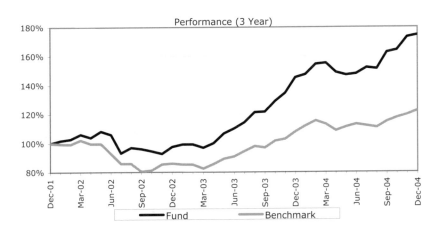

Performance (3 Year)

Fund —— Benchmark ——

Glossary of Terms

1-Day Return: Percentage change of the hedge fund NAV over one day, adjusted to distribution.

1 Mth: Percentage change of the hedge fund NAV over one month, adjusted to distributions.

1 Yr: The hedge fund's one-year performance.

10 Yr: The hedge fund's annualized rate of return over 10 years.

15 Yr: The hedge fund's annualized rate of return over 15 years.

3 Mth: Percentage change of the hedge fund NAV over three months, adjusted to distributions.

3 Yr: The hedge fund's annualized rate of return over three years.

6 Mth: Percentage change of the hedge fund NAV over six months, adjusted to distributions.

7-Day Return: Percentage change of the hedge fund NAV over seven days, adjusted to distributions.

Alpha: The abnormal (or manager specific) rate of return on the hedge fund in excess of what would be predicted by the market return and risk measure (beta).

Annualized Average Rate of Return (ROR): A calculation of the return on an annual basis from the beginning to the end of the holding period.

Annualized Standard Deviation (σ): A measure of the variability (volatility) of a fund relative to its mean return (i.e., its annualized rate of return). Annualized standard deviation indicates, on average, the degree to which the fund's performance deviates from its average annualized rate of return. Higher standard deviation means higher risk.

Appraisal Ratio: The signal-to-noise ratio of an analyst's forecasts. The ratio of alpha to residual standard deviation. A measure of portfolio management skill that is computed as 1) a portfolio's incremental return relative to a benchmark, divided by its incremental risk, or 2) alpha divided by non-systematic risk.

Beta: The measure of the systematic risk of the hedge fund. The tendency of the hedge fund's returns to respond to swings in the broad market.

Burke Ratio: A measure of the rate of return of a fund compared to the size of deep, extended drawdowns (as opposed to numerous mild ones). The greater the value, the better.

Compound Annual Return: The annualized rate of return of the hedge fund (provided that the fund is at least one year old).

Convergence Arbitrage: An investment sub-style in which the manager focuses on obtaining returns with low or no correlation to the market. The manager buys different securities of the same issuer (e.g., the common stock and convertibles) and works the spread between them. For example, within the same company the manager buys one form of security that he/she believes is undervalued and sells short another security of the same company.

Correlation: A statistic that scales the covariance to a value between -1 (perfect negative correlation) and +1 (perfect positive correlation).

CTA: Commodity trading advisor. A CTA runs separate commodity accounts.

Current Exposure—Long: Current percentage of long exposure.

Current Exposure—Net: Current percentage of net exposure.

Current Exposure—Short: Current percentage of short exposure.

Daily Change: The dollar move of the hedge fund's NAV.

Directional Trading: An investment style based upon speculation of market direction in multiple asset classes. Both model-based systems and subjective judgment are used to make trading decisions.

Discretionary Trading: An investment sub-style in which the manager rotates investment selection to different sectors of the economy as he/she sees fit.

Distressed Securities: An investment sub-style that involves buying the equity or debt of companies that are in or facing bankruptcy. The manager hopes to buy company securities at a low price and hopes that the company will come out of bankruptcy and securities will appreciate.

Distribution: The dates of distributions with dollar values (of distributions).

Down Capture Ratio: Calculated as the fund average return divided by the benchmark average return, considering only periods when the benchmark was down. The smaller the ratio, the better.

Early Redemption Fee: The percentage fee (usually 5%) applied in case of redemption of the hedge fund investment within a certain period of time (often six months).

Fund of Funds: A fund containing more than one hedge fund. Hedge funds used in a fund of funds could be classified in one or more main styles. Often a diversified portfolio of generally uncorrelated hedge funds.

Fund Size: Size of the hedge fund in millions of U.S. or Canadian dollars.

Gain Deviation: A measure of the volatility of the upside performance. It calculates an average return only for the periods with a gain and then measures the variation of only the gain periods around this gain mean.

High-Water Mark: Either the previous highest value of an investor's investment for which incentive fees have already been paid, or if no incentive fees have been paid to date, the original investment in a particular hedge fund adjusted for purchases and redemptions since the first buy. The high-water mark value indicates the point below which the fund cannot charge a performance fee to the particular investor, even in the case of over-hurdle-rate performance in the year. Should the high-water mark value be higher than the beginning-of-year value of the investment (adjusted to cash flows), the performance fees will only be calculated and paid based on the difference of the high-water mark and the end-of-year value of the particular hedge fund investment.

Hurdle Rate: A set calendar year rate of return above which performance fees are charged.

Inception Date: Month and year when a particular hedge fund was launched.

Information Ratio: A measure that explicitly relates the *degree* by which an investment has beaten the benchmark to the *consistency* by which the investment has beaten the benchmark.

Jensen's Alpha: Jensen's alpha measures the ability of a fund manager to generate a greater-than-expected return, given a fund's risk level. Jensen's alpha is used primarily to evaluate portfolio manager skill in selecting securities. It provides a basis for the comparison of portfolios with different risk levels. Positive alphas are a reflection of superior manager skill, while negative alphas indicate that the manager's efforts did not add value to the portfolio.

Kurtosis: Refers to the weight of the tails of the distribution. Positive kurtosis indicates a relative peak, while negative kurtosis implies a relatively flat distribution.

Long Bias: Long-bias sub-style hedge funds usually have more exposure to "long" financial instruments than to "short" financial instruments. Managers of these funds assume that the market goes up in the long run.

Loss Deviation: Calculates an average return only for the periods with a loss and then measures the variation of only the losing periods around this loss mean.

M^2 (Modigliani Measure): Expresses performance directly as a return figure. It adjusts the fund by leveraging or de-leveraging it, using the risk-free asset to equalize volatility (typically the market volatility). The higher the ratio, the better.

Macro Trading: This investment philosophy is based on shifts in global economies. Derivatives are often used to speculate on currency and interest rate moves.

Management Fee: Set annual fee the hedge fund company charges its fund for providing investment management services (usually ranges between 1.5% and 3%, similar to mutual funds).

Maximum Drawdown: Maximum percentage loss from the hedge fund's "peak to valley."

Maximum Number of Months Off Peak: Maximum number of months when the NAV was less than the former highest value. The time during which the NAV was below the "high-water mark."

Merger Arbitrage: An investment sub-style in which the manager seeks to capture the price spread between current market prices and the value of securities upon successful completion of a takeover or a merger. The price spread is due to the time value of money and a risk premium on the deal not closing. Returns in merger arbitrage arise from the correct anticipation of relative movements in stock prices.

Minimum Investment: Minimum initial investment in the particular hedge fund (normally $150,000 in Ontario for a non-accredited investor).

Monthly Rate of Return: Month-by-month performances of the hedge fund.

Month-to-Date: Percentage change of the hedge fund NAV since the last day of the previous month, adjusted to distributions.

NAV: Net asset value per share (of hedge fund).

No Bias: No-bias sub-style hedge funds usually have equal exposure to "long" financial instruments and to "short" financial instruments. Managers of these funds make no assumptions about the market direction in the long run.

Omega: This statistic measures the cumulative probability that a hedge fund's returns will be above a specified return threshold, compared to the cumulative probability that its returns will fall below a specified return threshold.

Performance Fee: A certain percentage that a particular hedge fund charges per year over and above the management fee. The performance fee is usually 20% over a threshold performance (hurdle rate) in a calendar year. Many hedge funds' threshold performance for an incentive fee is 0%; however, some charge over +10% or the T-bill rate of return in the calendar year.

Positive Carry: Positive carry exploits investment opportunities when the cost of borrowed funds is lower than the return earned on investments.

Possible Exposure Range—Long: Percentage range of possible long "exposures."

Possible Exposure Range—Net: Percentage range of possible net "exposures."

Possible Exposure Range—Short: Percentage range of possible short "exposures."

Private Placements: An investment sub-style in which the manager tries to take advantage of the short-term opportunities represented by investing in firms that need to raise capital quickly.

R² (R-squared): Statistical measure of how well a regression line approximates real data points; an R-squared of 1.0 (100%) indicates a perfect fit.

Relative Value: A style that focuses on the spread relationship between pricing components of financial assets. Market risk is kept to a minimum. Many managers use leverage to enhance returns.

RRSP Eligibility: Indicates whether a particular hedge fund is eligible for RRSP investment. If RRSP eligible, it can be classified as either Canadian or foreign content.

Semideviation: The semideviation is a downside measure of risk. Standard deviation of below-average returns.

Sharpe Ratio: Reward-to-volatility ratio. Ratio of the hedge fund's excess return to standard deviation.

Short Bias: Short-bias sub-style hedge funds usually have more exposure to "short" financial instruments than to "long" financial instruments. Managers of these funds do not assume that the market goes up in the long run.

Skewness: Characterizes the degree of asymmetry of a distribution around its mean. Positive skewness indicates a distribution with an asymmetric tail extending toward more positive values. Negative skewness indicates a distribution with an asymmetric tail extending toward more negative values.

Sortino Ratio: Also called the "upside potential ratio." In contrast to the Sharpe ratio, the Sortino ratio distinguishes harmful (downward) volatility from general volatility.

Specialist Credit: An investment style based on lending to credit-sensitive issuers. Funds of this style conduct a high level of due diligence in order to identify relatively inexpensive securities.

Standard Deviation: Statistical measure of volatility measuring the difference between a hedge fund's actual performance and its average performance.

Statistical Arbitrage: An investment sub-style in which managers perform a low risk, market neutral analytical equity strategy, believing that equities behave in a way that is mathematically describable. This approach captures momentary pricing aberrations in the stocks being monitored. The strategy's profit objective is to exploit mispricing in as risk-free a manner as possible.

Sterling Ratio: The Sterling ratio is defined as a portfolio's overall return divided by its maximum drawdown statistic. In finance, the Sterling ratio represents a measure of a portfolio's risk-adjusted return.

Stock Selection: Combining long and short positions, primarily in equities, in order to exploit under- or over-valued securities. Market exposure can vary substantially.

Systematic Trading: An investment sub-style that uses a proprietary computer program to make most or all decisions about the positions of the fund.

Tracking Error: Represents the standard deviation of the hedge fund's alpha over the benchmark for a specific period.

Treynor Measure: Per unit of risk, it calculates the fund's return over and above the risk-free rate. While the Sharpe ratio uses the standard deviation of return as a measure of risk, the Treynor ratio uses the fund's beta.

Up Capture Ratio: Calculated as a fund's average return divided by the benchmark average return, considering only those periods when the benchmark was up. The greater the value, the better.

Valuation Frequency: An indication of how often a particular hedge fund is valued (normally weekly).

Variable Bias: Variable-bias sub-style hedge funds frequently rotate their bias about the direction of the market and their exposure to "long" and "short" financial instruments. Managers of these funds assume either a bullish or bearish bias at different times and change their net exposure accordingly.

YTD: Percentage change of the hedge fund NAV since December 31 of the previous year, adjusted to distributions.

Resources

RELATED OR SIMILAR BOOKS ON THE CANADIAN MARKET:

Up until now, there has been no publication dedicated solely to the Canadian hedge fund industry. While some of the rules and regulations differ between Canadian and U.S. hedge funds, their strategies and styles are similar. The books below are available in Canada, but were all published in the U.S.

Author	Title	Publisher
Peter Temple	*Hedge Funds: Courtesans of Capitalism*	John Wiley & Sons, 2001
Mark Boucher	*The Hedge Fund Edge: Maximum Profit/Minimum Risk Global Trend Trading Strategies*	John Wiley & Sons, 1998
Joseph G. Nicholas Kristen M. Fox	*Investing in Hedge Funds*	Bloomberg Press, 1999
Francois-Serge L'habitant	*Hedge Funds: Risks and Returns*	John Wiley & Sons, 2001
Francois-Serge L'habitant	*Hedge Funds: Myths and Limits*	John Wiley & Sons, 2001
Lars Jaeger	*Managing Risk in Alternative Investment Strategies: Successful Investing in Hedge Funds and Managed Funds*	Prentice Hall, 2002

Author	Title	Publisher
Gordon de Brouwer	*Hedge Funds in Emerging Markets*	Cambridge University Press, 2002
James P. Owen	*The Prudent Investor's Guide to Hedge Funds*	Wiley Trade Publishing, 2000
Daniel A. Strachman	*Getting Started in Hedge Funds*	John Wiley & Sons, 1999
Beverly Chandler	*Investing with Hedge Fund Giants: Financial Times Profit Whether Markets Rise or Fall*	Financial Times Prentice Hall, 2001
Stefano Lavinio	*The Hedge Fund Handbook*	McGraw-Hill Ryerson Ltd., 1999
Jess Lederman Robert Klein	*Hedge Funds: Investment &Portfolio Strategies for the Institutional Investor*	Irwin Professional Publishing, 1995
William J. Crerend Robert A. Jaeger	*Fundamentals of Hedge Fund Investing: A Professional Investor's Guide*	McGraw-Hill (Health Professional Division), 1998
Laurence A. Connors	*Investment Secrets of a Hedge Fund Manager: Breakthrough Techniques Beat the Market*	Irwin Professional Publishing, 1995
Carl C. Peters	*Handbook of Managed Futures & Hedge Funds: Performance, Evaluation & Analysis*	Irwin Professional, 1996
Sarah Barhan	*Starting a Hedge Fund—A U.S. Perspective*	ISI Publications, 2001
Sarah Barhan Ian Hallsworth	*Starting a Hedge Fund—A European Perspective*	ISI Publications, 1999
Ron Lake	*Evaluating & Implementing Hedge Strategies*	American Educational Systems, 1996

INTERNET RESOURCES:

There are a number of excellent sources of information on hedge funds available through the Internet. Some of the most comprehensive sources are listed below.

In Canada:

http://www.canadianhedgewatch.com
http://www.aima-canada.org
http://www.hedgefunds.ca
http://www.fundlibrary.com
http://www.globefund.com
http://www.hedge.ca

Outside Canada:

http://www.thehfa.org (has a Canadian chapter)
http://www.hedgefund.net
http://www.e-hedge.com
http://www.hedgeworld.com
http://www.aiwa.com

Index of Hedge Funds

Index

blue chip stocks
  defined, 22
bonds
  defined, 51–52
  distorted value of, 12
  liquidity of, 39
broad market indices, 22
brokers, 75
  direct-access execution, 60
bull market
  defined, 24
buy and hold
  compared to Jones's strategy, 8
  defined, 2
  long only, 2
  strategy, 2
  strategy and mutual funds, 24

C

Canadian Hedge Watch, 70
Canadian Institute of Financial
Planners (CIFP), 70
Canadian Investment Fund, 19
capital
  preservation of, 2, 19
cash
  and mutual funds, 26–27
closed-end funds, 18
commodity trading advisors, 49
computers
  use in stock analysis, 23
Concordia Res Parvae Crescunt, 18
convertible arbitrage, 51–54
convertible bonds, 52
corporate bonds, 51
correlation to a benchmark, 87
Credit Suisse First Boston (CSFB)/
Tremont, 67, 71
CSFB/Tremont Hedge Fund Index, 71

currency
  value of, 37

D

declining market, 25, 26–27
  making money in, 4
direct-access execution brokers, 60
directional trading, 46–49
discipline, 106
discretionary trading, 47–48
distressed securities, 62–64
diversification, 17–18, 68–69, 93, 94
diversified long portfolio
  and mutual funds, 21
Dow Jones Industrial Average, 22
  and changing markets, 59
  index, 22
  as performance benchmark, 24
due diligence, 69, 74–75
  on fund of fund hedge funds, 92–94

E

Eendragt Maakt Magt, 17, 18
emotions and investing, 103
equity markets
  and mutual funds, 27–28
event driven approach, 66

F

fees, 94
  and hedge funds, 26
  incentive, 9
  management, of mutual funds, 26
  performance, 90
  referral, 44
fiduciary responsibility, 2, 19

New York Stock Exchange (NYSE), 22
no bias, 61
Nortel, 32–33

O

offering memorandum (OM), 77–78,
     79, 81, 94, 98, 100
  auditors, 90
  and hurdle rate, 91
Ontario Securities Commission, 25,
     43–44
open-end mutual fund, 18

P

past performance, 80–81
  and risk analysis, 89
performance
  and benchmark, 87
  of hedge funds, 40–42, 103
  measuring, 85, 86
  and mutual fund fees, 26
platinum
  as investment, 38
PlusFunds, 70
Portus Alternative Asset Management,
     25, 43–44
precious metals
  as investment, 36–38
price, distortions, 12
private placements, 65–66
prospectus offering, 65
purchasing process, 100–101

Q

Quantum Fund, 10

R

real estate
  as investment, 34–35
  liquidity of, 39
real estate investment trusts (REIT),
     35, 36
regulations
  of mutual funds, 25
relative performance
  in bull market, 24
  comparison among funds, 24
  defined, 22
  of mutual funds, 22–24
relative value, 49–57
  arbitrage, 50–51
  convertible arbitrage, 51–54
  merger arbitrage, 54–56
  statistical arbitrage, 56–57
research, 74–75, 94–95
  on fund, 77–81
  on fund of funds hedge funds, 92–94
  on World Wide Web, 70–71
resources, 94–95
returns
  consistency of, 39
  of hedge funds, 40–42
  and Jensen's alpha, 86
  and risk characteristics, 89
  and Sharpe's ratio, 85
Ridgeway Developments Inc., 50–51
risk
  adjusted return, 85
  analyzing, 86
  and beta, 86
  characteristics, 89
  controlling, 87–92
  and hedge funds, 28, 43, 74, 75, 77,
     80

choosing, 23, 24, 57–61
computer analysis, 23
liquidity of, 39
stop loss, 104
strategy
  of fund, 78–79
"style drift," 79
subscription agreement, 100–101
systematic trading, 48–48

T
tactical allocation, 49
TASS International Research, 71
tax shelters, 36
technical analysis
  and stock choices, 23
technology sector, 32–34, 47
Tiger Fund Management, 10
Toronto Stock Exchange (TSX), 22
trade claims, 62
trading strategies
  convertible arbitrage, 51–54
  directional, 46–49
  discretional, 47–48
  multi-process group, 66
  relative value, 49–57
  security selection, 57–61
  specialist credit, 61–66
  systematic trading, 48–49
  tactical allocation, 49
Tremont Advisors, 70–71
TSX Composite Index, 22, 31

U
unit pricing, 98

V
Van Hedge Fund Advisors International, 67, 71
van Ketwich, Andriaan, 17, 18
variable bias, 59–60
volatility, 83, 84
  and risk, 81–84
Voordeelig en Voorsigtig, 18

W
World Hedge Funds Summit, 70
World Wide Web
  source of fund information, 70–71

Z
Zurich Capital Markets, 71

I'm sorry
It was my fault
How do I make it Right
Don't complain.

Life you like your way, No dream
will come your way...

Author Bios

PETER BECK

Peter Beck is a well-known financial expert and President of Swift Trade Securities, Canada's leading direct-access trading firm.

A true entrepreneur, Peter started his colourful career as a chef in Hungary. He immigrated to Canada in 1979 where he started a number of successful businesses, including the country's first long-distance company in 1988, competing directly with Bell Canada. When he sold the company in 1993, there were offices coast to coast, making it one of the leaders in the industry.

In 1997, Peter read an article about a U.S. day trading firm and decided to bring the concept to Canada. In just four years, Swift Trade Securities grew from one office to 10 across Canada, used by over 400 full-time traders. Swift Trade Securities remains Canada's premier Direct Access Electronic Trading Centre, and today operates 38 offices around the globe with a further 25 slated to open in 2005. The company was named #2 on *Profit Magazine*'s 100 Fastest Growing Canadian Companies list for a remarkable 5-year growth of almost 9000%.

Mr. Beck has been featured in media across the country, including *The Globe and Mail*, the *Toronto Star*, CTV News, ROB TV, and *Canadian Business*. He regularly appears on television to offer commentary on the U.S. markets. He is also co-author of the bestselling *Canadian Income Funds*.